TWO POWERS IN HEAVEN

TWO POWERS IN HEAVEN

Early Rabbinic Reports
about Christianity and Gnosticism

ALAN F. SEGAL

BAYLOR UNIVERSITY PRESS

Published in 2002 by Brill Academic Publishers Inc. Copyright © 1977 by E. J.
Brill, Leiden, The Netherlands.
Reprinted in 2012 by Baylor University Press, Waco, Texas

Cover Design by Zeal Design for Baylor University Press
*Cover image is from a floor mosaic in the ancient synagogue at Beit
    Alpha, Israel.*

Library of Congress Cataloging-in-Publication Data

Segal, Alan F., 1945–2011
    Two powers in heaven : early rabbinic reports about Christianity and
Gnosticism / by Alan F. Segal
    337 p. cm.
    Originally published: Leiden : E.J. Brill, 1977, in series: Studies in Judaism in
late antiquity.
    Includes bibliographical references and index.
    ISBN 0-391-04172-X
    1. Heresies, Jewish. 2. Dualism in rabbinical literature. 3. Rabbinical
literature—History and criticism. 4. Church history—Primitive and early church,
ca. 30–600. 5. Gnosticism. I. Title.

    BM646 .S44 2002
    296.3'5—dc21

                                        2002018341

The Baylor University Press ISBN is 978-1-60258-549-2

Printed in the United States of America on acid-free paper.

For Meryl

TABLE OF CONTENTS

PREFACE

This study of the rabbinic heretics who believed in "two powers in heaven" began as a dissertation at Yale. The advantage of the topic, as Professors Goldin, Dahl, and I discussed it, was that it allowed me to explore some relationships between rabbinic Judaism, Merkabah mysticism, and early Christianity without becoming overly dependent on the complicated and uncharted Merkabah texts. Ironically, what seemed like a neat and carefully defined problem soon expanded in an almost unforeseen direction. It became clear that "two powers in heaven" was a very early category of heresy, earlier than Jesus, if Philo is a trustworthy witness, and one of the basic categories by which the rabbis perceived the new phenomenon of Christianity. It was one of the central issues over which the two religions separated. Furthermore, the reports of heresy began to clarify how gnosticism, Judaism, and Christianity related—a problem which has vexed scholarship for more than a century.

That systematic study of the reports of "two powers" in rabbinic literature might yield some interesting clues about the history of mysticism, gnosticism, and Christianity was not a total surprise. Previous scholarship had identified the heretics inconclusively as gnostics and Christians. The work of Gershom Scholem had emphasized a relationship to early Merkabah mysticism. Not unexpectedly, the sources showed that some mysticism and apocalypticism, as well as Christianity and gnosticism, were seen as "two powers" heretics by the rabbis. The key factor was not that all qualified as heresy but that, with prudent dating of the stages of the traditions, the development of the heresy could be reconstructed.

Dating the rabbinic reports was the most complicated problem. It depended on methods developed in New Testament scholarship for dating the sayings of Jesus. While the use of form criticism and tradition history has grown quite sophisticated in New Testament studies, Jewish scholars have been slower to pick up the methods. Jacob Neusner has consistently championed the use of form criticism and tradition history in Judaism. This study was influenced by his opinions but the application to the field of rabbinic polemic (where extra-rabbinic sources can be used for dating) has not been tried before. Due to the analogous task, the examples and experience of scholars trying to define the opponents of Paul were also useful.

Though it was difficult to date the rabbinic traditions accurately in many cases, the results showed that the earliest heretics believed in two *complementary* powers in heaven while only later could heretics be shown to believe in two *opposing* powers in heaven. The extra-rabbinic evidence allowed the conclusion that the traditions were earlier than the first century. Furthermore, in comparing the literature, it was possible to define a number of dangerous scriptural interpretations central to the heresy and show how the rabbis countered them by bringing in other scriptures which unambiguously stated God's unity. From this evidence it became clear that the basic heresy involved interpreting scripture to say that a *principal angelic or hypostatic manifestation in heaven was equivalent to God*. This heresy was combatted by the rabbis with verses from Deuteronomy and Isaiah which emphasized God's unity.

Common sense tells us to expect discussions of monotheism in rabbinic Judaism. After all, strict monotheism has been one of the central characteristics of Judaism throughout the ages. However, rabbinic literature, unlike Greco-Roman Jewish literature, does not often discuss theology directly. Most scholars, noting the lack of attention to theology in rabbinic writings, emphasize the rabbinic interest in "orthopraxy" rather than "orthodoxy." A few have even suggested that there was no concept of orthodoxy in rabbinic Judaism. Part of the importance of these reports about "two powers in heaven" is that they show us that the rabbis, in common with their brethren in the diaspora, were concerned about the theological and orthodox center of Judaism when other sectarian groups of their day seemed willing to compromise Judaism's integrity. This study gives us actual evidence of one of the central issues around which rabbinic orthodoxy formed.

Besides the obvious relevance of these findings for understanding the rabbinic movement, this study has ramifications for Christian historians in two important ares: (1) the development of christology and (2) the rise of gnosticism. On the subject of christology, the rabbinic information emphasizes the scriptural basis for christological discussion. According to rabbinic description, it does not seem necessary to believe that early Christians merely associated Jesus with some existent savior model who came equipped with a fixed title and job description. Rather, it appears that the debate between Christianity and Judaism proceeded partially on midrashic or exegetical lines. Ambiguous passages in scripture were clarified by each side of the debate through the use of other scriptural passages which mentioned the same vocabulary or concept. Consequently, this study supports a growing number of New Testament scholars who do not feel the need to postulate a pre-Christian "son of man" redeemer figure with which Jesus was identified. The character of the rabbinic debate makes it possible to see christology build through exegesis rather than through hypothetical, pre-existent titles. Christians, believing in his translation to heaven, could have applied to Jesus a number of passages describing either God's principal angel or some other divine but anthropomorphic manifestation described in Israel's scriptures. There is no need to postulate a previous title "son of man" or even outline a complete model of the figure. The unity could easily have been achieved in applying all the different traditions to Jesus. The title would then emerge later, as a result of the exegesis. To be sure, the New Testament never calls the Christ an angel and clearly argues that Jesus is higher than the angels. But, insistence on divine perquisites for God's principal assistant was apparently not unique to Christianity and became exactly the detail which put Christianity in the category of heresy from the rabbinic perspective.

The second area in which "two powers in heaven" traditions in rabbinic literature offer some clarification is in the history of gnosticism. Here we are on less speculative ground than when trying to understand the earliest christologies. It turned out that gnosticism picked up several of the heretical Bible exegeses of earlier "two powers" heretics. The gnostic interpretation of God's principal angel was a specialized answer against the rabbinic attack. The rabbis had pointed out that God said "there is no God but me" (as in Dt. 32:39, Is. 44–47, etc.). The gnostics invented a mythical scene in which those scriptures could have been said, yet not be evidence against gnosticism. They claimed that the God of the Jews said He was unique but He was an ignorant and limited God. In claiming this, they reserved half of the texts characteristic of the principal angelic mediator for their gnostic redeemer while attributing the other half to the evil demiurge who was the god of the Jews but not the author of salvation. This stage in the debate can only be traced to the second century and logically presupposes the earlier stages. Therefore it comes later than the debate in which Christianity participated. From the rabbinic perspective, both Christianity and gnosticism were virulent and vituperative varieties of "two powers" heresy but the heresy with a complementary divine economy arose earlier than the heresy with an opposing one. This evidence gives limited and disinterested support to the church fathers' contention that gnosticism arose later than Christianity. But it further implies that both Christianity and gnosticism arose out of Hellenistic and apocalyptic

Judaism by sharing heretical traditions of scripture interpretation which speculated on a principal angelic mediator of God. As I said, the inquiry has had ramifications quite far removed from the rabbinic material. I am not so naive to think that my conclusions about christology or the rise of gnosticism can be accepted without comment by people more specialized in these fields. Nor was that my desire. Rather, I only outlined enough of these specialized fields to date the rabbinic material and to suggest the relationship of the rabbinic texts to Christian history. Hopefully, I learned enough of the characteristics of these disparate bodies of text to stimulate constructive rather than destructive criticism. I realize that no single individual or body of material can fully explain this most complex and difficult period of history. The important thing, I think, is to perceive the relevance of the rabbinic material for solving traditional problems of New Testament and gnostic scholarship, even while maintaining the necessity of reading those literatures for dating rabbinic material. That rabbinic and Christian communities interacted antagonistically is an obvious and unfortunate part of centuries of Western history. This study has shown me that, ironically, in spite of the enmity, the witness of each community is necessary for understanding the history of the other.

Since this book started as a dissertation I have had the advantage of much significant advice. Anyone familiar with the study of Hellenistic Judaism or New Testament scholarship will recognize the debt I owe to Professor N. A. Dahl. I have cited his works when specifically relevant but his insight and knowledge extend far beyond explicit citation. His direction and encouragement underlie the whole. I also owe a debt of gratitude to many scholars who served as my advisers. Professor Judah Goldin, who served as co-director of the dissertation while he remained at Yale, was a considerable help. Professor Sid Leiman was a constant adviser throughout the research and writing. He was especially generous with his time and patience in commenting on the rabbinic evidence. I have also received much helpful direction from my colleagues and teachers at Princeton and Yale. Wayne Meeks and Rowan Greer read the manuscript when submitted for the degree in December 1975. I have tried to profit from their comments in revising for publication. Gilles Quispel, Jarl Fossum, Elaine Pagels, Ithamar Gruenwald, Donald Juel, John Gager, Richard Sarason, Matthew Black, and Jacob Neusner kindly read parts of the dissertation and offered suggestions for improvements. However my abilities are judged, these scholars have made theirs freely available to me.

I owe many people thanks for helping in the production of the manuscript. My wife, Meryl, aided me at several crucial moments even while her own career continued to make its normal demands on her. Beverly Jones and Lorraine Fuhrmann have been extraordinarily persevering typists while Elaine Mustain, though she also helped with the typing, should properly be considered an editor, since she both read critically and offered trained suggestions about the text. Particular thanks goes to Jenny Lehmann at Princeton's computer center, who adapted an indexing program to my needs, and to Len Galla, who helped me enter the data.

I would also like to express special gratitude to the institutions who granted me stipends for my research. The Memorial Foundation for Jewish Culture helped to defray part of the costs of typing and binding the dissertation. The Princeton University Committee on Research in the Humanities and Social Science helped pay for typing and binding towards publication and made a generous grant subsidizing the printing. A further grant to subsidize publication was made by the Max Richter Foundation.

Princeton, New Jersey   ALAN F. SEGAL
March 23, 1976
Adar 21 5736

LIST OF ABBREVIATIONS
(and frequently cited works)

AAJR	American Academy for Jewish Research
Ab.	Aboth
Abr.	De Abrahamo
Act. Pil.	Acts of Pilate
Acts	The Acts of the Apostles
Adv. Haer.	Adversus Haereses
Adv. Marc.	Adversus Marcionem
Aet.	De Aeternitate Mundi
Agr.	De Agricultura
AJSL	*American Journal of Semitical Languages and Literature*
Albeck	Enoch Albeck and Enoch Yalon, *The Six Orders of the Mishnah* (Jerusalem: 1959).
Alon, *Toledot*	G. Alon, *Toledot ha-Yehudim be-eres Yisrael betekufat ha-Mishnah we-hatalmud* (2 vols.) Tel Aviv: 1952-55
Am.	Amos
Ant.	Antiquities (as in Josephus, *Jewish Antiquities*)
Apoc. Abr.	Apocalypse of Abraham
Apocr. and Pseudepigr.	R. H. Charles, ed., *Apocrypha and Pseudepigrapha of the Old Testament* (Oxford: 1913)
Apol.	Apology
Aptowitzer	*Kain und Abel in der Agada: den Apocryphen, der hellenistischen, christlichen und muhammedanischen Literatur.* (Vienna and Leipzig: R. Lowit, 1922)
Aq.	Aquila
Arab. vers.	Arabic version
Arak.	Arakhin
Arm.	Armenian
ARN, ARNA, ARNB	Aboth de Rabbi Nathan, Texts A and B
Asc. Is.	Ascension of Isaiah
Ass. Mos.	Assumption of Moses
A. Zar.	Abodah Zarah
B.B.	Baba Bathra
b	Babli (Babylonian Talmud)
b.	ben or bar (son of)
Bacher, *APA*	Wilhelm Bacher, *Die Agada der Palästinensischen Amoräer* (Strassburg, 1892)
Bacher, *AT*	W. Bacher, *Aggadot Ha-Tannaim*, tr. into Hebr. by A. Z. Rabbinowitz (Tel Aviv: 5682)
Bar.	Baruch
BASOR	*Bulletin of the American Schools of Oriental Research*
B.C.E.	Before the Common Era
BDB	F. Brown, S. R. Driver and C. A.Briggs *Hebrew and English Lexicon* (New York: 1907)
Bekh.	Bekhoroth
Ber.	Berakhoth
Bergmann	J. Bergmann, *Jüdische Apologetik: im neutestamentlichen Zeitalter* (Berlin: Georg Reimer, 1908)

Bet. haMidr.	Bet haMidrash
Betz.	Betzah (or 'Yom Tob')
Bianchi, *Gnosticisimo*	Bianchi, ed., *Le Origine della Gnosticismo* (Leiden: 1967)
Bikk.	Bikkurim
Birnbaum	Philip Birnbaum, ed., *Daily Prayer Book* (New York: 1949)
BJRL	*Bulletin of the John Rylands Library*
B.K.	Baba Kamma
B.M.	Baba Metzia
Borgen	Peder Borgen, "God's Agent in the Fourth Gospel," *Religions in Antiquity.* Festschrift for E. R. Goodenough (Leiden: Brill, 1968) p. 137-148.
Buber	Martin Buber, *Eclipse of God: Studies in the Relations Between Religion and Philosophy* (New York: 1957)
Büchler, *Minim*	Adolph Büchler, "The Minim of Sepphoris & Tiberius in the Second and Third Centuries" in *Studies in Jewish History* (London: 1956)
CCARJ	*Central Conference of American Rabbis Journal*
C.E.	Common Era
Cher.	De Cherubim
1 Chr.	1 Chronicles
2 Chr.	2 Chronicles
c. Christ.	Julian, *contra Christianos*
CD	The Damascus Rule (The Zadokite Fragment)
C.G.	Cairo Geniza
C.G.L.	Coptic Gnostic Library at Nag Hamadi
Chron. Jer.	Chronicles of Jerahmeel
Col.	Colossians
Conf.	De Confusione Linguarum
Congr.	De Congressu Eruditionis gratia
Cont. Ap.	Contra Apionem
1 Cor.	1 Corinthians
2 Cor.	2 Corinthians
C.P.J.	Corpus Papyrorum Judaicarum
Dahl, *2 Cor.*	Nils Alstrup Dahl, "The Fragment 2 Corinthians 6:14-7:1 and its Context" unpublished paper
Dahl, "Christology Notes"	N. A. Dahl, unpublished "Christology Notes"
Dahl, "Conflicting Scriptural Passages"	N. A. Dahl, unpublished notes on Conflicting Scriptural Passages
Dahl	N. A. Dahl, "Der Erstgeborene Satans und der Vater des Teufels (Polyk. 7 und Joh. 8:44)," *Apophoreta: Festschrift—Ernst Haenchen* (Berlin: 1964)
Dan.	Daniel
Decal.	De Decalogo
Dem.	Demai
Det.	Quod Deterius Potiori insidiari soleat
Dial.	Justin, *Dialogue with Trypho*
d.o.	Direct object
D.S.	*Diqduke Soferim* (Variae Lectionis in Mischnam et in Talmud Babylonicum) recorded by R. Rabinowitz (Brooklyn: 5720 et. seq.)
D.S.S.	Dead Sea Scrolls
Dt.	Deuteronomy

Ebr.	De Ebrietate
Ec.	Ecclesiastes
Eduy.	Eduyoth
EJ	*Encyclopedia Judaica*
Elbogen	Ismar Elbogen, *Der jüdische Gottesdienst in seiner ge-schichtlichen Entwicklung* (Hildesheim: 1962)
Ep. Arist.	Epistle of Aristeas
Eph.	Ephesians
Epi.	Epiphanius
Epstein, tr.	*The Babylonian Talmud*, tr. I Epstein (London: Soncino, 1961).
Epstein, *MBW ᵓWT*	J. N. Epstein, *MBW ᵓWT LŚPRWT HTN ᵓYM.* (Jerusalem: 1957)
Eranos	*Eranos Jahrbuch*
E.R.E.	*Encyclopedia of Religion and Ethics*
Erub.	Erubin
Est.	Esther
Eus.	Eusebius
Evang. Quart.	*Evangelical Quarterly*
Ex.	Exodus
Ezek.	Ezekiel
Ezra	Ezra
Festugière	R. P. Festugière, *La Révélation d'Hermes Trismégiste* (Paris: 1949-54) in four volumes
Finkelstein	*Sifre on Deuteronomy*, ed., L. Finkelstein (New York: 1969)
Fischel	H. Fischel, *Rabbinic Literature and Greco-Roman Philosophy: A Study of Epicurea and Rhetorica in Early Midrashic Writings* (Leiden: 1973)
Flacc.	In Flaccum
Fossum	Jarl Fossum, Dissertation, Utrecht
Freedman, tr.	*Midrash Rabbah*, ed. and tr. H. Freedman and K. Simon (London: Sociano, 1961)
Friedländer, *Gnosticismus*	M. Friedländer, *Die vorchristliche jüdische Gnosticismus* (Göttingen: 1898)
Fug.	De Fuga et Inventione
Gal.	Galatians
Gen.	Genesis
Gen. Apoc.	Genesis Apocryphon
Gig.	De Gigantibus
Ginzberg, *Legends*	Louis Ginzberg, *The Legends of the Jews*, trans. Henrietta Szold (Philadelphia: 1968)
Gitt.	Gittin
Goldin, *Song*	J. Goldin, *The Song at the Sea: Being a Commentary on a Commentary in Two Parts* (New Haven: 1971)
Goodenough, *Jewish Symbols*	E. R. Goodenough, *Jewish Symbols in the Greco-Roman Period* (New York: 1942)
Graetz, *Gnosticismus*	H. Graetz, *Gnosticismus und Judentum* (Krotoschin: 1946)
Green	A. Green, "The Children in Egypt and the Theophany at the Sea: Interpretation of an Aggadic Motif," unpublished paper
Gruenwald, *Apocalyptic*	I. Gruenwald, *Apocalyptic and Merkabah Mysticism: A*

and Merkabah Mysticism   *Study of the Jewish Esoteric Literature in the time of the Mishnah and Talmud.* Unpublished dissertation (Jerusalem: Hebrew University, 1968/9) revised edition forthcoming from Leiden: Brill, 1978.

Gruenwald, *Visions of Ezekiel*   I. Gruenwald, ed., "The Visions of Ezekiel" *Temirin: Texts and Studies in Kabbalah and Hasidism*, ed., I. Weinstein (Jerusalem: 1972)

Gunther, *St. Paul's Opponents*   J. J. Gunther, *St. Paul's Opponents and their Background* (Leiden: 1973)

H.A.   Hypostasis of the Archons

Hab.   Habakkuk

Hag.   Hagigah

Harnack   A. von Harnack, *Marcion: das Evangelium vom fremden Gott: eine Monographie zur Geschichte der Grundlegung der katholischen Kirche* (Darmstadt: 1960)

Hall.   Hallah

Heb.   Hebrews

Hengel, *Son of God*   Martin Hengel, *The Son of God*, tr. J. Bowden (Philadelphia: Abingdon, 1976).

Herford   R. Travers Herford, *Christianity in Talmud and Midrash* (London: 1903)

Hip.   Hippolytus

Hist. Jud.   *Historia Judaica*

Holscher, *Anfängliches Fragen*   U. Holscher, *Anfängliches Fragen: Studien zur frühen griechischen Philosophie* (Göttingen: 1968)

Hor.   Horayoth

Hos.   Hosea

H-R   H. S. Horowitz & A. Rabin, *Mekhilta d Rabbi Ismael* (Frankfort: 1931)

HR   *History of Religions*

HSS   *Harvard Semitic Studies*

HTR   *Harvard Theological Review*

HUCA   *Hebrew Union College Annual*

Hull.   Hullin

Hyp.   Hypothetica

ICC   *International Critical Commentary*

IEJ   *Israel Exploration Journal*

Is.   Isaiah

JAOS   *Journal of the American Oriental Society*

Jas.   James

Jastrow   M. Jastrow, *Dictionary of the Targumim, the Talmud Babli & Yerushalmi and the Midrashic Literature* (New York: 1926)

JBL   *Journal of Biblical Literature*

JE   *Jewish Encyclopedia*

Jer.   Jeremiah

Jg.   Judges

JJGL   *Jahrbuch für jüdische Geschichte und Literatur*

JJS   *Journal of Jewish Studies*

Jl.   Joel

Jn.   John

1 Jn.   1 John

2 Jn.   2 John

3 Jn.	3 John
JNES	*Journal of Near Eastern Studies*
Job	Job
Joël, *Blicke*	M. Joël, *Blicke in die Religionsgeschichte zu Anfang des zweiten christlichen Jahrhunderts* (Breslau: 1880)
Jon.	Jonah
Jos.	De Josepho
Josh.	Joshua
JPS	*Jewish Publication Society of America*
JR	*Journal of Religion*
JSJ	*Journal for the Study of Judaism*
Jub.	Jubilees
Jude	Jude
Kasher	M. M. Kasher, *Torah Shelemah*, 23 vols. (New York: 5709 f.)
Kel.	Kelim
Ker.	Kerithoth
Ker. Pet.	The Preaching of Peter
Ket.	Ketuboth
1 Kg.	1 Kings
2 Kg.	2 Kings
Kidd.	Kiddushin
Kil.	Kilaim
Kinn.	Kinnim
Koehler-Baumgartner	L. Koehler & W. Baumgartner, *Lexicon in Veteris Testamenti Libros* (Leiden: 1948)
Krauss	S. Krauss, *Griechische und Lateinische Lehnwörter in Talmud, Midrash & Targum* (Berlin: 1898-9)
Lam.	Lamentations
Lauterbach	J. Z. Lauterbach, *Mekilta de-Rabbi Ishmael* (Philadelphia: 1949)
Lauterbach, *Clarifications*	J. Lauterbach, "Some Clarifications on the Mekhilta," *Sefer Klausner: A Collection of Science and Belles-Lettres gathered for Prof. Y. Klausner on his Sixtieth Jubilee*, ed., N. H. Torchyner, A. A. Kubek, A. Tcherikover, B. Shortman, (Tel Aviv: 1940)
Lauterbach, *Jesus*	J. Lauterbach, "Jesus in the Talmud," in *Rabbinic Essays* by J. Lauterbach (New York: 1973).
Lauterbach, *Rabbinic Essays*	J. Lauterbach, *Rabbinic Essays*
Leg.	De Legatione ad Gaium
Leg. All. i, ii, iii	Legum Allegoria
Lev.	Leviticus
Lieberman, *Greek*	S. Lieberman, *Greek in Jewish Palestine: Studies in the Life and Manners of Jewish Palestine in the II-IV Centuries C.E.* (New York: 1965)
Lieberman, *How Much Greek?*	S. Lieberman, "How Much Greek in Jewish Palestine?" *Biblical and other Studies*, ed., A. Altmann, (Cambridge: 1963)
Liddell-Scott	Liddell & Scott, *Greek-English Lexicon*, 9th ed., (Oxford: 1940)
Lk.	Luke
Loeb	Loeb Classics Edition, *e.g. Philo*, tr. F. H. Colson and G. Whitaker and R. Marcus (Cambridge: Harvard University Press, 1971)

LXX	Septuagint
m	mishnah
Maas.	Maaseroth
Makk.	Makkoth
Mal.	Malachi
Marmorstein, *Background*	A. Marmorstein, "The Background of the Haggadah," *HUCA*, 6 (1929)
Marmorstein, *Essays in Anthropomorphism*	A. Marmorstein, *Essays in Anthropomorphism*, vol. II of The Old Rabbinic Doctrine of God (New York: 1937)
Marmorstein, *The Old Rabbinic Doctrine of God*, also ORDOG	A. Marmorstein, *The Old Rabbinic Doctrine of God* (London: 1937)
Marmorstein, *RGS*	A. Marmorstein, *Religionsgeschichtliche Studien I Heft: Die Bezeichnungen für Christen, und Gnostischen im Talmud und Midras* (Schotschau: 1910)
Marmorstein, *Studies*	A. Marmorstein, *Studies in Jewish Theology* ed., J. Rabinowitz (Oxford: 1950)
Marmorstein, *Unity*	A. Marmorstein, *The Unity of God in Rabbinic Literature*, *HUCA*, 1 (1923).
Meeks, *The Prophet-King*	W. Meeks, *The Prophet-King: Moses Traditions and the Johannine Christology* (Leiden: 1967)
Meg.	Megillah
Meil.	Meilah
Men.	Menahoth
MGWJ	*Monatsschrift für die Geschichte und Wissenschaft des Judentums*
Mic.	Micah
Mid. Tan.	Midrash Tannaim
Midd.	Middoth
Mig.	De Migratione Abrahamo
Mikw.	Mikwaoth
Mk.	Mark
M. Kat.	Moed Katan
Moore	G. F. Moore, *Judaism* (Cambridge: 1927-40)
Mos. i, ii	De Vita Mosis
MRI	Mekhilta debe R. Ishmael
MRSbY	Mekhilta of R. Simeon b. Yohai
M. Sh.	Maaser Sheni
M.T.	massoretic text
Mt.	Matthew
Mut.	De Mutatione Nominum
Nah.	Nahum
Naz.	Nazir
Ned.	Nedarim
Neg.	Negaim
Neh.	Nehemiah
Neusner, *Traditions of the Pharisees*	J. Neusner, "The Rabbinic Traditions about the Pharisees before 70 A.D.: The Problem of Oral Transmission," *JJS*, 22 (1971).
NHW	J. Lewy, *Neuhebräisches & chaldäisches Wörterbuch über die Talmudim & Midrashim* (Leipzig: 1876)
Nidd.	Niddah
NT	*Novum Testamentum*

N.T.	New Testament
NTS	*New Testament Studies*
Num.	Numbers
Ob.	Obadiah
Ödeberg, *III Enoch*	H. Ödeberg, *III Enoch or the Hebrew Book of Enoch* (Cambridge: 1928)
Ohol.	Oholoth
Op.	De Opificio Mundi
Oracles Chaldaiques	*Oracles Chaldaiques,* (Paris: 1971)
Orl.	Orlah
OTS	*Oudtestamentische Studiën*
PA 1, 2, 3, 4, or 5	Palestinian amora of the first through fifth generation
PAAJR	*Proceedings of the American Academy of Jewish Research*
Par.	Parah
Pauly-Wissowa	*Paulys Realencyclopaedie der classischen Altertumswissenchaft...* hrsg. von G. Wissowa, (Stuttgart, 1894 f.)
P.E.	Praeparatio Evangelica
Peah	Peah
PEQ	*Palestine Exploration Quarterly*
Pe.	Pesahim
Pesh.	Peshitta
Pes. K.	Pesikta de Rav Kahana
1 Pet.	1 Peter
2 Pet.	2 Peter
P.G.	*Patrologia Graeca,* ed., J. Migne, Patrologiae cursus Completas Series Graeca (Paris, 1928-36)
PGM	*Papyri Graecae Magicae,* ed. K. Preisendanz (Leipzig: 1928-31)
Phil.	Philippians
Philem.	Philemon
Philos.	Origines, *Philosophumena* (Same as Hip. *Refutatio*)
Plant.	De Plantatione
Post.	De Posteritate Caini
P.R.	Pesikta Rabbati
Pr.	Proverbs
Praem.	De Praemiis et Poenis
PRE	Pirqe de Rabbi Eliezer
Prov.	De Providentia
Ps.	Psalms
Ps. Clem. Hom.	Pseudo-Clement, *Homilies*
Ps. Jon.	Pseudo-Jonathan
I Q Apoc.	Genesis Apocryphon from Qumran
4 Q Flor.	The Blessing of Jacob from Qumran
IQH	The Thanksgiving Psalms from Qumran
IQM	The Wars of the Sons of Light against the Sons of Darkness, the War Scroll from Qumran
11 Q Melch.	The Melchizedek Fragment from Qumran
I Q pHab.	The Habakkuk Commentary from Qumran
4 Q pNah.	The Nahum Commentary from Qumran
IQS	The Manual of Discipline from Qumran
4 Q Test.	The 'Testimonia' from Qumran
Quis Her.	Quis rerum divinarum Heres sit
Quispel, *Gnostic Studies*	G. Quispel, *Gnostic Studies,* 1, (Istambul: 1974)

Quod Deus	Quod Deus sit Immutabilis
Quod Omn. Prob.	Quod omnis Probus liber
Ref.	Refutatio
... R.	Rabbah (indicating a commentary in the Midrash Rabbah)
R.	Rabbi, Rab
RB	*Revue Biblique*
REJ	*Revue des Études Juives*
Rev.	Revelations
RHR	*Revue de l'Histoire des Religions*
Rom.	Romans
RQ	*Revue de Qumran*
R. Sh.	Rosh ha-Shanah
RSV	*Revised Standard Version of the Bible*
Ru.	Ruth
Sac.	De Sacrificiis Abelis et Caini
1 Sam.	1 Samuel
2 Sam.	2 Samuel
Sam. Pent.	Samaritan Pentateuch
Sanh.	Sanhedrin
SBL	Society of Biblical Literature
Scholem Festschrift	*Studies in Mysticism & Religion Presented to Gershom Scholem on his 70th Birthday by Pupils, Colleagues and Friends* (Jerusalem: 1967)
Scholem, *Major Trends*	G. Scholem, *Major Trends in Jewish Mysticism* (New York: 1961)
Scholem, *Jewish Gnosticism*	G. Scholem, *Jewish Gnosticism, Merkabah Mysticism and Talmudic Tradition* (New York: 1965)
Shab.	Shab.
Shebi.	Shebiith
Shebu.	Shebuoth
Shek.	Shekalim
Sib. Or.	Sibylline Oracles
Simon, *Verus Israel*	M. Simon, *Verus Israel: Étude sur les relations entre Chrétiens et Juifs dans L'Empire Romain* (135-425) (Paris: 1964)
SJC	Sophia Jesus Christi
Slav.	Slavonic
Smith, *Observations*	M. Smith, "Observations on Hekhalot Rabbati," in *Biblical and Other Studies*, ed., A. Altmann, (Cambridge: 1963)
Sob.	De Sobrietate
S. of S.	Song of Solomon
Som. i, ii	De Somniis
Soncino Midrash	H. Freedman & M. Simon, ed. *Midrash Rabbah*, trans. into English (London: 1939)
Sot.	Sotah
Sowers, *Hermeneutics*	S. Sowers, *The Hermeneutics of Philo and Hebrews: a Comparison of the Interpretation of the OT in Philo Judaeus and the Epistle to the Hebrews* (Zurich: 1965)
Spec. Leg. i, ii, iii, iv	De Specialibus Legibus
ST	*Studia Theologica*
Strack-Billerbeck	H. Strack & P. Billerbeck, *Das Evangelium nach Matthäus erlautert aus Talmud und Midrash.* vols., I, II, III, IV1, IV2, V, VI (München: 1922)

Strom.	Stromateis
Stud. Patr.	Studia Patristica
Sukk.	Sukkah
t	tosefta
T 1, 2, 3, 4, 5	Tanna of the first through fifth generations
Tam.	Tamid
Taan.	Taanith
Tanh. B.	Tanhuma in Buber's edition
TDNT	*Theological Dictionary of the New Testament*
Teb. Y.	Tebul Yom
Tem.	Temurah
Ter.	Tertullian
Test. Abr.	Testament of Abraham
Test. Ash.	Testament of Asher
Test. Ben.	Testament of Benjamin
Test. Jud.	Testament of Judah
Test. Lev.	Testament of Levi
Test. Naph.	Testament of Naphtali
Test. Reub.	Testament of Reuben
Test. Zeb.	Testament of Zebulun
Tg.	Targum
1 Th.	1 Thessalonians
2 Th.	2 Thessalonians
Theodor-Albeck	J. Theodor & C. Albeck, *Midrash Bereshit Rabba. Critical Edition with Notes and Commentary* (in Hebrew) 2nd printing, corrected. (Jerusalem: 1965)
1 Tim.	1 Timothy
2 Tim.	2 Timothy
Tit.	Titus
TO	Targum Onkelos
TJ	Targum of Jerusalem
TJ II	Fragmentary Targum
TP	Palestinian Targum (TJ, TJ II)
Toh.	Tohoroth
TWNT	*Theologisches Wörterbuch zum Neuen Testament*
Uktz.	Uktzin
Urbach, *Sages*	E. Urbach, *The Sages, their Concepts and Beliefs* (Jerusalem: 1969, in Hebrew)
Urbach, *Secret Torah*	E. Urbach, "The Tradition about Secret Torah" in *Studies in Mysticism and Religion presented to Gershom Scholem on his 70th Birthday by Pupils, Colleagues and Friends* (Jerusalem: 1967).
USQR	*Union Seminary Quarterly Review*
U.W.	"Ursprung des Welt" (The Origin of World) from the Coptic Gnostic Library (untitled work)
Virt.	De Virtute
Vit. Cont.	De Vita Contemplativa
VT	Vetus Testamentum
Vulg.	Vulgate
Weiss, *Dor*	I. Weiss, *Dor Dor WeDorshaw*, 5 vols. (Wilno: 1911)
Winston, *Iranian Component*	D. Winston, "The Iranian Component in the Bible, Apocrypha and Qumran: A Review of the Evidence," *HR*, 5 (1966), 183-216.
Wolfson, *Philo*	H. Wolfson, *Philo: Foundations of Religious Philosophy*

TRANSLITERATIONS

א = '	מ ם = M
ב = B	נ ן = N
ג = G	ס = S
ד = D	צ = '
ה = H	פ ף = P
ו = W	צ ץ = Ṣ
ז = Z	ק = Q
ח = Ḥ	ר = R
ט = Ṭ	שׁ = Š
י = Y	שׂ = Ś
כ ך = K	ת = T
ל = L	

Names and familiar words are spelled in conventional English.

Greek

Greek letters are transliterated by their Latin equivalents. But,

η = ē
θ = th
ξ = x
υ = y; u in diphthongs
φ = ph
χ = ch
ψ = ps
ω = ō
ᶜ = h

PART ONE

INTRODUCTION

CHAPTER ONE

TWO POWERS IN HEAVEN

The History and Importance of the Problem

The intention of this book is to collect and examine the rabbinic reports about the heresy of "two powers in heaven" and to identify the proponents of the heresy. Such a task will impress most readers as abstruse. What interest can there be in such an obscure group of heretics within the early rabbinic movement? This book will attempt to answer that question. My study has convinced me that reports of these heretics (in the talmudic and midrashic literature of roughly the first six centuries of our era) are of considerable relevance for any student of late Hellenistic religion, especially for those interested in Christianity during the first crucial centuries of its growth.

That is no small claim. Anyone familiar with the quantity of material written in the fields of Christian origins and early Judaism has the right to be skeptical of claims to novelty. Surely every shred of evidence in traditional bodies of material has been studied and noted already! Even the heretics who believed in "two powers in heaven" have been discussed several times in scholarly literature. Nor has their significance been entirely missed. The sectarians have been identified, albeit inconclusively, both as gnostics [1] and as Christians. Of course, were it established that the rabbinic reports dealt with one or the other of the groups, the reports about "two powers" would be unmistakably significant. Any new piece of evidence about the behavior of early Christianity would help us understand its cloudy beginnings as a movement. But what has continued to keep this peculiar rabbinic heresy obscure

---

[1] By gnosticism, I mean primarily that religion of salvation in late antiquity which posited an evil secondary god who created this world, making it impossible for any but the elect, by virtue of their knowledge (*gnōsis*) of the high god to find salvation. Gnosticism is the extreme form of a much broader trend in the centuries immediately surrounding Jesus' life. Social alienation, pessimism, other worldliness, secret societies, all may be loosely described as gnostic. But, for reasons which will soon grow apparent, anti-cosmic dualism will be taken as the primary criterion separating the phenomenon of *gnōsis* and the movement of gnosticism. See Yamauchi, *Pre-Christian Gnosticism*, pp. 13-28 for a discussion of the problems in defining gnosticism. (Full references for frequently cited works can be found in the list of abbreviations, p. xv f.)

is lack of firm proof that the term "two powers in heaven" referred either to Christians or to gnostics exclusively (as if they were separate movements!) compounded by a great deal of confusion about what the heretical doctrine was.

Unfortunately, I cannot claim to have identified the heretics in every case. In fact, many of my remarks will be cautionary—showing that an earlier scholar's identification of a report of "two powers" either as Christian or as gnostic cannot be firmly maintained. However, in one very early, very important text I can identify one group as the indicated heresy by excluding the others. This has significant implications for our understanding of the first century. More often, I will try to show that both Christians and gnostics (and others as well) became the targets of the particular rabbinic polemic which the title "two powers" denoted. Previous studies have tended to make identifications casually, so even negative conclusions or mixed conclusions will be significant. It would also be significant to demonstrate that the rabbis put Christianity and gnosticism in the same category to argue against them. Furthermore there is new evidence suggesting that Christians and gnostics were not the only targets for the title of "two powers" heretics. I will try to show where the reports can be related to other groups, whose lives or writings can be more firmly dated than the rabbinic tradition. Whenever it is possible to isolate reports and date them (a constant concern throughout the paper) I will try to sketch out a history of the various heresies in Judaism which, in turn, may illuminate the darkness regarding the origins of Christianity and gnosticism.

Needless to say, if the problem of the "two powers" heresy could be solved in a straightforward manner, it would already have been solved. However, writers like the Christian heresiologists, who composed special tracts against their enemies, were rare, and an intellectual like Origen, who actually quoted his opponent copiously, was unique. The rabbis stuck closer to a more effective procedure of their day for dealing with opponents—allusion and polemic. They did little to characterize their enemies, especially when to do so would have had the effect of spreading the error further. Such an exercise would have impressed them as unwittingly publicizing evil or, as they would have said, as "an opening of the mouth for Satan." Consequently, identifying any of the opponents of the rabbis in rabbinical texts is still a vexing problem.

We must realize that problems abound even in the definition and etymology of the rabbinic word for "sectarian" or "heretic." (Hebrew "*min*"; pl. "*minim*"). [2] In English the words "sectarian" and "heretic" express different degrees of disapproval and social distance. A sectarian is probably best described as a disapproved rival among many factions within the parent group, while a heretic is someone who began in the parent group but who has put himself beyond the pale with respect to some canon of orthodoxy. The transition between "sectarian" and "heretic" in rabbinic literature would have been apparent only when rabbinic Judaism was acknowledged to have become "normative." Unfortunately, there is no scholarly consensus about when rabbinic thought became orthodox. Furthermore the rabbis assume that their interpretation of Judaism was always orthodox and never distinguish clearly between "sectarians" and "heretics." So far as they were concerned, any interpretation not part of their accepted community was "heretical" though there was certainly a time when non-pharisaic interpretations were only "sectarian."

This is what one would expect generally in long conflicts within a community. Since any community includes people who may share only a few important norms and mutual connections, not every argument is grounds for fission. Rather, when a crisis arises, a period of debate takes place when the issues are clarified. New authority may develop to deal with the crisis. Temporary sanctions may be applied to warn the heretics of their behavior. Only at the end of a long process of definition will the heresy grow clear. However, after the limit has been set, the past history of the issue may be seen in much less ambiguous light. Once the end point is known the development takes on a different aspect.

---

[2] *Min* = heretic seems to have no convincing antecedents in Biblical Hebrew. Joël, *Blicke*, II, p. 71, derived it from MᵓMYN (believer, like *pistos*), which seems improbable. For a complete bibliography and discussion of the problems, see Elbogen, p. 36, Simon, *Verus Israel*, p. 217 f. and G. Hoennecke in the appendix to his study *Juden-Christentum*, p. 398. Levy, *NHW*, III, 104a derived the term from the arabic root meaning to lie, speak falsely, by comparing it with the assumed etymology of the Syriac, *mania*. However, *mania* is equally likely to have been a loan word from the Greek, meaning "madness." Herford, p. 362 suggested that the word came from a root shared by Hebrew and Aramaic (*min* in Hebrew, ZN in Aramaic). The word is associated with the Hebrew word, ZNH meaning "to commit adultery." Bacher's suggestion seems the most plausible to me. He derived the word from the Hebrew, MYN, meaning "kind" or "species," or "sex." From this it acquired the secondary sense of "sect." Finally, in rabbinic literature it became the word describing a member of that sect—a development paralleled by the word "GWY," which meant "nation" in Biblical Hebrew but evolved the meaning of "gentile" in rabbinic Hebrew. The *double entendre* that Herford noticed would hold in any case.

What we know about the rabbinic period seems to follow this general model. The standard, rabbinic modes of expulsion—ḤRM and NDWY—do not seem to have been formalized in the first and second centuries. [3] At least, we do not have good evidence to suppose their use against the *minim*. However, the process of exclusion was certainly well underway by the time of the Mishnah's codification (200 C.E.) for the Mishnah prohibits the leader of the service from saying certain benedictions associated with the *minim*. [4] Since the instrument of expulsion is liturgical in this case, perhaps we may trace the process back to the Yavnean community where Gamaliel (about 80-115) ordered Samuel the Small to compose a "benediction" against the *minim*. [5] This would have made participation in synagogue services impossible for anyone identifying himself as a *min*. Though the tradition is from a later source and may have been embellished in many respects, such a development would not be unexpected in the Yavnean community, which had to deal with the problem of understanding what the term "Jew" was to mean after the temple was destroyed. Therefore we are dealing with a definition of the limits of Judaism which developed over the time and which may not have reached uniform practice until the very end of the second century.

Logically, one would think that a non-Jew would qualify neither as a sectarian nor as a heretic. Unfortunately, strict logic does not apply to the situation. There is a certain amount of evidence that the rabbis occasionally used the word *"min"* loosely to describe gentiles whose beliefs and practices resembled the Jewish heresy under consideration.

One thing is certain. The earlier scholarly attempt to identify the *minim* as a single group was misled. [6] A variety of Jewish sectarian groups fell heir to the rabbinic designation, *min*. Depending on the context and epoch in which the specific tradition arose, *min* could refer

---

[3] See Goeran Forkman, *The Limits of the Religious Community: Expulsion from the Religious Community within the Qumran Sect, within Rabbinic Judaism and within Primitive Christianity* (Lund: 1972). He relies on the work of C. H. Hunzinger, *Die jüdische Bannpraxis im neutestamentlichen Zeitalter* (Göttingen: 1954) and J. E. Mignard, *Jewish and Christian Cultic Discipline to the Middle of the Second Century* (Boston: 1966).

[4] See p. 98 f.

[5] See Berakhoth 28b. An original reference to *minim* in the "blessing" is generally conceded even though the contemporary liturgy has omitted the phrase. It can be reconstructed from versions in the Cairo Geniza. See Elbogen, p. 37 f.

[6] Herford (p. 17 f.) tried to identify *min* with Christian but that is overly-simple, as will become apparent.

to Samaritan, Sadducee, gnostic, Judeo-Christian, and many others. [7] This contributes to much of the confusion in identifying heretical groups and makes the careful determination of the place and date of the rabbinic traditions all the more important. Furthermore, in order to identify the various sectarian groups, one must also identify the heretical doctrine espoused by those groups and find evidence that the doctrine can be clearly associated with an historical group at the time the rabbinic tradition arose.

Those heretics who believed in "two powers in heaven" present a more promising target in the identification of sectarian groups than do other heresies, because some kind of dualistic doctrine is inherent in the rabbinic designation. However, as we have seen, that definition of dualism must be broad enough to include Christianity as a referent. At its beginning, Christianity was rather more "binitarian" than trinitarian, emphasizing only Christ and the Father as God. Since Christianity has been suggested as a candidate for the heresy by scholars, we must be prepared to allow that the "two powers in heaven" were complementary instead of opposing deities as one normally expects. The heresy may have been "binitarianism" or "ditheism" depending on the perspective of the speaker, but not necessarily opposing dualism. Thus, propounding a strict definition of the heresy before looking at the evidence will be impossible. Instead I will continue to call the heresy "two powers in heaven" as the rabbis did. [8]

---

[7] According to j. Sanh. 10:5, there were 24 different kinds of *minim* at the destruction of the Temple. While the number "twenty four" must be purely conventional, it illustrates the complexities in identifying sectarian groups. The *"min"* who derided Alexander the Great for rising before the Jewish High Priest, thus showing him deference (Lev. R. xiii), is usually identified as a Samaritan, because Samaritans are reported in other legends to have criticized the Jews before Alexander. Ber. 9:5 refers to the institution of a benediction with the words "from eternity to eternity" which has been taken as a counter-measure against the Sadducees who rejected the concept of resurrection. A variety of Jewish Christians or gnostics have been seen as the opponents of the rabbis in b. Sanh. 39b. See *JE*, VIII, 595 for examples of these conventional identifications. S. M. Wagner has attempted to define several categories of deviation in rabbinic writings in *Religious Non-Conformity in Ancient Jewish Life*. Unpub. dissertation, Yeshiva University, 1964. However, the terms may have changed in meaning over their long history of use in tannaitic and amoraic literature.

[8] The ambiguous translation "two *powers* in heaven" has been maintained with the knowledge that the Hebrew term is only approximated by the English "power." Its different meanings should perhaps be noted at the outset. From the root R-Š-Y, it has the general sense of power of disposal, permission, authority. In detail, it means the right of possession to something (see Foerster, *TDNT*, *"exousia"* 565 for examples) the authority of commission, the right or the freedom to do something, as heirs and

Of course, most rabbinic passages just use "two powers" and assume the reader will know what it means. Only a few passages in rabbinic literature actually elaborate on the subject of "two powers in heaven," and even these few passages define it from a confusing variety of perspectives. Some of the passages treat "two powers in heaven" as one category of heretical doctrine. Sifre Dt. 329, for instance, mentions those who believe in "no power in heaven," followed by those who believe in "two powers in heaven," and finally, those who believe

---

descendants at law (in Ket., 9:5; a divorced women in Ned. 10:3; the marriage Ned. 10:3 etc.).

When contrasted with ḤWBH (obligatory) it means "optional" or "recommended" or "voluntary." It can mean "power" in the sense of "capability" or "ability," as when someone is able to move himself voluntarily, under his own power.

However, since the more normal word for power in the sense of "capability" is KḤ, RŠWT should be distinguished as power in the sense of "authority" as when a piece of land is within the power of a person or community. Indeed, the terms does have many legal ramifications, in the fixing of limits on property rights and obligations. Accordingly, ŠTY RŠWYWT BŠMYM has often been taken to mean "two dominions in heaven." I use the more ambiguous term "power" because the texts show that dominion is not its primary meaning. Rather, as I will show in reference to the Greek understanding of the term "authority," RŠWT often has the implication of a figure or person and means authority in the sense that the figure has capability independent of God. Indeed, "two gods" is a common synonym.

The implication of "personage" may clearly be seen in the New Testament use of the word. In Greek, *dynamis* (power, capability) and *exousia* (power, authority) may be synonymous (see Liddell-Scott, *TDNT*). The LXX often translates MLKWT (dominion) as *exousia* or *dynamis*, though sometimes with other words as well. Strictly speaking, *dynamis* would imply an impersonal power when predicated of deity whereas *exousia* would imply a personal power. However, these distinctions become clouded in Hellenistic Jewish texts where the dynamis of the deity is sometimes hypostatised as a separate person. (Grundmann, *dynamis TDNT*, II, 295). Thus the exercise of God's power may be personified in the forces of angels who bear different names, such as *archai, kyriotētes, eklektoi, exousiai, thronoi, dynameis.* (Cf., Bertholdt Stade, *Theologie des A.T.*, I (1911) 375, for examples). The Hebrew word and the NT usage of *exousia* seem parallel except in matters where the NT theologically differs from rabbinic discussions. (Foerster, *TDNT*). In the NT, *exousia* may also mean the power of Satan, though it is sometimes seen as a derivative of God's power. In relation to Jesus, where it denotes his divinely given power and authority to act, it goes beyond rabbinic theology where only God can act independently in the heavenly realm, and thus gives credence to the rabbinic use as a charge against Christian heretics. In Christianity, it may also be used for the authority imparted to the church. (Foerster, *op. cit.* for examples.) Then too, the NT uses *exousia*, together with *archai, dynameis,* and *kyriotetes* to describe supernatural beings.

It is clear that what the rabbis objected to was not other heavenly beings. They too told stories about angels. However, they were particularly scrupulous to avoid the connotation that any heavenly being could exercise *independent authority* and every detail in characterizing a heavenly being's personality made that danger more real. It will become clear, then, that the rabbis will object to "two powers" heresy because they view it as a "two authorities" theology.

that God has "neither the power to kill nor to preserve." Of course, the categories for defining the heretics lack consistency. The expected parallel—many powers in heaven—does not appear here though it is attested elsewhere. The third group is defined in different categories than the first and second. The reason for this is that the rabbinic source is primarily concerned with the exegesis of the scripture under consideration—Dt. 32:39—which turns out to be a powerful argument against heretics. It is only secondarily concerned with categories of doctrine. Throughout the paper considerable attention will be devoted to the pattern of scriptural citation because the scriptural supports for heresy and orthodoxy were of primary importance to the rabbis. Their attention to scripture will guide us in reconstructing the argument between the rabbis and the heretics, at least as the rabbis saw it. After this has been done, it will be possible to assess the rabbis' perspective about the content of the heresy.

By outlining the difficulties encountered merely in defining terms, I am suggesting that previous studies have artificially simplified the problem. Yet, I do not mean to imply that the previous research is irrelevant in the gargantuan task of identifying these heretics. Previous researchers have been mature scholars educated since youth in traditional texts. Rather, the passage of time has brought new information and new methodologies to light making it possible to refine their insights and correct their biases. To appreciate the problem of partiality, one must survey the approaches that scholarship has taken on the problem.

Heinrich Graetz began the study of "two powers" heretics. He was attempting to relate the reports of gnosticism and anti-gnostic polemic in the writings of the church fathers with reports of sectarianism and heresy in rabbinic texts. [9] Graetz's analysis of gnosticism centered on the figure of Elisha ben Abuya (ca. 110-135) whom tradition had branded the arch-heretic. Elisha ben Abuya was disrespectfully named "Aher" (Other), by the rabbis, as if he were too infamous to name directly. Graetz saw Elisha b. Abuya as the model antinomian gnostic. The relationship between Aher's apostasy and "two powers in heaven" is based on a long passage in the Babylonian Talmud (Hag. 14b) which

---

[9] The literature on Jewish gnosticism from Krochmal, *Moreh Nebukei Hazeman* (Lemberg: 1851) and Graetz, *Gnosticismus* can be found in Blau's article in *JE*, V, 686. See also Weiss, *Dor*, II, 125 ff. Some modern problems are summed up in R. Mcl. Wilson, *The Gnostic Problem* (London: 1958).

concerns four rabbis' mystical journey to paradise. For Graetz, the
passage became the paradigm of Hellenistic sectarian possibilities. In
this passage, four sages—Akiba, Simeon b. Zoma, Simeon b. Azai and
Aher—are credited with an ascension to Paradise (the *pardes*) while
yet alive; only Akiba is reported to have survived the journey unharmed.
For Graetz, Aher exemplifies of the antinomian wing of gnosticism;
Simeon b. Zoma and Simeon b. Azai are representatives of the moderate
Jewish-gnostic wing; only Akiba is exemplary of Jewish anti-gnosticism.
Graetz described Aher as an antinomian because he is elsewhere reported to have stopped observing the law. His gnosticism was supposed
by Graetz to derive from an incident on this heavenly journey. Having
successfully avoided the dangers of the voyage, Aher arrives at the
Pardes and sees the angel Metatron enthroned in heaven. Astounded,
Aher asks whether there are "two powers in heaven" and becomes a
heretic when he returns to earth. Graetz associated "two powers in
heaven" with the anti-cosmic dualism that appears in extreme gnosticism. To do so, he emphasized Metatron's resemblance to the gnostic
demiurge, who created an evil world and then tried to keep men from
discovering the good, high god beyond his influence. Since Metatron
is pictured as writing down the merits of Israel and since he is reported
to be Moses' teacher in kabbalistic literature, Graetz reasoned that he
must be equivalent to that gnostic god who has sovereignty over all
earthly things. He must also be seen as subservient to a higher god,
since the Talmud reports that he is punished by God for giving Aher
the wrong impression. Consequently, the reports of "two powers in
heaven" were seen by Graetz as extreme gnosticizing within Judaism,
a tendency exemplified by Aher and characterized by a rejection of
those aspects of Judaism which were difficult or dangerous to observe
in the Hadrianic persecution (which he dated before the Bar Kochba
Revolt). Even so, Graetz saw gnosticism as a Hellenistic phenomenon.
It arose outside of Judaism and entered it during a time when the
convenient adoption of its principles made life easier for those without
the courage to stand fast to Judaism's monotheistic "orthodoxy."

Graetz's dating and theories have deservedly been criticized because
of his speculative reconstruction of events. However, every scholarly
inquiry into Jewish gnosticism has continued to assume that reports of
"two powers in heaven" are part of its subject matter. [10] Other scholars
have blithely assumed that "two powers in heaven" refers to Christ-

---

[10] See p. 60 f. (Chapter 3) for a fuller discussion of the problem.

ianity. J. Z. Lauterbach, [11] suggested that refutations of those who believe in "two powers" are arguments against Christianity when it was still considered a Jewish heresy. To demonstrate this assertion he cited Dt. R. II, 33 where Solomon is reported by the rabbis to have stated categorically that the one God has neither son or brother. Since some texts associate this heresy with "two powers" Lauterbach felt that the second heavenly power must be Jesus. "Two powers" could only refer to Persian dualism if the parties were antagonistic, [12] while Christian theology might easily have been understood by the rabbis to posit a second divine figure working in harmony with and claiming to be the son of the one God.

R. Travers Herford [13] also dealt with the rabbinic evidence but was misled by prior assumptions. As he saw it, his task was to collect all the passages describing Christianity in the Talmuds and midrash. However, he quickly took up the thesis that all the references to the *minim* refer to Christians, a view which he maintained in spite of evidence to the contrary. Predictably, he came to the conclusion that the *minim* who believed in "two powers in heaven" were Christians, though probably gnostic Christians. Of course, like other scholars of this period, his conclusion was not wrong for the entire history of the heresy. Herford's primary mistake was methodological. Having taken up a theory, everything was made to fit it, despite information which contradicted his thesis.

Only one study in this period dealt solely with the heresy of "two powers in heaven." That was the work of S. Rubin. [14] His study defined "two powers" as any kind of dualism. Hence, he dealt with any philosophical dualism as "two powers in heaven," mentioning the talmudic period only superficially and without any real historical method. He also fancifully assumed that the talmudic dualists were Manichaeans because the term *min* resembles the name *Mani*.

A more significant direction was taken by A. Marmorstein [15] who studied eight tradition clusters concerning those who believe in "two

---

[11] Lauterbach, *Jesus*.

[12] Lauterbach is assuming that sons and brothers could not be antagonistic in the heavenly economy. However, he neglects to mention that Ahura Mazda and Angra Mainyu are spoken of as brothers in Persian literature and that a monotheistic heresy in Zoroastrianism, namely Zurvanism, assumed that there was a common father for both.

[13] R. Travers Herford, *Christianity in Talmud and Midrash*.

[14] Solomon Rubin, *The Belief in Two Powers* [in Hebr.] (Krakow: 1908-09).

[15] Marmorstein, *RGS*, I, pp. 66-81.

powers." His efforts were devoted to the interrelation between rabbinic Judaism and Christianity, but the passages themselves were discussed under the rubric of the *dogmata* (*Lehrsätze*) of the gnostics, implying a certain reticence to identify the traditions as referring strictly either to Christian or gnostic groups. Even in some later works, Marmorstein [16] found it impossible to reach any final conclusion about the identity of the rabbis' opponents, allowing both Christians and gnostics as possibilities from the internal evidence. According to Marmorstein, the critical evidence must come from external sources. He was most hopeful of developing "statistical data," by which he seems to have meant demographic and sociological information about the geographical proximity of various opponent communities to the rabbinic sages. Yet, Marmorstein tended in other writings to ignore his more cautious statements. He attributed the tannaitic reports of "two powers in heaven" to anti-gnostic polemic; those afterwards he attributed to anti-Christian polemic. [17] No good reasons were developed for the assumption of such a chronology. Rather he seemed to rely on the then new, but now outmoded, scholarly consensus that Christianity grew out of a hypothetical pre-Christian gnosticism. Viewed from our later perspective, his assumption of a pre-Christian gnosticism was premature. Proof of its existence has remained elusive, though there is growing evidence of non-Christian gnosticism. [18] With more careful examination of the data, and without making assumptions at the outset, it is hoped that a few more clues about the origin of gnosticism, and its relationship to Judaism and Christianity can be recovered in the reports of "two powers in heaven." But it is certainly counter-productive to assume any sequence or development for the data before it has been thoroughly analyzed.

Among more recent scholars, Adolf Büchler [19] made a most helpful contribution by asking why many statements attributed to heretics vilify Jews but not the biblical claims of Israel. He then suggested that these "sectarians," though called "heretics," must have understood themselves as non-Jews. Therefore, the term "heretic" must be comprehended in its historical context. As an example of this, he showed that Jewish

---

[16] Marmorstein, *Unity*, 467-99.
[17] See also Marmorstein, *Background*, pp. 141-204 for a discussion of Marcion and the problem of dualism in rabbinic literature.
[18] See Yamauchi, *Pre-Christian Gnosticism*.
[19] Büchler, *Minim*.

polemic against heretics sometimes was aimed at gentile Christians like Justin Martyr. [20] Only a person who wanted to place his group in the privileged position of Israel would attempt to discredit the Jews without doing damage to Jewish exegetical traditions. More interesting still for this study is the fact that some of the arguments of Justin are called "two powers" arguments by the rabbis. [21] When his evidence is fully seen it is sufficient to conclude that Christians were sometimes described as "those who believed in two powers," [22] but only in one particular time and place. We must still leave open the possibility that other groups at other times used the same arguments and hence warranted the same designation.

Even though these scholars did not solve the problem adequately, a great deal has been learned about the significance of the reports of "two powers in heaven" from them. The earliest studies tended to assume that the reports of "two powers" were evidence for their hypotheses about early Jewish heretics, whether they identified them as Christians or gnostics. As time went on, it became clear that more than one group could have been involved. What is needed now is an impartial study of the reports without any previous assumption about their referents or priorities.

The groundwork for impartial study of "two powers" tradition was begun by G. F. Moore. [23] Moore dealt with the problem of "two

---

[20] His argument for the association is made by reviewing the scriptural passages used to fight dualism. These would include Gen. 1:26 ("Let us make man in our image") where the possible interpretation of God's having an associate in creation proved difficult to the rabbis. Of course, the rabbis record many instances of these difficult passages. One such instance, Gen. 19:24, was discussed in Sepphoris around 200 C.E. by Ishmael ben Yosi. The verse reads "The Lord rained down fire and brimstone on Sodom and Gomorrah from the Lord from heaven." The difficulty here is a possible inference of two gods from the otherwise superfluous "from the Lord." As Büchler points out, Justin Martyr used this verse in his *Dialogue with Trypho* to demonstrate that the God who appeared to Abraham, Isaac and Jacob, was the Christ and a different divine figure from the God who had planned the creation. Further, one of the Jews accompanying Trypho admits that one of the two angels who had gone to Sodom was called "God" by Abraham. Apparently, Justin Martyr also knew of Jews who allowed one name of God to refer to something like a *logos* but refused to identify the *logos* with Jesus as he had done. Since Justin also lived in Tiberias at the same time as R. Ishmael b. Yose, we have the beginning of the kind of "statistical" or demographic evidence that Marmorstein was seeking.

[21] See p. 118.

[22] See p. 221 f.

[23] Moore, *Judaism in the First Centuries of the Christian Era: The Age of the Tannaim* (New York: 1971), I, p. 365 f.

powers in heaven" briefly and in philosophical rather than historical terms in his discussion of the Jewish concept of God. He showed that the rabbis basically criticized these heretics for compromising the mono-theistic center of Judaism. But he also reasoned that the designation of "two powers" could not refer to polytheism, for polytheism would hardly have been a danger within the Jewish community. However, there were two trends within sectarian Judaism which Moore felt might account for this peculiar rabbinic designation. Some theory of two deities might be related to the several descriptions in rabbinic literature of those who believed God to be the author of good only. Alternatively, a very sublime and transcendent concept of God might lead to a role as divine agent for intermediary heavenly powers, like either the demiurge of gnosticism or the Christ of Hellenistic Christianity. While he masterfully described the rabbinic understanding of monotheism, Moore found it impossible to decide between the two logical possi-bilities for the identity of the "two powers" heresy. Instead, he sum-marized the issues by commenting on the advantages of dualism for reconciling the evil and imperfection so perceptible in the world with the goodness and perfection posited of God. Since dualism was also a widespread solution to the problem of theodicy in Hellenistic philo-sophy, it was not surprising to Moore that dualistic heresies arose in Judaism.

Obviously all the scholars who have written on the problem of "two powers" have seen gnosticism, Judaism, and Christianity as related phenomena, but I have not discussed that aspect of their thought yet because no two scholars agreed completely on the causal nexus between them. It would go too far afield now to summarize the many relation-ships which scholars have posited between Judaism, Christianity and gnosticism. Perhaps since gnosticism was first described by church fathers, Christian scholars have been the most interested in the pro-blem. Although there is agreement among them in correlating Christ-ianity with gnosticism, there is hardly any agreement on a theory which would explain that correlation. Particularly thorny has been the problem of whether gnosticism or Christianity is the chronological predecessor. Did Christianity grow out of a gnostic environment or did gnosticism grow out of a Christian one? The early church fathers saw gnosticism as a Christian heresy and they first reported the term "gnostic" as a description of it.

But from Graetz's time forward it became clear that the question of priority could not be addressed without careful study of Jewish text.

In his book, [24] Moritz Friedländer put forth the thesis that gnosticism is a pre-Christian phenomenon which originated in antinomian circles in the Jewish community of Alexandria. [25] This was a clear statement of the priority of gnosticism to Christianity; it was also innovative in its suggestion that gnosticism originated in Judaism. [26]

Later in the twentieth century, the "History of Religions" school came to similar conclusions from different evidence for the priority of gnosticism to Christianity. They saw the predecessors of gnosticism in Persian and Mandaic texts and theorized that gnosticism grew out of Jewish thought that had absorbed Indo-Iranian themes. [27]

Based on this consensus, many New Testament scholars feel that Christianity actually adapted a pre-existent gnostic savior myth to the facts of Jesus' life. [28] The discovery of gnostic texts at Nag Hammadi has verified the existence of a non-Christian gnosticism in the third century, but no document of pre-Christian gnosticism (which according to Bultmann developed out of a combination of Persian mythology with Israelite traditions) has been discovered. Nor has any one document from the early periods evinced the entire so-called gnostic salvation myth. In fact, we lack any pre-Christian texts which evidence the kind of anticosmic, exclusivistic beliefs evident in the Nag Hammadi texts. Without some contemporary evidence we cannot be sure even of the major tenets of any possible gnosticism in Jesus' time. In order to point out this difficulty, a group of researchers, gathered at Messina, agreed to use "gnosticism" to refer exclusively both to the phenomena outlined by the church fathers and to the later developments of those phenomena, while using "gnosis" to refer to gnostic traits and themes occurring earlier. [29] No agreement was reached as to whether the *gnosis*

---

[24] Friedländer, *Gnosticismus*. Friedländer is also indebted to M. Joël, *Blicke in die Religionsgeschichte zu Anfang des zweiten christlichen Jahrhunderts* (Breslau: 1880).

[25] Philo speaks of these sectarians in Mig. 86-93. See Friedländer, *Gnosticismus*, p. 4-9.

[26] For a detailed analysis of this aspect of Friedländer's work see Birger Pearson, "Friedländer Revisited: Alexandrian Judaism and Gnostic Origins," *Studia Philonica*, 2 (1973), 23-39.

[27] The accomplishments of this school of scholarship are critically surveyed by Carsten Colpe, *Die religionsgeschichtliche Schule* (Göttingen: 1961).

[28] This theory particularly characterizes those scholars influenced by R. Bultmann, to mention the foremost scholar having held this view. For a short review of the evidence brought by scholars for the existence of a gnostic redeemer myth see Meeks, *The Prophet-King* (Leiden: 1967), pp. 6-17. The history of scholarship on gnosticism is summarized at greater length by Yamauchi, *Pre-Christian Gnosticism*, pp. 13-28.

which preceded gnosticism was proto-gnostic (that is, incipient gnost-icism), or only pre-gnostic (that is, a chronological but unessential predecessor to gnosticism).

Gilles Quispel has dealt specifically with the gnostic problem and "two powers" heretics in his essay on the significance of the Jung Codex. [30] His basic point is that, since Jewish sectarianism has lately been shown to be more extensive than previously thought, both our ideas of Christian and Jewish orthodoxy and the origin of gnosticism should be re-evaluated. In a tack which anticipates some of the con-clusions of this essay, he sees a relationship between "two powers" heresy and mystical traditions of the Merkabah type which hypostasize the "name of God" as a separate angelic being. At the same time, he sees a greater relationship than commonly recognized between these Jewish mystical traditions and Christian or apocalyptic works on the one hand and gnostic works on the other.

Several other scholars have seen a relationship between gnosticism and heterodox Judaism. R. M. Grant [31] promoted the position that gnosticism is to be explained as a response to the failure of Jewish apocalyptic. M. Mansoor [32] has seen Qumran especially as the source of gnostic speculation and his views have been corroborated by Ring-gren. [33] Hugo Ödeberg [34] and Nils Dahl [35] have pointed out the relationship between gnosticism and early Jewish mysticism, with Christianity serving as an intermediary between earlier mysticism and the later gnosticism. Good summaries of this new perspective have been published during the last few years. For instance, H. F. Weiss [36] has reviewed some of the "two powers in heaven" reports in rabbinic literature, together with the reports of early mysticism, in his study

---

[29] Bianchi, *Gnosticismo*. Unfortunately much of the clarity ostensibly achieved is not carried into practice since the adjective derived from both gnosticism and *gnosis* is "gnostic".

[30] "The Jung Codex and its significance," *The Jung Codex: A Newly Recovered Gnostic Papyrus,* 3 Studies by H.-ch. Puech, G. Quispel and W. C. Van Unnik, translated and edited by F. L. Cross, (London: 1955), pp. 35-78.

[31] R. M. Grant, *Gnosticism and Early Christianity* (New York: 1966).

[32] Bianchi, *Gnosticismo*, p. 379-400.

[33] Helmer Ringgren, *The Faith of Qumran* (Philadelphia: 1963), pp. 68-81.

[34] Hugo Ödeberg, *The Fourth Gospel* (Amsterdam: 1968) and *III Enoch*.

[35] N. A. Dahl, "The Johannine Church and History," in W. Klassen and G. Snyder eds., *Current Issues in New Testament Interpretation* (New York: 1962) and his student Peder Borgen, "God's Agent in the Fourth Gospel," in J. Neusner, ed., *Religions in Antiquity*, (Leiden: 1968), p. 137 f. as well as *Bread From Heaven*: Supplements to *Novum Testamentum*, X (Leiden: 1965), pp. 158-164. See also, Dahl, "Christology Notes."

of cosmology and creation in Hellenistic and Palestinian Judaism. He is especially interested in the parallels between the rabbinic reports and the impersonal kinds of mediation that parallel Greek philosophy. Martin Hengel has recently published a summary of the material as part of an argument that the title "Son of God" developed within the Jewish milieu of early Christianity. [37] In doing so, he reviews much of the evidence about angelic mediators which will become important in this study and mentions the rabbinic references to "two powers in heaven" as relevant.

Most of these works argue that extreme gnosticism cannot easily be shown to precede Christianity. Yet, some of the most difficult aspects of this thorny problem of the definition of gnosticism can be side-stepped in the study of "two powers." Our texts make a different distinction necessary. When the rabbis describe "two powers" in heretical beliefs which are antagonistic (and other opposing dualisms can be ruled out) extreme gnosticism is the indicated heresy. But, when the "two powers" are complementary, some other kind of heresy is indicated. A variety of concepts generally thought to contribute to extreme gnosticism—apocalypticism, Merkabah mysticism or *gnosis*—may be considered when the texts suggest two corresponding powers in heaven, but not extreme gnosticism. In other words, for rabbinic purposes, the key criterion separating extreme gnosticism from earlier phenomena —whether they be pre-gnostic or proto-gnostic—is the opposition between the two powers. All the configurations were heretical.

The rabbinic texts about "two powers" can yield new evidence in the controversy over the origins of gnosticism and its relationship to Christianity, if they are treated with these sensitivities in mind. For instance, sometimes it will be possible to isolate and date different strands of the rabbinic attack. In those cases, we will be able to tell whether opposing dualism or the moderate, corresponding "binitarianism" entered rabbinic purview first. On that basis, we will be able to sketch the outlines of a history of the heresy of "two powers," including an approximate date for the entrance of several different heretical groups into rabbinic scrutiny. This, in turn, will suggest a progression and relative chronology of apocalypticism, mysticism,

---

[36] See Hans-Friedrich Weiss, *Untersuchungen zur Kosmologie des hellenistischen und palästinischen Judentums*, DAWB 97, (Berlin: 1966). See also, I. Gruenwald, "Knowledge and Vision," IOS, 3 (1973), 102 n. 52-53.

[37] Martin Hengel, *Der Sohn Gottes, die Entstehung der Christologie und die jüdisch-hellenistische Religionsgeschichte*, (Tübingen: 1975). It has just been translated into English by John Bowden (Philadelphia: 1976).

Christianity and gnosticism as historical movements, at least as the rabbis saw them. Of course, this evidence by itself cannot be final. The rabbis may have missed some aspects of the phenomenon or have chosen not to record their earliest encounters. But the task of this paper is to explain what has been preserved, not speculate on what has not.

The research into the heresy of "two powers in heaven" has been done by illustrious scholars, though it should be evident by now that the time is ripe for formulating some significant new conclusions. New discoveries have brought to light important new information about the religious movements of that time. The known variety of dualistic possibilities for the identity of the heretics should now be explored. It would be helpful to the search for ditheistic sects to review each possibility, noting briefly what has been learned recently about each.

According to the *Jewish Encyclopedia* of 1901, [38] Zoroastrianism, Philonic theosophy, Manicheanism, and gnosticism were the dualistic phenomena opposed by the rabbis, while Essenism had improperly been consider a dualistic possibility. Twentieth-century scholarship has reversed these conclusions almost entirely. We have already seen the extent to which Christianity is implicated. Furthermore, while Zoroastrianism remains a *possible* referent for the antidualistic polemic of the rabbis, it cannot be considered the *probable* target any longer. For one thing, Zoroastrianism cannot be considered the classical case of dualism which it was once supposed to be. In the Gathas, Zarathustra evinced characteristics both of a monolatrist and a dualist [39]—monolatrist, because he worshipped only one God; dualist, because he seemed to believe in two aboriginal, opposing, moral principles, truth and falsehood. Zarathustra's supposed writing (the oldest writing to survive in the Avesta) is ambiguous enough on the subject of dualism to require clarification by strictly dualistic commentary of later texts. Unfortunately, while the younger Avestan texts develop the theme of moral and cosmological dualism, they also contain references to gods which are, at best, extraneous to Zarathustra's system and which appear logically to contradict most of his thought. Hence, dating the emergence of dualistic thought in Persia is quite difficult. Apparently, Iranian religion was able to subsume a variety of differing theological tendencies. Not

---

[38] Kaufmann Kohler and F. G. Hoffmann (*JE*, V, 5 f.) criticize Zeller (*Gesch. der Philosophie*, 2nd ed., iii, 250) for the notion that the Essenes espoused dualism.

[39] Exactly what Zarathrustra contributed to Zoroastrianism is still hotly contested. See, e.g., Ilya Gershevitch, "Zoroaster's Own Contribution to Zoroastrianism," *JNES*, 23 (1964), 12-31.

until after Zoroastrianism became the state religion of the Sassanian Empire (ca. 225 C.E. at the earliest) can strict dualism be documented as the end-product of a long development towards orthodoxy. The result is that some scholars now place the emergence of clear dualism as late as the end of the Sassanian Empire in the fifth century C.E. [40] On the other hand, dualism cannot be ruled out completely as a characteristic of early Persian religion. A fragment of Aristotle's *peri philosophias* cited by Diogenes Laertius reports that the Magi believed in two opposing moral principles. [41]

No doubt, Morton Smith is right to point out that Persian influence on Israelite culture has been generally underestimated because of the lack of textual evidence. [42] Since documentation of this influence is further hampered by lack of knowledge about when dualism became characteristic of Persian religion, stylistic rather than philosophical parallels have become important in pointing out the relationship between Persia and Israel. M. Smith [43] characterized a genre in II Isaiah as typical of the Persian court in Babylonia. In the oracle concerning Cyrus (Isa. 44:24-28, 45:1-7) YHWH's theophany is framed in terms similar to those that frame Marduk's praise of Cyrus. This suggests that the writing is meant to describe YHWH with the grandeur reserved for Babylonian royalty, though adapted for Cyrus's political purposes. These findings are important to us because they include the basic biblical polemic against dualism, for instance: (Is. 45:7) "I form light and create darkness, make weal and create woe, I, YHWH, do all these things." These statements represent a clear change from the creation story in Genesis where God creates light, but not darkness. Such insistence on God's authorship of all creation (even risking contradiction of other biblical traditions) would implicate Zoroastrian dualism as the target of the prophet's polemic. [44] Yet it is important to note that Persians are not the only people singled out as opponents of YHWH. The prophet argues in the same passage that the gods and religions of all the other nations have no power. This kind of

---

[40] E.g., R. C. Zaehner, *Dawn and Twilight of Zoroastrianism* (London: 1961), pp. 175-92.

[41] Diog. Laer. Proem., 8. See C. Clemen, *Fontes Historiae Religionis persicae* (Bonn: 1920), p. 75. Also *Die griechischen und lateinischen Nachrichten über die persische Religion* (Giessen: 1920).

[42] Morton Smith, *Palestinian Parties and Politics that Shaped the Old Testament* (New York: 1971), p. 73.

[43] Morton Smith, "II Isaiah and the Persians," *JAOS*, 83 (1963), 415-21.

[44] See, e.g., Claus Westermann, *Isaiah 40-66* (Philadelphia: 1969), p. 162.

polemic would certainly fit the new picture of religion in the Persian Empire of II Isaiah's time—a picture which sees Zoroastrianism as a small minority even within the Persian ruling class, who also tolerated both the traditional religions of its conquered peoples and several non-Zoroastrian strains of their own Persian religion.

The conclusions about Persian thought relevant to our study can thus be summarized in the following way: Although Zoroastrianism can be pinpointed with some probability in Isaiah's writings and although Isaiah's writing serves as the basis of the rabbinic polemic, it is not necessarily true that Zoroastrians were the heretics who believe in "two powers in heaven." Another piece of evidence which argues against the identification of Zoroastrians with "two powers" heretics is the fact that many rabbinic writings do not hesitate to identify Zoroastrians by name and to name their gods:

> A magi (sic) once said to Amemar: From the middle of your (body) upwards you belong to Ormazd; from the middle downwards to Ahriman. The latter asked: Why then does Ahriman permit Ormazd to send water through his territory? [45]

The Magi are openly defeated. There is no reason for the rabbis to use more obscure terms.

The Dead Sea Scrolls, however, have given us significant evidence of dualism within Judaism. Some scholars even claim that Qumran was a case of Jewish sectarian absorption of Persian thought. T. H. Gaster, for instance, sees Qumran as the Jewish form of Zoroastrianism. [46] Whether or not they were "Zoroastrian Jews" is still problematic, but it is growing clear that the Dead Sea covenanters were a kind of Essene. [47] Because of the Dead Sea Scrolls, we can be certain that some apocalyptic and sectarian movements within Judaism developed dualistic tendencies which could have been described as "two powers in heaven" by the rabbis. Even without raising the issue of their relationship to Zoroastrianism (which, in any case, was unnoticed by their contemporaries) the Qumranites can be seen as a contemporary source of dualism.

In the Manual of Discipline of the Dead Sea Scrolls, ethical dualism is boldly outlined:

---

[45] San. 39a. tr. Epstein.

[46] See Gaster, *The Dead Sea Scrolls in English* (New York: 1956), p. 190.

[47] Dupont-Sommer, *The Essene Writings of Qumran*. F. M. Cross, *The Ancient Library of Qumran* (New York: 1958), pp. 49-106.

He created man for dominion over the earth; and he set in him two spirits for him to set his course by them until the set time of his visitation. They are the spirits of truth and of perversity. In a dwelling of light are the generations of truth and from a well of darkness come the generations of perversity. In the hand of the prince of lights is the dominion of all the sons of righteousness; in the ways of light will they walk. In the hand of the angel of darkness is all the dominion of the sons of perversity and in the ways of darkness they will walk.

And by the angel of darkness are the errors of all the sons of righteousness; and all their sins and iniquities and guiltiness and deeds of transgression are in his dominion according to the secrets of God for his appointed time. All their afflictions and set times of their troubles are under the dominion of his hostility and all the spirits of his portion are set to trip up the sons of light, but the God of Israel and his angel of truth are the help of the sons of light. [48]

Just as the two spirits of truth and error vie for the rule of man's heart, so does a man belong to the good party of righteousness or the evil party of iniquity. From the War Scroll, it becomes quite clear that the Qumran group felt itself to be the elect which, though then few in numbers, would one day serve with the angels as God's divine army, vindicating their present outcast status with victory at the end of time.

Although the Dead Sea sectarians seem to be dualists, they also believed in one transcendent God above all the angels. For them, each of the moral forces, good and evil, had a captain. The angel of darkness and the angel of truth would correspond to the spirit of light and the spirit of darkness. Other apocalyptic documents contain similar dualistic statements. [49] Otzen, [50] for instance, pointed out dualistic phrases in the Testament of the Twelve Patriarchs: "Know, therefore, my children that two spirits wait upon man—the spirit of truth and

---

[48] A. R. C. Leany, *The Rule of Qumran and its Meaning* (London: 1966), p. 144 to I Q S 3:17 f.

[49] See the recent comprehensive article on extra-rabbinic dualism by John G. Gammie "Spatial and Ethical Dualism in Jewish Wisdom and Apocalyptic Literature," *JBL*, 93 (1974), 356-385.

[50] Otzen, "Die neugefundene hebräischen Sektenschriften," *ST*, 7 (1953), 135 f. For more possible "Two natures" arguments see Apoc. of Abraham 22, I Enoch i; 1, 38:1, 89:10 f., The Wisdom of Solomon 3:2 ff., 4:3 ff., 21:13 ff. See also Hermetic Writings I 18, 21. IX, 5. This same legend also occurs in pagan writing. Plato, *Phaedrus*, 248, among the Stoics see Arnim, j., *Stoicorum Veterum Fragmenta* (Stuttgart: 1958) I, 216; III, 658. *Diogenes Laertes*, ed. Hicks (Cambridge: 1958), VII, 127. Additional references provided by John Gager, unpublished paper on dualism. Also, S. Aalen, *Die Begriffe 'Licht' und 'Finsternis' im AT, im Spätjudentum, und im Rabbanismus* (Oslo: 1951).

the spirit of deceit," [51] and "Two ways hath God given to the children of men and two wills, two places and two goals." [52] Of course, there is room for saying that this dualism is less extreme than that of Qumran, merely reflecting a belief in two opposing human impulses. [53] Traces of this kind of dualism even occur in rabbinic thought where they are not regarded as heretical. The rabbis developed their own theory of man's two impulses, the impulse toward good, and the impulse toward evil. [54] In a *baraita*, R. Akiba is also supposed to have articulated a theory of extreme, ethical dualism:

> After his apostasy, Aher asked R. Meir [a question], saying to him: What is the meaning of the verse: *God hath made even the one as well as the other?* He replied: It means that for everything that God created He created [also] its counterpart. He created mountains, and created hills; He created seas, and created rivers. Said [Aher] to Him: R. Akiba, thy master, did not explain it thus, but [as follows]: He created righteous, and created wicked; He created the Garden of Eden, and created Gehinnom. Everyone has two portions, one in the Garden of Eden and one in Gehinnom. The righteous man, being meritorious, takes his own portion and his fellow's portion in the Garden of Eden. The wicked man, being guilty, takes his own portion and his fellow's portion in Gehinnom. R. Mesharsheya said: What is the Biblical proof for this? In the case of the righteous, it is written: *Therefore in their land they shall possess double.* In the case of the wicked it is written: *And destroy them with double destruction.* [55]

Aher had asked a question which implies he was thinking of an heretical dualism. Meir replied with an exegesis about God's plan for creation. Then Akiba is credited with a statement of ethical dualism which, while careful to preserve man's free will, nevertheless resembles many passages in apocalyptic and even some Qumranic literature. We should probably assume that these dualistic ideas were more commonly shared among all sects of Judaism than is evident from orthodox rabbinic texts. Since this passage also makes clear that aspects of op-

---

[51] Testament of Judah 20:1.

[52] Testament of Asher 1:3 ff.

[53] Wernberg-Moeller, "A Reconsideration of the Two Spirits in the Rule of the Community," *RQ*, 3 1961-2 and M. Travers, "The Two Spirits of the Rule of the Community," *ibid.*, 449, 541 believe that the Qumran community as well should be considered as believing only in two impulses within man. However, the hypostasization of angels overseeing these impulses as a major theme indicates the presence of metaphysical existence of the two forces, whatever they may be considered within the heart of man.

[54] See Urbach, *Sages*, pp. 415-427.

[55] *Hag.* 15a., Tr. Epstein.

posing dualism were subsumed by the rabbinic movement, it is less likely that any ethical or opposing dualism *per se* would become the target of the "two powers" polemic. In the course of the paper we will have to observe the specific criteria which made a dualistic system heretical.

Since the Christian messiah may have been a target of the "two powers" polemic, other mediating or intermediary divine helpers in Jewish tradition may also have offended rabbinic sensibilities. The Aramaic terms *Yeqara, Memra,* and *Shekhinah* could be included in the heresy to the extent that they were not verbal subterfuges and point to a metaphysical or theological conception. [56] However, it seems likely that these traditions represent rabbinic attempts to explain dangerous scripture rather than "heresy" itself.

In view of the lack of other evidence and because of his obvious genius, Philo has long been held to be the example *par excellence* of "Hellenistic Judaism" of the first century. His use of the term *logos* points to Jewish familiarity with Hellenistic philosophical schools. Philo's concept of the *logos* is a combination of Platonic ideas of divine intermediation and the Stoic world spirit. *Logos* is equivalent with the intelligible world; but, because it can be hypostasized, the *logos* can also be viewed as a separate agent and called *a* god. Hence any Jew who shared Philo's ideas of the nature of divinity could be a prime candidate for the charge of "two powers in heaven." [57]

Philo writes about the providence of God in another way as well— in terms of His powers summarized by the creative and ruling power. We shall see that these traditions may also have some bearing on the problem of "two powers in heaven."

Many scholars have pointed out that Philo's conception of *logos* is intimately related to other Hellenistic Jewish traditions about the

---

[56] The history of the argument about the nature of the *Shekhinah, Memra,* and *Yeqara* is ably summed up by A. M. Goldberg in *Untersuchungen über die Vorstellung von der Schekhinah in der frühen rabbinischen Literatur*, pp. 1-12.

[57] Several scholars have seen relationships between Jewish heresy and the various schools of Hellenistic philosophy. One should mention perhaps Joël, whose thesis is that the mystical texts discussed briefly above were the product of Jewish speculation in Platonic and neo-Pythagorean modes. H. Fischel has also pointed out many relationships between Jewish traditions and Epicurean, Stoic and Cynic thought. (Henry Fischel, *Rabbinic Literature and Greco-Roman Philosophy: A study of Epicurea and Rhetorica in Early Midrashic Writings*, Leiden: 1973). He feels that the traditions about the four who entered the *pardes*, which we discussed previously, are linked with Jewish epicureanism.

figure of Wisdom, the name of God, and the great archangel that mediated the Sinai theophany. It is possible that underlying Philo's philosophical language are exegetical traditions which he shares with many other Jews.

Any angel who assumed a primary role in heterodox Jewish tradition might have been the subject of the rabbinic injunction. This would include traditions about the angel Melchizedek, a heavenly Jacob, Michael, Gabriel, or the hero Enoch. The rabbis themselves associated "two powers in heaven" with Aher, who had travelled to heaven and seen the angel Metatron in a posture that suggested two powers.

The relevance of the "son of man" tradition reiterates what has already become obvious: Christianity must be considered as one of the prime candidates for the charge of "two powers in heaven," because the Christian community relied on many of the traditions of a principal angel for its exaltation christology. [58] Where a glorified christology developed, criticism of "two powers in heaven" could be levelled by the rabbis. The evidence has already been reviewed in discussing the work of Buechler and Marmorstein.

We have few clear references to Christianity in the talmuds and midrash. Presumably this is partly due to censoring of texts by medieval Church authorities. Most references to Jesus are late, such as: "On the eve of Passover they hanged Jesus and a herald went out before him for 40 days. Let him be stoned for he has committed sorcery and has deceived Israel and led it astray." [59] However the charge that Jesus was a magician was early: Justin [60] refers to it. The New Testament implies it. Since historical references to first-century Christians are unsure and obscure in the talmud and midrash, Christianity becomes an even better candidate for the charge of "two powers in heaven." [61]

Most of what can be said of Christianity as a candidate for "two

---

[58] N. A. Dahl, "The Johannine Church and History" in W. Klassen and G. Snyder, *Current Issues in New Testament Interpretation* (New York: 1962), suggests a relationship between *Merkabah*-traditions and Christianity, especially the Gospel of John. See also Dahl, "Christology notes."

[59] b. San. 43a. Notice the later rabbinic attention to halakhic procedure. Jesus should have been stoned for "sorcery" and "leading astray," not crucified, which was improper execution in rabbinic law.

[60] Dialogue 69:7.

[61] Herford, Marmorstein, Büchler all argue that polemics about men claiming to be gods reflect debates with Christianity. See also Lauterbach, *Jesus* esp. pp. 550-565 for more arguments. See also Winston, *Iranian Component*, pp. 183-216, appendix II for review of the literature on the Christian use of the Balaam oracles and the Jewish polemic against it.

powers" heresy may also be true of gnosticism, as we have seen. Where a demiurge and transcendent god are described, the rabbinic charge of "two powers in heaven" becomes plausible; where a complex system of archons and spheres is described, the closely associated charge of "many powers in heaven" becomes possible as well.

Marcion must be mentioned as an example of Christian dualism. He is often classified as a gnostic, but his gnosticism is of such an individual kind that he would be better defined as a radical, Pauline Christian with gnostic affinities. Almost all our information about Marcion is derived from the church fathers, who were hardly complementary, but not necessarily totally inaccurate. When the rabbinic description of "two powers" heresy warrants it, Marcion's thought will have to be investigated.

If growing knowledge of the Hellenistic world has widened the field of candidates for the identification of "two powers" heretics, the passage of time has also brought more sophisticated tools for study of the primary texts themselves. Methodological advances in the study of religion have had ramifications for the traditions about "two powers." In particular, insights gained from form, source, and redaction criticism of the New Testament have made new and more careful assumptions necessary for the study of rabbinic literature. The most emphatic spokesman for this enterprise is Jacob Neusner, whose approach to rabbinic literature is ground-breaking. [62]

Though the technical issues cannot be discussed in detail, the methods must be described. Source criticism tried to isolate the separate documents or traditions within the literature. Based on these results, form criticism presupposes and concentrates on the oral stage of development of folklore. It assumes that the sources of the traditional literature can be found in an oral genre which can be identified and whose properties can be studied in reference to the specific historical or social institution (*Sitz-im-Leben*) which produced it. The genre produced, however, is usually maintained even after the social institution

---

[62] Jacob Neusner, *Traditions of the Pharisees* pp. 1-18. Also see some of his longer works, as, *From Politics to Piety: The Emergence of Pharisaic Judaism* (Englewood Cliffs: 1973); *A Life of Johanan ben Zakkai* (Leiden: 1962, 1970); *Development of a Legend: Studies on the Traditions Concerning Yohanan ben Zakkai* (Leiden: 1970); *The Rabbinic Traditions About the Pharisees before 70* (Leiden: 1971); *A History of the Mishnaic Law of Purities* (Leiden: 1974 f.); See also W. Sibley Towner, *The Rabbinic "Enumeration of Scriptural Examples"* (Leiden: 1973); and B. Gerhardsson, *Memory and Manuscript: Oral Tradition and Written Tradition in Rabbinic Judaism and Early Christianity* (Lund: 1961).

has faded or after the tradition has been written down, although literary styles in turn influence the tradition in different ways. [63] These observations, however inexact, have been used extensively in European and biblical folklore. In the study of the New Testament they have been massively employed to distinguish between the traditions which go back to Jesus himself and those which are probably products of the early church. [64] The application of this technique has restricted our confidence severely. For instance, in the search for the Jesus-layer of the gospel traditions, the overriding criterion for authenticity has had to be that of dissimilarity. Only those traditions essentially dissimilar from the general ideological milieu and later tendencies of the church can be firmly allowed as authentic to Jesus. [65]

Redaction criticism is the name for scholarly analysis of the motives behind the editing of a document in its present form. It asks the question—*a cui bono*—to whose advantage is the preservation of the statement under discussion. As such, it often isolates the *Tendenz* characteristic not just of the literary redactor (as was originally hoped), but also of a long period of editing. Form criticism and redaction criticism, then, are complementary ways to study any tradition—the first emphasizing the context out of which the tradition arose, the second stressing the perspectives and biases of the people who preserved it.

Some rules of tradition formation, of course, hold for all folklore. Others are particular to specific cultures and must be examined individually. In the study of rabbinic literature, adoption of form and tradition criticism has not been quick. Consequently, there are few specific principles that can be generalized about rabbinic thought as

---

[63] Jan Vansina, *Oral Tradition: A Study in Historical Methodology* sharply distinguishes between oral traditions in preliterate and literate societies. Oral tradition in literate societies is limited to exchanges which take place in every day conversation and are handed down randomly, without special institutions. Rabbinic traditions are evidently an exception to these observations, as J. Gager points out, "The Gospels and Jesus: Some Doubts about Method," *JR* (1974), 250.

[64] The literature on form criticism of the New Testament is manifold. See Edgar V. McKnight, *What is Form Criticism?* (Philadelphia: 1969), for basic bibliography.

[65] Other criteria for authenticity—coherence, multiple attestation, and Aramaism are either more suspect or reducible to the criterion of dissimilarity. See J. Gager's article, cited above, for a discussion of these criteria. Obviously, the criteria for authenticity are not applicable to rabbinic traditions without adaptation. Probably, the criterion of dissimilarity can be used most fruitfully only with the traditions attributed to the most pre-eminent rabbis. The real work on establishing criteria for authenticity in rabbinic writing has yet to be done. See Neusner, *Eliezer b. Hyrcanus, The Tradition and the Man* (Leiden: 1974-5).

yet. Basically we shall only be able to use the method to distinguish between various levels of the traditions in the same rabbinic text.

Since consensus has not yet been reached about how to apply insights gained from other cultures' oral traditions to the study of rabbinic literature, scholars must make careful, cumbersome methodological suppositions concerning the date of rabbinic writings. In most cases this means that the wording of a tradition cannot be proved earlier than the second century. Therefore, it would not be out of place now to anticipate a specific dating problem in the "two powers" materials in order to exemplify the constraints which form and redaction criticism must place upon us until a consensus is reached. R. Simlai and R. Yohanan are credited with a principle for defeating heretics who based their belief on the plurality of divinities on scripture. [66] For instance, some heretics used statements like: "Let *us* make man... (Gen. 1:26)" as positive proof that there is more than one God. Either R. Yohanan or R. Simlai simply observed that wherever God is described in plural terms, a singular form follows closely in scripture, disproving the heretical exegesis. They are therefore credited with the principle that wherever the heretics base their arguments on scripture, their defeat is close at hand. The problem is not merely that the same principle is attributed to two different rabbis. They were close contemporaries and R. Yohanan was the teacher of R. Simlai. The problem is even more complicated. Although the principle is attributed to the third century rabbis, the argument also occurs frequently in texts attributed to second century tannaim, without reference to R. Yohanan or R. Simlai.

There are two basic ways to resolve this contradiction in attribution. Either R. Yohanan and R. Simlai's names are associated with an exegetical principle which is of greater antiquity, or the principle was added into the earlier traditions as a gloss because it dismissed the heresy in summary fashion. While pious Jews have always been disposed towards the former solution, careful historical methodology demands that we use the latter solution as the basis for inquiry. Since we are dealing with a culture which distinguished various levels of antiquity of traditions in order to formulate legal precedents and valued older traditions more highly, we must rule out the earlier dating by methodological premise *unless and until* other evidence warrants it. In other words, when dating is in doubt, the *onus* of proof is on the scholar who wants to maintain an early dating. The study of oral forms and the application of the criterion of dissimilarity forces a methodological skepticism of antique dating because cultures like the one in which the rabbis lived characteristically attribute new thoughts to more and more ancient authority as a way of expressing the value of the thought. In the particular case at hand, we will find that the third century principle is always recognizable by means of its unique wording. So whether or not the argument was more antique than the third century, R. Yohanan and his pupil impressed a datable form upon it.

Though this limitation on dating in rabbinic literature is strict, any attempt to reconstruct a first century form of the "two powers" traditions is not automatically precluded. When there are hints for the existence of an earlier form of the tradition than can be provided from the rabbinic evidence alone, (as will be true for the "two powers" traditions) there are warrants for searching other first century, non-rabbinic literatures for further evidence of it. The different varieties of early dualism have already been discussed, so both the magnitude and the possibilities inherent in such a task must already be evident. However, if we postpone that task until after the rabbinic material is surveyed, we can look through the extra-rabbinic documents for evidence of the specific beliefs which the rabbis opposed. In other words, even if the rabbinic evidence alone cannot demonstrate the existence of a heresy in the first century and before, it may yet give us hints about the earlier forms of the thought which were in the process of becoming heretical. It may not give us all the evidence, but we may only properly discuss phenomena indicated by rabbinic texts. Though the limitations of such a methodological attack must be evident, they will provide us with some important new information.

In some ways, the study of tradition formation in rabbinic Judaism is easier than the comparable and older study of tradition in the New Testament. In New Testament scholarship, one has to begin with complete skepticism of every statement attributed to Jesus because the positive benefits of attributing a church doctrine to its original, supernatural author were immeasurable. In rabbinic tradition not every thought needed to be attributed to an early sage, because the deliberations of every rabbi were considered divinely inspired. One must be alert to the specific gain in authority (for instance, in legal precedent) when an amoraic tradition is elsewhere attributed to a tanna. Then too, it is far sounder method to use the New Testament to corroborate a first century date for a rabbinic tradition than to use rabbinic literature to illuminate and date New Testament traditions, as is now often done.

With reference to the "two powers" heresy, I believe I can show some positive results from Christian and extra-rabbinic literature, even given the methodological precautions, if the reader is patient enough to follow a necessarily long and sometimes tedious argument. Unfortunately, not until one places the results of the analysis of rabbinic text in the context of extra-rabbinic, Jewish-sectarian, and Christian writing does the great antiquity and significance of the "two powers" traditions become manifest.

The proper procedure for this study, then, is to collect, collate, and consider all the evidence about "two powers in heaven," both in the tannaitic and amoraic periods. This corpus will itself be important because the collation has never been accomplished before. Close analysis will be necessary to isolate the various generic and formal characteristics of the traditions, to separate the stages in the development of the argument itself and to reveal clues about the identities of the heretics. Sometimes it will be necessary to distinguish many different layers of tradition in one passage. Often no firm dating will be possible. Particular attention will have to be paid to the scriptural passages from which the heretics derive their doctrines. But only after these considerations have been weighed can we discover whether the biblical passages were actually used by some contemporary dualistic group or were only biblical stylizations of heresy, invented by the rabbis themselves. This analysis will be carried out in Section II (The Rabbinic Traditions).

When the rabbinic evidence has been sifted, we will be in a better position to judge which of the dualistic communities reviewed earlier in this chapter were the likely targets for the rabbinic polemic at any isolatable time and place. With the extra-rabbinic evidence we will also be able to solve some of the ambiguities of the rabbinic texts. For this reason, many of the final conclusions about the significance of the rabbinic reports will necessarily be found in the chapters of Section III dealing with extra-rabbinic evidence. This is, admittedly, an inconvenient place to look for the conclusions about the rabbinic corpus, but this complex problem necessitates such a difficult form. I think the task worth the effort because a new clarity about the rabbinic view of the rise of Christianity and gnosticism can be gained by the end. This information is important for its own sake. But it becomes essential information when one realizes that the rabbis were among the closest, most expert, and most concerned contemporary observers of Christianity and gnosticism.

PART TWO

THE EARLY RABBINIC EVIDENCE

CHAPTER TWO

CONFLICTING APPEARANCES OF GOD

PASSAGE 1

MRSbY	MRI
The Mekhilta of R. Simeon b. Yohai, p. 81. Bashalah 15.	The Mekhilta of R. Ishmael Baḥodesh 5, Shirta 4.

Another interpretation: *YHWH is a man of war, YHWH is His name.*

I am YHWH your God: Why is this said?

Because, when the Holy One Blessed be He was revealed at the sea, He appeared to them as a young man making war.

Because When He was revealed at the sea, He appeared to them as a mighty hero making war. As it is said, *YHWH is a man of war.*

YHWH is His name. He appeared to them at Sinai like an old man, full of mercy:

He appeared at Sinai like an old man, full of mercy, as it is said: *And they saw the God of Israel.* (Ex. 24:10) And of the time after they had been redeemed what does it say? *And the like of the very heaven for clearness.* (Ex. 24:10).
Again, it says

I beheld 'til thrones were set down. (Dan. 7:9).

I beheld 'til thrones were set down (Dan. 7:9) And it also says *A fiery stream issued and came forth from him* etc.

So as not to give an opportunity to say "There are two powers in heaven" Rather *YHWH is a man of War.* (Another interpretation:) *YHWH is a man of War.* YHWH fought in Egypt. YHWH fought at the Sea. And He is at the Jordan, He is at the Arnon streams.

Scripture would not give an opportunity to the nations of the world to say "There are 'two powers' but declares *I am YHWH your God.*" (Ex. 20:2).
I was in Egypt.
I was at the Sea.
I was in the past, I will be in the future to come.

And He is in this world, And He is in the world to come. He is in the past and He is in the future to come.

I am in this world, I am in the world to come.

MRSbY	MRI

MRSbY

As it is said: *Behold now, that I, even, I, am He*, etc. (Dt. 32:39) *Thus says YHWH, the king of Israel*, etc. *I am YHWH, the first and the last*, etc. (Is. 44:6).

MRI

As it is said: *Behold now, that I, even I, am He*, etc. (Dt. 32:39). *Even unto old age I am the same* (Is. 46:4). *Thus says YHWH the king of Israel and his Redeemer the Lord of Hosts, I am the first and the last*, (Is. 44:6). And it says *Who has wrought and done it? He that called the generations from the beginning. I, the Lord who am the first, and to the end I am He.* (Is. 41:4).

PR Piska 21 100b [1]

(Another comment: *Face after face*) R. Levi said: God faced them in many guises. To one He appeared standing, and to one seated; (See Gen. 28:13 and Isa. 6:1) to one as a young man, and to one as an old man. How so? At the time the Holy One, blessed be He, appeared on the Red Sea to wage war for His children and to requite the Egyptians, He faced them as a young man, since war is waged best by a young man, as is said *The Lord is a man of war, the Lord is His name* (Ex. 15:3). And when the Holy One, blessed be He, appeared on Mount Sinai to give the Torah to Israel, He faced them as an old man, for Torah is at its best when it comes from the mouth of an old man. What is the proof? The verse *With aged men is wisdom, and understanding in length of days* (Job 12:12); and therefore Daniel said: *I beheld till thrones were placed, and one that was Ancient of days did sit* (Dan. 7:9). In regard to God's guises R. Hiyya bar Abba said: If a whoreson should say to you, "They are two gods," quote God as saying in reply: I am the One of the sea and I am the One of Sinai.

(Another comment) R. Levi taught at Sinai the Holy One, blessed be He, appeared to them with many faces, with a threatening face, with a severe face, with an angry face, with a joyous face, with a laughing face, with a friendly face. How so? ... In regard to God's many faces, R. Hiyya bar Abba taught: Should a whoreson say to you, "They are two gods," reply to him, Scripture does not say "The gods have spoken ... face after face" but *The Lord has spoken with you face after face.*

Passage 1 may be found in several places in midrashic literature and is alluded to in many more. The primary reference is in *MRI* where the passage occurs in two places (Bahodesh 5 and Shirta 4) in virtually identical form. In Bahodesh alone a closely related tradition, adduced in the name of Rabbi Nathan, was added because of its obvious rele-

---

[1]. See also Pesikta Rabbati de Bahodesh, Ex. 20:2 together with Dt. 5:4. Tr. Braude, p. 421 f. The later midrashim tend to fill in the gaps in reasoning in the earlier ones. For a description of the rabbis ambiguous style, see Goldin, *Song, ad loc.*

MRI, in comparison to *MRSbY*, has developed an elegant argument based on the unstated rabbinic doctrine of the Two Attributes of God. [7] This rabbinic doctrine derives two different aspects of God—one merciful (MDT HRHMYM) and the other, just (MDT HDYN)—from the two Hebrew names of God, YHWH and Elohim. [8] Ex. 20:2, the first line of the Ten Commandments, since it contains both Hebrew names, proves not only that one God was present, but that He was present on Sinai in both His just and His merciful manifestations. The complete argument allows that God can appear in different manifestations—either as a just or as a merciful God or as both—but that it is always the same God and that He was present in both His manifestations when He gave the Torah to Israel.

Although this elaboration is quite sophisticated, there are some difficult aspects to it. For one thing, the two locations adduced in scripture for the doctrine of God's two attributes are puzzling. They imply that YHWH should be seen as the just attribute, while Elohim should be the merciful attribute, which is exactly the opposite of the standard rabbinic identification. That problem will be addressed later, but one point can be clarified now. The argument that two figures or manifestations of God are possible (one ostensibly old, the other young) is separable from the argument that God has two attributes, one just and the other merciful. Of course, they are related ideas. But what they share is a dependence on exegesis either of the repetition of the name of God or the different names of God in the scripture.

Other variations in *MRI* should be noted. Just as Ex. 15:3 and Ex. 24:10 f. are introduced as separate but related cases of theophany in *MRI*, so Dan. 7:9 is treated as a separate case of the phenomenon of God's changing manifestations, as was suspected in reading *MRSbY*.

Scriptures known as the Baraita of Rabbi Ishmael and found in the introduction to the *Sifra*, a tannaitic midrash on Leviticus. See Nils A. Dahl, "Widersprüche in der Bibel: Ein altes hermeneutisches Problem," *Studia Theologica*, 25 (1971), 1-19.

[7] Lauterbach maintains that the doctrine of God's mercy and justice may be seen even in *MRSbY* where YHWH = A man of war would be a problem since YHWH should symbolize God's mercy. This seems correct to me. The point of bringing in Ex. 24:10 f. here is to prove God's mercy at the giving of the law, not merely his appearance as an old man in Dan. If any problem can be said to be more basic I suspect it is the very idea of God portrayed as a man. That is what all the passages have in common. Not only Dan. 7:9, Ex. 15:3, but also Is. 42:13, Ez. 1:26 would also qualify as dangerous, because they figure God in human form. We shall see that many of these are implicated in other descriptions of the heresy as well.

[8] For a complete summary of the Rabbinic Doctrine of the "Two Aspects of God," see Urbach, *Sages*, pp. 396-407.

Here the details of the argument are worked out. In the apocalyptic vision ascribed to Daniel, two thrones appear in heaven, which imply two different figures to fill them. After referring to this dangerous idea, the midrashist has also inserted a specific remedy to the misconception that "two powers in heaven" are being described by Daniel. In Dan. 7:10 scripture states that "a fiery stream... came forth from *Him*" where the singular pronoun shows that only one personage is present, although there may be two manifestations. [9]

A further elaboration in *MRI* must also be explained. Ex. 24:10 f. was quoted because Ex. 24:11b contained the proof that God was merciful to the Israelites at Sinai. However, the midrash also makes a special point of quoting Ex. 24:10b ("And the like of the very heaven for clearness"), which is irrelevant to the argument that God is merciful, the point of the proof-text. However, this biblical verse contains an anthropomorphic description of YHWH, (probably understood to describe a glorious enthronement). [10] That it contains another merkabah (chariot-throne) description similar to Dan. 7:9 f. is perhaps of itself enough to explain the reference. However, in this case, the midrashist must also be alluding to other rabbinic traditions which explain how God's throne could be both constructed of brick-work and be "the like of the very heaven for clearness." This possible contradiction in the deity's appearance is solved by assuming that when Israel was in bondage, God's Shekhina or presence shared their fate symbolically by resting on the brickwork, but when they were freed, His throne rested on the clear blue heaven. [11] The redactor then must have been reason-

---

[9] The argument of the rabbis is not completely convincing for the text may only be referring to one of the two figures at this point. In fact, the rabbinic argument is characteristic of the method for combatting the heresy developed in the third century by R. Yohanan. In chapter 1 we decided that it must be considered a gloss. See pp. 27 and 121.

[10] It can be hown that Dan. 7:9 f. and Ex. 24:10 f. were seen together by early interpreters. T.O. states that a throne (KRSᵓ) is present in the vision of God at Ex. 24:10 f., a detail which is missing in MT and LXX but can be supplied by assuming the influence of other enthronement traditions. The detail could have been supplied from Dan. 7:9 f. but more likely both Ex. 24:10 f. and Dan. 7:9 f. were seen in the light of Ez. 1 and Is. 6 which contain descriptions of the throne, resting on a precious stone with a figure like a man sitting on it. The TJ declares that the whole vision was mediated by the angel Michael whose name means "Who is like God" and who appears as a man.

[11] In the MRI Pisḥa XIV, the following legend is recounted: Whenever Israel is in bondage, the Shekhina is, as it were, in bondage with them; as it is said, "and they saw the God of Israel; and there was, under His feet (the like of brick-work) etc.," i.e., even as they were engaged in making brick during their bondage,

ing that, since the contention under discussion is that God's aspect changed in the various visions He gave to man, the legend of the Shekhina's change of aspect at Ex. 24:10 should be included as well.

The peroration at the end of *MRI* has also been expanded over the version in *MRSbY*. It comprises a list of biblical passages which combat the idea that two deities rule the cosmos, together with an elaboration of the many aspects of God which, nevertheless, remain descriptions of only one deity. As in MRSbY, it appears to be based on Ex. 3:14, the revelation of His name. Although God may be viewed in various aspects, there is a limit to how far one may go in ascribing independent motives to His different hypostases. [12]

MRI, in effect, has defined more carefully than *MRSbY* what the problem of "two powers in heaven" entails, by giving us three different texts from which the heresy can be derived: Dan. 7:9 f., Ex. 15:3, and Ex. 24:10 f. Furthermore, it has identified the people who believe in "two powers in heaven" as gentiles. In the final peroration against the doctrine, it does not know about the reference to the River Arnon which was present in *MRSbY* and adds Is. 46:4 to the list of scriptural passages which may be used as a corrective against the false doctrine. *MRI* and *MRSbY* must have a sophisticated "legend" in common together with some independent development.

The last recension of these traditions, *PR* 21 (100b) is very late. It records similar objections against "two powers in heaven" ascribed

---

so He had at His feet, the likeness of a brick, symbolizing His sharing of their fate.) But when they were redeemed, it was, as the verse says, "The like of the very heaven for clearness"—i.e., the brightness of the skies symbolizing God's joy. See for a complete presentation of the argument Goldin, *Song*, p. 127, who bases his well argued suggestion on I. Levy, "Ein Wort über die Mikhilta des R. Simeon," p. 9 n. 1. See also the rabbinic discussion in j. Suk. 4:5.

12 *MRSbY* introduces these thoughts as another interpretation (DBR ᵓHR.) It also makes the name of God a part of the explicit commentary by saying: The Lord is a man of war—(this means) He makes battle in Egypt; the Lord is His name—He battles at the sea and is the same at the Jordan and the same at the Arnon, the same in this world and the same in the world to come, the same in the past and the same in the future age. The passage, hence, has been further expanded by *MRSbY* to include the events of the Arnon. (For description of saving events at Arnon see, Tan B., IV, 126-27, Tan. Hukhat 19, Nu. R. 19:24, SZ 23-24, b. Ber. 59a-59b. Also Ginzberg, *Legends*, III, p. 337 f. and VI, p. 116 f.) The proof-texts have been expanded as well, by the addition of two more biblical quotations—Is. 44:6 between Dt. 32:39 and Is. 41:4 and also Is. 48:12 at the end. It is possible that each of the four scriptural quotations is to be taken as a specific proof for the corresponding previous statement of God's immutability. (See Goldin, *Song*, p. 128.) In the Bahodesh traditions, the statements of God's constancy are present but the proof-texts are Dt. 32:39, Is. 46:4, Is. 44:6, and Is. 41:4.

to a third generation amora, R. Hiyya b. Abba (290-320 C.E.) therefore is later than him. Notice that the midrash is occasioned by Moses'
vision of God "face to face," confirming that theophany and anthropomorphism are basic issues in the tradition. Moses' special gift in
somehow seeing God or His angel, though it may contradict Ex. 33,
remains a central preoccupation. R. Levi (290-320 C.E.) first contributes the midrash that God appears in whatever form is appropriate
to His action. He uses Ex. 15:3 as his proof-text that God appeared as a
young man at the Sea. Interestingly enough, he seems at first not to
be interested in Ex. 24:10 f., which demonstrates elsewhere that God
appeared in His merciful form. Rather, he emphasizes the youth-age
contrast by quoting Job 12:12 to the effect that age denotes wisdom.
Hence, it was appropriate for God to have appeared in aged form on
Sinai. This exegesis effectively splits the tradition into its two logical
aspects—the first only concerning the forms in which God appeared;
the second, which follows, concerning His attitude of grace or anger
at each manifestation. To each of the separate strands of the tradition,
R. Hiyya b. Abba answers in Aramaic, rather than Hebrew, that if a
heretic says that there are "two gods" based on Dan. 7:9 f., one is to
remind him that God stated that He is the same at the Sea and at
Sinai. [13] Here, both the Sinai theophany and the Daniel vision are
central texts. In the second midrash, R. Hiyya b. Abba uses Dt. 5:4 as a
proof-text that all God's faces (i.e., aspects) are present at Sinai. Ex.
24:10 f. does not appear, but R. Hiyya b. Abba refers to the same
theophany given to Moses, as it is reported in Deuteronomy instead of
Exodus. He also deals with the same troublesome report that the elders
saw God. All of this leads to the conclusion that this version of the
tradition is quite late. The themes of God's appearance and human
form have been divided into separate issues in order to deal with each
more conveniently and fully, but the relationship to the name of God
has grown more obscure.

In just three passages, then, we have become aware of the development of a tradition over a vast period of time. Traditions with so
many different layers present immense dating problems. Each layer
can only be dated by approximation. Later, I will show that extra-

---

13 Since God never directly says in scripture that He was at the Sea and at Sinai,
one must conclude that R. Hiyya is referring to an earlier midrash which resembled
the text in MRSbY or MRI or even to targumic exegesis of Ex. 3 since R. Hiyya
quotes in Aramaic. Note that the term "two gods" (ditheism) can be equated with
"two powers" (binitarianism) in this passage.

rabbinic writings contain similar traditions making a first century origin plausible on external grounds. To anticipate only a fraction of the evidence, Philo attests to the pervasiveness and antiquity of the problem of God's apearance and His different aspects. [14] Since Philo states that he relies on ancient Jewish tradition, his writings, including those pertaining to the exegesis of the names of God, may indicate the antiquity of the tradition. That Philo knows the issue suggests a possible origin well before the birth of Jesus. But Philo's writing suggests more than a continuing issue. He employs very similar scriptures and suggests the existence of widespread scriptural traditions, since the rabbis, a century later, know nothing of him directly and are not indebted to him for their exegesis. Yet Philo and the rabbis independently interpret the different names of God both as signifying different figures and as symbolizing His attributes. Preliminary indications are, therefore, that many parts of the Jewish community in various places and periods used the traditions which the rabbis claim is an heretical conception of the deity.

Although we shall see that Philo uses both traditions about different manifestations of God and traditions about His contrasting attributes in his exegetical discussions, the rabbis emphasize the latter and warn against the former. We can see how the two different manifestations of God present in Daniel's vision might trouble the rabbis. It is not too much to suppose that some kind of argument about contrasting manifestations of God in different theophany texts was known to Philo and used by him but that it was later opposed by the rabbis who called other people who espoused that kind of argument "two powers" heretics.

It is not possible to decide exactly when rabbinic opposition to such doctrines started. For one thing, it is nearly impossible to be sure of the wording of rabbinic traditions before 200 C.E. much less before 70 C.E., when the rabbis became the leaders of the Jewish community. Most rabbinic traditions, at least as we have them, were written subsequently. [15] So we cannot blithely assume that the rabbinic reports date from the Second Commonwealth.

However, with Philo's evidence, we have reason to suppose their

---

[14] See p. 159 f.

[15] Jacob Neusner, *Traditions of the Pharisees*, claims that it was the academies after 70 that developed the forms of recording traditions. This argument has much merit and even if there are exceptions to his rule, it is best to earn them, instead of conveniently assuming that any passage is early.

antiquity. Furthermore some attempts at dating are possible. We can be sure that the root argument is quite ancient. This is because the doctrine of the two attributes (MDWT) of God is important to the rabbinic defense against the argument that God has two manifestations. Yet, the doctrine about the two attributes of God in the text under consideration is not quite consonant with the orthodox version. Ex. 15:3 contains the name of YHWH, which signifies mercy in the rabbinic system, while the sense of the passage requires the aspect of justice to be present. (YHWH is a Man of War.) Ex. 24:10 contains the construct form of the name Elohim, which signifies justice in the rabbinic system, while the interpretation requires that God show mercy ("And they saw the God of Israel..." yet remained alive!). The rabbis would certainly not have discussed such a contradictory passage, had it not already become a *crux interpretationis* on independent grounds. Whether or not the Mekhilta reflects an earlier rabbinic notion of the identification of attributes with the names of God, [16] or merely heretical understanding of such a tradition, the fact that it differs from the orthodox tradition allows us one conclusion: The tradition must have preceded the firm fixing of the rabbinic doctrine of the two attributes (MDWT) of God. After the tradition was fixed, no rabbi would have considered the consequences of this alternative identification of divine names, without noting that he knew what his forebearers had believed. It is, therefore, probable that the doctrine was characteristic of the heretics themselves. Since no one believes the rabbis knew of Philo, these heretics must have known of an exegetical tradition like Philo's.

The date of the origin for the rabbinic doctrine of the two attributes (MDWT) of God has been the subject of some controversy. A. Marmorstein [17] tried to maintain that R. Meir and R. Simeon b. Yohai

---

[16] There is evidence that other kinds of Jews identified traditions in different ways. Philo identified the names and attributes in ways opposing to the accepted rabbinic doctrine. See N. A. Dahl and A. Segal, "Philo and the Rabbis on the Names of God," *JSJ*, forthcoming. There is certainly a case to be made that the rabbis knew of an earlier doctrine, congruent with the Philonic one and that they subsequently fought against it.

[17] Marmorstein, *The Old Rabbinic Doctrine of God* showed that the "old" phrases, attribute of punishment (MDT HPWRᶜNWT), and attribute of good (MDT HṬWB) occur in discussions between R. Gamaliel II (80-110) and R. Akiba (110-135). Midr. Ps. 119 f. cf., San. 81a, Makk. 24a. They are also used once by R. Simeon b. Abba (290-320) (Gen. R. 9), although these latter may be a repetition of older speculation. In some of the sayings of R. Meir (*ARN* 30) (135-170) and R. Simeon b. Yohai (135-170) (Tan. 1:34), the older sayings are used, although in other traditions they also use the new terms. R. Jose b. Halafta (135-170) and R. Judah b. Ilai

(middle second century) were the first to use the terms MDT HDYN (attribute of justice) and MDT HRḤMYM (attribute of mercy). He suggested that MDT HṬWB (attribute of good) and MDT HPWRᶜ-NWT (attribute of punishment), synonyms for the accepted doctrine found in some tannaitic documents, were actually the technical terms of an earlier doctrine and were discarded by the rabbis, under the pressure of the gnostic menace. This much has been widely accepted. He also suggested that the surviving rabbinic doctrine was not antique and had been deliberately altered from an earlier one, out of polemical and apologetic motives. He even tried to prove that traces of an earlier, Philonic correlation of divine names and attributes were still to be found in some rabbinic texts. For instance, he tried to show that R. Akiba was unaware that "Elohim" could have the implication of "judge." However, that conclusion is too hasty. The same passage may be interpreted to indicate that R. Akiba was aware of the standard doctrine. [18] That would mean that the standard rabbinic doctrine could have been developed even earlier than R. Akiba. What is more important, the orthodox doctrine was massively developed by rabbis like R. Simeon and R. Meir only a few years after Akiba's death.

Now, since Marmorstein's time we have had to become more skeptical of attributions to tannaitic sages. Though they are not necessarily later, the attributions themselves cannot be the final proof of a tannaitic date. So far, we know only that rabbinic use of "justice

---

(135-170) still can use the old designations for the two attributes, but the new terms are also reputed to be in use by the same masters. These rabbis, then, are supposed by rabbinic tradition to be the beginnings of the transition of the use of the new terms (MDT HDYN and MDT HRḤMYM). From this Marmorstein deduced that the terms "attribute of mercy" and "attribute of justice" are no older than the middle of the second century and are probably younger than that.

18 Marmorstein maintains that R. Akiba did not know that Elohim meant judge because in Mekhilta Kaspa 1 (Mishpatim 19; H-R, p. 317 and Lauterbach III, p. 151) he treats the name of God as holy. But he would have had to be aware of the issue in order to have made such a ruling. So the opposite is the case. Furthermore, the origin of the current vocabulary is even attributed to earlier sages than Marmorstein thought. It can be seen in the sayings of R. Yosi Hagelili (Gen. R. 26:6, b. Sanh. 38b). In fact, some aspects of the tradition linking God's names and His attributes are biblical. In Jonah 3:8 and 4:3, God's change of mind in regard to the punishment of Nineveh is interpreted by means of God's interpretation of His name to Moses in Ex. 34:6: "YHWH, YHWH is a God merciful and gracious, longsuffering and abundant in goodness and truth." So the interpretation of the names of God as related to mercy is ancient. However the scripture is ambiguous enough to be used equally by the rabbis or by Philo as a demonstration of their respective systems of interpreting the names of God.

and mercy" arguments to counter heresy were attributed unselfconsciously to Akiba or earlier. We shall see that some of the attributions are likely to be accurate. The heated debates about mercy and justice are entirely appropriate to the gnostic menace of the early and middle second century. We will have to wait for the extra-rabbinic evidence to see that some Jews discussed such doctrines as early as Philo.

Marmorstein has been severely criticized and largely dismissed because he maintained that the rabbis actually used the Philonic identification of divine names, only changing to the received tradition in the face of gnostic opposition of the second century. As I tried to indicate above, his critics were right to question his arguments in several places. There is not sufficient evidence to reach his conclusion. But, having dismissed his arguments about a prior rabbinic formulation of the doctrine of God's two attributes, Marmorstein's critics failed to come to terms with the larger questions which he raised [19]—the relationship between the Philonic and rabbinic tradition of the names of God. The ancient terms for the attributes—attribute of goodness and attribute of punishment—do parallel Philo's normal vocabulary to discuss God's powers. [20] Furthermore, the important point is not the disagreement between the rabbis and Philo over the interpretation of the names of God but their fundamental agreement that God is the author of both justice and mercy. Both would say that God does mercifully even when He is administering strict justice. It is the mixture that is important. That is certainly the moral of the passage in the Mekhilta as well. Furthermore, that is exactly the issue over which the received terminology of the rabbinic doctrine was formulated. This would suggest that "Hellenistic" and "Palestinian" Judaism were not separated by as wide a gap as is usually maintained. But for now, it is not germane to discuss how the similarity came about. Our problem is the date of the traditions. We have already seen that the "justice and mercy" traditions were added onto the basic Mekhilta argument about a manlike hypostasis of God in order to defeat the heretical implication that there is more than one God. Rabbinic literature attributes the debate over mercy and justice to R. Akiba and his successors of the mid-second century. The received vocabulary for discussing such questions did not develop

---

[19] For more detail see N. A. Dahl and Alan F. Segal "Philo and the Rabbis and the Names of God," *JSJ*, forthcoming.

[20] MDT HṬWB = *dynamis agathotētos*, MDT HPWRᶜNWT = *dynamis kolastērios*. See p. 173.

that Moses is supposed to have seen either God or an angel of God. This might imply that the God of Israel was equivalent with the angel of YHWH. If so, was YHWH an angel or God? [27] In the second century C.E., R. Judah b. Ilai warned against translating this verse at all. To translate literally would falsify the meaning, since no man can see God and live. To insert the word "angel" for God would be blasphemous (and imply two powers?). The only possible rendering of the verse according to him is, "And they saw the glory of the God of Israel." Accordingly, almost all the targumim make such a translation. [28]

These traditions in the targums are explicitly related to the rabbinic polemic about the interpretation of divine names. At Ex. 3:14 the Palestinian targums point out that the newly revealed name of God means, "I am He who was with you in the bondage of Egypt and who will be with you in every bondage." This language is meant to interpret the divine name itself. [29] Apparently, whenever a second figure, either in the Pentateuch or in Dan., could be identified as a quasi-divine or independent angelic figure, the rabbis would fight vociferously against

---

[27] See p. 60 f., 182 f., 196 f., 244 f.

[28] The same mechanism was used with reference in Isaiah's vision of the figure on the temple throne (Is. 6:2 f.). Thus it is possible to find the Gospel of John 12:42 state that Isaiah saw the glory of Christ (for God), as the prophet's book says. The Fourth Gospel is surely an example of what the rabbis found heretical. See p. 214 f.

[29] These concepts are associated with personifications even when they are not described as the Shekhina. For instance, TO to Ex. 24:10 has: "The footstool of His feet as the work of pure sapphire stones, and as the aspect of the heavens when they are cleared from clouds." But TP has: "And Moshe and Aharon, Nadab and Abihu and seventy elders of Israel went up. And Nadab and Abihu lifted up their eyes and saw the glory of the God of Israel; and under the footstool of His feet which was placed beneath His throne, was like the work of sapphire stone—a memorial of the servitude with which the Egyptians had made the children of Israel to serve in clay and bricks, there had been women treading clay with their husbands; the delicate young woman with child was also there and made abortive by being beaten down with the clay. And thereof did Gabriel, descending, make brick, and, going up to the heavens on high, set it, a footstool under the throne of the Lord of the World, whose splendour was as the work of a precious stone, and as the power of the beauty of the heavens when they are clear from clouds." (See also T.P. to Ex. 15:3.)

Here the throne belongs to the "Lord of the World," who is God's principal angel (see p. 67, 189, 214, 256 f.) and evidently has the angel Gabriel under his control.

In discussing the youthful appearance of God, the rabbis might reflect some anti-merkabah or anti-Christian arguments. See Song of Songs R. 2:14 and TJ Ex. 24:10. Ps. 110, central to Christian exegesis, is normally interpreted to refer to Abraham, but a possible defensive folktale countering Christianity or apocalyptic messianism may be found in the M. Ps. to Ps. 110 where the verse is interpreted to mean that the Messiah will sit and study while God goes out to conquer Israel's enemies.

it. Once it was clear that this divine figure who seemed to be God, who carried His name, and who acted for God, could be called the *Shekhina* or the *Kavod* and not an independent deity, the rabbis accepted and expanded the tradition.

Thus it is not impossible that some of the tradition of the Mekhilta can go back to the second century. Let us return to the Mekhilta tradition for a moment to summarize what may be concluded. When all the traditions which must be later than R. Akiba are removed from *MRI*, we are left with an argument that looks rather like the argument common to both *MSbY* and *MRI*. The argument would serve to oppose any repetition of the divine name "YHWH" which could be construed as implying two independent deities. It would also oppose any identification of the two Hebrew names for God with two different independent divinities. To be sure, the peroration that God will continuously manifest himself ("He was in the past and He will be in the future") is present in both recensions but it is listed as a separate tradition in *MRSbY* and probably develops as an interpretation of YHWH based on Ex. 3:14. That leaves us with a kernel of traditions which associate the heresy with the warrior figure in Ex. 15:3 or the unspecified merciful figure at Sinai, together with the text of Dan. 7:9 f. The Dan. passage does, in fact, supply two figures in heaven, one old and one young. It seems likely, then, that the rabbis were opposed to any tradition of a manlike figure in heaven, acting independently of God.

The biblical passages are important in themselves. Dan. 7:9 f. can certainly be seen to allow for a "two powers" interpretation. Traditions about the human figure (YHWH's angel, but still God of Israel) seen at Ex. 24:10 f. allow for "two powers" interpretations without reference to other scripture. The same can be said for Ex. 15:3 (at least according to *MRSbY*). It is therefore probable that the rabbis have put these Exodus theophany passages together because some opponent also saw a reason to connect them.

The traditions of intermediation also seem appropriate to other rabbinic discussions attributed to the mid-second century. The problem is to relate the "mercy and justice" issue with the "intermediation" tradition. But the issues or mercy and justice are not necessarily related to the intermediation tradition in any definite fashion. The connection between "mercy and justice" and the "intermediation" is being made by the rabbis, because both traditions depend on an exegesis of the names of God. The rabbis are offering the mercy-justice exegesis as a substitute for the heretical implications of the intermediation tradition.

It is also clear that the intermediation tradition should be dated earlier since it is basic to the polemic. Therefore, dating the first redaction could depend on finding out when issues of mercy and justice became important to the rabbinic community. If it can be shown with reliable tannaitic sources that issues of mercy and justice actually are tannaitic and not merely ascribed to the tannaim by the later rabbis, then we have better reason to trust at least some of the attributions of the legends in this chapter. If arguments about mercy and justice do characterize tannaitic thought, then the heretical traditions are likely to be even earlier, since they logically must antedate the intermediation tradition.

There are several famous mishnahs which discuss mercy and justice, or good and evil, and thus show with a reliable source that these issues were important to the tannaim. [30] Some of these discussions were even linked to the heresy of "two powers in heaven" by the amoraim, so they will discussed below. [31] There, it will become evident that the link between mercy and justice and a heresy explicitly called "two powers in heaven" cannot be demonstrated from the mishnah alone. *But we do not know yet when the heresy was explicitly named "two powers in heaven."* All that is required for the moment is to show that the issues of mercy and justice are traceable to the tannaim. That is sufficient to imply that the original heresy is probably older than the second century, for we know that the tannaim linked the issue of God's appearance in different forms with the issue of His justice and mercy in order to defeat the idea that two divine hypostases operated independently. The clearest statement of tannaitic concern is in Ber. 9:5:

> Man is bound to bless (God) for the evil even as he blesses (God) for the good, for it is said, *And thou shalt love YHWH thy God with all they heart and with all they soul and with all thy might.* (Dt. 6:4). *With all thy heart*—with both impulses, thy good impulse and thy evil impulse; *and with all thy soul*—even if He take thy soul; *and with all thy might*—with all thy wealth. Another interpretation is: *With all thy might*—for whichever measure (MDH) He measures out to thee (MWDD), do give him thanks (MWDH) exceedingly.

This is a very interesting mishnah. It states the rabbinic and biblical notion that God is the author of good and evil. It explicitly argues that no personage other than God is to be acknowledged for evil. It brings in Dt. 6:4 as the salient scriptural citation. Dt. 6:4 was exceptionally

---

[30] See, e.g. Ber. 5:3, 9:3, Meg. 4:9.
[31] See p. 98 f.

helpful to Philo in the context of God's uniqueness and will appear frequently in rabbinic discussions of "two powers in heaven." Furthermore, the mishnah links its discussion of divine providence to the technical terminology for God's attributes (MDWT). Since the mishnah is an unimpeachable tannaitic source, a mid-second century date is quite probable for a discussion of mercy and justice, just as the midrash attributions imply. Furthermore, the mid-second century is likely as the date for the combination of the two traditions in the Mekhilta and implies that the basic issue of the form of God's appearance to man is older still. Of course the texts themselves are later and alternative reconstructions can be imagined, but a second century date and gnostic impetus has become likely as the cause of the redaction. Since the rabbinic attributions can probably trusted, at least in part, the whole tradition would fit the following chronological scheme: (1) A second manifestation of God can be shown in Hellenistic mystical and apocalyptic Judaism as early as the beginning of the Common Era (e.g., Philo). (2) Extreme varieties of this kind of speculation came to be opposed by the rabbis. (3) By the mid-second century, R. Akiba or his admiring successors in his name were using the doctrine of God's aspects of mercy and justice to counter the heresy. The defense went as follows: The contradiction between Ex. 15:3 and Ex. 24:10, can be reconciled by means of Ex. 20:2. Thus Dt. 32, Is. 44 f. and Ex. 20:2 are the main rabbinic proof-texts for the unity of God. Since the argument about God's justice and mercy is not consonant with the normative rabbinic doctrince, it seems probable that the rabbis were responding to opponents with a tradition associating justice and mercy with the names of God in a different fashion. (4) The issues which Passage 1 raise are discussed often by R. Akiba and his pupils—making the situation of the Bar Kokhba Revolt (ca. 135 C.E.) not impossible as a setting for the growth of a consolation theme. (5) Many parts of the traditions are obviously later elaborations and the final redaction may have been medieval. But at least one more part of the argument (that the singular of any verse counteracts the dangerous implications of a divine plural) is typical of the early amoraic period and attributed alternatively to R. Simlai and R. Yohanan. (6) The peroration at the end of Passage 1 could testify to the ferocity of the argument as early as the second century because it is targumic as well as midrashic. At any rate it represents an interpretation of the divine name YHWH which is extraordinarily relevant to the argument with the heretics.

Determining the identity of the group of heretics in question remains a serious problem. The many versions contain two different descriptions of possessors of the doctrine. While *MRSbY* describes only the doctrine, *MRI* describes those professing belief in the doctrine as "gentiles" and *PR* calls a person with such beliefs either a "whoreson" or "son of heresy" depending on the translation. Each of these terms will have to be investigated.

MRI: "gentiles," *lit.* "the nations of the world." Even though there are no major variants to these lines in *MRI*, Herford [32] suggested that the earliest version of the tradition must have read *minim* "sectarians" instead of "gentiles." It must be remembered that Herford identified all *minim* with Christians. According to him, "nations of the world" was inserted in the place of "sectarians" because the discussion in *MRI* in reference to the Ten Commandments (Bahodesh 5) contained many other traditions that dealt with the "gentiles."

Herford's arguments are misdirected in several respects. First of all, there is no conclusive evidence that *minim* always meant Christians. [33] Nor is it clear that the substitution of "gentiles" for sectarian can be supported. Although the context allows for a *possibility* of confusing "gentile" with "heretic" in the version of *MRI*, no such confusion can occur in the Shirta version. Furthermore, there is no textual evidence for such an assertion. Its only virtue is that it advances Herford's thesis. I see no reason to ignore the *prima facie* evidence that "gentiles" is the correct reading. That would seem to eliminate the immediate targets for the rabbinic charges "heterodox Jews" whose philosophy resembled Philo, together with apocalyptists, or mystics. However this is only one description of the heresy.

Though "the nations of the world" is the best rendering of the text, they must have been gentiles well-versed in Jewish tradition to have offered such a dangerous and sophisticated interpretation of Dan. 7:9 f. To be sure, the rabbis often put biblical quotations in the mouths of gentiles, stylizing in Jewish idiom a view which gentiles may well have had. However, here the heresy is not just proof-texted by reference to Dan. 7:9 f., Ex. 15:3, and Ex. 24:10 f. It actually rests on an exegesis of those texts, to which the rabbis have offered their own exegesis as a corrective. Thus, the argument may have originated in the Hellenistic milieu with people who were interested in Judaism but had not yet become Jews according to rabbinic definition.

---

[32] Herford, p. 301.

[33] Places where *minim* cannot mean Christians consist of places where *minim* are described as disbelieving in resurrection of the dead. See e.g., j Ber. 9c.

In the second century, this group would certainly have contained gentile Christians [34] who are the best contenders for this charge, though they are not the only group who could have been designated. We know some gentiles were "God-fearers" but had not accepted circumcision, thus invalidating their conversions in the opinion of most rabbis.

R. Hiyya b. Abba (290-320), a Babylonian amora who was contemporary with R. Levi and who immigrated to Palestine to study with R. Yohanan, is portrayed as calling whoever would believe in two gods "the son of harlot." Marmorstein suggested that either gnosticism or Christianity may be implied by such a term. [35] Both Herford [36] and Lauterbach [37] felt that the polemic was occasioned by Christianity. They argued that the reference to a son of a harlot is a stock denial of the virgin birth. However, the Aramaic word for harlotry could be associated either with the Hebrew word *min* (for sectarian) or the Hebrew root ZNH which could mean "to go whoring" which was associated with sinful, Canaanite (i.e. gentile) religion. We know it could be used with the sense of sectarian in the rabbinic period. [38] Hence, in the fourth century, the opponents could either have been gentile opponents of the rabbis or sectarian Jews. There is no reason to associate the heresy explicitly with either Christianity or gnosticism on the basis of the term alone.

There is some more evidence to connect this argument with a rabbinic polemic against Christianity. Elsewhere, M. Ps. 22 comments on "My God, my God, why hast thou forsaken me?," which in its Aramaic translation is supposed to have been Jesus' last words (Mt. 27:46). The Rabbis say that the first "My God" refers to the Sea and the second "my God" refers to Sinai. Since no other group found this verse suitable, this is enough to infer that Christianity was identified as "two powers" heresy, but the rabbinic charge of "two powers" may not have been originally or exclusively used against it.

In these traditions then, gentiles or gentile Christians seem to be the earliest recorded targets of the charge, probably because they were most vociferous contemporaries when the text was fixed in its present

---

[34] In fact, Justin Martyr uses similar arguments to portray the Christ. See Section III, p. 221 f.

[35] Marmorstein, *RGS*, II, p. 103.

[36] Herford, p. 304.

[37] Lauterbach, *Jesus*, p. 549.

[38] See b. A. Zar. 7a, where Prov. 5:8 is discussed. The passage in Prov. personifies Wisdom and moral rectitude as a woman and compares her with "the strange woman" who would represent moral folly, and is clearly described as a whore.

form. But we must also allow that where gentile Christians are involved, Jewish Christians, hence Jewish sectarians, are almost certain to have been their teachers. Nothing completely conclusive can be demonstrated from the internal evidence. But one aspect of the heretical beliefs can be of further use—the biblical passages which formed the basis of the heretical exegesis. An examination of the use of biblical exegesis in various Jewish sectarian groups of the first few centuries will yield further information about the identity of the heretics in question. That investigation will be carried out in Section III.

PASSAGE 2

Mekhilta Bahodesh 5

Rabbi Nathan says: From this one can cite a refutation of the heretics who say: "There are two powers." For when the Holy One Blessed be He, stood up and exclaimed: "I am the Lord thy God," was there any one who stood up to protest against Him? If you should say that it was done in secret—but has it not been said: "I have not spoken in secret," etc. (Isa. 45:19)? "I said not unto the seed of Jacob" (*ibid.*) that is, to these alone will I give it. "They sought me in the desert" (*ibid.*). Did I not give it in broad daylight? And thus it says: "I the Lord speak righteousness, I declare things that are right" (*ibid.*). [39]

R. Nathan's (ca. 135-170 C.E.) argument immediately follows passage 1 in *MRI* Bahodesh 5. Indeed, it assumes an exegesis of Ex. 20:2 for it is a further comment on the fact that only one God gave the Law. At the giving of the Ten Commandments, he argues, no other deity contradicted YHWH's statement that He is Israel's God. Since He made this statement openly and was not contradicted, there could be no other deity. R. Nathan uses further quotations from Isaiah to show that the statement in Ex. 20:2 was spoken publicly and openly. From this one may infer that the criticism on the part of those who believe in "two powers in heaven" was that the God who gave the Law acted secretly or deviously. This, in turn, suggests an opposition between the two deities in the doctrine of the heretics. It becomes possible to posit an opponent for R. Nathan who believed that the God of Israel did something in secret as a scheme against a higher God. There was only one kind of group in Palestine during that time that could hold such doctrines—the gnostics. R. Nathan's remark may oppose gnostic sectarians, either of a Christian or a non-Christian variety.

---

[30] Tr. Lauterbach, II, 232.

While it must be admitted that R. Nathan's remarks are a good defense against radically gnostic opponents, it is not clear that R. Nathan must have had radical gnostic opponents in mind. His defense also may imply heretics who are detractors of the Law. The rabbis, in this very pericope, are concerned to defeat the idea that the Torah is a parochial Law. They relate that every nation was offered the benefits of Torah; Israel alone accepted the responsibility. They claim that the Torah was given in open country, so that no nation could claim it for a private possession. R. Nathan's remarks ought to be seen within the context of this argument as well. But the argument has been expanded beyond the issue of the scope of Torah. R. Nathan specifically condemns the idea that any power can contradict God. Furthermore, he quotes a passage from Isaiah in which creation, not the gift of Torah, is the context in which God's unity is claimed. This suggests that a more serious problem—cosmic dualism from creation onwards—is being linked with the defense of the Law. Though one can never be certain of R. Nathan's actual opponents it seems clear from the expansion of the argument that his midrash would be very useful against radical gnostics.

R. Nathan directs his remarks against the *minim* or sectarians, who are obviously viewed as heretics by the rabbis. However, gnostic Jews or Jewish-Christians could still be included under the rubric of "sectarian" or "heretic" (as opposed to "gentile") at the end of the second century. [40] Since we know from the previous passage that "two powers" referred to Christians and not extreme gnostics, we have to conclude that "two powers" was a catch-all term for many different groups—including Christians, gnostics and Jews. We shall see that it grew to be a more popular and conventional designation as time went on.

It is important to note that the rabbis are dealing with a complex theological question by relying on biblical exegesis. The importance of the theological question should not be overlooked because the basis of the discussion in the rabbinic text is exegetical. The rabbis are saying that many varieties of Jewish sects—including Christians and

---

[40] As Büchler has shown (*Minim*, p. 252), *min* must have referred also to non-Jews at some point for arguments are ascribed to them which no Jew who wanted to maintain his relationship to the people Israel (of whatever interpretation) could maintain. From a methodological point of view then, one has to assume that *minim* are always Jewish sectarians, viewed as heretics by the middle of the second century, unless they are specifically accused of anti-Israel propaganda.

gnostics—are guilty of violating an essential premise of Judaism, even while they think they are exegeting scripture correctly. The rabbis are involved in the formulation of orthodoxy—a task necessary in their view because some Jewish sects have ceased to understand the theological center of Judaism. But the rabbis are not using philosophical tools to formulate orthodoxy; they are employing exegetical techniques.

The strategy of the rabbis in using the term "two powers" was quite sophisticated. First, there is a sense in which the designation is apt. Christians and gnostics did posit a second divine hypostasis. Second, the rabbis subsumed at least two different groups under one category. This policy implies that the rabbis either could not distinguish between the two or wanted to view various sectarians not as different groups but as one group sharing a single, basic misunderstanding. Putting all heretics in one category and dismissing them is an effective way of dealing with opposition. Third, although the designation is apt from the rabbinic perspective it is also exaggerated from the Christian one. In fact, neither apocalyptic, mystical, nor Christianized Judaism affirmed two separate deities. Each understood itself to be monotheistic, giving special emphasis to one divine hypostasis or manifestation. Only extreme gnosticism posited two different and opposing deities. In effect, the rabbis were classifying the other groups together with extreme gnosticism and treating them all alike. This tactic was effective because it was based not only on a plausible description but also on one which was a heinous charge from both the rabbinic and Christian perspective. In calling the sectarians "those who say there are two powers in heaven," the rabbis were stating that the sectarians violated the most basic tenet of Israelite faith—the unity of God. In view of this evidence, together with the mercy and justice traditions surveyed previously, it seems possible to frame the hypothesis that the rabbis may have always opposed Christian and other apocalyptic messianism but that the battle with "two powers in heaven" intensified when extreme gnosticism demonstrated the direction this kind of speculation might take.

CHAPTER THREE

AHER, METATRON, MERKABAH AND THE ANGEL OF YHWH

The heavenly enthronement texts (Ex. 24:10 f., Dan. 7:9 f., perhaps even Ez. 1:26 f.) whose interpretation separated orthodoxy from heresy in passage 1 are suggestive of Merkabah mysticism and its antecedents. As we have seen, this controversial phenomenon in Jewish history has been implicated from the beginning of research on Jewish gnosticism. [1] The midrashic passages discussed here will affirm a relationship between "two powers in heaven" and Merkabah mysticism. But, at the outset, justification for including such texts in a discussion of tannaitic evidence can be made on the basis of the ostensible subject of the next passage, Elisha b. Abuya (110-135 C.E.). We shall see that the attribution is certainly to be distrusted, but that relevant aspects of Maaseh Merkabah must be quite early.

PASSAGE 3

b. Hagigah 15a

Aher mutilated the shoots. Of him Scripture says: (Ecc. 5:5). Suffer not thy mouth to bring thy flesh into guilt. What does it refer to?—He saw that permission was granted to Metatron to sit and write down the merits of Israel. Said he: "It is taught as a tradition that on high there is no sitting and no emulation, no back and no weariness." Perhaps God forfend!—there are two divinities (powers). Thereupon they led Metatron forth, and punished him with sixty fiery lashes, saying to him: "Why didst thou not rise before him when thou didst see him?" Permission was (then) given to him to strike out the merits of Aher. A Bath Kol went forth and said: "Return, ye backsliding children" (Jer. 3:22)—except Aher. [2]

The tradition is a late addition to the Babylonian Talmud. It reports that Aher entered the *pardes* [3] and received a mistaken impression

---

[1] For more recent discussions, Scholem, *Major Trends*, pp. 40-79; also *Jewish Gnosticism*, and his articles in *EJ*. A good summary of scholarship on merkabah may be found in J. Greenfield's introduction to *III Enoch*, ed., H. Ödeberg. The outstanding essay on the relationship between the Sinai theophany and merkabah speculation is by Lieberman, Appendix D of Scholem's *Jewish Gnosticism*, 118-126.

[2] Tr. Epstein. See also III Enoch 16:2.

[3] The story of the *pardes* has been often discussed by commentators interested in defining the nature of Jewish gnosticism or mystical practice among the rabbis.

about the events he saw taking place there. Whatever the original meaning of *pardes*, the scene here is obviously the heavenly court with Metatron depicted as sitting to write down the merits of Israel. Apparently being seated is more than an infringement of protocol, for it is serious enough to give Aher the impression that Metatron is enthroned as equivalent to God Himself, hence able to act independently of God. Accordingly, the angels lead Metatron out to be punished, demonstrating that he is susceptible to divine commands and punishments, in no sense equal to God. Finally, the text claims that the prophecy of Jer. 3:22 does not apply to Aher and that he will be both unrepentent and unforgiven for getting an heretical impression about Metatron.

In this well-known story, much is revealed about one kind of thought to which the designation "two powers in heaven" was applied. There are some strikingly unexpected turns in this story, which makes its authenticity dubious and its purpose obvious. In the first place, Aher's observation that Metatron's seated posture gives the impression that there are "two powers" is not illogical. It stands to reason that divine and exalted creatures seated in heaven are enthroned. The rabbis are determined to refute the whole idea of heavenly enthronement by stating that such things as "sitting" and other anthropomorphic activities are unthinkable in heaven. Yet we have already seen that the rabbis are not reluctant elsewhere to talk of divine enthronement *per se* or the seats of mercy and justice. Nor does Aher present his observation as a challenge to the rabbis. He is horrified by it. *"Heaven forbid* that there are two powers," he exclaims. [4] Furthermore, Metatron, who is in no way responsible for Aher's assertion, and who apparently had the right to be seated, is punished as an object lesson for Aher. [5] In spite of this, Aher, whose statement at the beginning

---

The meaning of the term itself has been hotly contested. Those commentators who suspect early mysticism to have been present define the term as synonymous with heaven. Those who see the term to be originally non-mystical or philosophical and only later mystical tend to stress that it is Greek loan word (*paradeisos*) and could mean only garden, and, in fact, was quite often used in Epicureanism.

[4] This is certainly a gloss occasioned by the rabbinic sensitivity to recording heresy, even in the mouth of a heretic. For a more credible version of the tradition see III Enoch 16:2. Of course neither recension should be viewed as *ipssima verba* of Aher!

[5] "Fiery lashes" is the translation of PWLŚY DNWRᴐ which are circular plates or rings heated and strung on a lash. See B.M. 85b, also Yom. 77a. Rashi here and in the other places comments that bringing out fiery lashes is a way of threatening excommunication. The punishment itself seems to be reserved for rebellious heavenly

was full of pious indignation, remains willfully unrepentent at the end. As a purely moral tale, the plot leaves something to be desired! Rather, in its present context it is an etiology of heresy. It explains how certain people, who had special Metatron traditions, risk the heretical designation of "two powers in heaven." Aher functions as the heretic *par excellence*, as Simon Magus does in Christian anti-heresiological tracts.

Elisha's apostasy so contradicted his teachings that it fired the rabbinic imagination. By the time of the redaction of Ecc. R. a charming and poignant short romance had formed. [6] In this Hagigah passage, as we remember from Graetz, [7] Elisha was one of the four rabbis who tried to make the dangerous journey to paradise—the other three being Simeon b. Zoma, Simeon b. Azzai, and Akiba. Of these four, the Talmud tells us only Akiba makes the journey to the *pardes* successfully; the two Simeons meet catastrophic ends for failing to perform the correct procedures. Although Aher returns safe and sane, he is lost as well because he becomes a heretic.

The stories about Aher and the other rabbis have been arranged around the garden metaphor and are obviously ramified by later sages. Many modern interpreters of the *pardes* traditions have asserted that originally they had nothing to do with mystical speculation, only later to be unjustly claimed by mystics, because they were interested in finding tannaitic justification for their practices. [8] One of the foremost critics sharing this opinion is Ephraim Urbach, who is a strong modern apologist for the rationality of tannaitic thought and attempts to use text critical tools to demonstrate his points. He isolates the kernel of the *pardes* story as the parable of a king who has made a garden on high which commoners might see but not enter or use. [9] He concludes his analysis by saying that these stories originally had nothing to do with

---

creatures. Rashi senses the moral of the story for the Jewish community. It is a heavenly warning against heresy.

[6] See Ecc. R. VII, 8 and Ruth R. 6:4 f. as well as here, b. Hag. 12b f.

[7] See p. 9.

[8] The following have all suggested that the *pardes* story involved philosophical speculation (about *materia prima* usually) which was later misdirected into mystical thought: Graetz, *Gnosticismus*, pp. 94-95, Joël, *Blick*, I, p. 163, Bacher, *AT*, I, p. 233. See also Fischel, pp. 1-34.

[9] Urbach, *Scholem Festschrift*, p. 12-18. David Halpern is studying the midrashic and talmudic traditions in great detail in his dissertation at Berkeley. The parable that Urbach finds at center of the *pardes* tradition may be found in j. Hag. 73c near the bottom.

apocalyptic or mystical traditions. But that is not the same as saying there is no mystical speculation in first century Judaism. What he isolates is the parable at the core of the legend, the metaphor around which the legend was redacted on the basis of a word play between "paradise" and garden. His analysis implies nothing about the historicity of mystical tales about Akiba and his successors or even about the date that the parable of the *pardes* was associated with mysticism. [10]

Morton Smith [11] and Gershom Scholem, [12] on the other hand, show that the traditions in the Talmud and mystical texts are not out of place in the apocalyptic or the theurgic context of the second and third centuries. Scholem goes further, saying that the traditions are integrally related to apocalyptic lore. He even supposes a link with first century mystics like Paul, who claimed to know of a man who was taken up into the third heaven. Scholem's problem like Urbach's is to discover the specific part of the legend of "the four who entered paradise" which could go back to the first or second century.

We can best locate the early levels by peeling back the later ones. Whatever the origin of the story of the four who entered the *pardes*, it is likely that the part dealing with Aher has been extensively revised by later redactors. Firstly, the language of the story is Babylonian Aramaic. Next, it is not unlike the rather lengthy cycle of stories which were built up about Aher by later sages except that it has a moral particularly suitable for instruction against heresy. Lastly, the name of the angel, Metatron, argues for a Babylonian redaction and late date. [13]

We know that the story was meant to show the error of the doctrine which Aher espoused and to classify that doctrine as "two powers in

---

[10] To be sure, he addresses himself to just this problem in the legends concerning ben Arak. But his conclusions there are based on his previous argument that the stories are late.

[11] See Smith, *Observations*, where he argues that the theurgic magic in the so-called Mithras liturgy is of a piece with the heavenly journey of Hekhaloth Rabbati and hence the latter, which is not a talmudic report but an actual mystical book, may go back to the third century.

[12] See Scholem, *Jewish Gnosticism*, "The Four Who entered Paradise and Paul's Ascension to Paradise" where he traces mystical themes to Paul and II Enoch. See also J. W. Bowker, "Merkabah Visions and the Visions of Paul," *JSS*, 16 (1971), 157-73; A. Neher "Le Voyage de Quatre," *RHR*, CXL (1951), 59-82; J. Neusner, "The Development of the Merkabah Tradition," *JSJ*, 2 (1971), 149-60.

[13] Ginzberg first promulgated this argument. He denied all historic worth to the story because he thought Metatron to be a name otherwise completely limited to Babylonian sources. See *JE*, "*Merkabah*." It is probable, however, that Metatron is a rabbinic name first evidenced in Babylonia for a principal angel known by many names in Palestinian sects. See below, p. 64 f.

heaven." We also know from the previous chapter that the earliest isolatable heresy involved a divine hypostasis of God, somehow derived by exegesis from the Hebrew names of God. The rabbis maintained that such conceptions implied an independent will for one of God's creatures, hence compromised monotheism. But there is no reason to suppose that the heretics themselves would have said so. Here we have a similar tradition involving a specific angel, Metatron. The conclusions of the previous chapter make it seem likely, on grounds completely independent of Scholem or Smith, that angelic speculation led to heresy in Palestine. But that is not all. There is further evidence in rabbinic literature that opposition to principal angelic mediators is quite early. For instance, the rabbis often emphasize that some of God's actions in behalf of Israel were accomplished "not by an angel and not by a messenger." Judah Goldin [14] shows that the formula was applied to texts when the Hebrew syntax indicates that the subject (most often God, but once Moses!) should be specially emphasized. The contexts in which the formula occurs are five-fold: (1) God's redemption of Israel from Egyptian bondage, (2) God's punishment of Israel, (3) God's providing for Israel on its land, (4) God's revelation of the law to Moses at Sinai, and finally, (5) Moses' instruction to Israel about the convenantal value of the sabbath. These areas tend to show specifically where the rabbis were most concerned to emphasize that God himself, (once Moses) and not an angelic mediator, was responsible for the action. The comments by the rabbis are quite consonant with the teachings of R. Akiba's pupil, R. Simeon b. Yohai, perhaps even with R. Akiba himself [15] which were discussed in the previous chapter. But the letters of Paul give us certain proof that some Jews of the first century thought that the law was given by angels, an idea which would certainly have been opposed by the rabbis as well. [16]

It is not clear that the proto-Merkabah mystics would have identified their candidate for mediating angel or messenger with Metatron. To be sure, Metatron is an exceptionally important figure in later merkabah

---

[14] Judah Goldin, "Not by means of an Angel and not by Means of a Messenger," in *Religions in Antiquity: Essays in Memory of E. R. Goodenough*, ed. J. Neusner (Leiden: 1968), pp. 412-424. The language itself is likely to be related to LXX of Isaiah 63:9, or even a targumic rendering of the verse. In its augmented form this verse is a crucial part of the Christian discussion of the trinity. See Jaroslav Pelikan, *The Christian Tradition*, I, p. 177 f.

[15] See above (p. 45 f.) and also Urbach, *Sages*, pp. 116 f., 156 f. Also see Lieberman in Scholem, *Jewish Gnosticism*, p. 118-126.

[16] See Galatians 3:13 f. and below p. 211 f.

speculation. In *The Third* or *Hebrew Book of Enoch*, Metatron is set on a throne alongside God and appointed above angels and powers to function as God's vizir and plenipotentiary. These traditions are related to the earlier Enoch cycle in apocalyptic literature because Enoch is described by the mystics as having been caught up to the highest heaven (based on Gen. 5:24), where he is transformed into the fiery angel, Metatron. This is clearly dependent on the ancient "son of man" traditions which appear in Ethiopian Enoch 70 and 71, but they have been expanded in Jewish mysticism so that Enoch and Metatron are now *alter egos*, while neither the titles "son of man" nor "son of God" appear at all. Instead the principal angel is given the title "YHWH HQTWN" (YHWH the lesser) or the "NᶜR" (youth) and possibly even "SR HᶜWLM" (Prince of the World). [17] Martin Hengel suggests that titles like "youth" actually function as substitutes for the original titles in *I Enoch*, which had taken on christological significance and could not be used in Jewish mysticism. [18] Since these mystical descriptions of Metatron are later traditions and Metatron is described in orthodox, amoraic rabbinic writings as well, not every appearance of the angel Metatron can be heretical, and most of them are probably not antique. Scholem claims that only the concept of a principal angel, underlying the name of Metatron, [19] is Palestinian and antique. He points out that the names Yahoel, "Lesser YHWH" or YHWH HQTWN, which are quite often attributed to Metatron in Merkabah tradition and occasionally occur in Coptic-gnostic literature, must underlie the Aher story. [20] If Metatron were also known as YHWH HQTWN, Aher's mistake would have been both more understandable and more dangerous because the name of the angel would contain

---

[17] See my article "Prince of the World - Angel or Demon?: Towards a Sociology of Gnosticism," forthcoming.

[18] Martin Hengel, *The Son of God*, p. 46.

[19] See Cyrus Gordon, *Archiv Orientalni*, VI (1934), 328 and IX (1937), 95, for occurrences of Metatron on Babylonian libation bowls. Metatron is called "Great Prince" and "Great Prince of His Throne." See now Charles Isbell, *Corpus of the Aramic Incantation Bowls* (Missoula, Montana: SBL and Scholar's Press, Dissertation Series 17, 1975). pp. 34.4; 49.11; 56.12. For the various views on the derivation of the name, Metatron, see Ödeberg, *III Enoch*, 125-142 and Scholem's explanation, *Maj. Trends*, p. 68. Urbach shows (*The Sages*, p. 119, n. 15) that Scholem must be wrong in deriving the name from *vox mystica* phenomena. The fact that Metatron equals Shaddai in Gematria, which is in keeping with the tradition "My name is in him," argues for deliberate choosing of the name. See further words by Lieberman on metathronos in Gruenwald *Apocalyptic and Merkabah*.

[20] The Lesser Yah or Yahoel are also related terms and, being composed from YHWH, would contain the name of God, hence resemble the angel of Ex. 33:20 f. as well. See p. 195.

the tetragrammation and might indeed be taken as a second deity. [21] These observations allow Scholem to push the date of these Merkabah traditions back to the third century for sure and possibly the second, but certainly into the Hellenistic (hence Palestinian) cultural milieu. [22]

According to Scholem, YHWH HQTWN was only one name for the mediator. Many of the legends told about the archangel Michael in earlier aggadic sources were transferred by Merkabah mystics and by the rabbis to Metatron. The process of identification, says Scholem, can be traced to the fourth and perhaps the third centuries. The evidence for this identification is an apocalyptic, mystical document known as the "Visions of Ezekiel," which is based on a description of the seven heavens more or less parallel to the rabbinic account of the heavens in *Hag.* 12b and ARN.

As quoted by Scholem, the key passage reads as follows:

> And what is there in *Zebul*? R. Levi said in the name of R. Hama bar Ukba, who said it in the name of R. Johanan: The Prince [obviously Michael as in the Talmudic passage] is not dwelling anywhere but in *Zebul* and he is the very fullness of *Zebul* [i.e., fills all of it?] and before him are thousands of thousands and myriads of myriads who minister to him. Of them it is said in Daniel: I beheld till thrones were placed, etc.; a fiery stream issued, etc. (7:9-10). And what is his name? Kimos [or Kemos] ... is his name. R. Isaac said: Ma'atah [or me'atah] is his name. R. Inyanei bar Sisson said: Bizbul [meaning: in *zebul*] is his name. R. Tanhum, the Old said: Atatiyah..., is his name. Eleazar Nadwadaya said: Metatron, like the name of the (divine) *Dynamis*. And those who make theurgic use of the (divine) Name say: *Salnas*, ... is his name, Kasbak, ... [a different reading: *Baskabas*] is His name, similar to the name of the Creator of the World. And what is the name of the Merkabah of *Zebul*? *Halwaya*, ... it its name. [23]

The setting is the seven-tiered heaven, mentioned in b. Hag. 12b and ARN. The passage implies that Metatron, whatever the derivation of the name, is to be understood as a secret name for the archangel Michael. At least this is the interpretation that Eleazar Nadwadaya offers. At the same time, the passage states that the name Metatron is also like the name of God, here also called (GBWRH = *dynamis*) or "the power." The passage was composed by Jewish mystics, not

---

[21] Ödeberg, *III Enoch*, pp. 188-192. See also Scholem, *Major Trends*, p. 68 f. and *Jewish Gnosticism*, p. 41.

[22] Scholem's conclusions have been criticized by Lieberman (ŠQYᶜYN, 5699, p. 15) who questions the manuscript evidence he brings and by Urbach, *Sages*, (p. 119, n. 5). See Gruenwald, *Apocalyptic and Merkabah Mysticism*, and *Visions of Ezekiel*.

[23] Scholem's *Jewish Gnosticism*, p. 46.

their rabbinic colleagues, so the appearance of the now familiar reference to Dan. 7:9 f. further substantiates that other groups besides Christians were making "dangerous" interpretations of that verse, and that Daniel's vision substantiated the mystical doctrine. The mystics of the third and fourth centuries inherited these esoteric traditions about the night vision of Daniel and used them in an exegesis central to their position. [24] The passage shows that there were traditions about a principal angel of God, whatever the name, that are older than the Babylonian texts testifying to such traditions. We also know something of a quite similar heresy reported by rabbis in the second century. Whatever else the heresy may have been, it contained some of the kinds of traditions which would later become Merkabah mysticism, making it appropriate to describe the heretics as proto-Merkabah mystics. Of course we cannot be sure merely from the rabbinic title "two powers" that these traditions are historically related to the apocalyptic, Christian and later gnostic heresies we discovered in the last chapter. The rabbis may have associated many groups on the basis of phenomenological similarity, rather than common history. The fact that they use similar exegeses suggests some kind of relationship, as yet unspecified, among the various groups.

With these conclusions, we can now look at another text in the Babylonian Talmud related to the problem of "two powers in heaven":

[24] Perhaps the relationship between Metatron and Daniel 7:9 as shown by the quotation from the *Visions of Ezekiel* makes clearer the predicate of N^cR or "youth" for Metatron which Scholem finds so puzzling. It occurs in 3 Enoch 3:2 and is referred to in the *Shiur Koma* in the phrase MŠKN HN^cR. The young figure in Daniel 7:9 and Ex. 15:3 is never called N^cR in rabbinic literature. He is called GBWR, BḤWR, ꜣŠ MLḤMH. However the midrash does use the word ZQN, old man, explicitly to describe the Ancient of Days and the manifestation of God at Sinai, Ex. 24:10 f. and Ex. 20:2. Perhaps the missing step in the development is the use of Ps. 37:25 which states: "I have been a youth and now I am old." Thus the young figure in the heavenly visions could be identified as N^cR and the meaning of "servant" (as in servant of the altar) would be derivative. One should also mention that the contrast between God in youth and in old age was developed eloquently by appeal to passage in the Song of Songs (see, *e.g.*, Hag. 14a), an extremely popular book, and the Shiur Koma literature produced by Merkabah mystics. See Green, "The Children in Egypt and the Theophany at the Sea: Interpretation of an Aggadic Motif." The theme has also occurred in liturgy of later periods e.g. the *Shir Hak-Kabod*. Some evidence that such an hypothetical reconstruction is in accord with the history of the tradition comes from Yeb. 16b where Ps. 37:25 is put into the mouth of a figure called the "Prince of the World" because "only he who was present during the history of creation from its beignning to its end coul dhave spoken these words." The Prince of the World, as we shall see, is another figure intimately bound upin the traditions of Metatron and Michael and YHWH. See p. 50 f., 60, 64 f., 189, 214. See also Lieberman in Scholem, *Jewish Gnosticism*, as noted.

Sanhedrin 38b

R. Nahman said: "He who is as skilled in refuting the *Minim* as is R. Idith [MS. M: R. Idi] let him do so; but not otherwise. Once a *Min* said to R. Idi: 'It is written, *And unto Moses He said: Come up to the Lord* (Ex. 24:1). But surely it should have stated, *Come up to me!*'—'It was Metatron,' he replied, whose name is similar to that of his Master, for it is written, *For My name is in Him.* (Ex. 23:21). 'But if so, we should worship him!' 'The same passage however,' replied R. Idi, 'says: *Be not rebellious against Him* [i.e., exchange Me not for him.'] 'But if so, why is it stated: *He will not pardon your transgression?*' (Ex. 23:21). He answered: 'By our troth [lit: we hold the belief] we would not accept him even as a messenger, for it is written. And he said unto him, *If Thy presence go not* etc.' (Ex. 33:15)." [25]

The passage is ascribed to R. Nahman, a Babylonian who lived in the late third century. He, in turn, praises the rhetorical skills of R. Idi (or Idith), [26] who apparently lived in Palestine in the generation previous to R. Nahman. R. Nahman warns that it is dangerous business to get into arguments with the heretics. [27] One should refrain unless one has the skill of R. Idi.

The demonstration of R. Idi's competence is exceedingly interesting. Without naming the heresy, he describes a passage conducive to the "two powers" heresy (Ex. 24:1). In that scripture, God orders Moses and the elders to ascend to the Lord. Since the text says, "Come up to YHWH" and not "Come up *to me*," the heretic states that two deities are present. The tetragrammaton would then be the name of a second deity, a conclusion further supported by the lack of an explicit subject for the verb "said" in the Massoretic Text. The high god can refer to his helper as YHWH because the helper is the same figure of whom it is said, "My name is in him" (Ex. 23:20 f.).

Obviously this is another case of heretics believing in a principal angel with divine perquisites because the Lord's name is in him. Now we see how the name of YHWH was associated with the mediator. [28] The language is Babylonian Aramaic so the text itself can only be dated

---

25 Tr. Epstein.

26 Not even Urbach, *Sages*, p. 119 is sure of the identity of this rabbi.

27 If the identity of the group here is merkabah mystics, it is the only place in midrash that implies they are heretics. Note also the common pseudo-correction of Sadducee for sectarian.

28 Scholem argues that this implies that the earliest name for the angel here described must have been YHWH HQTWN or Yahoel, (or, at the very least Michael, whose name means "Who is like God!"). Rashi and R. Hananel *ad loc* say that Metatron refers to God as "Lord," thus avoiding the heretical implication.

to the third century with any surety. But the tradition must be based on older traditions in apocalyptic or proto-Merkabah or proto-gnostic texts where the principal angel has a theophoric name.

A most significant question is whether or not such ideas were ever current within rabbinic Judaism. As we have seen, Urbach [29] says that they existed only on the outskirts of rabbinism and only at the end of the second century. Scholem [30] says that they were central and early. It is quite possible that our texts are too refractory for definite answers but rabbinic opposition to extreme forms of speculation can be outlined by looking at their arguments.

The defense against the heretical doctrine is based on a *double entendre*. According to R. Idi, scripture should be understood as saying, "Do not exchange me" (from M-W-R) rather than, "Be not rebellious or provocative" (from M-R-H). Therefore, it is scripture itself that offers the best caution against the heretical doctrine. We learn from this defense that the heretics, in rabbinic eyes, were seen to confuse an angel with God!

The heretic then asks why the Bible needed to say that "he will not pardon your sins." As it is stated, the heretic is challenging the rabbi to apply a rabbinic doctrine that each phrase in scripture must be interpreted in such a way as to add its own specific piece of information. Although this stylizes the heretic in a rabbinic idiom, the heretical argument itself can certainly be discovered. More is at stake than a heretic challenging a rabbi to observe the proper rules of rabbinic debate. The heretic is saying that since the angel is described as not pardoning the Israelites at this one place, normally the angel must offer pardons. Hence, in heretical eyes, he has an independent share of God's power. Furthermore, the last polemical remark of the rabbi makes this implication clear. Were he only a messenger or agent— *parvanka* [31]—he should not be received.

---

[29] Urbach, *Secret Torah*, throughout.

[30] Scholem, *Major Trends* and *Jewish Gnosticism*, esp. pp. 20 f., 31 f., 43 f., 75 f.

[31] The word *"parvanka"* is a loan word from Mandaean and ultimately from Persian where it meant a forerunner or messenger or the normal word for letter carrier. In Hebrew, it seems to be used in the sense of messenger (Heb. *shaliah*), used in respect to both prophecy and liturgy to describe a representative of the people or to the sovereign. Since *shaliah* was a readily available word, one wonders why the rabbis did not use it, relying instead on the less familiar *"parvanka."* Ödeberg suggests that *shaliah* had already started to receive the connotation of savior, liberator, or deliverer, as it has in Mandaic. But Ödeberg is mistaken for *parvanka* also has soteriological connotations in Mandaic. See Nöldeke, *Man. Gram.* 417, n. 1, for its

If we take the literature in the New Testament as characteristic of some kinds of heresy in the first century, we find that this is not an entirely inaccurate description of Christian exegesis. Ex. 23:20 is most often taken to refer to John the Baptist (Mk. 1:2, Mt. 11:10)— that is, purely an earthly messenger. But the point of Mt. 11:10 is precisely that Jesus, for those who truly believe in him, is greater than John the Baptist and is in the same category as eschatological figures like Elijah. Furthermore, one of the things which, according to the New Testament, most upsets the Jews about Jesus is precisely that he does claim the power to forgive sins (Mk. 2:7 f.).

This is not intended to say that the pericope which has been described as characteristic of the third century at the earliest must be speaking about first century Christianity. There are some obvious differences between the two uses of Ex. 23:20. I only maintain that arguments like those which we find opposed by the rabbis in the third century and later were already present in heretical writings of the first century, as represented by Christians. The rabbis, then, accused heretics (some who resembled Christians, but probably others as well) not merely with the charge of believing in angels (which the rabbis themselves certainly acknowledged) but with the charge of believing that a certain principal angel was a special mediator between God and man. The mediation might have involved the forgiving of sins, which, in any case, was enough for the rabbis to conclude that the principal figure of the heretics was supposed to be more than an angel. Or it

_____

use in Kolasta and L. Ginza, as a guide for the spirit when it leaves its earthly life. Widengren ("Heavenly Enthronement and Baptism," *Religions in Antiquity*, 566) translates *parvanka* as "companion" because of its soteriological connotations and remarks on the relationship to M. Ir. *"Parvanak."* Another more probable reason for using *parvanka* rather than *shaliah* is that the word *"shaliah"* had the legal status of "agent" in rabbinic law. As an agent, a person acting for someone else should be treated *as if he were* the person he represents. Some considered an agent as a *partner* of the person that he represents. (B.K. 70a). In fact, there are accounts of "two powers" heretics who thought that the second power was God's partner in creation (see p. 111 f.). Accordingly, it was probable that the rabbis were avoiding the terms which would explicitly validate the heresy in rabbinic law. It is also possible that they used a word which the heretics themselves used to describe the second power. That would mean that the heretics are similar to Mandaean gnostics, or to the group who brought gnosticism to the Mandaeans. The rabbis did not employ the word *shaliah* to describe the angel described in Ex. 23:20, but the Persian loan word would be suitable because it contained the connotation of mediator without giving rabbinic approval to the concept. For the concept of God's agency as used in the Gospel of John to describe Jesus' mission on earth, see Peder Borgen, *Bread from Heaven*, Supplements to *NT*, X, (Leiden: 1965) 158-164 and "God's Agent in the Fourth Gospel," *Religions in Antiquity*, pp. 136-148.

might have involved the belief that the angel participated in God's divinity by appropriating one of His names. It seems clear therefore that some varieties of the heresy go back to the first century, even if the rabbinic texts do not.

It is important to note that the two powers worshipped by the heretics were complementary rather than opposing, as gnostic deities were. On the basis of this evidence, we must conclude that the earliest traditions which the rabbis opposed were of the complementary variety, since we have no hint that the opposing variety of heretical traditions (like the kind that R. Nathan may have described) had a similar, ancient history. Because of this, we should be prepared to accept the conclusion that the heretics, among whom Christians were certainly included, would not have agreed with the rabbinic charge that they were dualists. By the third century, which is the earliest possible period of our text, the rabbis seem to be fully aware of the kinds of claims that could be made about a "son of man" or Metatron or any other principal angel. So they reject the idea of divine intermediaries totally, except as dependent agents of punishment. In place of the "two power" understanding of Ex. 23:20, they offer the opposing verse Ex. 33:15, "If Thy presence go not with us, carry us not up hence," which they interpret as Moses' prayer that God himself should always be Israel's guide. [32]

The final stage in the rabbinic argument against angelic mediation may be found in Ex. R. 32:9 where it is recorded that wherever an angel of YHWH is mentioned one should understand that the Shekhina (i.e., God's presence) was manifested. The effect is to remove any doubt that the manifestation of divine force can be separate from God.

Identifying the specific group about whom the rabbis were concerned in this passage can not be successful. Scholars have answered the question in a variety of ways. Friedländer [33] erroneously saw the passages themselves as dating from the tannaitic period. In accordance with that theory, he could regard the rabbinic opponent as a gnostic. He then proposed that "Metatron" should be identified with a gnostic

---

[32] Philo offers an interesting and "dangerous" exegesis of these verses in Quae. Ex. II 46: When Moses was called above at the theophany on the seventh day (Ex. 24:16), he was changed from earthly man to heavenly man. The gospel of John (3:13) seems to contain a polemic against that idea. John says that the vision of God's kingdom and the second birth from above are not brought about by ascent into heaven to the son of man, but rather the heavenly man's descent brings the vision and the second birth. See Borgen, p. 146.

[33] Friedländer, *Gnosticismus*, p. 103.

god, "Horos." Of course, this overlooks the important fact that the rabbis (R. Aher and R. Idi), not the heretic, mention Metatron. Further, there is no hint of gnostic opposition of deities in any of the material. It seems likely that Metatron, chief of God's angels, who acts as His messenger and representative but is never regarded as God, is the rabbinic name for many mediators in heretical thought.

Herford [34] saw the heretical doctrine as belonging to the Christian camp, which was in accordance with his general theory that all *minim* are Christians. He suggested further that the type of Christianity involved would have to be the Jewish-Christianity outlined in the Epistle to the Hebrews. There, the Christ is seen as the heavenly High Priest "after the order of Melchizedek," who, in turn, is a kind of supernatural mediator. This ignores the fact that the Epistle to the Hebrews argues that the Christ, as Son, is superior to any angel. Urbach [35] also suggests that the opponent is a Christian. However he does this only because he feels that Merkabah mysticism must be excluded as a possibility during the tannaitic period. None are prepared to say that a variety of phenomena fit the bill of particulars.

With the information and study which Scholem has brought to the subject comes the most complete understanding of the opponents. His study has made it clear that these traditions were quite generalized and went through different phases in different Jewish sects. Nor were reports of heavenly journeys exclusively confined to Judaism, as the reports about Julian the Theurgist show. At first they were fairly widespread in apocalyptic, mystical, and ascetic groups. In Jewish circles they are always associated with theophany texts in the Old Testament, the same texts we have been tracing. They were witnessed by Philo, who, as we shall see, recast them as the *logos* and used them to describe the rewards of the mystical ascent. But the traditions were also present in the Qumran Community. [36] There is no reason to doubt that R. Yohanan b. Zakkai and his disciples, to whom the earliest Merkabah traditions are attributed in talmudic sources, were familiar with some

---

[34] Herford, p. 285 f.

[35] *The Sages*, p. 118 f.

[36] See Jonas Greenfield's prolegomenon to the new edition of *III Enoch*, ed., H. Ödeberg for a fine review of the evidence linking merkabah mysticism with various Palestinian apocalyptic traditions in the first century. See also G. Quispel, "The Jung Codex and its Significance" in *The Jung Codex*, H.-ch. Puech, G. Quispel and W. L. van Unnik (London: 1955), pp. 35-78. See Lawrence Schiffman, "Merkabah Speculation at Qumran: The ᶜ4Q Serekh Shiroth ᶜOlat ha-Shabbat," *Festschrift for A. Altmann*, forthcoming.

of the Essene and apocalyptic traditions that circulated in their day. [37] Whether or not the rabbis also indulged in mystical *praxis* at first is unknown. By the third century, however, all evidence shows that such practices were known to be dangerous by the rabbis. The traditions which did survive within Judaism only did so in secret conventicles of esoteric knowledge which collected and redacted the later documents of Merkabah mysticism. [38] The repression of such dangerous ideas in Judaism must date from the same period as the mishnaic rules in Hagigah strictly governing the transmission of Merkabah lore—that is, the late second century at the latest. The germ of the story about Aher then may be authentic or come from the period when such ideas were less restricted, though the heretical charge must be later and based in Aher's presumed antinomianism. The story about R. Idi and the *min* must come from the amoraic period when those who espoused the tradition could be subject to the charge of the "two powers in heaven." The heretical opponent of R. Idi in the third century could be either a Christian or Merkabah mystic. The former is somewhat more likely, because nowhere else are Merkabah mystics explicitly called *"minim."*

If one allows that either Christians or Merkabah mystics could have espoused these "two powers" doctrines in the third century, one must be willing to grant that the heretical traditions themselves are quite a bit older than the amoraic period, and that the title "two powers" could be applied to a variety of related doctrines.

---

[37] See Urbach, *Secret Torah* for an analysis of how these apocalyptic traditions ramified into the traditions now present as *beraitot* in Hagigah. See especially N. A. Dahl, "The Johannine Church and History," in *Current Issues in NT Interpretation*, ed., Klassen and G. Snyder (New York: 1962), p. 124-142, especially 131 for the impetus to see the roots of Johannnine Christology within Jewish traditions of the visionary ascent to heaven, as witnessed in merkabah and Christian apocrypha like "The Ascension of Isaiah." This work develops the observations of Ödeberg in *III Enoch* and *The Fourth Gospel*.

[38] It is difficult to tell how much of the later mystical ascent practice through ecstasy was present in the earliest period. However, theurgic ascent practices can be traced to the Julian the Theurgist (author of the Chaldaean Oracles) at the end of the second century, and hence to his father, in the middle of the same century (See Smith, *Observations*, H. Lewy, *Chaldaean Oracles and Theurgy* (Cairo: 1956) and *Oracles Chaldaiques*, ed., des Places (Paris: 1971) and subsequently became quite widespread throughout the Roman Empire. Whether earlier Jewish apocalyptic heavenly journeys could have existed without such theurgic practices is a moot question, but it seems to me to be quite unlikely that the literary traditions could circulate without some basis in ecstatic experience.

CHAPTER FOUR

A CONTROVERSY BETWEEN ISHMAEL AND AKIBA

We have learned a considerable amount about the early character of binitarian heresy from the "two powers" midrashism surveyed so far. However, as we will now see, much material not originally part of the heresy came to be associated with the "two powers" tradition. Hence it becomes especially difficult from this point onward to identify one specific group or doctrine with the heresy. Instead, a variety of different groups inherit the title. This can be shown clearly in the case of one debate between two tannaim, Akiba and Ishmael. In this particular case, an originally ambiguous story was only associated with the heresy of "two powers" in a later recension. The editor who associated the two traditions was, in effect, offering an interpretation of the ambiguous tradition by saying that it concerned "two powers" heresy.

PASSAGE 4

Genesis Rabba 1:14, b. Hag. 12a, Tan. 8

ᵓ*T the heavens and* ᵓ*T the earth* (Gen. 1:1) R. Ishmael asked R. Akiba: 1 Since you have studied twenty-two years under Nahum of Gimzo [who formulated the principle that] ᵓ*K* and *RQ* are limitations while ᵓ*T* and *GM* are extensions, [tell me], what of the ᵓ*T* written here? Said he to him: "If it stated 'In the beginning created God heaven and earth' 2 we might have maintained that heaven and earth too are divine." Thereupon he cited to him. 3 "*For it is no empty matter for you* (Dt. 32:47)" and if it is empty, it is so on your account—because you are unable to interpret—rather:

---

1 Hagigah: when they were walking in the way.

2 Hagigah: If "heaven and earth" (alone) were said I would have thought that "heaven" was the name of the Holy One Blessed be He. Now it says "ᵓ*T the heaven and* ᵓ*T the earth*" (Gen. 1:1)—"heavens" the real heavens; "earth," the real earth.

Tanhuma: "In the beginning created God heavens and earth" is not written rather, "ᵓ*T the heavens and* ᵓ*T the earth*" to show the logic of the divine writ.

3 Tanhuma: R. Akiba said to him! For it is no empty thing for you (Dt. 32:47) "If heavens and earth (alone) were said, we would have thought that THERE ARE TWO GODS, rather ᵓT the heavens and ᵓT the earth'—them and what is described with them."

ᵓT *the heavens* is to include the sun and the moon, the stars and the constellations, the ᵓT *the earth*—to include the trees and the grasses and the garden of Eden. 4

As the text stands, R. Ishmael is challenging the method by which R. Akiba interprets scripture. R. Akiba was taught by Nahum of Gimzo that every use of ᵓT signifies an inclusion in the meaning of the text. 5 "ᵓT the Torah"—one might hypothesize, would mean both the oral and written laws. R. Ishmael, however, challenges the principle with the first verse in scripture. But R. Akiba says that he does not interpret the scripture to include or exclude anything here. Rather the ᵓT signifies only that "heaven" and "earth" are definite direct objects of the verb "created," not the subject of "created." Hence, in no way can one assume that "heaven" and "earth" are deities. R. Ishmael replies that "This is no empty thing for you" (Dt. 32:47) presumably meaning that the occurance of ᵓT in this verse cannot remain without special significance in R. Akiba's system of interpretation or it would show a failure of that system. As he says, "If it is an empty thing for you, it is because you do not know how to interpret."

The next phrase of R. Ishmael is ambiguous. Either he says (1) ᵓT "the heaven already includes the sun and moon, stars and constellations..." meaning that R. Akiba's system has to fail because "heaven and earth" is already a synecdoche for all creation, or (2) he helps R. Akiba's argument by offering an explanation which R. Akiba has

---

4 The end of this quotation differs from Freedman order to convey the ambiguity of the Hebrew. See Theodor-Albeck I, 12 for complete references.

5 This is the Hebrew particle signifying the definite direct object which, therefore, like a case ending, has syntactical value but no lexical meaning. The verse in question is Genesis 1:1 ("In the beginning, God created heaven and earth.") Because of the Hebrew accusative particle ᵓT, we know that "heaven and earth" are to be understood as definite direct objects of the verb "created." If the Torah were written in ordinary Hebrew, the sole function of the ᵓT would be to point out this definite direct object. But the kind of Hebrew that comprised the Torah is precisely the point at issue between Ishmael and Akiba. (See Epstein, MBWᵓWT, pp. 521-526 and Bacher, *Aggada der Tannaiten*, I, p. 67 f.) R. Ishmael stated that DBRH TWRH KLŠWN BNY ᵓDM. The words of Torah are like ordinary speech (lit.: is like the language of men) (Sifre bashalah 112, San. 64b). This means that one should not pay any special attention to the seemingly pleonastic words in the text or even things that seem repetitious. R. Akiba, on the other hand, had learned his exegetical methodology from Nahum of Gimzo, who taught that all particles, indeed, every jot and tittle of the Torah held some special meaning which must be unlocked. In particular, conjunctions employed in the Torah were intended to indicate the extension or limitation of its provisions. Hence this system was called extension and limitation RBWY WMYWṬ. The particles KL, ᵓP, were regarded as implying extensions while ᵓK, MN, KK were regarded as limitations.

not himself considered but which would support R. Akiba's system. Or (3) the last phrase can be understood as being spoken by R. Akiba. The first possibility (1) has two difficulties: (a) it leaves the matter wholly undecided; (b) it involves translating the definitive LRBWT as "already does include." The second possibility (2) seems most likely to me because it involves the least textual change but it has the difficulty of attributing to R. Ishmael an argument for a system of interpretation which he is known always to have opposed. The third possibility (3) involves a change of speakers without any indication in the text. It also involves assuming that R. Akiba is the first to bring up the idea that heaven and earth are *pars pro toto*, Ishmael not having a suspicion of it previously. The third possibility is the route most scholars have taken, by assuming that the text is in disarray and that another "ᵓMR LW" should be added in the text somewhere, indicating that the speaker did change. ⁶

The ambiguity in the text is quite old; even the elaborations of the tradition in *Tanhuma* and *Hagigah* may be seen as separate attempts to resolve it. In *Tanhuma* R. Akiba is reported to have said the last phrase and, by using the "eth" to have included all the things in heaven and earth. This statement closes the argument. He also maintains that heaven and earth might be taken to mean "two gods"—which is the exact phrase used in the statement of R. Elisha b. Abuya in Hagiga, and, as we have seen previously must be equivalent to saying that the heresy of "two powers" is involved. But the text is late, relative to

---

⁶ See e.g., Theodor-Albeck, *ad loc.*; Marmorstein, *Essays in Anthropomorphism*, p. 11 interprets the paragraph based on an emendation. Marmorstein is most articulate about how the passage should be read... "The original text can be reconstructed by consulting all the available parallels and manuscripts." Tanchuma ed. Buber, Gen., 5 f., has the following reading in which R. Ishmael says: "The expressions (eth) in Gen. 1:1 surely cannot be explained according to your method; it is, however, the usual expression of the text. R. Akiba says: 'Thou canst not explain it according to your method, cf. (v. Deut. 32:47) but I can, for if the particle would be omitted one would think that heaven and earth are Godheads; now, since the texts puts "eth," the teaching can be derived that heaven and earth were brought into existence fully furnished with their complete equipment.' It is noteworthy that the rendering of the verse from Deuteronomy, which is quoted here in the dialogue in the name of R. Ishmael or R. Akiba respectively, is cited in the Palestinian Talmud four times in the name of one of the younger Palestinian Amoraim, R. Mana, v. Peah 1:1, Shebiit 1:6, Shabbath 1:1, Sukka 4:1 and Ketuboth 8, end. This looks strange unless we take it as a later gloss. The Midrash Abkir published by me in Dwir, pt. 1, pp. 127-128 enables us to render the question and answer in this way: R. Ishmael asks what is the meaning of "eth" in the verse? Surely no one of us will go so far as to suggest that heaven and earth are deities or that man is God, or that God is a lad? Therefore R. Akiba gives his interpretation."

the other versions, and the Genesis Rabba text, which is supported by all the other versions, has neither a direct mention of "two deities" nor an additional marking that the speaker changes. If R. Akiba is the author of the last statement, he speaks without a definite mark of the change in speakers. [7]

Whatever the solution to the textual problem and the structure of the argument, the crucial point for studying rabbinic heresiology is to understand what is meant by calling heaven and earth gods. The heresy—or more exactly the faulty interpretation of scripture—was puzzling to later rabbinic interpreters as well. In the Hagigah version of the text, for instance, the dangerous doctrine is described as believing that "heaven" and "earth" are *names* of God. Only in the late midrash, Tanhuma, is the heretical belief explicitly called "two gods." The only thing immediately apparent from the Tanhuma evidence is that the heresy of "two powers" was taken by later tradition as being equivalent to saying there are two Gods—i.e., ditheism. Discovering the character or practitioners of any hypothetical heretical doctrine and its dubious relationship to "two powers in heaven" will not be easy. It is sure that, despite the similarity in language, Tanhuma cannot have the same heresy in mind as we have traced in the first two chapters. Ishmael and Akiba can not be talking about "two deities or powers *in heaven*." Only one is in heaven,—or, more exactly, *is* heaven. One suspects, then, by the time of the redaction of Tanhuma, the charge of "two gods" or "two powers" had become completely conventional and could be used against a variety of unorthodox opinions, without the slightest deference to the original sources of the heresy.

Heaven and earth were seen as deities by every polytheistic culture surrounding Israel. Even Persian and Greek philosophy maintained that they were divine. However, no culture around the Jews during that period maintained that heaven and earth were the only two gods. It is not likely that either polytheism or strict dualism is the doctrine attacked in this passage.

The same tradition is attached to a variety of different scriptural verses: Gen. 4:1, and Gen. 21:20, to name the principal ones. All of

---

[7] The Soncino Midrash (in English) appears to understand the passage in this third way. Freedman and Simon translate ᵓLᵓ as "No" and see the sense of the passage as follows: "No! ᵓT the heavens is to include the sun and the moon, the stars and the planets WᵓT the earth is to include trees, herbage and the garden of Eden." Thus they see an implied change of speaker for this last paragraph.

these occurrences, as we shall see, are designed to combat some unstated heresy, although no unified conception of the heresy can be discovered. In view of this, one must suspect that the redactor brought a perfectly innocent, non-polemical, exegetical controversy between Ishmael and Akiba into a new context where the controversy could have a polemical ramification.

We cannot tell which context is the original location for the argument. Ishmael and Akiba's argument makes more sense at Gen. 1 than at other places, as we shall see. But the state of the text makes one hesitant to associate it with any one scripture. After all, there are thousands of "ʾT's" in the Bible.

Only when one abandons the idea that the "tannaitic" argument itself condemns heresy can one rely on what previous scholars have said. Ishmael and Akiba were arguing over an exegetical principle. Any other issue remains ambiguous. Nevertheless, somebody saw it as a convenient foil against a variety of unstated heretical beliefs.

Scholars have suggested a relationship between the argument between Akiba and Ishmael at Gen. 1 and gnosticism. [8] Joël was the first to see a relationship between the passage and the report of the Marcosian Gnostics by Irenaeus. (Adv. Haer. 1:18). According to this report, the gnostics held the belief that "God," "beginning," "heaven," and "earth" in the first verse of the Bible were all to be considered part of a divine tetrad.

Actually, many other doctrines could have been the subject of the polemic as well. For instance, in the *Apophasis Megale*, ascribed to Simon Magus, the Samaritan from Gitta, there is a doctrine which sounds even more suitable. The creation is accomplished by the *logos*, "who stands, stood and will stand." He creates all the other powers, the first two of which are identified with heaven and earth. They, in turn, become allegorized as male and female principles in the formation of embryos, through an allegorical reading of the narrative of the garden of Eden. Wherever heaven and earth are hypostasized creatures in any fantastic gnostic system, not just the Simonian system, one could expect the rabbinic argument to be relevant. Furthermore, as is growing clear from the Nag Hammadi texts, Gen. 1 was a favorite Bible passage in almost every variety of gnostic exegesis. Practically any kind of gnosticism could be suitably answered in the polemic.

---

[8] The scholars who see this passage as referring to gnosticism are Joël, *Blicke*, p. 169; Marmorstein, *Essays in Anthropomorphism*, p. 10.

However, the most widespread sectarian doctrine derived from the first chapter of Genesis had to do with a second power, the *logos*, and not with gnosticism specifically. Of all the terms in the first sentence of the Bible, "In the beginning"—not either "heavens" or "earth"—was the most commonly used to derive a second divine creature. "In the beginning" is often understood as "by means of 'The Beginning,' " thus hypostasizing a principal angelic helper in creation. Even in the gnostic systems mentioned above, the *logos* is present as creator of the many divine archons. These themes seem to be based on the well-known identification of Wisdom as God's helper in creation (See Gen. R. 1, for instance). Furthermore, in the fragmentary targum [9] we find an interesting variant of the theme. Because it was assumed that God's Wisdom had mediated the creation, the targum translated "In the beginning" as "By wisdom." The Samaritan liturgy also contains that reading. [10]

This also may be the basis of the Sophia legend among the gnostics. The *Tractatus Tripartitus* of the Jung Codex emphasizes that though Wisdom fell from grace she had done so independently, by her own authority (*exousia*, 1:3). Furthermore, Christians, as exemplified by the church father Theophilus, maintained that "in the beginning" actually meant "Christ" because the gospel of John had identified the *logos* with the messiah. So many dangerous doctrines depend on the first verse of the Bible that one is reluctant even to specify which one is the most likely to have been the target of the polemic. [11]

If Akiba wanted to defend against any of these doctrines, he picked a weak and indirect argument. Pointing out that "ʾT" rendered "heaven and earth" direct objects would be little help against such well-developed heresies. Either the original dispute between Ishmael and Akiba was unrelated to this conflict or it was imperfectly transmitted. I suggest it was both.

However, the text makes more sense as an anti-heretical polemic when one assumes that later rabbis wanted to defeat a variety of heresies about the creation of the world. First of all, they could rely on a tradition about two great rabbis. Secondly, while the discussion actually does not demonstrate that the only divine being in the first

---

[9] H. K. Weiss, *Untersuchungen zur Kosmologie des hellenistischen und palästinischen Judentums* (Berlin: 1966), p. 199 and Gilles Quispel, "From Mythos to Logos," *Eranos Jahrbuch*, 29 (1970), (pub. 1973, 323-340), now in *Gnostic Studies*, 1, 163.

[10] Samaritan Liturgy, XVI, 1 (ed., Heidenheim, 25).

[11] This will be discussed further in Section III. See p. 184 f.

verse of the Bible is God, it could be maintained by later sages that the great rabbis had had that issue in mind. Furthermore, the history of the text's transmission shows just such a trend toward more and more explicit reference to heresy. It seems unlikely that the original issue of the text (or even the original target of the polemical understanding) can be recovered, but the ambiguity of the tradition allows it to be used broadly against heresy.

The other midrashim concerned with this dispute of Ishmael and Akiba also reflect a later polemical intent, although it is not always clear that gnosticism was the heresy implied. Apparently the rabbis quickly saw that the argument between Akiba and Ishmael about the meaning of "ʾT" was a good counter argument to speculation in Genesis 1:1, where it makes a certain degree of sense. But they also used it in reference to various other Scriptural passages, where the discussion between R. Akiba and R. Ishmael is almost completely irrelevant.

In reference to Genesis 21:20 ("And God was with the youth," i.e., Ishmael) the rabbis noticed the problem posed by an incorrect interpretation of the "ʾT." In this case, when the ʾT is interpreted as introducing the direct object, one is left with the meaning "The Lord became a youth." Orthodoxy interpreted the phrase to mean "and the Lord was *with* the youth as ʾT must have originally been understood. If the ʾT had been left out, they say, "the verse would be very difficult." Indeed so! But this is not analogous to the Genesis verse because what is really at stake is the interpretation of ʾT (d.o. or "with"), not strictly its presence or absence. If ʾT were present and being used to introduce the direct object, the question would still be difficult. One has to assume that the tradition about Ishmael and Akiba was grafted conventionally onto this section because it was seen as a defense against heretical arguments. Yet strictly speaking, Ishmael and Akiba's argument is not applicable to the biblical verse. Of course, a number of different groups maintained that God became a youth. Merkabah mysticism may be implicated. The NᶜR of Gen. 21:20 is a technical term for the younger figure in the mystical speculation. [12] However, any Christian group which believed in divine incarnation could also have been the target of such a tradition. There is no sure way to distinguish between the various opponents at this time. The only thing which can be said with reference to this passage is that the opponent would have to read Hebrew.

---

[12] See p. 67 f. for a discussion of NᶜR in Jewish mystical writings.

Another context for the argument between Ishmael and Akiba over the use of the "ʾT" is Gen. 4:1, the folk etymology for the name "Cain." In this case there is a clear polemical setting for the discussion. Cain's name is understood by means of the phrase: "With YHWH('s help) I have acquired a son." However, the statement could also be taken to mean "I have acquired a son through YHWH," or even, "I have received YHWH as husband." Notice again that the presence or absence of ʾT is not the issue; the meaning of the word is in dispute. Were the ʾT absent, the word would yield the sentence "I have acquired a man of God," which is irrelevant for the argument.

There is a long history of exegesis about the offspring of Cain, [13] who were regarded, like Cain himself, as wholly evil. [14] Many heretical groups came to be associated with Cain. [15]

N. A. Dahl has suggested a plausible theory of how heretical groups came to be identified with Cain and also how the gnostic group, the Cainites, may have taken such a figure for their hero or eponymous ancestor. Perhaps another example of understanding the tetragrammaton as one of the angels lies behind this passage. [16] In orthodox eyes, the angel is no longer good. Rather he is Satan and he is seen as the angel who commits adultery with Eve. Therefore, the defensive tradition would be based on the idea that Cain is the first-born of Satan, making his offspring anathema. Such a defensive argument was used not only by the rabbis but also by the evangelists (John 8:44) and the church fathers (Polycarp 7:1). In the evangelist's case, the appellation is used against Jews: Whoever does not want to believe in Jesus has Cain for a father instead of Abraham. The Jews who are the target of this charge were accusing Jesus of being a Samaritan. It is possible that the accusation of being an offspring of Cain was first a Jewish charge against Christians (and others such as Samaritans)

---

[13] Seth-Cain typology in Arm. Adam 63-64, W. Sol. 2:24, Post. 42, see also 35, 38, Det. 78, see also 32, 68, 103.

[14] JE, III, 493 ("demiurge"); Comp Gen. R. 8:9. Marmorstein, Unity, p. 483; Background, p. 156.

[15] See Aptowitzer, p. 11. In the fragmentary targum a tradition is recorded that Cain said to his brother in the field "I believe that the world was not created with the attribute of mercy." See also Aptowitzer, p. 12 and p. 122, n. 63, and A. J. Braver, "The Debate Between a Sadducee and Pharisee in the Mouths of Cain and Abel," Beth Mikra, 44 (1971), 583-585 (Hebr.). More importantly in Tg. Ps. Jn 4:1, 5:3 and PRE 21, 22 Cain is not viewed as the offspring of Adam.

[16] See Dahl, p. 72; based on Gen. 16:7-13; 22, 11-16; Ex. 3:27, Ki. 6:11-24; Zach. 3:1 f.; and Ödeberg, III Enoch, Intro. 82 f., 90, 117, 119, 188-192.

which was here reversed by the Christians as a defense against the charge.

The heresiologists knew of a gnostic group which actually called themselves Cainites and traced their lineage back to him. According to them, Cain had a greater power than Abel because his power came from above. This idea may have been based on some other tradition about angelic agency in Gen. 4:1. The heretics would have regarded a good angel as the father of Cain. Philo, who sees Cain as a symbol for evil, admits a similarity with Enoch and Melchizedek in that the scripture does not record his death. [17] No doubt this fact was not lost on the Cainites either. It would not be improbable for Cainites to have based traditions about Cain's translation to heaven and enthronement on scriptural grounds, since we find enthronement traditions about Enoch and Melchizedek based on scriptures' omission of a report of their death.

Nor was the positive evaluation of Cain restricted only to the Cainites. The Perateans suggested that it was only the demiurge, the god of this world, who did not accept the offering of Cain. [18] Marcion taught that the high god accepted Cain, leaving Abel and Abraham and their descendants behind unsaved. [19]

The groups who viewed Cain positively had merely accepted the charge of being the first-born of Satan which was hurled at them by orthodoxy. However, they turned it into a positive attribution. The later church fathers also said that Cainites took Judas Iscariot as well as Cain as a hero. [20] This "negative value" kind of Judaism or Christianity was a product of the intense three-way polemic going on between Judaism, gnosticism and Christianity—with the gnostic groups being opposed by both sides.

That the paragraph of rabbinic discussion between Ishmael and Akiba could be associated with all these different heretical arguments makes sense best in a polemical environment. The biblical Ishmael and Cain became allegorized as the ancestors of groups who had fallen away from the truth while Genesis 1:1 was the source of most all of the gnostic cosmologies.

The exact conflict between Akiba and Ishmael is unclear. The

---

17 Fug. 64.
18 Hippolyt. Ref., V, 16:9.
19 See p. 234 f.
20 Friedländer, Gnosticismus, p. 19-24. Puech ascribes the Gospel of Judas to the Cainites. (Dahl, p. 80).

evidence is that it was unclear to early tradition as well. Some rabbis later remembered an historical argument between the tannaim in a new context and used it as a convenient counter to cosmological, angelological, ascension, and gnostic traditions. The redactor seems to be the one who made sure that the argument appeared at Gen. 4:1 and 21:20. It is possible that Akiba and Ishmael actually argued about Gen. 1:1. But from the state of our texts, it is impossible to isolate the original issue exactly. The original disagreement seems to have concerned exegetical methodology, later reinterpreted under the pressure of the gnostic controversy. Both heresy and orthodoxy accepted the metaphor that they were brothers—but ironically, vilification, not brotherhood, was the purpose of the identification. As far as "two powers" is concerned, it is clear that only some of the possible heretical traditions deal specifically with doctrines about a second, angelic helper for God. The term is quickly brought into a variety of contexts, many of which are anti-gnostic, and some of which have nothing to do with the earliest level of the heresy.

CHAPTER FIVE

MIDRASHIC WARNING AGAINST "TWO POWERS"

PASSAGE 5

Sifre Deuteronomy 379

See now that I, even I, am He. (Dt. 32:39). This is a response to those who say there is no power in heaven. He who says there are two powers in heaven is answered: "Has it not elsewhere been said: '*And there is no God with me.*'" And similarly (for one who says) "There is no power in it (heaven) to kill or to revive, none to do evil or to make good," Scripture teaches: "*See now that I, even I, am He. I kill and I revive*" (Dt. 32:39). And Again, "*Thus says YHWH, the king of Israel and his deliverer, YHWH of Hosts. I am the first, I am the last, and besides Me there is no God.*" (Is. 44:6).

Another interpretation: "*I kill and I revive*" (Dt. 32:39). This is one of four sure allusions to resurrection of the dead: *I kill and I revive* (Dt. 32); *Let my soul die the death of the righteous*; *Let Reuben live and not die* (Dt. 33); *After two days he will revive us* (Hosea 6). I might think that death was by one (power) while life was by another. Scripture teaches: "*I wounded and I will heal.*" Just as wounding and healing is by one (power), so is death and life by one (power alone). [1]

None escape my hand: No father can save his sons. Abraham could not save Ishmael and Isaac could not save Esau. From this example, I know only that fathers cannot save their sons. From where do I learn that brothers may not save their brothers? Scripture teaches: "No man can ransom his brother" (Ps. 49:8). Isaac did not save Ishmael, Jacob did not save Esau. Even if a man were to give all the money in the world, it would not give him atonement, as it is said: "No man can ransom his brother... his ransom would cost too much..." (*Ibid.*). A soul is dear. When a man sins with it, there is no compensation.

---

[1] Midrash Tannaim: Another interpretation: *See now, I, even I, am He.* R. Eliezer said: Why is it suitable for Scripture to say "I" twice? The Holy One, Blessed be He said: 'I am in this world and I am in the world to come. I am He who redeemed Israel from the hand of Egypt and I will redeem it in the future at the end of the Fourth Kingdom.'" *And there is no God with Me*: Every nation who says there is a second god will I prohibit from eternal life, and every nation who says, there is no second god, I will give them resurrection in the future. I will kill these and revive those, as it says "*I kill and I revive.*"

This anonymous passage in Sifre cannot be shown to be aimed merely at one heretical group. It is a cleverly designed anthology of arguments against various views which the rabbis opposed. Something about the character of the heretical doctrines can be learned, but the final identities of any groups espousing the doctrines is elusive. The best we can do is note the form of the argument. First, those who deny the existence of God are refuted by reference to Dt. 32:39a. This is obviously an important scriptural weapon because immediately thereafter those who believe in "two powers" in heaven are refuted with the continuation of the same verse. Finally, those who believe in God but deny His ability to kill or bring to life are refuted by reference to Is. 44:6.

Great difficulty is encountered when one attempts to find hints of the identifies of the opponents. Büchler [2] argued that the opponents in this passage must be either Jews, Judeo-Christians or gnostics by reasoning that the use of biblical passages would be little help in combatting gentiles, for whom the Bible held no authority. Büchler's guess is hardly a specific identification, yet even this argument must remain open to question. This particular passage (as opposed to the earlier traditions) might have been only a rabbinic stylization of various arguments and used only within the Jewish community.

Nor does it seem likely that the rabbis could have had only one group of heretics in mind. The first opponents mentioned seem to be atheists. Other passages in rabbinic literature are amenable to the suggestion that there were atheistic Jews. For instance, Sifre to Dt. 32:21 [3] says "I will vex them with a foolish people" as a reference to *minim*. Then it further characterizes the heresy by applying Ps. 14:1 "The fool says in his heart, there is no God." Of course, few people in the ancient world denied deity completely, but Epicureans were often called atheists because they felt the gods could effect nothing in the world and were irrelevant to men. Furthermore, the midrash knows of Jews who believed that the world operated "automatically," [4] which implies that some Jews of the period were students of Epicurean philosophy. [5]

---

[2] Büchler, *Minim*, p. 267. Stauffer, *TDNT*, III, p. 99 associates the verses with Marcion. See Marmorstein, *EJ* (1931), VII, 564.

[3] Finkelstein, p. 367, Sifre Deut. 32:21 (pp. 320, 137a).

[4] Midr. Psalms, I, 5 see Krauss, II, p. 4. See also Sifre Deut., pp. 221. Josephus, *Antiquities*, 10, 278. Lieberman, *How Much Greek?* p. 130.

[5] Sifre Num. 112, m. San. X i; m. Aboth II 14; b. San. 99b and 38b; Gen. R. ch. 19:1; Sifre Dt. 12, t. Sanh. XIII, 5b (17a); also A. Marmorstein, "Les Épicuriens dans la littérature talmudique," *REJ*, LIV (1907), 181-193; Yalk. Zach., pp. 582,

These atheists may be related to the opponents who either deny that "God neither kills nor brings to life," or those who felt that He "neither causes evil nor good." Since two separate heretical arguments are mentioned, it is possible that there were really two distinct heresies, the first of which denied resurrection, the second of which denied reward and punishment or even divine providence entirely. However, in that case, those who deny reward and punishment could have easily been included under the first category of "those who believe that there is no authority in heaven."

Even leaving aside the atheists who may be separate from the others, the same group who believed in "two powers" could not have also believed that God had no power to do either evil or good. Some hypothetical heresy may have believed that one god did not supervise activities, leaving all immanent functions to another god, or that one god was the author of evil while the other god created good; but it is not likely that any group accepted both dualism and the lack of punishment and reward at the same time. No specific relationship between the three types of doctrines is implied in the passage, beyond the rabbinic opposition which they all share. The thread of the argument comes from the scriptural quotation rather than logical argumentation. The different doctrines opposing the rabbis are so tied to the exegesis of the passage that one must suspect that some of the doctrines are completely theoretical, derived merely from the words of scripture and do not reflect actual heretical doctrines.

However, this suspicion cannot be entirely demonstrated either. The "two powers" argument is brought up because the Hebrew word אֲנִי (I) is repeated twice, possibly implying two speakers. This is the kind of scripture which might have appealed to various heretical groups. Even the LXX translates the verse by repeating "see" twice instead of the "I," implying an early sensitivity to the verse.

The second paragraph of this section may reflect some real debates. It gives four pericopae in scripture from which one can demonstrate the doctrine of resurrection. [6] The heretical doctrine is elaborated by

---

Yalk. num., pp. 764 b. Hag. 5b, Gen. R. 8:9; b. Ned. 23a, Krauss, p. 107. See Marmorstein, *RGS*, I, p. 52, and especially Urbach, *Sages*, pp. 73, 311, 588. Talmudic uses of the word "apikoros" are compiled by S. Wagner, *Religious Non-Conformity in Ancient Jewish Life*, (unpublished dissertation: Yeshiva University, 1964), 124-144. A relationship between Epicurean philosophy and resurrection, providence, mercy and justice is provided by Fischel, pp. 35-50.

[6] Midr. Tan. expands the list to ten pericopes in scripture but the additional

the charge that one god might be thought to be in charge of killing while another is in charge of revivification. This charge is countered by use of Hos. 6:2 where God says that He has struck down and will heal. Just as one God alone strikes down with sickness and heals, so too only one God is responsible for life and death. [7] Of course, logically and historically, healing and resurrection may be separate ideas connected only by their similar form. They also have no absolute connection with dualism and may just as well imply polytheism or merely the existence of a doctrine of a demonic world opposing the divine plan. In that case one set of divine creatures would be responsible for all the sickness in the world, while another would be responsible for healings. [8]

In the first paragraph of the text we had a clear reference to "two powers in heaven" but no clear evidence that the doctrine was related to any of the other heresies mentioned. In the second paragraph of the text, there is an ambiguous reference to a doctrine which might be dualistic but might as well be polytheistic, together with a discussion of the doctrine of the resurrection of the dead. No historical information may be concluded from such an anthology.

Based on Hoffman's research, it is generally assumed that the additional midrash appearing in Midr. Tan. is a secondary elaboration stemming from a later period and perhaps dating as late as the eighth century, because the first other appearance of that tradition is the Pirke of Rabbi Eliezer (hereafter *PRE*) which is commonly understood to have been edited in the eighth century. [9] This additional midrash does record evidence about "two powers in heaven." It assumes that those who believe in a second god are from gentile nations (*goi*) and links that doctrine with the discussion of resurrection in the following way: Those gentiles who deny a second god will be saved to enjoy resurrection, but those who do not deny the second god will not enjoy the benefits of the world to come. It seems that an eighth century midrashist

---

passages do not always seem appropriate for proving a doctrine of resurrection from Torah.

[7] See Marmorstein, *Unity*, p. 447 and Ex. R. 28:3. God's revelation takes different shapes but this variety does not in the least imply the theory of "two powers." In regard to Moses, see p. 145. Elsewhere the same God wounds and heals, reveals himself in the same moment in the East, West, North and South. See p. 1317.

[8] For the operation of this kind of belief in the Hellenistic world see E. R. Dodds, "Man and the Demonic World," *Pagan and Christian in an Age of Anxiety* (Cambridge: 1965), pp. 27-68.

[9] M. D. Herr dates PRE to the first half of the eighth century in Palestine just prior to the fall of the Omayyad dynasty, see *EJ*.

has simply assumed that the two paragraphs of the midrash (the first describing atheists, dualists, etc., and the second describing resurrection) are related. Probably he did so on the basis of m San. 10:1 which states that all Israel has a share in the world to come, then defines those sinners who have lost their portion. The Epicurean, he who denies the divine origin of the Law, and he who does not admit that resurrection is prophesized in the Torah are all condemned by the Mishnah. But since "two powers" heresy is not explicitly mentioned by the Mishnah, the midrashic commentator wants to make sure that the penalties for ditheism are clearly spelled out as well. He does so by connecting the discussion of resurrection at the beginning of the second paragraph in *Sifre Dt.* with the *caveat* against dualism at the end.

In the third paragraph of the Sifre passage, there are a few clues to the identity of the unspecified sectarian groups, but there is no implied relationship between the sectarian practices in any of the other paragraphs. In the third paragraph the midrashist warns that fathers cannot save their sons nor brothers save their brothers from retribution for sin. That families will be split up on the day of judgment is a standard motif appearing many times in the literature of the day and, in fact, in many different religious systems throughout the world. [10]

That no father can redeem his son and no son redeem his father is a tradition present in other rabbinic writings as well. [11] Elsewhere, the dictum is modified to allow that a son can redeem his father, although no father can redeem his son. Rabbinic literature does record that the patriarch Abraham redeemed his father, Terah. Ginzberg feels that this type of statement is a warning against excess in the doctrine of "the Merits of the Fathers," by which the goodness of the patriarchs in the past was believed to atone for an individual's misdeed in the present. [12] This suggests that some of rabbinic opposition in this passage could be directed against abuse of rabbinic doctrines or against the far more serious problem of the exaltation of Abraham or Jacob found in apocalyptic documents and pseudepigrapha.

There is no clear evidence, then, that the three paragraphs in this section can be viewed as speaking about only one group. What unites them is only that the rabbis use the quotation from Deuteronomy as

---

[10] See vivid descriptions of heart-rending family separations in Mt. 24:40, Lk. 17:34, Quran 23:103, 80:33 f., b. San 104a, 4 Ezra 7:102, Bundahisn 31. Winston, *Iranian Component*, 196.

[11] M. Ps. 46:1, San. 104a, for example.

[12] Ginzberg, *Legends*, V, 274 f., 419, see II Enoch 53:1.

an opportunity to discuss and dismiss conclusively various doctrines which they oppose. It is clear that the redactor of the *Sifre* felt that the doctrines could readily be grouped together but the exact basis of the grouping, and hence, the exact character of the groups under discussion, became quickly muted in the transmission of the tradition and remains elusive.

Although no one group can be definitely identified, the fact that more than one group can be seen in the passage is a positive conclusion. What may be certainly concluded is that Herford and Buechler were hasty in applying these passages only to Christians. Christians do remain a possibility for the subject of some of the traditions. However, Samaritans, gnostics and Jewish apocalyptic groups cannot be excluded. It seems likely that such editorial redactions of Midrash were responsible for the expansion of the term "two powers in heaven" by later rabbis until it could cover many heretical groups. The problem is to discover which of the heretical groups were actually called "two powers in heaven" by the earliest tannaitic sages before the designation became common. Because of the ambiguity of the passages, no evidence can be found for changing the conclusion that the earliest traditions posited a separate, principal, angelic helper, of God on the basis of scriptural theophany texts. The other traditions seem to be later additions to the polemic. However, from this pericope, we can conclude that Deuteronomy 32:39 became a favorite scripture—like Exodus 20, Dt. 6:4, Isaiah 44-47—to defeat heretical notions of the godhead. There are important correlations between arguments of God's justice and mercy and "two powers" heresy in this passage. But the exact relationship cannot be defined. All we can say is that after a certain point in time, many forms of mediation—from binitarianism to extreme, opposing dualism—were subsumed under the title "two powers in heaven."

PASSAGE 6

Numbers 15:30

But the person who sins presumptuously, native or alien, he insults the Lord.

Sifre Zuta Shalah 15:30

The person—This refers to him who says: "There is no power in heaven!"
The person ... and the person—This refers to him who says: "There are two powers in heaven."
Who sins presumptuously—to include him who sins intentionally.

he insults the Lord—Why do idolators resemble one who empties a pot while stirring it, so that nothing remains. [See p. 92 n. 18 for this translation].

This passage in Sifre Zuta (passage 6) resembles that in Sifre Deuteronomy (passage 5) in that it uses the repetition in the wording of scripture as an occasion to discuss "two powers in heaven." It is generally supposed that Sifre Zuta is from the "school of R. Akiba" and is part of the traditions handed down through the academy of R. Eliezer b. Jacob II (135-170 C.E.). This would contrast with the previous passage in Sifre Deuteronomy (passage 5) which has been attributed by Epstein to "the school of R. Ishmael." [13] In any event like the last tradition, the redaction is quite late and specific information about the tannaim will be difficult to come by. We may assume that the concern to safeguard the community from those who believe in "two powers in heaven" was evidenced in both "schools" of midrash and that similar exegetical means were found to show that such a heresy was forbidden in scripture. In Sifre Deuteronomy (passage 5), the fallacy of "two powers" doctrines was outlined. Here scripture is used to occasion a discussion of the penalties for the heresy. In Sifre Deuteronomy (passage 5) the views might be seen as sectarianism. Here it is clearly heresy and punishable by severe means.

Nu. 15:30 is quite well suited for use as an attack against inhospitable doctrines. It is from the part of Nu. which outlines the procedures for the various sacrifices which all residents in the Holy Land should bring to the Lord to atone for various transgressions, both accidental and willful. Nu. 15:30 states that any person "who sins presumptuously," whether he be born in the land or a stranger, is a reproach to the Lord. The penalty for such an offense is KRT. The stern wording makes the verse ideal for use against heretics. In fact, the passage in Nu. makes such good sense against rabbinic opponents that it has been used by many teachers to apply to many different enemies. In the *Sifre*, [14] for instance, "he who sins presumptuously" is taken to signify he who makes perverse interpretations of scripture (MGLH

[13] Mielziner, *Introduction to the Talmud* (New York: 1969), p. 285. Epstein, NBWᵓWT, pp. 625-633, esp. 628, where the passage in question from Sifre Dt. is attributed to R. Ishmael's school although the majority of Sifre Dt. is from R. Akiba's school. It should be noted that the schools mentioned indicate two differing redactional principles but not any real connection to the academies of these two sages. See *EJ*, "Midrashei Halakha," "PRE," "M.T." and "Sifre Zuta" (M. D. Herr). A summary of critical opinion on each midrash will also be found there.

[14] Sifre 120.

PNYM BTWRH) while "he reproaches the Lord" is taken to mean he who indulges in fatuous interpretations (YWŠB WDWRŠ BHG-DWT ŠL DWPY). [15] These apparently refer to unacceptable exegetes or parties within the rabbinic movement. On the next verse, the *Sifre* records that "because he despised the word of the Lord" refers to Sadducees while "he broke His commandments" refers to the Epicureans. [16] R. Simeon b. Eleazar (170-200 C.E.) felt that the "soul shall be cut off" should be taken to refer to the Samaritans "who believe that the dead do not revive." He makes evident an ironic principle in attempting to fit each heretical deed with its proper punishment. From the rabbinic perspective, the Sadducee has despised the word of the Lord because he rejected the oral Torah. Epicureans have broken the commandments because they felt that the gods were irrelevant to man's existence. The punishment meted out to Samaritans also fits their crime: they are cut off from eternal life. In Sifre the opponents seem to refer to people who do not respect accepted traditions about the meaning of scripture within the academy. All of the groups opposed to the rabbis, then, seem to have real knowledge of scripture and can be called either rabbinic sectarians or Jewish heretics.

The passage in Sifre Zuta (passage 6) also includes those who believe in "two powers in heaven" among those to whom the penalty of KRT applies. How much of the characterization of the heretics in the paragraph actually applies to those who believe in "two powers in heaven" is uncertain, just as it was uncertain in passage 5. However here, even the characterization of the heresy is somewhat unclear. There is a rabbinic debate about the meaning of the word MGDP, (which I have been translating as "He reproaches the Lord"). The rabbis were concerned to define the exact nature of the reproach. In our passage, it is assumed that MGDP means "idolator," which is the majority opinion among the rabbis. This would imply that the rabbis were protesting the community from Jews who went over to gentile ways. But R. Akiba is supposed by tradition to have dissented from this view. He believed that MGDP referred to a blasphemer, as indeed is its usual meaning in the targums (II K 21:13) and many places in the Mishnah. [17]

But the problem is not just one of definition. There is also a problem

---

[15] Bacher, *Exegetische Terminologie*, p. 149.

[16] Sifre 121.

[17] E.g., Ker. 1:2, Sanh. 7:5, j. A. Zar. 3 (42d) as well as Tosefta and Targum on Kings *ad loc.* (Sperber, v. 2, p. 310).

in the consistency of penalties in the law. In b. Ker. 7b the rabbis decide that MGDP must be an idolator in order for the law's penalties to be applied consistently. This explains the irony that in Sifre Zuta, a document from the "school of R. Akiba," those redacting in R. Akiba's name list only the opposing, later predominant perspective that the crime is idolatry, not mentioning what was thought to have been R. Akiba's own understanding of the term—blasphemy. [18]

In the received edition it seems clear that two crimes are assumed for the purpose of deciding the penalties, so both the characterization

---

[18] Though this reading testifies to the outcome of the dispute, other places in tannaitic literature show that the dispute continued for some time before the authoritative ruling was made, for R. Akiba's position on the question is often remembered. As the tradition developed, other closely associated traditions became included and added to the confusion. In *Sifre Zuta*, for instance, the etymology of G-D-P is taken as proof that the meaning of the reproach is idolatry. The proof rests on what must have been an expression in common usage. "After doing something to the bowl, a man has scraped it so clean that nothing remains." This self-defeating process is compared to idolatry, but neither the vehicle nor the tenor of the comparison is completely clear.

First the vehicle of the metaphor: Horowitz suggests that the text should be amended from NṬR to NṬL so that the phrase would mean, "after *receiving* the bowl." Lieberman (*Sifre Zuta*, p. 5 n. 12) takes issue, saying that the correct emendation is to NᶜR (on the pattern of m. Kelim 28:2) which then would make the metaphor to empty the pot by means of stirring it and, in the process, scraping it out of impatience. Lieberman's emendation is the most carefully reasoned.

Other recensions of the tradition have tried to clarify the problem *vis-à-vis* the tenor of the metaphor. In the Sifre to this passage, the same difference of opinion is mentioned as an issue between R. Eleazar ben Azariah (T2) and Issi ben Akabiah (T5!). The earlier sage says that it is as if a man said to his compatriot "You scraped the bowl and nothing remains of it." Both seem to be implying that the damage was done in the process of emptying. In j. San. 25b Simon b. Eleazar (T5) is quoted as saying that the MGDP and the idolator scrape out everything and don't leave a commandment. He allows two different categories of sinner, MGDP and idolator, but sees that the etymology implies only that both violate all the commandments. In b. Keritot 7b each of the two etymological explanations are split up on corresponding sides of the debate about whether MGDP means idolator or blasphemer. The rabbis here report that Elazar b. Azariah was understood to say MGDP is one who scrapes the dish and does not impair it while R. Issi said MGDP refers to one who scrapes the dish and does impair it. Then the talmud goes on to say that R. Elazar b. Azariah meant the passage to refer to those who worship idols while Issi and some other sages as well said that the phrase referred to blasphemers. According to this tradition the basic metaphor is as follows: Even if one may still believe and recognize the supremacy of the creator (a much more sophisticated understanding of the worship of *eikons* than the rabbis usually evince), when one has committed blasphemy, one has deprecated the creator himself. Blasphemy then becomes the more severe crime in the eyes of the rabbis, though both blasphemy and idolatry were equally severe in point of law. It seems probable then that this passage comes from a time when Jewish idolatry was not a problem and the rabbis wanted either to emphasize the crime of blasphemy or explain some practice as being less harmful than blasphemy.

and the penalties refer to both crimes. The rabbis seem to be saying that the people who sin presumptuously include either those who intentionally deny the authority in heaven or promote "two powers in heaven," whether they be part of Israel or outsiders. Atheism and dualism were linked in this verse to apply the penalties of idolatry to both. They were both seen to be perverters of the truth of the Bible and could be discredited with the same scriptural reference.

In passage 5, the previous anthology of heresy, it was discovered that more than one group was condemned in the passage and that "two powers in heaven" was only one of the many. Not all doctrines in that passage could then be applied without scruple to those who believed in "two powers in heaven." Any of several different groups of people—Sadducees, Samaritans, gnostics, Christians—might be implicated if the second paragraph, which concerned resurrection, could be taken as relevant to "two powers." If the third paragraph about the redemption by various relatives were also describing the "two powers" heresy, then any group which believed in the exaltation of its hero or patriarch could be implicated.

The next logical step is to compare passage 5 with passage 6 and ask if any of the groups in passage 5 could have been opposed, characterized and punished by the rabbis as idolators or blasphemers. Such an exercise can only cut down the logical possibilities to the strongest candidates, not yield a firm rejection of any group or a firm identification. But a determination of the strongest candidates is a relevant consideration.

The Sadducees are not prime candidates, for they do not appear to have been opposed by the Pharisees in those terms. The accusation is probably conventional. The Samaritans, however, were charged with both crimes. The idols of the Samaritans were mentioned in 2 Kings 17:30-31. Accordingly, Sanhedrin 63b informs us that the Samaritans continued to worship the gods of their native lands, even after their conversion to Judaism. Those from Babylon worshipped a hen, the Cuthians a cock, those from Hamath a ram, the Avvites a dog and an ass, the Sepharvites the mule and the horse. The Samaritans are even said to have fashioned images of Jacob and Joseph to whom they paid divine honors, [19] a particularly interesting fact in view of the rabbinic warning against reliance on forefathers for salvation. Samaritans are also accused of blaspheming God—as, for instance, in j. San. 25d

---

[19] Ginzberg, *Legends*, V, pp. 274 f., 419.

where R. Simeon b. Lakish (2A) is continuously obliged to rend his
garments because of a Samaritan's language. In the same passage,
gentiles who blaspheme are mentioned so the implication is that some
Samaritans blaspheme just as some gentiles blaspheme. Yet blasphemy
is characteristic enough of Samaritans to raise the question among the
rabbis of whether it is worthwhile continuing the practice of rending
the garments after hearing it.

One great difficulty in allowing that Samaritans could have been
included under the rubric of "two powers in heaven" is to discover if
anything in their beliefs could be interpreted dualistically or as binitarianism. While they were certainly viewed as schismatics by the end
of the mishnaic period, [20] how they would have been characterized
as "two powers" heretics is not at all clear. It is possible that the
veneration of Jacob or Joseph along with God, as mentioned above,
could point to apocalyptic doctrines seen by the rabbis as "two powers
in heaven." Another possibility is to stress the link between Samaritanism and gnosticism, as is so often done by the sources. For instance,
Simon Magus, the legendary founder of all Christian heresy, was a
Samaritan. According to Epiphanius [21] the Samaritans were the first
to identify Shem with Melchizedek and hence Melchizedek's city of
Salem with Shechem. [22] It is known from 11QMelch at Qumran that
Melchizedek was often viewed as an eschatological salvation figure,
similar to the archangel Michael in in many parts of sectarian
Judaism. [23]

That Christians are included among those who say there are "two
powers in heaven" has been established previously. Blasphemy was
one charge levelled at Jesus by Jews according to the New Testament.
When Jesus was arrested and brought before the High Priest, he is

---

[20] See J. Purvis, *The Samaritan Pentateuch and the Origin of the Samaritan Sect*
(Cambridge, Mass: 1968). Also see M. Smith on Alt and Montgomery's view of
Samaritanism in *Palestinian Parties and Politics that Shaped the O.T.* (New York:
1971), pp. 193-201. See especially J. Fossum, dissertation Utrecht.

[21] Haer 55:6.

[22] See Ginzberg, *Legends*, V, 226. Also see pseudo-Eupolemus in Euseb. P.E. 9,
17, 5 where the holy city of Melchizedek is identified with Har Garizim instead of
the usual Salem or Jerusalem. Epiphanius attributes the Shem-Melchizedek identification to the Samaritans while the Jews declare Melchizedek to be the son of a
prostitute probably on the basis of the tradition that he was "without mother, father
or genealogy." This report is particularly relevant when one remembers that "son
of a prostitute" was also used to describe "two powers" heretics. See p. 54. See
J. Fossum, dissertation Utrecht, for Samaritan demiurgic traditions.

[23] E.g., T. Levi 17:7. See p. 197, n. 31.

asked if he claims to be the messiah. Jesus answered, "I am and you shall see 'the son of man' sitting on the right hand of power and coming in the clouds of heaven." (Mk. 14:62). According to this version of the story of Jesus' trial, he may have associated himself with the "son of man" in Daniel 7:9 f. The reaction of the High Priest was to rend his garments and accuse Jesus of blasphemy. Whether or not this was the original form of the saying is questionable. The church clearly associated Jesus with the son of man, therefore making the story's authenticity problematic. But, by the end of the tannaitic period, the claims of the church and not the actual event would have been the issue of any debate. If the rabbis heard and accepted the Christian story they might have regarded Jesus' crime as blasphemy, although it was not blasphemy in the name of God and hence could not carry the penalty of death. The trial of Stephen shows the same emphasis. Stephen sees a vision of the heavens opening with Jesus standing next to God's glory, [24] which is meant to refer to Jesus' words during his trial as well. Whatever these traditions imply about the actual events, they signify that the Christian community, earlier than 70 C.E., [25] identified Jesus with the figure of the "son of man" in the dream vision at Daniel 7:9 f. which they said the Jewish community regarded as blasphemy.

Idolatry may also have been a charge levelled at Christianity by Jews insofar as even some Christians thought other Christians idolatrous for eating meat sacrificed to idols. [26]

Christianity and Samaritanism are both closely linked with the gnostic movement, for gnosticism was first defined by church fathers (notably Irenaeus) as a Christian heresy. Irenaeus explained that the arch-heretic responsible for the rise of gnosticism was Simon Magus. Since many gnostics believed in the return of the elect to the highest God, it can be said that they believed in the immortality of the soul (or at least of some souls) but not necessarily in the resurrection of the body, which is impure in their speculation. [27]

Of course, these represent only the logical possibilities, not estab-

---

[24] C. K. Barrett, "Stephen and the Son of Man," *Apophoreta* (Berlin: 1964), pp. 32-38.

[25] Willi Marxsen, *Mark the Evangelist*, pp. 151-206.

[26] I Cor. 10:14 f.

[27] The Valentinians, however, are evidently an exception. See, e.g., Elaine H. Pagels, " 'The Mystery of the Resurrection': A Gnostic Reading of 1 Corinthians 15," *JBL*, 93 (1974), 276-88.

lished identifications. But the increasing range of possibilities seems to be characteristic of the history of the tradition. The result of viewing these passages, then, is not only to realize that various groups may be possible candidates for the title of "two powers in heaven," but also to see that groups which we would define as different might have been put into a single category by the rabbis. By the time of the editing of the midrash, the doctrines of atheism and dualism were being associated with proofs about punishment for idolators and blasphemers. Various groups charged with these crimes must have been gnostics, Christians, Samaritans, and apocalyptists, all of whom are recognized by modern scholarship as speculating on related scriptures, although Sadducees and Dead Sea Scroll sectarians may have been earlier targets for the same charges.

We cannot definitely identify a single group as the target for these charges by the end of the tannaitic period. By that time, and perhaps under the influence of these passages, the term "two powers in heaven" became a completely conventional, stereotypic term. It no longer referred to one group (if it ever did) and became relevant to a whole series of groups, becoming a homologous term with "those who say there is no power in heaven" and "those who say there are many powers in heaven." The rabbis must have used it deliberately rather than the synonymous term "two gods." Given the similarity in terms and the results of the previous chapters, it seems likely that the vocabulary itself was standardized in the middle or late second century at the earliest, to be used systematically only by the third and succeeding centuries. [28]

After the charges against heretics were anthologized in this manner it is unlikely that "two powers" could have continued to be used to denote a specific group. Too many conflicting doctrines were put together. Furthermore, the plethora of terms and doctrines in these texts implies that the term "two powers" itself was coined to be elastic—fitting any number of different groups which might not otherwise answer to the description under strict definitions. That, no doubt, explains the confusion of modern scholars in isolating a group with the doctrines charasteristic of "two powers in heaven." In the earlier periods, we were dealing with specific dangerous scriptures; here we are dealing with a number of dangerous doctrines and groups, some

---

[28] The advantage of RŠWT is that it is ambiguous. It can denote an angelic presence, or it can be used to designate domain. See Shab. 1:1 and j. Shab. 1:1. Thus, it may imply ditheism or a doctrine of archontic rulers without giving any details.

of whom could be characterized as believing in "two powers" but who were indiscriminately put together with a variety of different heretics. They were all defeated by the use of Nu. 15:30. Thus, the original referent of the charge was lost. But the blasphemous and idolatrous implications of the heretical beliefs had now been clarified. [29]

---

[29] In the introduction, various means available to the rabbinic community for controlling deviance were discussed (see p. 6). Contemporary research on this subject has grown more wary of reading rabbinic excommunication—NDWY and HRM—into historical descriptions before the third century. Here, in traditions which must be later than the third century in their present context, the rabbinic modes of excommunication are not mentioned either. Rather the *minim* who believe in "two powers" were said to be worthy of KRT, extirpation. This suggests that rabbinic excommunication was reserved for offenders who still viewed themselves as part of the community. Crimes worthy of extirpation would include not only blasphemy and idolatry, as we have already seen, but also magic, sorcery, and "leading astray." There is no way to tell whether this association in Sifre to Nu. 15:30 was made for polemical effect, to show the community how bad the heresy was, whether it reflects theoretical, legal precedent, or the results of actual cases. It seems most likely that these midrashic traditions reflect accusations alone. According to Christian texts, such charges were made by the Jews. The New Testament, which tends to look for a Jewish religious charge against Jesus rather than a Roman, political one, claims that Jesus and Stephen were executed for blasphemy. Church fathers attest that Jews called Jesus' miracles sorcery while the New Testament itself may be sensitive to the charge (e.g. Mark 1:23 f., 5:7 f., 7:32 f., 9:23 f.). Even so, such traditions do not necessarily reflect actual Jewish reactions to Jesus, rather have been taken by Jews and Christians alike through the ages as descriptions of the events. Therefore linking groups like Christians with KRT is not illogical. The punishment of KRT is extremely elastic and variable. In different forms, different periods, and under different situations, it might entail the death penalty or, as is the far more normal interpretation, death at the hands of God, who would cut off the life of the offender before his appointed time.

CHAPTER SIX

MISHNAIC PROHIBITIONS
AGAINST UNORTHODOX PRAYER

Like the tannaitic midrashim, the Mishnah has preserved various traditions related to "two powers" heretics. The Mishnaic evidence can be dated to the late second century for sure, but, like the midrash, the Mishnah has been edited in such a way as to obscure the exact relationship between "two powers" heresy and the sectarian practice it describes. The *mishnayot* describe relevant heretical practices under the rubric of forbidden prayer. Various unacceptable prayers and practices described in the Mishnah are ascribed to "two powers" heretics by the amoraim, so we can only be sure of the presence of a named heresy in the amoraic period after the codification of the Mishnah. Clearly the heresy itself and exegesis of the dangerous scriptures on which it depended were earlier than the end of the second century.

The identity of the opponents in the tannaitic tradition is more obscure once the amoraic term "two powers" has been removed. The tannaim are concerned with some repetitions in prayer and with various heretical concepts of justice, goodness and mercy. By the end of the tannaitic period, these issues were associated with the "two powers" polemic. In passage 1, we saw that it was the rabbis themselves who made the association. They offered an exegesis of the names of God which emphasized his qualities of justice and mercy counter to, and in place of, an heretical doctrine which apparently hypothesized two different visual manifestations of God. These passages seem to show that the heretics themselves were quite concerned with the problems of mercy and justice.

PASSAGE 7

Mishnah Berakhot 5:3

He who says: (in a prayer) (A) "Even to a bird's nest do your mercies extend" or (B) "May your name be remembered for the good" or (C) "We give thanks, we give thanks"—is to be silenced.

Mishnah Megillah 4:9

(D) He who says: "May the good bless you."—this is the manner of sectarianism.

Jerusalem Talmud Megillah 4:10 75c

He who says: "May the good bless you—this is two powers."

Babylonian Talmud Megillah 25a and Berakhot 33b

Gemara: We understand why he is silenced if he says "We give thanks, we give thanks." because he is manifesting (a belief) like two powers; also if he says, "Be your name mentioned for the good," because this implies, for the good only and not for the bad, and we have learnt, a man must bless God for the evil as he blesses Him for the good. But what is the reason for silencing him if he says 'Your mercies extend to the bird's nest?' Two Amoraim of the West, R. Yosi b. Abin and R. Yosi b. Zebida, give different answers; one says it is because it creates jealousy among God's creatures, the other, because he presents the measures taken by the Holy One, Blessed be He, as springing from compassion, whereas they are but decrees...

This tradition occurs in two places in slightly altered form, once at Ber. 5:3 and again at Meg. 4:9. The passage apparently condemns various liturgical formulas in Palestinian Judaism. Whoever says that (A) God's mercy extends to a bird's nest or that (B) His name should be remembered for the good or who (C) repeats a "modim" prayer should be silenced. The Meg. passage contains the additional tradition that "He who says (D) 'May the good bless you' is acting in the manner of sectarianism." This fourth tradition (D) often appears in the manuscripts of the Talmud to Ber. as well as Meg.

The Mishnah makes no further statement about these forbidden prayers. It only includes them in part of the discussion of various heterodox liturgical practices to which the rabbis objected. Whether they were characteristic of one single group or related in some other way is left undiscussed by the rabbis. Elbogen [1] suggested that phrases (A), (B), and (D) were additions to the end of the "modim" prayer while (C) referred to a repetition of the words at the beginning. The basis for this assertion is the record of over three hundred different additions to the "modim" prayer from various texts and manuscripts of it. A person who uses benediction (A) is described as going before the ark, which implies that he was leading prayers. But there is no firm evidence that the synagogue was the only setting for all the heretical invocations. Before rejecting or accepting Elbogen's conclusions, let us look at each benediction.

(C) "We give thanks, we give thanks."

The Modim prayer is now one of the last parts of the Amidah, a prayer containing eighteen benedictions and one curse, which is

---

1 Elbogen, p. 57.

essential to every Jewish service. The whole prayer is conventionally recited silently, facing Jerusalem, but if a quorum of ten is present, the reader of the service repeats the entire prayer aloud. When the Modim prayer is read aloud, the congregation responds to it by saying the MWDYM DRBNN in an undertone. The two Modim prayers themselves differ slightly from one another—the first, emphasizing God's mercies at the end; the latter, the MWDYM DRBNN, emphasizing God's creative powers at the beginning. [2] The MWDYM DRBNN is, however, from a period later than the Mishnah, being composed out of several phrases suggested by the amoraim. [3] Even assuming without evidence that the current method of employing the prayer is roughly as ancient as the composition of MWDYM DRBNN, we must conclude that among the earliest commentators on the mishnah, it was not the repetition of the Modim prayer *per se* which was the mark of sectarianism, for the service began to require a repetition. It must have been the intent or content of the repetition, rather than the repetition itself, which was the problem. If so, we may suspect that the orthodox repetition of the modim prayer in the synagogue emphasized themes of mercy and justice as a corrective to an heretical repetition.

The amoraic traditions concerning the prayer do not clarify the heresy. Although they assume that such prayers are to be silenced because they manifest "two powers in heaven," they do not explain how. We may suspect that they themselves were guessing. We must also be prepared to allow that the tannaim in their day were worried by different phenomenon from the amoraim.

Yet some scholars have dismissed any doubts and seen the tannaitic report and the ascription to "two powers" to be both antique and trustworthy. Because of this, they can note a relationship between this *mishnah* and a passage in the Qumran Thanksgiving Psalm. [4] The column reads:

> I Thank Thee, my God, for Thou has dealt wondrously to dust and mightily towards a creature of clay!
>
> I thank Thee, I thank Thee. [5]

---

[2] Birnbaum, p. 91.

[3] Sotah 40a and j. Ber. 1:5 (3d) Elbogen, p. 58.

[4] This reference was brought to my attention by Jonas Greenfield, who also remains skeptical of the identification. It comes from Jacob Licht, *The Thanksgiving Scroll: A Scroll from the Wilderness of Judaea: Text, Introduction, Commentary and Glossary* [In Hebr.] (Jerusalem: 1957), p. 161.

[5] I Q H XI, 3.

Licht brings up the rabbinic charge casually in reference to the MWDH, MWDH in l. 3. There is good reason for Licht not to stress the identification. First of all, MWDH, MWDH is not the same as MWDYM, MWDYM. Secondly, there is nothing in the passage which the rabbis would have found heretical. There is nothing in the passage that is even specifically characteristic of Qumran. Finally, Licht himself observes in his critical notes that the repetition of MWDH looks like a gloss because it is written below the line. Lohse [6] suggests that the repetition is a dittography. Now it is still possible that the Qumran sectarians would have been called "two powers" heretics by the rabbis. But we have no evidence that they were the ones who said "MWDYM... MWDYM" or even that they prayed to the angelic captain of evil.

Moreover, other groups remain just as plausible contenders for the charge. Christianity may be implicated because early Christian liturgy contained characteristic and crucial prayers that began with the word "Eucharistoumen." "We give thanks" which is a very plausible Greek translation for any Hebrew prayer, beginning MWDYM ᵓNHNW. For instance, the Didache reports that the Eucharist was performed in the following manner:

> And concerning the Eucharist, Hold Eucharist thus: First concerning the cup, "We give thanks to Thee, our Father, for the holy vine of David, thy child, which Thou didst make known to us through Jesus Thy child; to Thee belongs glory forever." And concerning the broken bread: "We give thanks, our Father, for the life and knowledge which Thou didst make known to us through Jesus, Thy child. To Thee be glory forever." [7]

These two benedictions were to be said previous to what appears to be a normal meal. After the meal, an additional benediction was said. Beginning the two blessings before the meal with MWDYM instead of BRWK may well have caught rabbinic attention. Although there is no further evidence to support the identification of this heretical prayer with Christianity, the parallel is so striking that it demands serious consideration. Of course, there is considerable critical agreement that the wording of the eucharist prayer was taken from Jewish sources. [8]

---

[6] Eduard Lohse, Die Texte aus Qumran: Hebräisch und Deutsch (München: 1971), p. 152. He suggests the following translation: Ich preise dich, mein Gott. Denn du hast wunderbar am Staube gehandelt und am Gebilde von Lehm dich überaus herrlich erwiesen.

[7] Didache, IX, X, tr. Lake, p. 323.

[8] See, for example, Jeremias, The Eucharistic Words of Jesus (New York: 1966), p. 255 f.

If Christianity is to be considered a candidate for the heresy in the second century, it would have involved not praying to two different deities in the synagogue service, as the amoraim assumed, but actually referring to a second power in the blessing before the meal.

If it is true that Christians were the target of this ordinance because they repeated a "modim" prayer (albeit not the "Modim" of the Amidah), then the Babylonian amoraim, who did not know of the earliest identification, assumed that the "two powers" allegation referred to two different gods. Apparently, such dualists were believed to exist in the Babylonian synagogues of their day. Rab Abaye, the illustrious authority of the fourth generation of amoraim in Pumpeditha, adds an exegesis which helps clarify the heretical belief insofar as the amoraim are concerned.

> R. Huna says: Whosoever prays at the rear of a Synagogue is called wicked. For it is said: *The wicked walk round about.* Abaye says: This only applies where he does not turn his face towards the Synagogue, but if he does turn his face towards the Synagogue there is no objection to it. There was once a man who prayed at the rear of a Synagogue and did not turn his face towards the Synagogue. Elijah passed by and appeared to him in the guise of an Arabian merchant. He said to him: "... *As if there were two powers?"* and drew his sword and slew him. 9

The setting is the synagogue. Probably the Amidah is being discussed in this passage because Ṣ-L-Y was used to denote this prayer. What is important to note is, first, the severity of the charge of "two powers" in the folk tale. The man is not necessarily guilty of the charge. He only appears to be guilty of it. But it is enough to cause his death. One suspects that this story has no actual connection with the original heresy. There is no awareness of the earlier tannaitic traditions. Rather, for the amoraim, the issue was the orientation of the congregation towards Jerusalem, not merely that a man was praying in the rear or repeating the prayer. The man must have been praying toward the back of the synagogue, implying that he was worshipping a divine power other than the God of Israel.

---

9 b. Ber. 6b, tr. Epstein. The expression for "two powers" here is KDW BR. Something appears to have been left out of the text. Probably the expression was KDW BRY ᵓLHYN or possibly KDW BRYᵓYN (two creators!). This raises the possibility that the term "two powers" might have been used as a euphemism for a stronger term. At any rate, it shows that the older terms for the heresy could have been used even after the term "two powers" became virtually standard in referring to phenomena of this sort. I have altered Epstein's translation to suit the context.

Quite probably, this a late folk-tale. If so, it is another piece of evidence for the process of conventionalization of heresy which is evident in other texts. The phenomenon described as "two powers" by the amoraim in fourth century Babylonia is certainly different from the one characterized by the tannaim in second century Palestine. This has to be true, whether or not one accepts Christianity as a likely target for the charge. In the late tradition only the term "two powers" (and not any consistent description of the heretic) has initiated the Elijah folk-tale.

The amoraim, however, continued to be very conscious of the relationship between the repetition of the "modim" prayer and "two powers." The third century Babylonian sage, R. Zeira, who studied at the Academy in Tiberius, links the Modim prayer with the Shema, the central prayer in Jewish liturgy. According to R. Zeira, there were those who said the Shema twice as well. But the rabbis distinguish this from the "two powers" controversy. The person who repeats the Shema is treated as a fool, not as a heretic, for the rabbis attribute the repetition to a lack of attention.

(D) "May the good praise you"

The Jerusalem Talmud identifies (D) with "two powers in heaven." All sources agree that saying such a thing is heresy but the character of the heresy is indistinct. Commentators have suggested a series of possible candidates for the heresy, based on guesses about the meaning of the saying. It could mean "May the (Lords of) the good bless You," suggesting at least two powers because the mention of powers of good (angels?) implies that powers of evil exist as well. It is also possible that the heretical groups were saying that certain angels had usurped God's power. In both cases the rabbis could have been objecting to a benediction which emphasized God's providence through various mediating figures like angels.

If the amoraic commentators had good information, it may be that the benediction encouraged only good men to praise God, while evil men presumably would praise Satan. In this case, the Qumran documents and associated movements like the covenanters of Damascus and the Therapeutae might be indicated, since in their *Weltanschauung* men were split into two camps in this way. But the early heresies are not as likely candidates as some later ones. One heretical group which might have been implicated is the gnostic sect described in the Book of Baruch. The gnostic Justin outlines a system where both the high

8

god and his supporters, once they ascend to heaven, are called "the good." [10] Of course, we know if this group from a Greek report, but we do not know whether they or their predecessors or others like them could have expressed their prayers in Hebrew. In that case, the charge of "two powers in heaven" brought by the Palestinian rabbis would have been occasioned by a gnostic system. [11]

(A) and (B)

The other two heretical phrases have no articulated connection to the heresy of "two powers in heaven" but they may be implicated by being grouped by a redactor with heretical prayers that do. We already know that arguments about the justice and mercy of God were brought into rabbinic polemic by the middle of the second century. This is additional evidence that the tannaim were interested in stressing God's authorship of both mercy and justice.

(A) "Even to a bird's nest do Your mercies extend."

Perhaps most puzzling is the first phrase (A), which states that anyone who says, "Your mercies extend to the nest of a bird," is to be silenced. The Mishnah is alluding to the law of Dt. 22:6, 7 stating that the mother bird may not be taken when scavenging for bird's nests. One can take the fledglings but not the mother with the young, killing the whole family. No doubt this law is meant to set an humanitarian example. Pointing to it in a benediction could, of itself, have been no cause for alarm. Consequently, there is considerable discussion in the gemara as to the exact nature of the heresy. Two fifth generation Palestinian amoraim, R. Yosi b. Zebida and R. Yosi b. Abin (350-375 C.E.) argue over the nature of the heretical views: The first says that such a phrase creates jealously among the various works of God's creation—presumably meaning that man and beasts would be jealous of the mercy shown to birds. The second says that such a doctrine makes the commands of the Lord into acts of grace when they are His decrees, to be obeyed whether they are merciful or not. [12]

A further tradition from Babylonia includes Rabba and Abaye (320-350 C.E.) in a discussion of the same text. A man uses the following benediction in front of Rabba: "Thou hast shown pity on the bird

---

[10] Hippolytus, Ref. V 26, 1-27, 5. This may be related to Jesus' statement in Mk. 10:18.

[11] See p. 248 for a discussion of the Gnostic Book of Baruch.

[12] Herford, p. 202 sees a protestation against the Pauline antithesis of law and grace in this doctrine. There is no evidence to support it.

and his nest, do Thou have pity and mercy on us!'' Abaye points out correctly that the benediction, as admirable as it may seem, is none-theless to be forbidden because of the tannaitic precedent. This points out that the ruling against this benediction was enforced even when the amoraim were hard pressed to discover the justification.

We thus have no real evidence from the explanations of the amoraim that they knew the actual historical situation of the tannaitic decree. It seems likely that the original argument was over some aspect of the doctrine of God's mercy and may even, as R. Yosi b. Zebida states, have to do with the emphasis of God's aspect of mercy when He must be understood as master of both justice and mercy. The amoraim's perplexity about the severity of the ruling ought to alert us to the deep tannaitic concern to attribute both justice and mercy to the one God.

(B) "May Your name be remembered for the good."

Good and evil is the obvious subject of this heretical benediction. The amoraic commentary unanimously points out that such a benediction is illegal because it conflicts with the mishnaic ruling in Ber. 9:5 that man is to praise God both for evil and for good. On this basis, many scholars have seen this statement as a safe-guard against a strict dualism. It implies an opposition which attributed only good to God while evil was attributed to other agencies. Depending on the hypo-thetical identification of the other power, scholars have seen a variety of different groups as the target for this charge. Maurice Simon [13] feels that the evil force should be Ahriman, hence Zoroastrians, are involved. Most scholars feel that some variety of gnosticism is involved.

This brings to mind the related phenomena of Qumran, the Thera-peutae and the Essenes as well. Philo describes the Essenes as believing that God is the source of good alone and not evil. [14] Neither did the Qumran sectarians always seem to ascribe evil to God. [15] Similar views are ascribed to various Jewish heresies by treatises found at Nag Hammadi. [16] Here then is ample evidence that problems of good

---

[13] Soncino Meg. p. 149.

[14] Quod Omn. Prob. 84. Moore, *Judaism*, I, 364, n. 3. Lehmann (REJ, 30 (1895), 180 f.) suggested that our mishnaic tractate was meant to counter Essene, (ḤṢWNYH) beliefs. Since then more of the Essene type of dualism has become known from the Qumran texts. Furthermore, the identification of Essenes with ḤṢWNYM is un-founded.

[15] E.g., I QS 2.

[16] Quispel, "Christliche Gnosis und jüdische Heterodoxie," *ET* (1954); "Der gnostische Anthropos und die jüdische Tradition," *Eranos*, 22 (1954), p. 201.

and evil, justice and mercy were being discussed constantly in the environment around the tannaitic Jewish community, as we discovered even in the first passage about "two powers."

The heretical doctrines have some congruence with the heresies described together with "two powers in heaven" in the midrash. For instance, there may be some relationship between (B), (D) and the heretics of the midrash who deny that God has the power to do either good or evil.

The relationship to the question of God's attributes of mercy and justice is even more interesting. In the four heretical benedictions brought together in this place, problems of dualism, good and evil, justice and mercy are all combined. (B) and (D) are definitely involved with some heretical understanding of God as the source of good and evil. Some heretical understanding of justice and mercy is definitely involved in (A). (C) seems to be related to ditheism, but not necessarily to opposing dualism. Rather it seems to imply a complementary ditheism where both deities could be expected to listen to psalms of praise. One way to explain the assembling of various disparate texts of this sort and understanding them together is to assume that, whatever their separate origins, they were all viewed together by the rabbinic community at the end of the second century.

It is certainly true that concepts of God's justice and mercy were discussed in Judaism by Philo and even earlier. But the rabbinic evidence allows us only to date reports to the late second century when Marcionism, gnosticism, apocalypticism, and Christianity could all be seen together. This would correspond to the phase of traditioning in passage 1 and 2 (MRI, MRSbY, PR) when the doctrine of God's justice and mercy became tied into an independent exegetical argument against two heavenly figures.

One further relationship between the development of liturgy and the charge of dualism may be found in a later gemara:

> What benedictions does one say [in the morning]? R. Jacob said in the name of R. Oshaya: "[Blessed art Thou] who formest light and createst darkness." Let him say rather: "Who formest light and createst brightness"?—We keep the language of the Scripture. If that is so, [what of the next words in the text]. *Who makest peace and createst evil*: do we repeat them as they are written? It is written "*evil*" and we say "all things" as a euphemism. Then here too let us say 'brightness' as a euphemism!—In fact, replied Raba, it is in order to mention the distinctive feature of the day in the night-time and the distinctive feature of the night in the day-time. It is correct that we

mention the distinctive feature of the night in the day-time, as we say, "Who formest light and createst darkness." [17]

The question is over the wording of a prayer which is taken from scripture. R. Oshaya has asked whether one should not say, as a kind of euphemism, "who forms light and creates brightness," instead of the scriptural "darkness." The questioner is told that Is. 45:7 is the basis for the phrase in the liturgy and it must remain as is. The questioner then asks, "Why do we not follow Isaiah in another case?" He compares that part of the verse with the second part of the blessing-formula: "Who makes peace and creates all things." He claims rightly that, if Isaiah's wording is decisive, we should follow it all the way and not now replace "evil" by "all things." The answer is that "all things" is an effective euphemism for evil. However, if that is so, why then should "brightness" not be a euphemism for darkness? [18] The gemara seems to be prepared in principle to accept the argument but, in practice, states that darkness should be retained in the blessing so as to mention the qualities of both day and night. [19]

It is interesting to note that the first substitution of language was not an issue to R. Oshaya. He accepted it as a principle and wanted to apply it further. If this is R. Oshaya the Great, the first generation amora, rather than the later amora of the same name, it would imply that such a substitution was in effect by the end of the tannaitic period. In any event, his suggestion that "brightness" also be accepted as a euphemism for darkness is rejected. This suggests that the previous substitution was accepted as antique and could not safely be contravened. On the other hand, the later rabbis were not going to let scripture be changed again in liturgy, even when it was convenient for their perspective. The net effect of such considerations is to conclude that the change of Is. 45:7 must have dated considerably before R. Oshaya's time.

Something more is at stake than the type of euphemism acceptable for prayers in synagogue. Here we have evidence that the verses in Isaiah were seen as dangerous enough to be slightly altered in liturgy.

---

[17] Ber. 11a-b.

[18] In suggesting this substitution the questioner has relied on the use of an antonym by way of completing the euphemism. This common practice, as e.g., calling a blind man ŚGYᵓ NHWR, appears to us to be an oxymoron but in its context was apparently a perfectly acceptable euphemism.

[19] See, e.g., Finkelstein, "La kedouscha et les bénédictions du schema," REJ, 93 (1932), 21.

The change was carried out to emphasize that one God created all things, both day and night, both light and darkness, both good and evil. This softens the theological problem raised by calling God the creator of evil and may indicate opponents who charged that YHWH was solely a good or an evil god.

CHAPTER SEVEN

"MANY POWERS IN HEAVEN"
AND MISCELLANEOUS REPORTS

Mishnah Sanhedrin 4:5

Therefore but a single man was created in the world, to teach that if any man has caused a single soul to perish from Israel [some texts omit "from Israel"], Scripture imputes it to him as though he had caused a whole world to perish; and if any man saves alive a single soul from Israel [some texts omit "from Israel"], Scripture imputes it to him as though he had saved alive a whole world. Again [but a single man was created] for the sake of peace among mankind, that none should say to his fellow, "My father was greater than your father;" also that the heretics should not say, "There are many ruling powers in heaven." ... 1

Mishnah Sanhedrin includes this very interesting report of a doctrine of "many powers in heaven" during the tannaitic period. Though it is called heresy, and it becomes an even greater problem for Judaism in the amoraic period, the manifold references to Adam speculation in the gemarah to this passage show as that a good deal of latitude was allowed by the rabbis.

The Mishnah includes the tradition in the middle of a discussion of the differences between witnesses in capital and non-capital cases. Witnesses are to be apprised of the fact that any mistake or perjury in testimony in capital cases is much more serious than in non-capital cases. If a man is killed unjustly, the witnesses are liable eternally, just as Cain was eternally liable for the crime he committed in murdering his brother. He who takes a life has acted as if to destroy the entire world, while he who preserves a life has preserved the entire world.

The last puzzling statement is explained by comparing each man with the first man. If Adam had been killed, all his potential progeny —that is, all mankind—would have died with him. Therefore, Adam was created singly in order to show that the life of each man is equal to the whole world. As was the case with Adam, so is the case with every man alive, according to the Mishnah. Each life is as important as Adam's. But, since the theme of the first man has been broached,

---

1 Tr. Danby, p. 388, with modifications. See also Ex. R. 29:2 and Dt. R. 2:13 also p. 121 f., 137 f.

the Mishnah includes several other traditions on the subject. All men are said to have one father to keep anyone from saying that he comes from better stock. [2] Also, men have one father, so that the heretics cannot say that there are "many powers in heaven." From these two brief statements, it is impossible either to tell the identity of those heretics who expressed such a doctrine or to define their relationship to the "two powers" heresy. It is impossible even to define their relationship to Adam speculation.

The brief comments in the Mishnah are discussed at length in the gemara both on the subject of Adam and on the issue of heresy. Nor are the two themes completely separate subjects, for we know from external sources that Adam speculation was a great part of heretical beliefs. Many of the legends reproduced in this place are interesting but not immediately relevant. We shall have to come back to them later. First, we must investigate legends which specifically clarify the refractory text of the Mishnah.

How does one progress from the idea that more than one man was created to the idea that there are many powers in heaven? One answer would be as follows: The Mishnah suggests that if the world's peoples were descended from different ancestors, there would be constant discord in the world. One could extrapolate from that statement to the idea that many different first men would imply that many different gods made them. This is the route taken by some rabbinic commentators to explain the connection. [3] It is easy to see how traditional commentaries come to this conclusion by combining the two traditions of the gemara, but the gemara itself lists them separately.

The gemara develops the idea of the Mishnah in quite a different way, while adding some new material in order to make a short anthology of beliefs about Adam. It says:

> Another answer is: for the sake of the righteous and the wicked that the righteous might not say: Ours is a righteous heredity and that the wicked might not say: Ours is a wicked heredity.

---

[2] Philo seems to argue that there were two Adams (*Leg. All.* 1:31, 53, 55), one heavenly and one earthly. Elsewhere he says that the good have Seth for a father, while the evil are the progeny of Cain. (Post. 35, 38, 42, 43, 45; Det. 32, 68, 78, 103; Fug. 64.) But there is considerably more Adam speculation in heretical and gnostic literature. See Urbach, *Sages*, p. 180 f. and especially Hans-Martin Schenke, *Der Gott "Mensch" in der Gnosis: Ein religionsgeschichtlichen Beitrag zur Diskussion über die paulinische Anschauung von der Kirche als Leib Christi* (Göttingen: 1962). See also J. Fossum, dissertation, Utrecht.

[3] See Bertinoro, *ad loc*, for instance.

the rabbis pronounced the biblical Adam a heretic because they wanted to call heretical anyone who harbored exalted beliefs about him.

None of the traditional commentaries have offered a credible derivation of the term "many powers in heaven" as applied to these "two powers" creation traditions. However, based on the evidence it is possible to offer a hypothesis. It seems plausible that the rabbis called the heresy "many powers" rather than "two powers" when the context involved the creation story and when more than God and his primary agent populated the heretical cosmology. This suggests that the creation legends nurtured by the "many powers" heretics were the elaborate angelologies and systems of archontic rulers characteristic of many gnostic and Jewish-Christian sects. This hypothesis would certainly be an appropriate understanding of the heresy during the late tannaitic period, a time when the church fathers tell us that such schemes were common. But that would logically suggest that "two powers" heretics were the ideological predecessors of the "many powers" sects. Since that heresy seems related to similar texts and seems later than the earliest traditions about "two powers," the basic heresy would appear to involve thinking that God needs help to carry out His commands in the world. The earliest level of the tradition would testify not to a gnostic or a Jewish-Christian configuration only but to two corresponding figures. Only at the end of the tannaitic period, here and in the story attributed to R. Nathan (passage 2), do we have even a hint of evidence for the gnostic configuration. Even in the case of "many powers" speculation we cannot be sure that extreme gnostics were the only heretical groups involved. Jewish-Christians without gnostic pretensions also adopted such complex cosmologies. The earliest sure tannaitic title for the heresy appears to be "many powers" but the development of the heretical tradition is similar to the "two powers" traditions, where there is good reason to claim greater antiquity, and where we have seen that the original layer of heresy involved two corresponding divine manifestations. The later tannaim apparently expanded the argument so that the heresy could also be called "two powers in heaven" when the deities were opposing, or "many powers in heaven" when the divine economy contained many characters.

Another relevant controversy over monotheism appears in a tannaitic context and seems at first to be stimulated by the comment of a pagan emperor. Upon careful consideration, it becomes clear that the opponent is neither pagan nor an emperor, that the heresy is "two powers" and that the tradition is only dubiously tannaitic. Furthermore, it presents us with further evidence that traditions about the creation of man can be associated with "two powers" as well as with "many powers" speculation:

> Again the Emperor said to Rabban Gamaliel, "He who created the mountains did not create the wind, for it is written, *For lo, there is a former of mountains and a creator of wind.*" (Amos 4:13). According to this reasoning, when we find it written of Adam, *And He created...* Gen. 1:27) *and He formed...* (Gen. 2:7) would you also say that He who created this did not create that? Further, there is a part of the human body just a handbreath which contains two holes, and because it is written "*He that plants the ear, shall He not hear? He that forms the eye, shall He not see?*" (Ps. 94:9). Would you maintain there too that He who created the one did not create the other?" Even so he answered. Yet he (R. Gamaliel) rejoined "At death, both are brought to agree." [16]

Some versions of this text list KWPR (denier) instead of KᵓYSR (emperor) as Gamaliel's opponent in this controversy. Rabbinowitz [17] lists KᵓYSR as the most likely original reading. Furthermore, it is one of a number of discussions between Gamaliel and the emperor. However, when we turn our attention to the actual tradition rather than the text, we shall see that the original participants in the dialogue were not likely to have been either R. Gamaliel or a Roman emperor. Apparently, the various stories ascribed to R. Gamaliel constitute a small folk-romance of dubious historicity.

The issue in this controversy seems to be the existence of many creators or gods, which would imply pagan polytheism. However, when one looks at the scripture involved, one sees that there are actually only two gods at issue both in Amos 4:13 and Genesis 1:27 vs. 2:7. Ps. 94:9 allows only two gods but a later editor infers "many creators" based on the number of human limbs. That editorial statement, together with the textual ascription to the emperor, makes it seem as if polytheism is the problem. Actually the issue is whether two creators can be inferred from the different verbs used of God by scripture.

This argument becomes clear when we look at another version of the same story:

> A certain *min* once said to Rabbi, He who formed the mountains did not create the wind, and he who created the wind did not form the mountains, for it is written, *For lo, He that formeth the mountains and*

---

[16] Sanh. 39a; tr. Epstein.
[17] *D.S. ad loc.*

createth the wind. (Amos 4:13). He replied, "You fool, turn to the end of the verse, *'The Lord [The God] of Hosts is His name.'* " Said the other, "give me three days time and I will bring back an answer to you." Rabbi spent those three days in fasting; thereafter, as he was about to partake of food he was told. "There was a *min* waiting at the door. Rabbi exclaimed, *Yea, they put poison in my food.*" (Ps. 69:22). Said [the *min*] "My master, I bring you good tidings; your opponent could find no answer and so threw himself down from the roof and died." He said, "Would you dine with me?" He replied "Yes." After they had eaten and drunk he [Rabbi] said to him, "Will you drink the cup of wine over which the benedictions of the Grace [after meals] have been said, or would you rather have forty gold coins?" He replied, "I would rather drink the cup of wine." Thereupon there came forth a Heavenly Voice and said, "The cup of wine over [which] the Benedictions [of Grace have been said] is worth forty gold coins." R. Isaac said, "The family [of that *min*] is still to be found amongst the notables of Rome and is named the Family of Bar Luianus." [18]

In this version it is a *min* (and some texts have Sadducee) who uses the argument. It is Rabbi (i.e., Judah the Prince, ca. 200 C.E.) who counters the arguments by saying that the continuation of the pericope in Amos clearly implies only one God. By the time of R. Judah the Prince no Sadducee could have participated in the argument. Rather, the opponent was a member of a sect which also contained the son of an acculturated family in Rome known to the narrator. Since the method of argument is characteristic of third century rabbis and later, it is likely that even the ascription to Judah the Prince should be distrusted. [19] But it is clear that the issue is "two powers." However, the defense against the heresy based on Amos 4:13 involves stressing the name of God, showing that the issue may be related to the earliest varieties of the heresy.

This suggests that the original setting for the tradition was possibly the second century, but probably the third century in Galilee, where a heretic and an unknown rabbi (probably not Judah the Prince, certainly not Gamaliel and Caesar) debated the question. The incident may never have happened at all but, if not, the creator's imagination was fired by a real issue in the third century community. The tradition was eventually ascribed both to R. Judah and to R. Gamaliel, since it seemed like an argument of sufficient ingenuity for these great teachers.

---

[18] Hullin 87a; tr. Epstein.
[19] See p. 26 f., p. 121 f.

One possible clue to understanding heretical explanations of this scriptural passage is to realize that there is a well-attested and early tradition that Amos 4:13 is messianic in character. For instance, the LXX translates as "announcing to men his messiah (*Christos*)." Obviously the LXX has taken MH SYHW (his thought) as MSYHW (his messiah).

The heretic may also have combined the messianic interpretation of this verse with the argument about the number of deities. This constellation of issues would be fully appropriate to the "two powers" controversy. But if the story originated in the context of "two powers" controversy, the original connections must have been obscured in transmission. After all, it was the moral of the story, not the description of the heresy, which interested later exegetes. If a connection between the messiah and the "second power" can be maintained, the most likely candidate for this heresy is orthodox Christianity or Christian gnosticism.

One last passage must be considered under the rubric of tannaitic evidence because it appears in a *baraita*. The entire passage in which it appears is relevant but will be considered in more detail in the amoraic section of this work. The passage itself does not mention "two powers." The context, however, assumes it.

> A min once said to R. Ishmael b. Yosi (170-200 C.E.): It is written: *Then the Lord caused to rain upon Sodom and Gomorrah brimstone and fire from the Lord.* But "from Him" should have been written. A certain fuller said: "Leave him to me, I will answer him." He then proceded: "It is written. *And Lamech said to his wives, Ada and Zillah, 'Hear my voice, ye wives of Lamech.'* But he should have said my wives. Such is the scriptural idiom.—So here too, it is the scriptural idiom." [20]

In its present context the passage is one of a number of examples supposedly illustrating R. Simlai's contention that the scriptural refutation of heretics can always be found close by the place in scripture from which their heresy is drawn. [21] The passage attributes this particular argument to a tanna of the second century and his contemporaries, even though R. Simlai's principle would have to come from the third century. When one looks carefully, however, one sees that

---

[20] San. 38b, tr. Epstein.

[21] R. Simlai's or R. Yoḥanan's principle was outlined on p. 27 and will be dealt with at length on p. 122 f. It is awkward to discuss R. Ishmael's contribution before the context into which it has been inserted. But the insertion is tannaitic and ostensibly earlier in time than its amoraic context.

although the purpose is similar—to defend against dangerous interpretation of scripture—the method is quite different. The fuller in the company of the tanna wants to defeat an argument which suggests that two gods could be derived from this verse because of the repetitious style. He shows that the passage cannot bear a "two powers" interpretation merely on the basis of language, because biblical style is normally repetitious. It would be absurd to think that there are two Lamechs when Lamech addresses his wives as "wives of Lamech" instead of "my wives." So too, it is ridiculous to think that there are two different Gods because the tetragrammaton appears twice in the sentence instead of once with a subsequent pronoun. This would be quite an unusual argument for the rabbis, who based on R. Akiba's principles, were ordinarily quick to point out the intricacies of style in order to support their points. The fuller is allowed a more naive argument.

Normally, early datings of talmudic evidence are suspicious because traditions tend to be attributed to earlier rabbis though they do not actually come from that period. Here, however, there is less reason to remain suspicious. The naive defense is slightly embarassing. The form of the story separates it from the context, abruptly interrupting the examples brought in the name of R. Simlai. In fact, the example contradicts his principle in some respects because the proof-text against the error is fifteen chapters away from the dangerous passage. The tradition must already have assumed its final form before it was inserted into the amoraic evidence. It may be an authentic discussion in the presence of R. Ishmael b. Yosi, inserted into R. Simlai's sermon.

This passage is a very important piece of evidence because we have external evidence to show that Gen. 19:24, was used by a contemporary of R. Ishmael b. Yosi to show that two divine figures rule the universe. Justin Martyr [22] used Gen. 19:24 to prove that Christ (taking YHWH as *Kyrios*) operates as the agent of punishment against Sodom because he is God's messenger in the world of men. This is remarkably firm proof that even orthodox Christians were seen as "two powers" heretics.

We have discovered that many "two powers" traditions ostensibly from tannaim are actually amoraic in their present form. The problem has been to discover if any aspect of the tradition could have existed during the tannaitic period. Because of that, much of the ostensibly tannaitic evidence has turned out to be datable only to amoraim and has

---

[22] *Dial.* 56. See p. 221 f.

necessarily already been surveyed. Now we can turn to the remaining amoraic evidence. Of course, any heretical argument first attested by the rabbis during the amoraic period may yet have existed earlier. The report may signify that the rabbis only commented on it in a later period or that the other comments by rabbis have been lost. However, without some outside verification of an earlier date (as will be discussed in more detail in the last section) it is wise to assume that the rabbinic defense against heretical arguments should be best dated by its earliest report in rabbinic literature.

CHAPTER EIGHT

HOW MANY POWERS CREATED THE WORLD?

The major arguments against "two powers" heresies were laid down during the tannaitic period. The amoraim accepted these categories, expanded them greatly, and added new arguments. The increasing number of biblical passages regarded as dangerous testifies to the expansion rather than diminution of the heretical challenge. At the same time, as was clear already at the end of the tannaitic period, the term, "two powers" had come to signify a variety of apocalyptic, Christian and gnostic heresies. In the amoraic period the gnostic and Christian opponents dominated the Palestinian scene. [1] But all the rabbinic evidence should be considered before trying to discover the identities of the various kinds of sectarians who were discussed together under this category by the rabbis.

PASSAGE 8

Tanhuma Kadoshim 4 (Buber, 37a) [2]

Another interpretation: *Say to the whole congregation of the Children of Israel "You shall be holy for I am Holy.* (Lev. 19:2). The Holy One Blessed Be He told them "Be holy for I am Holy in every matter. Look at what is written: *'For God is Holy (pl.)'* " (Josh. 24:19). What is the meaning of "For God is Holy?" This verse gave an opportunity to the heretics for it appeared *like two powers.* The heretics asked R. Simlai about "For the Lord is Holy (pl.)"—You yourselves don't say that He is one power, rather there are *two powers.*" He said to them "What fools the world contains! Look at what is written: 'For *He* is a Holy God.' If it had said 'They are Holy Gods,' you might have thought there were *two powers.*"

This passage is recorded in Tanhuma, a later document which is sometimes believed to contain ancient traditions. [3] However, the version

---

[1] Büchler, Marmorstein, Lauterbach and Herford discuss all these amoraic traditions though not with equal skill. In general, it will be difficult to distinguish heretical from orthodox Christianity except in those cases where a definite, opposing gnostic system can be postulated.

[2] Versions of this text occur: Ber. 9:1; j. Ber. 12b; San. 38b; Gen. R. 1:13 ms. 8; Gen. R. 8:9; Ex. R. 29:1; Dt. R. 2:13; M. Ps. 50:1; Tanhuma Bereishit 7; Tanhuma Kadoshin 4. For Yalkut, Pugia Fidei, and other later midrash see notes to Gen. R. 8:9 in Theodor-Albeck edition (I, p. 63).

[3] S. Buber, *Midrash Tanchuma: Ein Agadischer Commentar zum Pentateuch von*

which names the heresy as "two powers" is not even the earliest version of this particular tradition. In fact, although the tradition occurs in many places in reference to many different biblical passages, this is the only version which names the heretical doctrine as "two powers." It is obvious that the term "two powers" was not central to the tradition at its inception and was perhaps added during one redaction of the Tanhuma midrash, not earlier than the fourth century.

Furthermore, the language of the passage does not identify the heresy as "two powers" in a straight-forward way. Rather, it says only that the arguments are "similar to the heresy of two powers." (KŠTY RŠWYWT). Apparently the designation "two powers" was already well known to the amoraim. These heretical arguments were seen to be of the same type by the rabbis, confirming what we already know —that "two powers" had become a conventional term for a variety of heresies whenever scripture could be interpreted to imply plural forms for divinity. Here the argument seems confined to grammatical plurals.

However, there is nothing in the traditions to indicate that the heretics themselves would have argued solely from plural grammar. Wherever we know that a scriptural passage was used by heretics, the arguments of the heretics were much more complicated.

The most complete version of this particular tradition is found in b. Sanhedrin 38b where almost all of this type of dangerous scriptural passages were brought together.

> R. Yohanan said: in all the passages which the minim have taken (as grounds) for their heresy, their refutation is found near at hand. Thus: let us make man in our image (Gen. 1:26)—and God created (sing) man in His own image (*ibid.*, 27); Come, let us go down and there confound their language (Gen. 11:7)—and the Lord came down (sing) to see the city and the tower (*ibid.*, 5). Because there were revealed (Gen. 35:7) to him, God. Unto God who answers me in the day of my distress (*ibid.*, 3); For what great nation is there that has God so nigh (pl.) unto it, as the Lord our God is (unto us) whenever we call upon Him (Dt. 4:7). And what one nation in the earth is like Thy people, like Israel whom God went (pl.) to redeem for a people unto Himself (sing.) (2 Sam. 7:23). 'Til thrones were placed and [one that was] the ancient of days did sit (Dan. 7:9). 4

Here the passage was attributed to R. Yohanan (250-90 C.E.). In most other versions, the teaching was attributed to R. Simlai, his

---

Rabbi Tanchuma ben Rabbi Abba (Jerusalem, 1963/64 from Vilna: 1885), p. 3. Most scholars date it considerably later.

� Tr. Epstein.

student. Possibly the name of R. Yohanan, the more famous rabbi, found its way into the text because this section of Talmud contains many other anti-heretical traditions ascribed to R. Yohanan. [5] Since Simlai was Yohanan's student and colleague it is also possible that R. Simlai learned the tradition from his teacher and carried it on. [6] The third century attribution of the traditions remains unaffected in any case.

Whatever the authorship, the process of exegesis is clear. A grammatical plural form in scripture is used by heretics to demonstrate duality or plurality in the deity. The rabbi suggests that the remedy to the heresy, always a grammatical singular, invariably occurs close to these plurals, proving the heretical doctrine wrong. Some of the dangerous scriptures must reflect real arguments between orthodox and heretical communities, but other passages may have been added purely by analogy, as the tradition grew. More importantly, we have no evidence that any actual heretical argument took the form in which it is reported. While the heretics might have used the passage, their beliefs were no doubt more sophisticated than the rabbis reported.

We already have had some indication that the arguments were more complex than the rabbinic reports suggest. Gen. 1:26 and Dan. 7:9, for instance, provide real support for many different kinds of heretical beliefs. In the earlier traditions we have seen that the heretical arguments based on these verses were wide and varied. The rabbinic response was always directly relevant to the heretical argument. When the rabbis also pointed to a singular in the verse, it could be shown to be a secondary layer of the rabbinic defense. For instance, in passage 1 the plural in Dan. 7:9 is countered with a singular in some of the versions, but that argument would seem to belong to the amoraic stratum. The original heretical argument based on this particular scripture must have involved the two manifestations—the "son of man" and the "Ancient of Days." The reduction of the argument to a conventional pattern reflects a later stage of the tradition, when the issue itself was no longer primary and a developing literary or oral genre had begun to

---

[5] Rabinowitz, *Dikduke Soferim, ad loc.* notes that the text was frequently censored here.

[6] Reuven Kimelman has shown that R. Yohanan and Origen, both living in third century Caesarea, were likely to have known about the arguments of each other. He feels this tradition should be attributed to R. Yohanan. See "Origen and R. Yohanan on Canticles," paper; AJS Conference, Boston, Dec. 1975, also.

dictate the form in which the tradition would be preserved. We may suspect that an earlier layer existed, but we can only describe it where we have good textual evidence of an earlier issue. The plural was probably noted by the heretics but we know that the "son of man" exegesis was far more elaborate than an explanation of the plural. The rabbis, on the other hand, did not allow themselves to be put in the position of helping to spread the heretical ideas. They simply located the plural in scripture, showed that it referred to the single God and avoided any further characterization.

A similar collection in the Jerusalem Talmud shows that the tradition evolved in a slightly different form in the Palestinian academies.

> The minim asked R. Simlai "How many gods created the world?" He said to them, "Do you ask me? Go and ask the first man, as it is written, (Deut. 4:32) *'Ask now the former days which were before thee, since God created man upon the earth.'* It is not written here,' *(they) created,* 'but,' *(he) created.'* " They said to him, "It is written, *'In the beginning God created* (Gen. 1:1)' "Is it written, *'(they) created?'* It is only written, *'(he) created.'* "
>
> R. Simlai said, "In every passage where the minim go wrong, the answer to them is close by."
>
> They (the minim) returned and asked him, "What of that which is written (Gen. 1:26) *'Let us make man in our image, after our likeness.'* " He said to them "It is not written here *(ib.* 27) *'And they created man in their image,'* but *'And God created man in His image.'* " His disciples said to him, "Rabbi, thou has driven away these men with a stick. But what dost thou answer to us?" He said to them, "At the first, Adam was created out of the dust, and Eve was created out of the man. From Adam onward (it is said) *'in Our image according to Our likeness.'* It is impossible for man to exist without woman, and it is impossible for woman to exist without man, and it is impossible for both to exist without the Shekhina."
>
> And they returned and asked him, "What is that which is written: (Josh 22:22) *'God, God, the Lord, God, God, the Lord He knoweth.'* " He said to them, "It is not written here, 'they know,' but it is written *'He knoweth.'* " His disciples said to him, "Rabbi, thou hast driven these men away with a stick. But what dost thou answer to us?" He said to them, "The three (names) are the name of one, just as a man says, 'Basileus,' 'Caesar,' 'Augustus.' "
>
> They returned and asked him, "What is that which is written (Ps. 50:1) *'God, God, the Lord hath spoken and He called the earth?'* " He said to them "Is it written here *'(they) have spoken and have called?'* It is only written, 'He hath spoken and hath called the earth.' " His disciples said to him, "Rabbi, thou hast driven these men away with a stick. But what do you answer to us?" He said to them, "The

three (names) are the names of one, just as a man says, 'labourers,' 'masons,' 'architects.' "

They returned and asked him, "What is that which is written (Josh 24:19) *'For He is a holy God* (where the word holy is plural)' " He said to them. "It is written there not 'they are holy,' but 'He is holy.' (He is a jealous God.)" His disciples said to him, "Rabbi, thou hast driven these men away with a stick. What dost thou answer to us?" R. Isaac said, "Holy in every form of holiness." For R. Judan said, in the name of R. Aha, "The way of the Holy One, Blessed be He, is in holiness. His word is in holiness, His sitting is in holiness, the baring of His arm is in holiness. He is fearful and mighty in holiness. His ways are in holiness, as it is written (Ps. lxxvii 13): *'Thy way, O God, is in the sanctuary.* His footsteps are in holiness: (Ps. 68:24). *'Thy goings O my King, my God, in the sanctuary.'* His sitting is in holiness: (Ps. 47:8) *'God sitteth upon the throne of His holiness.'* His word is in holiness: (Ps. 108:7) *'God God has spoken in His holiness.'* The bearing of His arm is in holiness: (Ps. 51:10) *'The Lord has made bare His holy arm.'* He is fearful and might in holiness: (Ex. 15:11) *'Who is like Thee, glorious in holiness, (fearful in praise?)'* "

They returned and asked him, "What is that which is written: (Dt. 4:7) *'For what great nation is there that hath a God so near to them, as the Lord our God, whensoever we call upon Him?'* " He said to them, "It is not written here, *'Call upon them,'* but *'Call upon Him.'* " His disciples said to him, "Rabbi, you have driven away these men with a stick. What do you answer to us?" He said to them. "He is near in every manner of nearness." [7]

R. Simlai's method for defeating heretics is slightly different from the description of R. Yohanan's in the Babylonian Talmud. But the principle he espoused is similar to the Babylonian Talmud's version—countering the mysterious plurals with a nearby singular to show that there is only one God.

In one place this argument seems especially appropriate. The singular verb in Genesis 1:1 does prevent one from getting the wrong impression about the number of deities present at creation. In fact, the Palestinian rabbis seemed satisfied with the argument in this one place and made no further comment on that verse. Significantly, the rule of R. Simlai is adduced from that place. It is possible that the argument actually arose in regard to that verse and was later extended to others.

When the heretics appeal to Gen. 1:26, R. Simlai's principle is used to "drive away the heretics" but it is not sufficient to end the discussion within the academy. Apparently, although the "two powers"

---

[7] j. Ber. 12d-13a.

heretics could be defeated easily, the correct understanding of Gen. 1:26 was not evident. Orthodox argument had the further advantage of justifying marriage as a divinely sanctioned institution. So R. Simlai's doctrine was not a sufficient exegesis of the passage, although it apparently sufficed to refute the heresy. It looks as if the doctrine of R. Simlai was applied quite automatically as a defense against any heretical passages, but the dangerous scriptural passages also received separate explanations which the rabbis found useful to proclaim. R. Simlai's principle could not be the final word on each passage.

To these already familiar traditions in midrash are appended several new scriptural passages which support heresy. These traditions add Jos. 22 and Ps. 50 to our list of places from which heretical doctrines could be derived—not this time from a grammatical plural, but from the repetition of the various divine names. These arguments, in fact, might be as old as the oldest "two power" arguments which we have traced since the oldest traditions also depended on an exegesis of the different names of God. R. Simlai defeats the heretical arguments with his versatile principle. But, the further question about the real significance of the divine names then arises for the rabbis. After these examples follows one last occurrence of the grammatical plural argument, obviously out of place and suggesting that the three previous examples were inserted in the text haphazardly from another source.

To summarize, in the first crux (Gen. 1:1), R. Simlai's principle is completely satisfactory. It is not clear that R. Simlai himself would have adduced the following cases where his principle is not the final word. Further use of his principle may have been made by modest exegetes working under his inspiration and hence attributed to him.

In the passage from the Babylonian Talmud where the tradent may have been either R. Simlai or R. Yohanan, the context concerned both heresy and heretical views of the creation separately. In the Jerusalem Talmud the link between heresy and dangerous views of creation is made explicit since R. Simlai is asked by the heretics "How many deities (or powers) created the world?" R. Simlai's response differs slightly in the many versions of this tradition. He either tells the heretics to inquire of the first days (Gen. R. 8:9) or the first man (j. Ber. 12b) or the record of creation (Dt. R. 2:13) or the Torah (Gen. R. 1:13 Mss 8, Tan. 7). In each case the directive is to seek a primeval authority, based on Dt. 4:32 ("Search into days gone by, long before your time, beginning at the day when God created man on earth; search from one end of heaven to the other and ask if any deed as mighty as this has been seen or heard.") [8] Emphasizing different aspects of that verse yields the different primeval authorities.

Each version of the tradition has a slightly different anthology of biblical passages. But, in each case, the argument is most aptly used against the idea of two creators and later extended to apply to other ideas of two deities in heaven. [9] This extension is facilitated by Dt.

---

[8] The verse in Dt. can also be used as additional proof that one God only was responsible for the creation. Dt. is talking about the Mosaic revelation, a fact not lost on the rabbis. "Did any people ever hear the voice of God speaking out of the fire as you heard it and remain alive?" Dt. asks. This theme was strongly emphasized in reference to the Exodus passages in the Mekhilta (passage 1.) There, the elders of Israel saw God, yet lived—which showed God's aspect of mercy, a different aspect of deity than was present at Sinai and the sea. Apparently, in the case of Dt. R. as well, heretical speculation about the number of Gods arose. R. Simlai explains that Dt. 4:33 (sing.) contradicts Dt. 4:32 (plural) (Ex. R. 29:1), and that only one God can be derived from the passage. The argument has become conventionalized in the rabbinic texts. The heretics surely did not rest content after merely observing the plural form.

[9] *Ber. 9:1; j. Ber. 12b* Ask the first man (Dt. 4:32)
Gen. 1
Gen. 1:26
Josh. 22:22
Ps. 1:1
Josh. 24:19—Ps. 77:13, 68:24, 47:8, 108:7, 51:10, Ex. 15:11
Dt. 4:7

San. 38b: R. Yohanan gives the rule
Gen. 1:26
Gen. 11:5 f.
Gen. 35:5 f.
Dt. 4:7
2 Sam. 7:23
Dan. 7:9 f.
R. Idi Ex. 24:1 (Ex. 23:21)
Exchange me not: He will not pardon (Ex. 33:15)
R. Ishmael b. Yosi (Gen. 19:24)
Gen. 3:23

Gen. R. 1:13 Ms 8. Ask the Torah
Dt. 4:7
Josh. 24:19

Gen. R. 8:9 Ask the first days (Dt. 4:32)
Gen. 1:1
Gen. 1:26
Ex. R. 29:1 Ex. 20:1 and Dt. 4:33
Dt. 4:6
Dt. R. 2:13 the record of creation
Dt. 4:7
Gen. 1:1 also 1:3 1:6
Gen. 1:26
Dt. 4:6-7

4:34, which is telling proof against any dualistic doctrine not just two creators, because it states: "You have had sure proof that the YHWH is God; there is no other... This day, then, be sure and take to heart that the YHWH is God in heaven above and on earth below; there is no other." Of course, heretical distinctions between YHWH and God can be the target of such polemic.

Thus, we can derive a list of scriptural passages which were viewed as dangerous in the third century, contemporary with R. Simlai or R. Yohanan. [10] These are Gen. 1:1 f., Gen. 1:26 f., Gen. 11:5 f., Gen. 19:24, Gen. 35:5 f., Dt. 4:7, 2 Sam. 7:23 f., Dan. 7:9 f., Josh.

M. Ps. 50:1
Dt. 4:24 Prov. 3:19-20
Josh. 22:22

[10] *Gen. 1:1*
Gen. R. 8:9
Dt. R. 2:13 (here also Gen. 1:3, 1:6)

Gen. 1:26
Gen. R. 8:9
San. 38b
Dt. R. 2:13
Yalkut

Gen. 11:5 f.
San. 38b

Gen. 19:24
San. 38b (R. Ishmael b. Yosi)

Gen. 35:7
San. 38b

Dt. 4:7
Ber. 9, j. Ber. 12b
Dt. R. 2:13
San. 38b
Gen. R. 1:13 ms. 8
Ex. R. 29:1

Dt. 4:32-3
Ex. R. 29:1 (with Ex. 20:1)

Josh. 22:22
M. Ps. 50:1

Josh. 24:19
j. Ber. 12b
Tan. 7
Tan. kaddoshin 4 (with Lev. 19:2)
Gen. R. 1:13 ms. 8

2 Sam. 7:23
San. 38b

22:22, Josh. 24:19, Ps. 50.1. We can review these verses as they appear in other parts of rabbinic tradition to see whether there are any further hints characterizing the heresy in a less conventional way.

Gen. 1:1 f.: This verse was supposed to be at issue in tannaitic times. [11] Ishmael and Akiba are reported to have argued about whether the ʾT in the first verse of the Bible was inclusive or exclusive, which was interpreted later to defeat the idea that either heaven or earth were deities. That a plurality of deities could be derived from the first verse because the word for God (Elohim) is plural (Dt. R. 2:13) was the way this issue was expressed during the third century. One wonders if the conflict between Ishmael and Akiba (which may have been purely grammatical) became associated with heresy during this period. [12] Also relevant to this scriptural passage are Gen. 1:3 and 1:6 where the same word is at issue. Since the word God, *Elohim*, occurs so often in the Bible, the defenders must have had in mind a specific doctrine of plurality of deities present at the creation. These verses were used to advantage by many groups using Hellenistic Jewish traditions and cannot be said to be exclusively gnostic, apocalyptic or Christian. [13]

Dan. 7:9
San. 38b
Ps. 50:1
j. Ber. 12b
Prov. 3:19-20
M. Ps. 50:1
[11] See p. 74, Ishmael and Akiba on Gen. 1:1.
[12] See 83 f.
[13] See p. 226 f. and p. 257 f. Meg. 9a, J. Meg. 71d cf., also Gen. R. 8:11. The rabbis report that the Greek version of the Bible contained another translation of Gen. 1:1—i.e., "God created, in the beginning." Rashi and *tosafot ad loc.* say that this was to avoid the difficulty of "two powers." *Tosafot* says that "In the beginning" itself could have been taken as the name of a deity, were it not for the inversion of the familiar grammar.

Meg. Taanit, Massekheth Soferim 1:7-10, j. Meg. 1:71d (cf., Mekh. Ex. R. 12:40) Meg. 9a also Gen. R. 8:11; 10:9, 38:10, 48:17, 98:5, Ex. R. 5:5, Lev. R. 13:5 all report several passages where the rabbis believe that the LXX changed the MT. Of these more than 13 alterations, only four actually appear in surviving manuscripts of the LXX, some more attestations surviving in African versions. None of the attestations are in verses relevant for us. However, Irenaeus does state that some heretical groups made "In the beginning" into a God (see p. 78). Frankel (*Vorstudien*, 31) suggests that all may have been variants of a Hebrew text presented to King Ptolemy and not basically a Greek translation of the text. See also Geiger, *Nachgelassene Schriften*: (herausgegeben von Ludwig Geiger), IV. Band (Berlin: 1876) p. 50 f. Against Frankel, A. Aptowitzer, "Die rabbinischen Berichte über die Entstehung der LXX," *Hak-kedem*, St. Petersburg: II (1908), 11-27 and 102-122 and III (1909), 4-17. Also see Towner, *Rabbinic Enumeration of Scriptural Examples*, pp.

Gen. 1:26: has already been studied in great detail by many scholars. The tradition of sectarian exegesis goes back to Philo and before. [14] It is mentioned in Gen. R. 8:9, San. 38b, Yalkut Shimoni, and Dt. R. 2:13 as being among the phrases in scripture against which R. Simlai cautions. In his view, the problem is the plural of majesty with which God ordered the creation of man. Simlai's answer is that only one God is involved in the process because the verb in the next verse is in the singular. Of course, it is hardly a detailed answer to every heresy based on the verse, but it has the advantage of not broaching any of the other (sectarian) understandings. For instance, the problem of the likeness between man and God is not mentioned. Nor is the question broached of the identity of the being addressed. The repetition of the word "Adam," implying a plurality of creators or creations, is not mentioned. So many dangerous doctrines find support in this verse that one can easily see its refutation by R. Simlai's principle to be meant to counter them all by prudent dismissal with as little characterization as possible on the part of the amoraim.

Gen. 11:17: contains the same difficult plural of majesty as in Gen. 1:26. The report of LXX translators also occurs at Gen. R. 39:10 for this verse. [15] Here God says "Let us go down and confound their language." (The plural is translated literally by the received text of the LXX.) Targum Onkelos is embarrassed by the idea that God descends, so it translates, characteristically, "was revealed" instead.

Gen. 19:24: contains the seemingly pleonastic repetition of "from YHWH" in the account of the punishing of Sodom and Gomorrah. This possible source of heresy has been added to R. Simlai's group but can actually be traced to a Tanna, R. Ishmael b. Yosi. [16] Elsewhere, R. Hilfi (PA 2) the son of Samkai, reports that R. Judah (PA 2) felt the repetition meant that divine punishment was carried out by the

---

206-213, who rightfully stresses the history of the tradition within the midrash itself instead of the purported historical incident underlying it. It is enough for current purposes to note that rabbinic tradition assumed that battle over these verses went back to the second century B.C.E. and to the foundation of Hellenistic Judaism.

[14] Gen. 1:26 (and Gen. 2:7 as well) is fully dealt with in the following places: Jervell, *Imago Dei*; M. Smith, "On the Shape of God and the humanity of the Gentiles," in J. Neusner, ed., *Religions in Antiquity*, pp. 315-26. Also R. Mcl. Wilson, *Studia Patristica*, I 1 (1957), 420-37. See p. 27 f., 113 f., 143 f. See also Birger Albert Pearson, *The Pneumatikos-Psychikos Terminology* (Missoula: SBL Dissertation Series 12, 1973), p. 51 f.

[15] See note 13.

[16] See p. 118.

angel Gabriel. [17] Thus, he must believe that one of the "YHWH"'s in that passage refers to Gabriel. While Gabriel was not considered a separate, independent power by the rabbis, the tradition attests to the existence of exegeses which allowed the tetragrammaton to signify a being other than Israel's one God. [18] Obviously that very doctrine was enough to worry the rabbis. Though this midrash does not mention "two powers," it involves a concept coming perilously close to that heresy, stopping only before the overt postulation of separate authority. This is followed by the exegetical principle of R. Eleazar who believed that "and YHWH" refers to both God and his heavenly court. R. Yohanan had espoused a similar idea but R. Eleazar has refined that intuition to a rule based on the occurrence of the word „and" (W). R. Yohanan, for his part, maintains that God always consults His heavenly court. Of course, this eliminates the problem of principal hypostases of God whose divinity could be confused with Him and also explains the plurals of majesty in Genesis. This verse is important in some Christian exegesis as well. [19]

Gen. 35:7 and 5: "There he built an altar and called the place El Bethel, because it was there that God had revealed Himself to him when he was running away from his brother." The problem is, again, the grammatical plural referring to God in the verse. The rabbis explain it by saying that 35:5 contains the singular to prove that God is really one. However, this is not an innocent occurrence of a grammatical plural either. It is bound up with the immense speculation about Jacob and the revelation at Bethel, which is based on Genesis 29:10 f. In different writers, notably Philo, the word "place" itself is taken as a name for God, just as MQWM (place) became the name for God within early rabbinic tradition. Philo himself discussed a "second god" in reference to the Bethel revelation. [20]

Josh. 24:19: "Joshua answered the people, 'You cannot worship YHWH. He is a holy (pl.) God, a jealous God, and He will not forgive your rebellion and your sins.' " The rabbis point out the singular forms which contradict the one plural in the verse. The interpretation of the verse is puzzling and it is possible that some detractors of the

---

[17] Gen. R. 51:2.

[18] See p. 134 f., p. 201 f. See also Fossum dissertation, Utrecht.

[19] See p. 113 n. 10 for a discussion of this principle behind the tradition in Gen. R. 21:5 that Adam became like the angels when he learned the difference between good and evil.

[20] See p. 159 f., p. 170 f.

God of Israel derived two gods—one just and one merciful, or one who created, another who forgives—from this verse.

2 Sam. 7:23: "And thy people Israel, to whom can they be compared? Is there any other nation on earth to whom thou, O God, has set out (pl.) to redeem from slavery to be your people?" The rabbis again show that the sense of the verse requires a single God to be present even though a plural is implied by the grammar. However, there are many other things in the verse which might give the impression of more than one God. The phrase GWY WᵓLHYW presents a problem to the rabbis. R. Eliezer suggested that it refers to idols which the Israelites took out with them from Egypt, namely the idol of Micah. As we have seen before, R. Akiba thought that this verse must refer to the Shekhina, who is to be redeemed along with Israel. Thus, there is room in the verse for understanding a divine manifestation other than God, as long as that manifestation is within the ken of orthodoxy.

Dan. 7:9 f.: The rabbis point out that the singular form in the verse counteracts the earlier plural. A good deal more speculation in heretical communities was based on these verses than is implied by the comment. [21]

Ps. 50:1 and *Josh. 22:22*: have a different character from the citations above. They are mentioned by R. Simlai expressly (in j. Ber. 12df) but their distinct character makes one suspicious of ascribing them originally to him. They may easily have been added to the tradition. Both of these examples involve the expression "God, God, YHWH," which the *minim* took to exemplify plurality of deity. In this case it is not a grammatical plural which presents the dualistic possibility but the different names of God. Since three names of God —El, Elohim and YHWH—are suggested in the verses, various scholars [22] postulate that Christianity with a well developed trinitarian doctrine was the heresy under attack. However, the LXX had already translated the Hebrew in such a way as to imply that "two powers," rather than three, were present. We have seen that the linking of different names of God to different manifestations is quite ancient. It is probable that all the recorded midrashic traditions served as a defense against more radical doctrines.

At the beginning of the section, I noted that it was unclear whether

21 See p. 33 f., p. 66 f. and 201.

22 See Marmorstein, *Unity*, p. 491; Büchler, *Minim*, p. 258; Bacher, *APA*, I, pp. 555 f.; Herford, p. 261; and Bergmann, p. 89.

"two powers" or "many powers" was the heresy of interest to R. Simlai. The actual phrase "two powers" appears only in a late version in the Talmud. We discovered that the traditions ascribed to R. Simlai make an anthology of scriptural passages useful to defeat heresy. The rabbinic traditions have been reduced to a conventional form, where the heretical group merely pointed to a plural and the rabbis retorted with a singular. But we have seen that the actual doctrines were more complex. Behind the sectarian designation of plurality are traces of traditions either about a second principal figure in heaven, or about the meaning of the repetition of God's name, all of which go considerably along the way towards "two powers" heresy. After comparing these passages with the other rabbinic traditions about the same scriptures, it even seemed that some rabbinic writings contained traditions related to the heresy. Two passages may have had three powers in mind. They may have been describing a trinity of sorts, as some scholars have suggested but, whether of the gnostic or Christian variety is difficult to decide. However, the Greek translation of these passages implies two rather than three powers. So if the heretics read their Bible in Greek, they may have recognized only two powers. Only the two passages describing the creation—Gen. 1:1 and Gen. 1:26—definitely support the idea that more than two powers were involved. That interpretation is not necessary, rather suggested by what we know of "many powers" traditions of the creation. [23] This leads to the conclusion that the basic distinction in rabbinic thought even in amoraic times, was between "one power" and "two powers" in heaven. This basic distinction divided heresy from orthodoxy, Jewish monotheism from groups which read scripture but, from the rabbinic perspective, were outside of the community of believers.

Possible interpretations of "many powers in heaven" continue to correlate with the biblical creation account. This further suggests that the term "many powers in heaven" was coined after the term "two powers in heaven" had been in use and that it described a more complex heavenly hierarchy specifically derived from the creation account as in some varieties of apocalypticsm, Christianity and gnosticism.

If it is true that "two powers in heaven" was the basic category of heresy, it is still not necessarily true that the term described only Christians while "many powers" described only gnostics. We know that there were Jewish-Christian groups with elaborate systems of

---

[23] See Ex. R. 29:2 and Dt. R. 2:13 as well as p. 109 f., 137 f., and 141.

cosmology and intermediaries, which could have been named as "many powers in heaven," even though they had no specifically gnostic character. On the other hand, some gnostic groups preserved only two gods, the high god and the demiurge. [24]

---

[24] See p. 244 f.

CHAPTER NINE

DIVINE POWERS AND ANGELS

PASSAGE 9

Genesis Rabba 1:7

R. Isaac commenced with, *The beginning of Your word is truth; and all Your righteous ordinance endures forever* (Ps. 99:160). Said R. Isaac: From the very commencement of the world's creation, *"The beginning of Thy word is truth."* [Even], *In the beginning God created* (Gen. 1:1) [shows that] YHWH *Elohim is the true God.* (Jer. 10:10). Therefore, *And all your righteous ordinance endures forever* (Ps. *loc. cit.*). For, in regard to every single decree which You have promulgated concerning Your creatures, they affirm the righteousness of Your judgment and accept it with faith. And no person can dispute and maintain that two powers gave the Torah or two powers created the world. For "And the Gods spoke" is not written here, but, *And God spake all these words* (Ex. 20:1). In the beginning Gods created is not written here, but *In the beginning God created.* (Gen. 1:1). 1

The Rabbi Isaac in question is R. Isaac b. Nappaha (250-320 C.E., so called only in the Babylonian Talmud) the famous Palestinian amora of the second and third generation. His identity is confirmed by the midrash, which has captured the type of exegesis characteristic of the Palestinian sage—making a proemium or introduction to the Bible reading of the week. 2 R. Isaac was a student of R. Yohanan and is portrayed in such a way as to bear out his teacher's lessons. He combatted both the now familiar heresy that two gods might have been present at creation and the additional problem that the ordinances of God might be unjust.

The defense against these doctrines was accomplished by associating another verse with the first verse of the weekly Bible reading in order to clarify the meaning of that verse. R. Isaac associated Ps. 119:160 with Gen. 1:1, both because of a similar subject matter and because of a similar word. Gen. 1:1 begins with BRʾŠYT (in the beginning) and Ps. 119:160 contains a word derived from the same root RʾŠ (head). Instead of "the principle of Your word is truth," he translated: "The beginning of Your word is truth." Hence Ps. 119:160 is applicable

---

1 Tr. Freedman, with modifications.
2 Bacher, *APA*, II, p. 275.

to the first words of the Bible—by a substitution, somewhat like a *gezerah shavah*. However, just which aspect of Ps. 119:160 is applied to Gen. 1:1 is ambiguous, and has occasioned two different interpretations among the traditional commentators. The first possibility is to reason that since "The beginning of Your word is truth," we know that the beginning of the Bible is true when it says that one God (sing.) created the world, hence the statement that "YHWH is God" is true. [3]

This interpretation is the popular one, but has the disadvantage of not adequately explaining why R. Isaac quotes Jer. 10:10. It rather seems to me that R. Isaac was using a more elaborate system of substitution. He could be saying: "Since we know that the first statement of the Bible is true (Ps. 119:160) and since we know that YHWH as well as Elohim is the true God (Jer. 10:10), we can be sure that both God's names—YHWH and Elohim—were present at creation. Therefore both His qualities of mercy and justice were also present." From the very beginning God's ordinances were both just and merciful. The only proper response is to accept them all faithfully. The conclusion of the argument is taken from the second part of Ps. 119:160 —that every decree always shows justice and mercy (SDQH) at the same time. [4]

This immediately occasions a warning against the idea that two powers created the world or that two powers gave the Law. Then R. Simlai's exegetical device is utilized to show the grammatical difficulty in propounding a "two powers" heresy.

If the second interpretation is right, the rabbinic doctrine of the two attributes of God—MDT HDYN and MDT HRHMYM—is being used apologetically against a heretical argument. That heresy may have taken two forms. The first possibility is that the creator was unjust. The second possibility is that the God who created is simply not the same God who saves.

Either possibility involves "two powers." Both identify the names YHWH and Elohim as different deities. R. Isaac, using the rabbinic doctrine of the attributes of God as a defense, showed that only one

---

[3] *Rashi* and *Etz Yosef* (Enoch Zundel b. Joseph of Bialistock, 19th century) both assume that the opening statement of the Bible proclaims the truth that the Lord is God, and there is none beside Him, for it is He alone who created the world.

[4] The Mahartzu (Ze'eb Wolf Einhorn, 19th century) understands *Elohim* (God) to signify God's attribute of Justice. The opening verse of the Bible "In the Beginning *Elohim* created" then is an assertion that He created the world on the basis both of justice and mercy.

God is present and proved his contention by using the method current with R. Simlai and R. Yohanan. The complete structure of his argument is considerably more complex than R. Simlai's principle, which is again appended as an after-thought.

> R. Luliana b. Tabri said in R. Isaac's name: Whether we accept the view of R. Ḥanina or of R. Yoḥanan all agree that none were created on the first day, lest you should say, Michael stretched the world forth in the South of the firmament and Gabriel in the North, while the Holy One, Blessed be He, measured it in the middle: but I am the Lord that makes all things, that stretched forth the heavens alone, that spread out the earth by myself.—*Mi Itti?* (ib. 44:24)—who was with me? is written; who was associated with me in the creation of the world? [5]

Another series of traditions, evinced in Gen. R. 3:8, is attributed to R. Isaac. In this tradition, R. Isaac cites the discussion between R. Hanina and R. Yohanan, Isaac's teacher, about the day on which the angels were created. Since it ought to be clear that the angels were not created on the first day, R. Isaac maintains that we can be sure that God accomplished creation without any angelic help. Hence, no angel can be his equal. R. Isaac gives an example of heretical belief, testifying that some people alleged that Michael and Gabriel were associates of God in creation. God may have created the middle, but each angel created other parts of the firmament. By means of a double entendre, R. Isaac uses Ps. 44:24 to ask the rhetorical question: "Who was associated with me in the creation of the world?" The answer, of course, is that no one, not even an archangel was given such an honor. This unnamed doctrine seems related to the Gabriel, Michael and Metatron speculation discussed previously. [6] However, other elaborate angelologies may have been involved, for beliefs in angelic mediation were commonplace throughout Judaism. What is dangerous, of course, is the notion that some principal angel could be said to usurp God's independent power.

This tradition also helps explain the relevance of the next midrash in Dt. Rabba, concerning the meaning of Dt. 6:4:

> R. Isaac opened (his discourse) with the text: *"The Lord is my portion,"* said my soul; therefore will I hope in Him (Lam. 3:24). R. Isaac said: "This may be compared to a king who entered a province with his

---

[5] Gen. R. 3:8 repeated 1:3. See also M. Ps. 24a, Tan. B. 1:12.

[6] See p. 112 f., p. 141. The use of the word ŠWTP implies a separate divinity which makes use of the name of God. This is especially clearly brought out in Ex. R. 29:2 where such ideas are expressly called "many gods" and condemned by means of Ex. 20:2.

generals, rulers and governors. Some of the citizens of the province chose a general as their patron, others a ruler and others a governor. One of them who was cleverer than the rest, said, "I will choose the king." Why? All others are liable to change, but the king is never changed. Likewise, when God came down to Sinai, there also came down with Him many companies of angels, (Num. 2:3). Michael and his company, Gabriel and his company. Some of the nations of the world chose for themselves (as their patron) Michael, others Gabriel, but Israel chose God for itself, exclaiming, "The Lord is my portion," said my soul. This is the force of "Hear, O Israel, the Lord, our God, the Lord is One." [7]

The passage, again from R. Isaac, does not mention "two powers in heaven." It does discuss Michael and Gabriel as if they had been accepted as deities by groups other than Israel.

The testament of God's unity in Dt. has allowed the redactor of Deuteronomy Rabba to assemble many rabbinic teachings against angelic and binitarian dangers.

Another explanation: *Hear, O Israel*. This bears out what Scripture says, "Whom have I in heaven but Thee? And besides Thee I desire none upon earth (Ps. 73:25)." Rab said: "There are two firmaments, the heaven and the heaven of heavens." R. Eleazar said: "There are seven firmaments: Heaven (ŠMYM), Heaven of Heavens (ŠMY ŠMYM), Firmament (RQYᶜ), Sky (ŠḤQYM), Habitation (MᶜWN), Residence (ZBWL), Thick Cloud (ᶜRPL); and God opened them all unto Israel in order to show them that there is no God but He. The Assembly of Israel said before God: 'Master of the Universe, whom have I in heaven but Thy glory? As in heaven I have none but Thee, so too upon earth I desire no other; as I have not associated another with Thee in heaven, so upon earth, too, I have not associated with Thee any other God but daily I enter the synagogues and testify concerning Thee that there is no other God but Thou, and I exclaim, *Hear, O Israel: the Lord our God, the Lord is one.*'" [8]

The passage is an interpretation of Dt. 6:4, "Hear, O Israel, YHWH is our God, YHWH is One," a statement of God's unity which has assumed central importance in Israel's liturgy. The passage combines several traditions in a sophisticated way. First, it quotes Ps. 73:25, "Whom have I in heaven but Thee, and besides Thee I desire none upon the earth." The questions raised by the psalmist are used to proclaim God's complete unity.

The first question, "Whom have I in heaven but Thee?" is answered

---

[7] Dt. R. 2:34, tr. Rabbinowitz.

[8] Dt. R. 2:32, tr. Rabbinowitz, with modifications. See also Gruenwald, *The Visions of Ezekiel*, ad loc.

by reliance on a description of heaven, transmitted elsewhere in rabbinic literature in the name of Rab and R. Eleazar. 9 In this version, a new edge has been put on the traditions by the rabbis, who are obviously reacting hostilely to some idea of a heavenly figure of major status. According to them, God opened each heaven to Israel to show to them that there is no other God but Him. The word used to describe that figure is ᵓLWH (God) rather than RŠWT (power) showing that the terms could be used interchangeably. By continuing the exegesis of Ps. 73, the possibility of another earthly God is also denied. This is a convenient argument against a number of beliefs, among which, especially in this context, would be incarnation. In order to counteract those heretical tendencies, the orthodox position marshalled the Shema (Dt. 6:4), the very center of synagogue liturgy.

The next passage in Dt. Rabba is also based on the Shema and contains information attributed to earlier times. It begins with a quotation from Pr. 24:21.

PASSAGE 10

Dt. Rabba 2:33

Another explanation: What is the force of, *"And the King?* Make [God] King over you. *And meddle not with them that are given to change"* (Prov. 24:21). Do not meddle with those who declare that there is a second god. R. Judah b. Simon said: [Scripture says], *"And it shall come to pass, that in all the land, saith the Lord, two parts therein shall be cut off and die* (Zech. 13:8); the mouths that declare that there are two powers shall be cut off and die. And who will survive in the future? But the third shall be left therein. This refers to Israel who are termed 'thirds,' for they are divided into three groups: Priests, Levites and Israelites and are descended from the three Patriarchs, Abraham, Isaac, and Jacob." Another explanation: Because they praise God with the threefold expression of holiness, "Holy, holy, holy (Isa. 6:3)." R. Aha said: "God was angry with Solomon when he uttered the above verse. He said to him: 'Why do you express a thing that concerns the sanctification of My name by an obscure allusion' [in the words] 'And meddle not with them that are given to change' (ŠWNYM)? Thereupon immediately Solomon expressed it more clearly [in the words], 'There is one that is alone, and he hath not a second; yea; he hath neither son nor brother' (Eccl. 4:8); He hath neither son nor brother, but *Hear O Israel: the Lord our God, the Lord is one."* 10

---

9 See Lev. R. 29:11; Hag. 12b, ARN 37 (Goldin, *ARN*, p. 154); Ginsberg, *Legends*, V, 10 f. where it is ascribed to R. Meir. See p. 66 f.

10 Tr. Rabbinowitz.

"Meddle not with them that are given to change" is seen as relevant to the Shema by means of a double entendre: "Meddle not with those who say there is a second God." This is done by understanding the root Š-N-Y/H to imply two, or a second, instead of "change," its usual meaning in this form. [11] Instead of reading "Two parts therein shall be cut off and die," he suggests the alternative meaning: "The mouths that say there are 'two powers' shall be cut off and die." Having done that, the exegete is left with the difficult problem of interpreting the significance of the last third. This he deftly calls Israel because Israel is the last third of two conventional groupings—both priests, Levites and Israel, and Abraham, Isaac and Jacob (who is Israel). Though the argument may be ingenious, the rabbis expressed their own disapproval by imagining God's displeasure at such an indirect proof.

The next paragraph is thus taken to be a more direct attack on the same problem. It is based on Proverbs, but is adduced in R. Aha's name (PA4). R Aha seems to identify those who believe in "two powers" as Christians. The earliest form of this tradition is actually tannaitic, appearing in Sifre 329 where the relationship to "two powers" is unstated. R. Aha attributes his exegesis to Solomon because the book of Proverbs, from which the text is taken, is attributed to Solomon. Therefore, the meaning of the verse can be clarified in light of another work attributed to Solomon—Ecc. 4:8, where Solomon is supposed to have stated that God has neither brother nor son. [12] By itself, the denial of the idea that God has brothers could have been a reference to any polytheistic system or Persian religion where the good and evil inclinations were sometimes conceived of as twin brothers. But the idea that God has no son seems to be best understood as a response to Christian or gnostic doctrine, even if there is no firm evidence for deciding between the two.

The text differs significantly in the version occurring at Ecc. R. 4:8:

> *There is one that is alone, and He hath not a second* (4:8). *There is one*: i.e., the Holy One, blessed be He, of whom it is said, The Lord our God, the Lord is one (Deut. 6:4). *And He hath not a second*: He has no partner in His universe. Yea, *He hath neither son nor brother*: since He has no brother, whence should He have a son? [13]

---

[11] A similar exegesis on Zech 13:8 is attributed to R. Judah b. Simon (PA 1).
[12] See p. 11 f.
[13] Ecc. R. 4:1, Tr. Rabbinowitz.

The traditional understanding is that ᵓH is not just to be construed as "brother," rather as "consort." The meaning of the phrase would then be that God could not possibly have a son because he has no consort. [14] This interpretation satisfies the sense of the passage. In fact it functions as a commentary because it places a logical progression on the tradition which is unsupported in any other version. Significantly, the phrase used to describe the second power in heaven is ŠWṬP, partner, which we have seen was the term for the heretical second figure present at the creation in Adam speculation. [15]

In other places as well, the amoraim attached the issue of "two powers" to some loosely related earlier tradition. In the following pericope, they added the issue because the earlier tradition dealt with other kinds of frivolous speculation. The tradition occurs four times in rabbinic literature. Each of the four occurrences demonstrates growth in the tradition towards more specification about the heresy involved. The earliest traditions are from Sifre and the Midrash Tannaim, two ostensibly tannaitic sources which appear to be stressing the perfection of the human body.

PASSAGE 11

Midrash Tannaim p. 187	Sifre Dt. 307
	The Rock, Perfect in all His actions: The former because he formed the world first and formed man in it.
His work is perfect. His work is perfected with all those who come into the world.	*His work is perfect.* His work is perfected with all those who come into the world. No one can speculate about his attributes, not even the most insignificant reason. And none can look and say: "If only I had three eyes, if only I had three hands, if only I had three legs, if only I could walk on my head, if only my head faced backwards, how pleasant that would be!" Scripture teaches, *All His ways are justice.*
No man in the world can say, "If only I had three eyes, if only I had three legs, if only I had three hands, if only my head faced backwards, if only I could walk on my head, then I would be pleased!" Why? Because *All His ways are justice.*	

---

[14] The root (ᵓHY) is not attested in Hebrew or Aramaic with the meaning of consort.

[15] See the technical use of the term in relation to sharing God's name in j. Taan. 2 (65d) b. San. 63a, b. Suk. 45b, Ex. R. 42 (to Ex. 32:4). The power could be a partner in that he shares the divine name. See p. 112, p. 137, p. 183 f.

Ecc. R. 2:12	Gen. R. 12:1
R. Simeon b. Yohai said: this is compared to a king of flesh and blood who built palaces and all who visited it said: "If only the columns were higher, it would be more pleasant. If only the walls were higher, it would be more pleasant. If only its ceiling were higher, it would be more pleasant!" As if a man were to come and say: "If only I had three arms, or three eyes or three ears or three legs, I would be pleased." Scripture does not say: "that which he has already made him but," *that which they have already made him.* The supreme King of Kings, Blessed be He, and his court, took a vote, so to speak, on your every limb and plan. And if you should say: "There are 'two powers,' has it not already been said: *He has made you and established you.*" (Dt. 32:6).	R. Simeon b. Yohai said: This is compared to a king of flesh and blood who built palaces and his comrades visited it and said: "If only the columns were higher, it would be more pleasant. If only the walls were higher, it would be more pleasant. If only the ceiling were higher it would be more pleasant." Yet if a man came and said: "If only I had three eyes, or three legs we would be astonished!" It is not stated: "that he has already made him," but *"That which they have already made him.* The supreme King of Kings, blessed be He and his court, took a vote, so to speak, on your every limb, and set it up according to your plan: (Thus it is written) *He has made you and He has established you.* (Dt. 32:6).

The exegesis is based on Dt. 32:4, "The Rock, His work is perfect." Understanding "rock" (ṢWR) as "shaper" (ṢYYR). The exegete applies the verse to Genesis and teaches that no one has the right to criticize the perfection of the human body. This moral lesson is proof-texted by means of other statements emphasizing that God has confidence in His creation, that He judges each creature equally, and that the purpose of all men is to be righteous. We have seen that these themes are sounded against the heresy of "two powers" especially after it becomes impossible to distinguish between the gnostic and principal angel varieties. There is no attempt within Sifre to make any connection with "two powers" explicit. However, later rabbis were sensitive to the theme and spelled out the danger of "two powers" heresy.

The version in Genesis Rabba develops in a different way. The midrash arises in reference to Ecc. but the exegesis is occasioned by quoting Gen. 2:4, the summary of the creation story. It is attributed to R. Simeon b. Yohai and his moral is to avoid criticizing man or any other work of the creator, since that implies a criticism of God. [16]

---

[16] The defensive argument may have been spurred by the notion that ṢYYR

Yet the analogy between divine and human motives is portrayed slightly differently than in the earlier version. Men stupidly criticize grand edifices. How much more stupid is it when they criticize man himself, who is God's magnificent edifice? An interesting addition to this passage is the explanation of the plurals in Genesis by saying they refer to God in consultation with His angelic court. God and His heavenly court decide by vote to create each human member, citing Dt. 32 as proof because it contains the seeming redundancy "He made you and established you." [17] Based on what we know of "two powers" traditions, we can say that there would be a possibility of deriving two deities in two different places in this story—one from the two verbs used for creation in Genesis, and the other from the two verbs used for creation in Deuteronomy. However, the specific charge of heresy is not mentioned.

In Ecc. R. the latest version, approximately the same text is repeated with the significant addition of a warning against "two powers." After the description of God and his heavenly court, the midrash adds Dt. 32 as protection against the idea that there are "two powers." One editor has obviously picked up the dangerous implication of the repetition of verbs for creating in Dt. 32, since he specifically reiterates these words. He maintains that God's consultations with the heavenly court is the correct interpretation of the repetition but is not satisfied with this explanation either. So he then tries to remove all possibility of heresy by reading the verse in a slightly different manner, understanding the repetition as emphasizing that one God has made all creation.

From this midrashic development, one may infer that the original discussion had something to do with the creation of man and may have had some connection to heresy. Further discussion linked it significantly with "two powers." Clearly, although the elaboration is secondary, the amoraim were associating creation, "two powers" and different words for "creator" with heresy. They did so for good reason but we cannot be sure that the original tradition had to do with such matters.

In many places in rabbinic literature, defense against "two powers" may be implied, although there is no direct statement of it. Of course,

---

("formed") signifies that a different and lower creator than the high God, who can "create." (Elohim). See the controversy between Gamaliel and the Emperor, p. 116 f.

[17] See p. 131 f. where R. Eleazar discusses also the heavenly court in regard to ambiguous passages of this type.

such passages are easily missed and there is no way to control rabbinic literature for all of them. But there is one that is very provocative:

> Rabbi Zeira, the son of R. Abbahu. R. Abbahu in the name of R. Elazar: " 'Happy the man whose helper is the God of Jacob' (Ps. 146:5). Why does scripture seem redundant [in saying]: 'He who made heaven and earth' To what is this related? It is like a king of flesh and blood who employed a governor to rule one estate but who had no authority over another. Similarly, lest you should say the *cosmokrator* rules the land, but not the sea, the Holy One, Blessed be He rules over both dry land and sea, saving from water in the sea, and from fire on the dry land. He who saved Moses from the sword of Pharaoh and saved Jonah from the belly of the whale, Hananiah, Mishael and Azariah from the fiery furnace and Daniel from the lions' den—He it is about whom it is written, 'He is the maker of heaven and earth, the sea and all that is therein.' " [18]

The tradition comes from R. Elazar b. Pedath (PA 2 250-290) who is seeking to explain the relationship between Jacob's prayer for help in scripture and the answer that God is the creator of heaven and earth. A king of flesh and blood might appoint governors over various parts of his realm, but God does not. He rules all parts of His realm at the same time. Unlike a *kosmokrator,* God does not rule the earthly part of the world, leaving the sea to another ruler. Rather God saves both on land and sea, showing He is omnipotent. The term *kosmo-krator* has technical meanings in some varieties of pagan thought, Christianity, and finally gnosticism where it became the title of the demiurge. At the base of all these traditions is probably the LXX, which often translated YHWH Sebaoth, "the Lord of Hosts" as *kosmo-krator.* The late date of the tradition would argue for gnostic or Christian opposition. But it may also have been occasioned by an exegetical problem, without specific reference to heretical or gentile belief. An argument against figures helping God in His maintenance of the world may be implicit, but any relationship to "two powers in heaven" remains unstated. Therefore, this may only be an argument against polytheism generally.

One last occurrence of the term "two powers" uses the heresy incidentally but links the heresy to its corrective, the first of the Ten Commandments:

---

[18] J. A. Zar. 3, 42c bottom.

PASSAGE 12

Pesikta Rabbati 20, 4

Then a troop of angels of destruction, strong and mighty, who are set round about the throne of glory, met him. When Moses reached them, they sought to burn him with the breath of their mouths. What did the Holy One, Blessed be He, do? He spread something of His own splendor about Moses, stood him up before His throne, and said: "Moses, make a reply to the ministering angels—speak up to them!" (The words: *"He causes (him) to take hold of the face of His throne and spreadeth His cloud upon him (Job. 26:9),"* prove, according to R. Nahum, that the Almighty spread about Moses something of the splendor of the presence of God, which is His cloud. Moses said to Him: "Master of the world, I fear that they will consume me with the breath of their mouths." God said: "Take hold of the throne of My glory and turn them back with thy words." Thereupon Moses made bold and gave a reply to the ministering angels. He said: "You have no cause to burn me with the breath of your mouths (in your wish to keep the Torah for yourselves.) In the Torah it is written (for the guidance of mortals) *'I am the Lord your God. (Ex. 20:2).'* But you, (who live in the very presence of the one God)—how could you have many gods? In the Torah it is written Thou shalt have no other Gods (Ex. 20:3). [Have you divided minds?] Have you 'two powers' (such as mortals are likely to have)?..." [19]

This late report in *Pesikta Rabbati* contains a passing reference to "two powers in heaven." The legend began as a commentary on Ex. 20:2 and related how Moses went up to heaven in the cloud on Sinai to get the Ten Commandments for Israel. This legend recounts a heavenly journey, a primary motif of Merkabah mysticism and implies, as Philo did, that Moses shared in God's divinity, though here it is solely for his protection. The reference to "two powers" occurs when Moses confronts the ministering angels, who, knowing a good thing when they see it, want to keep the Torah for themselves. Moses is forced to persuade them that the Torah is meant for Israel. He argues that the laws are designed only for man because the angels do not need them. They do not covet, have neither father nor mother, nor do they practice idolatry. He asks the angels whether or not they believe in "two powers," since they selfishly want to keep the first commandment for themselves. The first commandment is obviously viewed as a firm defense against dualistic or binitarian heresy. It is also clear that these traditions must be late since the charge of "two powers" is conventional, only used as a folkloric motif and presupposes no live heretical issue in the community.

---

[19] Tr. Braude, p. 408-9 with changes to express the direct reference to "two powers" in the Hebrew.

Marmorstein mentions two further places, not yet discussed, where he feels the heresy of "two powers" is implied. In one place I can agree that the issue is "two powers," but the passage itself seems to be an interpolation. His second occurrence is less sure. [20]

Marmorstein quotes a version of M. Ps. to Ps. 53:9:

> According to worldly custom, a king of flesh and blood has a duke for each domain and they carry on the burden of government with him. When the princes are assisting they also share in his grandeur. But the Holy One, Blessed be He is not like that. He has neither duke, nor governor nor second-in-command, as it is said: "What god is there in heaven or on earth who can match your works and mighty deeds?" (Dt. 3:24). "I am the Lord who made all things, by myself I stretched out the skies, alone I hammered out the floor of the earth." (Is. 44:24 f.) None else shares His burden, as it is said: "I performed it and carried it out." [21]

Since Braude has left the version out of his English edition of M. Ps., he must view it as secondary. However at whatever point it entered the tradition, it is an argument against "two powers" of the conventional sort we have noticed. Marmorstein also listed another place which he feels is relevant to the heresy and which should be mentioned, M. Ps. 51:8.

"Only He alone knows, which wonderful deeds He will perform." is the key phrase for Marmorstein, who believes it to be a covert argument against gnostics. This is certainly possible, but that does not seem to be a necessary conclusion. The passage only argues against people who claim to prophesize, without mention of the cosmology to which they adhere. Even less evident is the relationship to "two powers" heresy. It rather seems to me that the "alone" in scripture occasions what is now a conventional remark taken from rabbinic "two powers" polemic.

These last two passages have been mentioned because they were linked with the heresy by the last generation of scholars. However, most editions of M. Ps. do not even print these few lines. Passages of this sort can be discovered in other, less obscure places as well, but they will yield no further information for our study. It is best now to summarize what has been found in the rabbinic texts and then turn to the extra-rabbinic evidence, which solves some of the ambiguities we noted in the rabbinic texts.

---

[20] Both may be found in Marmorstein, *RGS*, 1, p. 71.
[21] Ps. 53:9.

CHAPTER TEN

SUMMARY OF RABBINIC FINDINGS

The rabbinic evidence is now before us. Many questions remain; but a number of new observations about "two powers" can be made. First, we should note that the heresy is almost entirely confined to Palestine. Not one historical tradition is set in Babylonia. The defense against the heresy is attributed only to Palestinian sages or to Babylonian sages who emigrated to Palestine. This suggests not only a Palestinian locale for the heresy, but a date for the battle which would precede Judaism's intensive contact with orthodox Zoroastrianism in amoraic Babylonia.

More importantly, we can differentiate several early stages of the rabbinic defense against the heresy. Heretical doctrine was only infrequently attacked by direct phenomenological or doctrinal characterizations—like "those who say there is no power in heaven," or "those who say there are two powers in heaven," or "many powers in heaven." No doubt the rabbis debated about doctrine, for such doctrinal characterizations provided the technical terms for the various heresies. However they recorded their legal-exegetical discussions more carefully. The beginning of the long battle can be seen best in two different, equally early areas—polemical exegesis and liturgical orthopraxy.

The earliest differences of opinion for which we have evidence were centered on scripture. The rabbis attempted to defeat a growing body of sectarian biblical exegesis supporting a binitarian heresy by suggesting an orthodox understanding of the crucial scripture. We also have evidence of an attempt to exclude various heretical understandings of providence from the synagogue by silencing prayers associated with them from use in public services. The association between the "two powers" heresy and the various liturgical formulae about God's providence is made by the amoraim, but the tannaitic material implies that the themes of justice and mercy were united with the themes of the appearances of God by the mid-second century.

The earliest datable manifestations of the heresy are to be found in exegetical battles:

Dangerous Scriptural Passages

Tannaitic Evidence

Chapter 2: *Conflicting Appearances of God*:
Exodus 15:3 vs. Ex. 24:10 f.
Daniel 7:9 f., later Ps. 22:2
defense: Ex. 20:2
           Dt. 32:39
           Is. 46:4 ⎫ i.e. Is. 44-47 generally
              44:6 ⎬ as well as other II
              41:4 ⎭ Isaiah passages

Chapter 3: *Aher and Metatron*
Daniel 7:9 f.
Exodus 24:1 f.
possibly: Ps. 37:25   (LXX 36:25)
           Ps. 104:31 (LXX 103:31, see Hull. 60a)
           Ex. 23:21

Chapter 4: *A Controversy between Ishmael and Akiba;*
Heaven and Earth as Divine Powers:
Genesis 1:1
Genesis 4:1
Genesis 21:20

Chapter 5: *Midrashic Warnings Against Two Powers*
Deuteronomy 32:39 (?)
defense: Dt. 32:39
          Nu. 15:30

Chapter 6: *Liturgical Prohibitions in the Mishnah*
Deuteronomy 22:6 (?)
defense: Deuteronomy 6:4, 22:6

Chapter 7: *Many Powers in Heaven;*
Adam as a Divine Creature
Genesis 1:26   Gen. 2:7 etc.
Genesis 19:24
Amos 4:13

Amoraic Evidence

Chapter 8: *How Many Powers Created the World?*
Gen. 1:26   *defense*:   Gen. 1:27
Gen. 11:7   Gen. 11:5
Gen. 35:7   Gen. 35:3
Dt. 4:7   Dt. 4:7
2 Sam. 7:23

Dan. 7:9	Dan. 7:10
Gen. 1:1	
Gen. 1:26	Gen. 1:27
Josh 22:22	Josh 22:22
Ps. 50:1 (LXX 49:1)	
Josh. 24:19	
Dt. 4:7	Ps. 77:13
	Ps. 78:24
	Ps. 47:8
	Ps. 108:7
	Gen. 4:23

Chapter 9:   *Divine Partners and Angels*

Gen. 1:1	*defense*:	Ps. 119:160
Gen. 1:1		Jer. 10:10
		Ps. 44:24
Gen. 2:4		Dt. 6:4
		Dt. 32:6

The crucial issues which can be dated early are: (1) a dangerous understanding of Dan. 7:9 f.; (2) dangerous contradictions between the portrayal of God as heavenly warrior (especially in Ex. 15:3) and the figure of an old man on a heavenly throne assumed to be described in various theophanies (especially Ex. 24:10 f.); (3) a tradition about a principal angel, based on Ex. 20 f., said to be Metatron in the amoraic traditions but whose real significance is that he is YHWH or the bearer of the divine name (using Ex. 23:21 f.).

These passages may have little in common in their origin. But they all picture God Himself as a man or posit a principal angel, with the shape of a man, who aids God in the governance of the world. Since the passages share a revelatory vision of the angelic figure or picture God sitting on His throne, other major biblical texts, describing God's angel or His enthronement could also be relevant. The angelophany and theophany passages of Genesis and Exodus might be included, as well as Is. 6 and Ex. 1. Besides Ex. 23:21 f. which the rabbis discuss at length, it might include Gen. 16:7 f., 21:17 f., 22:11, 31:11 f., Ex. 3:2 f., Ju. 2:1 f. where references to the angel of YHWH and Elohim are confused in the text.

The earliest isolatable rabbinic opposition to "two powers," then, is not against ethical dualism, but against a principal angel or mediator. While it seems possible that the angelic or anthropomorphic creature has some relation to the problem of theodicy, the helping angel is in no way evil. The portrayal of the second figure does not explain the existence of evil so much as the appearance of a sublime divinity to men. Therefore it is apt to call such beliefs "binitarianism" or "ditheism" rather than "dualism."

The rabbis counter the dangerous angelologies by suggesting different interpretations of the passages under discussion. They maintain that the two different descriptions of God can be resolved into one just and merciful figure—just as Ex. 15:3 and 24:10 refer to one God, once Ex. 20:2 is taken into account.

Is. 44 f. and Dt. 32 are seen as especially helpful for the rabbinic defense in order to show that the Bible explicitly forbids "binitarianism" when it says that only one God rules the world. In the amoraic period, an additional, highly conventional response to the heretical arguments develops, which dismisses the scriptural passages important to the heresy but avoids any detailed description of the heretical beliefs by concentrating on grammar. Rabbis Yohanan and Simlai are probably the first to teach that wherever a grammatical plural in scripture modifies God, the counter-argument of God's unity can be deduced from the singular grammatical forms which are invariably associated with that plural.

By the middle of the second century the doctrine of God's justice and mercy is combined with the name of God traditions. There is evidence of several sets of terminology to discuss the relationship between God and His attributes, but the received identification of names and attributes is apparently already in effect by then. This development is coterminous with rabbinic discussions of heretical views of God's justice or mercy. Whenever they developed, the basic traditions concerning the angelic figure are older than the time of R. Akiba and R. Ishmael because the rabbinic defense against the heresy contradicts the rabbinic doctrine of divine mercy and justice which was known to both of them. [1]

R. Nathan defends Jewish scripture against the heretical idea that God has created in secret. When put together with the issues of God's justice and mercy, this defense may imply complementary binitarianism but is more appropriate to the controversy either with Marcion or with extreme gnosticism. It is datable to the second century and probably served as the impetus to rapid development of rabbinic doctrines of mercy and justice. These issues were probably not totally unknown, however, before the mid-second century, since we shall see that Philo records many traditions concerned with such subjects.

---

[1] See p. 44 f.

Other traditions are associated with "two powers" in more obscure ways. These include notions about the process of creation or about Adam, who, in this context, is seen as a gigantic, mythic creature—possibly even an angel or a helper of God in creation. These traditions, only hinted at in the rabbinic writings and associated with "many powers in heaven" by the tannaim, centered around the creation story in Genesis. Though they appear in tannaitic writings, they are greatly elaborated upon by the amoraim, who first link them specifically with "two powers." Apparently at some point, a whole variety of different exegetical traditions are grouped together under the category of "two powers." From the rabbinic evidence alone, *it is not possible to show that any one heretical group combined all the different doctrines associated with the heresy.* Rabbinic literature presents a composite picture with many different positions being subsumed as heresy throughout the rabbinic period. It is possible to isolate some of the early tannaitic evidence but in the amoraic period all is melded. Thus even the historicity of the various attributions to amoraic rabbis is a moot point.

To summarize the exegetical front of the battle against "two powers" from the texts then, we see that the earliest isolatable layers of tradition can be discovered only as an early stratum in the Mekhilta and related passages (passages 1 and 2). Similar traditions of great antiquity may be safely supposed to lie behind the mystical traditions in the Talmud (passages 3 and 4). However, it cannot be assumed that the leading tannaim practiced mysticism in the way it is described. In the rest of the tannaitic passages, that exegetical sophistication developed in the earlier passages is put to use in fighting a variety of enemies. In the amoraic period the following passages are recorded as important in the heresy: Gen. 1:1, 1:26, 2:7, 11:7, 19:24, 35:7, Dt. 4:7, 2 Sam. 7:23, Dan. 7:9, Josh. 22:22, Ps. 50:1. Many of these were evident or implied in the tannaitic discussions. In most of the late cases the heretical issues are left obscure by the rabbis, so we must reconstruct them where we can. A number of the heretical arguments, however, are not attested in the tannaitic discussions. It is even probable that traditions originally having nothing to do with "two powers" were brought under the rubric in amoraic times. Clearly then, by the amoraic period, "two powers" was a broad enough category to include a number of different binitarian sectarians, some of whom could be described as radical, cosmic dualists.

The mishnaic evidence emphasizes the second thrust of the rabbinic offensive against heresy—ostracism from the synagogue. It is likely that the "two powers" sects were among the heretical groups excluded from the synagogue during earliest times, but it is not easy to characterize or date the entire battle.

The process of ostracism probably received its first impetus from Gamaliel—who expanded the curse against enemies of the synagogue in the liturgy to include the *minim*. [2] People who led prayers in the synagogue were admonished not to use a number of heretical prayers, among which was the "MWDYM... MWDYM" formula. But that formula is clearly related to "two powers" only at a later date when scholars agree that Christianity was included in the curse in the Amidah as well. [3] Since we are sure that Christians were called "two powers" heretics by the late tannaim, we have some good reason to suspect that believers in "two powers" traditions were also among those cursed by the synagogue, even if they were not yet associated with the other heretical behaviors ennunciated by the Mishnah. Yet the Mishnah does not identify the heretics who say "MWDYM... MWDYM" with the term "two powers." We must conclude that this is an oversight, or that the prayer formula was not associated only with the "two powers" heresy at first, or that the term "two powers" became conventional only at a later time. The last possibility seems most likely, but all of them could be partly true.

Besides the mishnaic reports about rabbinic supervision of liturgy, we know that the later rabbis relied on the first commandment (Ex. 20:2), once a part of the liturgy, [4] as a defense against dualism. The midrash to Deuteronomy points out that the Shema (Dt. 6:4 f.), together with its antiphonal answer, were also seen as the pronouncements *par excellence* against "binitarian" heresy. The rabbinic texts only associate "two powers" with the liturgical passages during the amoraic period, but the use of the same scriptures in exegetical battles

---

[2] See Elbogen, p. 36 f. for a discussion of the Birkat Haminim written by Samuel the Younger under the direction of Gamaliel. Samuel's text was probably appended to an earlier, version against the "arrogant," and other enemies of the synagogue. Joseph Heinemann, *Prayer in the Period of the Tannaim and the Amoraim: Its Nature and its Patterns* [in Hebrew] (Jerusalem: 1966), p. 142-4.

[3] A synagogue curse offensive to Christians is mentioned by several church fathers.

[4] Ber. 1, 3c. See Geza Vermes, "The Decalogue and the Minim," *Post-Biblical Jewish Studies* (Leiden: 1975), pp. 169-177 .

is demonstrable in the tannaitic period. Furthermore, extra-rabbinic sources suggest the antiquity of the tradition. [5]

Other liturgical rulings point out the rabbinic strategy for excluding heretics from the synagogues. For instance, the ruling about hearing the whole benediction before pronouncing "amen" (Ber. 8 end) prevented any sectarians from gaining a measure of acceptance by inserting their prayers into synagogue benedictions and having them ratified with an "amen." The ruling is mentioned specifically with regard to Samaritans, but Christians used the suspect formulae in their creeds as well. [6] Even The Apostles' Creed would have been completely orthodox in its beginning and closing. Only the middle contains material heretical from the Jewish perspective. Furthermore, "Samaritan" and "sectarian" are often confused in the manuscripts of rabbinic texts. From our study of tannaitic times it has become clear that Samaritans, Christians and other sectarians were grouped together and condemned in rabbinic heresiological writings and in liturgical ordinances because there was a phenomenological similarity between them from the rabbinic perspective: they all compromised monotheism by positing more than one authority in heaven. [7]

The term "two powers" may once have designated a specific group and circulated in various individual traditions but it appears to have become a stock characterization of heresy toward the end of the tannaitic period and to have lost any specificity it may have originally had. In some texts either "two powers" or "two gods" is used to describe the dangerous exegeses. The difficult passage at b. Ber. 11b (which calls the heresy DW BR) appears to be a defective rendering of some alternative denomination for "two powers." Toward the end

---

[5] The Shema, like much of the Deuteronomist perenesis, contains the proclamation of God's unity emphasizing particularly the fear and love of God, which in turn were associated with the two aspects of justice and mercy in midrashic literature. The same structure of thought is found as early as Philo. There is some evidence that Philo was relying on even more ancient tradition in discussing this matter (see p. 178 f.), suggesting a very early origin for the relatively late discussion of fear and love that we find in our present texts.

[6] See *Didache* 82 and Elbogen, p. 253.

[7] Even methods of exegesis against dangerous scriptural passages found their way into the liturgy. According to Mann's reconstruction of the triennial cycle of the scripture readings which was current in Palestine, the *haftarah* for the Ten Commandments was chosen in order to deal with the same issues that we are discussing. Jacob Mann, *The Bible as Read and Preached in the Old Synagogue* (New York: 1971), believed that the Ten Commandments *sidrah* actually began at Ex. 20:2 in the triennial cycle, because the ten commandments actually began there. Mann believed that the *haftarah* for Ex. 20:2 f. must have started with Is. 43:11 and continued through v. 21.

of the tannaitic period, and into the amoraic, the term "two powers" became more popular, possibly because it defined the heresy doctrinally, but did not reveal much information about it. It could be easily contrasted with "no power in heaven" on the one hand and "many powers in heaven" on the other. By the beginning of the amoraic period "two powers" was the clearly understood title for all binitarian or dualistic heresies and doubtlessly no longer referred to any one particular sect.

It seems clear, then, that the synagogue and academies in Palestine were the locus of the debate and defense against "two powers." Exegesis was the earliest battleground of the conflict. Although the answers to the heretics were worked out by the academies, the question must have been raised in relation to Bible-reading and by groups who were interested in hearing the Jewish Bible expounded. Since we know that some "two powers" heretics were among those cursed in the synagogue, we can assume the following tentative reconstruction of the evidence: Either contemporary with the exegetical problem or immediately after it, a successful campaign was mounted to silence various sectarians in the synagogue by regulating the content and procedures of prayer. Among those silenced were some evincing "two powers" interpretations of scripture. The sectarians may not have called themselves "two gods" or "two powers" heretics. Only the offended party, from a new position of authority, described these doctrines as heresy. When the rabbis insisted that prayers in synagogue meet specific standards of monotheism, the incipient heretics and the rabbis withdrew from each other by mutual consent but certainly on less than peaceful terms. Although they separated, the groups encountered each other in debate frequently, showing that the heretics continued to proliferate and that they remained in close proximity to the rabbinic community. Since the *provenance* of the debate was largely Palestine, when the center of Jewish life moved to Babylonia, the debate slackened. The heretics were entirely outside of the synagogue and probably were no longer in active conflict with the Jewish community. The late occurrences of "two powers" traditions may have been occasioned by sporadic encounters with heretics but seem primarily meant for the encouragement and edification of believers rather than for defense against a threatening heretical group.

The next step in the investigation should be clear. At the beginning of the discussion of this heresy, several candidates for the charge of dualism were surveyed. In the next section, I will try to identify the most likely candidates among the groups mentioned in Section I. Those using scriptures found dangerous by the rabbis will figure prominently in the discussion. Of course, particular note will be taken of Christianity and gnosticism which have frequently been implicated by the evidence (as well as by the suggestion of previous scholars).

To be sure, other apocalyptic and mystical groups have been implicated as well. But some tentative observations are possible at the outset, based on what we know about Christianity. Since Christian documents can be read as representative of one "two powers" group's experience, the reconstruction of the controversy previously outlined gains support. The book of Acts stresses that Christian evangelism began in the synagogues and expanded as the Jews rejected it. The Christian documents do not go into detail about the rabbinic grounds for the rejection. I feel the rabbinic evidence examined in this study clarifies that issue. It shows us that the rabbis opposed any group which emphasized a primary mediator. Christians were probably not uniquely condemned for there is nothing uniquely anti-Christian in the polemic. But it does not tell the whole story. The tentative reconstruction of events will continue to grow in attractiveness as the extra-rabbinic evidence unfolds. In due course, I think it will be possible to clarify some important historical relationships between Judaism, Christianity and gnosticism. The rabbinic polemic, when placed in the context of the known and datable extra-rabbinic evidence, suggests a chronology for the origin of extreme gnosticism and some of the reasons for its development.

One of the conclusions about gnostic origins is already evident: a full-blown gnostic salvation myth is unlikely to have existed in the first century. A number of reasons support this judgement. First, in the earliest rabbinic records the heretics do not seem to believe in two opposing gods, implying that the heretics were not dualistic in the usual sense. Second, nothing specifically or uniquely Christian or gnostic can be discovered in the heresy at first. Third, a number of groups were involved so there need not have been a unified mythology behind the heresy. Fourth, rather than a savior descending and rising there is much evidence that the angelic figure was to guide mystics and saints to the throne or to punish and forgive sins. Some of the gnostic versions of the "two powers" heresy, as we shall see, make more sense as a later stage of tradition designed to answer the rabbinic defense against the earlier binitarianism.

PART THREE

THE EXTRA-RABBINIC EVIDENCE
AND CONCLUSIONS

CHAPTER ELEVEN

PHILO

The survey of rabbinic traditions about "two powers" has given us some clues for discovering the identity of the heretics whose beliefs became the target of the charge of "two powers." The major criterion must be the use by sectarian candidates of the same biblical verses which the rabbis associate with the heresy. We can now survey the dualistic phenomena outlined in the introduction. This time, we can concentrate on those extra-rabbinic traditions which support the ideas of a second figure in heaven by means of the scriptural passages at the center of the rabbinic controversy. Of course, in a work of this size, only the broad outlines of the history of the tradition can be suggested. Specialists in each of the extra-rabbinic literatures should be able to work through the arguments in more detail.

The first significant extra-rabbinic evidence of "two powers" traditions is from Philo. He actually uses the term "two Gods" which was a synonym for "two powers" in rabbinic thought. [1] Yet his opinion of the idea, when we look carefully, is not entirely negative:

> Yet there can be no cowering fear for the man who relies on the hope of the divine comradship, to whom are addressed the words "I am the God who appeared to thee in the place of God." (Gen. 31 : 13). Surely a right noble cause of vaunting it is, for a soul that Gods deigns to show himself to and converse with it. And do not fail to mark the language used, *but carefully inquire whether there are two Gods*; for we read "I am the God that appeared to thee," not "in my place" but "in the place of God," as though it were another's. What then are we to say? He that is truly God is one, but those that are improperly so-called are more than one. Accordingly, the holy word in the present instance has indicated Him who truly is God by means of the articles, saying "I am the God," while it omits the article when mentioning him who is improperly so called, saying "who appeared to thee in the place" not "of the God" but simply "of God." [2]

---

[1] See p. 60, 74.

[2] *Som.* i 227-229 (Loeb, V, 417, tr. Colson and Whitaker). The translation, unless otherwise noted will be that of the Loeb edition. — Italics added.

Philo discusses the concept of a second deity as an explanation of the many anthropomorphisms in the Bible. Strictly speaking, "second God" is an improper designation for the divinity described in Genesis 31, the God of Beth-El. But Philo takes a tolerant view of such improprieties because the Bible itself uses anthropomorphic language to describe God. Immediately after discussing "the second God," Philo brings up the problem of anthropomorphism directly:

> And the sacred word ever entertaining holier and more august conceptions of Him that is, yet at the same time longing to provide instruction and teaching for the life of those who lack wisdom, likened God to man, not however, to any particular man. For this reason it has ascribed to Him face, hands, feet, mouth, voice, wrath and indignation, and over and beyond these, weapons, entrances and exits, movements up and down and all ways, and in following this general principle in its language it is concerned not with truth, but with the profit accruing to its pupils. For some there are altogether dull in their natures, incapable of forming any conception whatever of God as without a body, people whom it is impossible to instruct otherwise than in this way, saying that as a man does so God arrives and departs, goes down and comes up, makes use of a voice, is displeased at wrongdoings, is inexorable in His anger, and in addition to all this has provided Himself with shafts and swords and all other instruments of vengeance against the unrighteous. For it is something to be thankful for if they can be taught self-control by the terror held over them by these means. Broadly speaking the lines taken throughout the Law are these two only, one that which keeps truth in view and so provides the thought "God is not as man" (Num. 23 : 19) the other that which keeps in view the ways of thinking of the duller folk, of whom it is said, "The Lord God will chasten thee, as a man should chasten his son" (Dt. 8 : 5). Why then do we wonder any longer at His assuming the likeness of angels, seeing that for the succour of those that are in need He assumes the likeness of man? Accordingly, when He says, "I am the God who was seen of thee in the place of God" (Gen. 31 : 13) understand that He occupied the place of an angel only so far as appeared, without changing with a view to the profit of him who was not yet capable of seeing the true God. [3]

An anthropomorphic divinity is thus one of the two basic ways in which God can be conceived by man. The other is through pure intellectual activity. But both ways are based on an exegesis of scripture as far as Philo is concerned. Philo distinguishes the two understandings of God on the basis of two scriptural references. The first, summarized

---

[3] *Som.* i 234-237. (Loeb, V, p. 421-23, tr. Colson and Whitaker.)

in Dt. 8:5, involves the description of God in terms appropriate to men, so that men may see him and the unsophisticated may learn of Him. The second, summarized in Nu. 23:19, is the conception of God available to those who have come to perceive Him truly, and is available only to those who are well enough trained by philosophical discipline to receive revelation. Philo takes these two contradictory ideas in scripture—figuring God as man, and knowing that He is not—as summaries both of man's knowledge of God and of the whole process of exegesis. [4] They explain and justify the differences between the literal and allegorical methods of reading scripture. Therefore Philo finds it inappropriate to speak of God, the ultimate transcendent being, in anthropomorphic terms, yet justifies the language of the Bible as a valid pedagogical adaptation to the minds of people who have not learned otherwise. On the other hand, he will not abandon the importance of the text as it stands, sacrificing all literal meaning to the allegory. Thus God can actually appear to men as a man or angel. Any Jew or gentile would be able to call God's angels divine, or a "second God," as Philo himself does, while only the most trained would be able to see that this title does not compromise monotheism. [5]

The remark about a "second God" was occasioned by the angelic theophany which Jacob witnessed. The existence of the second figure is necessary exegetically, because the angel which appeared to Jacob was both shaped like a man and called a god. Of course, the story is important to Philo not only for discussing anthropomorphism, but also because Philo is interested in characterizing the type of vision vouchsafed to the mystic seeker of God, here symbolized by the patriarch Jacob-Israel. Philo takes the story to mean that the mystic can see a figure of God which is a "second God," but that figure does not compromise monotheism.

The identity of the second figure is especially interesting. Philo's exegesis relies on the Septuagint translation of "place of God" for the place-name of Beth-El (lit. house of God). For Philo, "place" is an important concept which may have three different meanings. [6] The first definition corresponds to a physical space filled with a material

---

[4] See, e.g., *Quod Deus* 53 f., 56 f., 61-62. *Leg. All.* iii 204-207. See also N. A. Dahl, *Widersprüche*.

[5] See discussions of Philo's allegorical method in J. Pépin, *Mythe et Allégorie* (Paris: 1958), p. 238. Sowers, *Hermeneutics*, p. 238. Wolfson, *Philo*, I, 25, 37, 55-86; II, 94-126.

[6] *Som.* i, 62.

form, our normal understanding of the term. The second corresponds to the *logos*, [7] the hypostasized intelligence of God, and the third corresponds to God himself. [8] Although he defines the terms philosophically, Philo's terminology bears striking resemblance to the early rabbinic designation MQWM for God. His concept of *logos* is similar to the rabbinic doctrine of God's *Shekhinah*, each of which is often used to explain the same difficult scriptures. [9]

When "place" refers to something divine revealed to man, as it did in the passage above, for Philo, it may mean God's image, His *logos*. It is, in fact, impossible for man to see God and live (Ex. 33:20). However, Moses and the elders see the image of God or everything "that is behind me" (Ex. 33:23). These are equivalent to the *logos* which as a second God can also be given the title "Lord." (*kyrios* = YHWH). [10]

This doctrine, which allows that "place" is a divine creature called Lord, cannot strike us as innocent, especially when we know that "Lord" is synonymous with the tetragrammaton and when the structure of the argument resembles the heretical argument which R. Ishmael b. Yosi countered at Gen. 19:24. We remember that R. Ishmael opposed the exegesis of Gen. 19:24 which derived a second power in heaven, (who was the agent of God in the destruction of Sodom) [11] from the second appearance of the divine name YHWH. By a similar method, Philo derives the idea that the *logos* is a separate, second divine hypostasis from the fact that "God" is repeated in "place of God" instead of using the pronoun (i.e., *My* place) as one would normally expect. Because of this, the *logos* is properly a god and may be called by the divine names. Philo is using an argument which R. Ishmael found dangerous. Furthermore he has paralleled the structure of the argument in the Mekhilta. [12]

The reasoning by which the name of God and the *logos* become

---

[7] *Op.* 20 (C-W I 6, 9, 11), *Som.* i, 66, i, 117 f., I, 229 (C-W III 219, 6; 23, 4 f. cf., 253, 24 f.). See Koester, *"topos"* in *TDNT*.

[8] *Leg. All.* i, 44 (C-W I, 72, 5) *Fug.* 75 (C-W III, 125, 25) *Fug.* 77 (III, 126, 8) *Som.* i, 64 (C-W III, 218, 24) *Leg. All.* iii 1 (C-W I, 114, 4) *Sob.* 63 (C-W II, 227-32).

[9] Wolfson, *Philo*, I, 200-294.

[10] See, e.g., *Fug.* 164 f., Mut. 8-10. This can be profitably compared with the rabbinic legend in the Mekhilta.

[11] See p. 118 f.

[12] See p. 35 f.

equated is also familiar to us. In this same passage in *On Dreams*, Philo states:

> Here it gives the title of "God" to His chief Word, not from any superstitious nicety in applying names, but with one aim before him, to use words to express facts. Thus in another place, when he had inquired whether He that is has any proper name, he came to know full well that He has no proper name, [the reference is to Ex. 6 :3] and that whatever name anyone may use for Him he will use by license of language; for it is not the nature of Him that is to be spoken of, but simply to be. Testimony to this is afforded also by the divine response made to Moses' question whether He has a name, even "I am He that is (Ex. 3 : 14)." It is given in order that, since there are not in God things which man can comprehend, man may recognize His substance. To the souls indeed which are incorporeal and are occupied in His worship it is likely that He should reveal himself as He is, conversing with them as friend with friends; but to souls which are still in a body, giving Himself the likeness of angels, not altering His own nature, for He is unchangeable, but conveying to those which receive the impression of His presence a semblance in a different form, such that they take the image to be not a copy, but that original form itself. 13

It is by virtue of the revelation of the divine name to Moses that the *logos* comes to be equated with the name of God. Of course, Philo is again dealing with the same biblical citations and issues which gave the rabbis so much trouble in succeeding centuries. Though Philo maintains no human characterization is properly applied to God, he also says that the *logos* may be called God, since it is in the form of the *logos* that God has chosen to reveal himself. Philo also seems to imply that certain men are actually able to see God directly, if they can transcend materiality. Conversely, he knows of men who know only the *logos*, who "take the image to be not a copy, but that original form itself." It takes but a small leap of the imagination, based on Philo's discussion of those "incapable of forming any conception of God whatsoever without a body" to suspect that there were others in Philo's day who spoke of a "second god," but who were not as careful as Philo in defining the limits of the term.

The importance of this kind of argument to the rabbinic texts ought to be clear. The parallel remains striking even when the biblical context is unfamiliar. Philo can use the same argument and the same term "second God" (Greek: *deuteros theos*, Latin: *secundus deus*)

---

13 *Som.* i, 230-33. (Loeb V, p. 419-21, tr. Colson and Whitaker).

whenever the biblical text might imply the existence of a second deity, not just when the term "place" is present:

> (Gen. IX : 6) Why does (Scripture) say, as if (speaking) of another God, "In the image of God He made man" and not "in His own image"?
>
> Most excellently and veraciously this oracle was given by God. For nothing mortal can be made in the likeness of the Most High One and father of the universe *but (only) in that of the second God, who is His logos.* For it was right that the rational part of the human soul should be formed as an impression by the divine *logos*, since the pre-*logos* God is superior to every rational nature. But He who is above the logos exists in the best and in a special form—what thing that comes into being can rightfully bear His likeness? Moreover, Scripture wishes to show that God most justly avenges the virtuous and decent men because they have certain kinship with His logos, of which the human mind is a likeness and image. [14]

Here Philo makes no disclaimer about the metaphoric quality of the terms he is using. He unabashedly calls the logos a "second God." Thus, in calling attention to various similar scriptural passages, the rabbis were not just stylizing theoretical arguments. Real traditions of a "second God" were present in Judaism as early as the time of Philo. Though the rabbis are opposed to the whole notion, Philo seems only to be opposed to the naive forms of the belief.

Of course, the idea of a "second God" raised the problem of compromising monotheism with Philo as well. Philo's answer to the problem was, as we saw in *On Dreams*, entirely unique. He said that when one looks carefully at the articles before the nouns in the sentence, one sees that "a god" merely refers to the divinity present at that moment, while the high God is signified either by the noun "God," without the article, or "the God" with a definite article.

In other words, Philo allows for the existence of a second, principal, divine creature, whom he calls a "second God," who nevertheless is only the visible emanation of the High, ever-existing God. In doing this, he has an entirely different emphasis than the rabbis. He is clearly following the Greek philosophers. [15] Like them, he is reluctant

---

14 Italics added. *Quest. in Gen.* ii, 62 Philo Supplement I, p. 150, tr. R. Marcus. Eusebius (*P.E.* VII, 13, 1) credits Philo with the term "second God," denoting the *logos*.

15 See Wolfson, *Philo*, I, ch. 4 to whom I am heavily indebted for the following discussion. See also Festugière p. 162 and E. Peterson, *Der Monotheismus als politisches Problem* (Leipzig: 1935).

to conceive of a pure, eternal God who participates directly in the affairs of the corruptible world. So he employs a system of mediation by which God is able to reach into the transient world, act in it, fill it, as well as transcend material existence, without implying a change in His essence. In these passages, Philo has suggested that the mediation is effected by the *logos*, who is the sum total of all the forms of the intelligible world and equal to the mind of God.

Philo uses the stoic word *logos* in place of the Platonic word *nous* to mean the mind of God, in which all the ideas or forms of our world are conceived. Possibly in doing so he wishes to emphasize both the intradeical and extradeical aspects of this concept. That is to say, as the mind of God, *logos* is equivalent to the intelligible world itself. But Philo also wishes to speak of *logos* as an extradeical hypostasis of God. That transition is possible because divine thought is different in quality from human thought. For God, thinking is equivalent to acting. So the *logos*, defined as the thinking faculty of God, can easily be described also as an incorporeal being, created for the purpose of carrying out His thoughts, having existence outside of God as well as containing the forms of the whole world. Thus, Philo can use his concept of *logos* both for philosophical argumentation and for explaining the anthropomorphisms in the Bible. The *logos* becomes the actual figure of God, who appears "like a man" in order that men may know His presence. [16]

It is clear that Philo uses and approves of the term "second God" which the rabbis later would find repugnant, because it allows him to maintain the truth both of his philosophy and of his scripture at the

---

[16] The vocabulary Philo uses is not unlike some other mystical, philosophical systems. Gilles Quispel (*Gnostic Studies*, I) points out that the Paternal Intellect of the *Chaldean Oracles* (which is the receptical of the sensible forms and the image of the godhead) is called a "second God" (*deuteros theos*) by Pletho. Quispel's point is that the conception of the second deity in the *Chaldaean Oracles* (a second century document) handles the problem of visible manifestation of godhead in a Platonic fashion. At the same time, this presupposes the relationship between mystical theurgy and neo-Platonism that E. R. Dodds has suggested. He further maintains that these doctrines can be discovered in the gnostics who opposed Amoheus in the third century A.D. and even in the work of Basilides earlier. Exploring this suggestion at this moment would take us too far afield. But if his analysis is correct, it appears that Philo, in some ways, would represent an early example of this supposed mystical-philosophical tradition which sanctioned the concept of a "second God" to describe some aspect of the godhead.

The idea of a "second God" also shows up in Christian neo-platonism and in many philosophical discussions in the church. See p. 229 for Origen and the modalist controversy.

same time. However, it is possible that the correspondance between Philonic and rabbinic terms is accidental. In order to show that the correspondance is significant, as I believe it is, one has to ascertain that the rabbis and Philo had specific traditions in common. It would be nice to have some statement of direct reliance. Unfortunately, we have little. Therefore we must discover a more indirect relationship. One way to reveal the reliance is to demonstrate that Philo has a continuous, not a merely fortuitous, interest in interpreting the same scripture as the rabbis. If his interest in these scriptures is constant and his arguments are parallel to the rabbis, there is a great chance that he was using traditions current in his environment which were also known to the rabbis a century later.

The best way to begin demonstrating that Philo evinced the scriptural traditions both useful and abhorent to the rabbis is to trace Philo's use of the scriptural passages dangerous to the rabbis and to see the great similarity in exegesis, technique and methods. In reviewing these passages, the rabbinic traditions of "two powers" will be constantly relevant. In looking at Philo's exegesis, I think one can see not just similar themes but a direct parallel with the rabbis.

For instance Philo stresses that there is no God besides God the Most High and uses Dt. 4:39, as the rabbis do, to deny that any other figure can be considered a God.

> But let Melchizedek instead of water offer wine, and give to souls strong drink, that they may be seized by a divine intoxication, more sober than sobriety itself. For he is a priest, even Reason, having as his portion Him that is, and all his thoughts of God are high and vast and sublime: for he is the priest of the Most High (Gen. xiv. 18), not that there is any other not Most High — for God being One "is in heaven above and on earth beneath and there is none beside Him" (Deut. 4 : 39) — but to conceive of God not in low earthbound ways but in lofty terms, such as transcend all other greatness and all else that is free from matter, calls up in us a picture of the Most High. [17]

In this particular case, Philo denies that any other being can be God's agent, for there is only one God. It is interesting that Philo picks the context of the story of Melchizedek to discuss this issue, since elsewhere he allows that the *logos* can be considered as a "second God" and divine mediator. It appears as though Philo is opposed to

---

[17] *Leg.* iii, 81.

some concepts of mediation, even while he maintains the agency of the *logos*. [18]

In explicating the significance of God's descent to the Tower of Babel, Philo comments on another of the biblical passages against which the rabbis warn—namely Ex. 24:10 f., the beginning of the Sinai theophany. The verse, so puzzling in rabbinic exegesis, is used by Philo to represent the gloating comment of Israel's enemies:

> Behold ... the eye of the soul, so translucent and pure, so keen of vision, the eye which alone is permitted to look upon God, the eye whose name is Israel, is imprisoned after all in the gross material nets of Egypt and submits to do the bidding of an iron tyranny, to work at brick and every earthly substance with labor painful and unremitting. [19]

Philo's understanding of the phrase describing God's throne in Exodus is, first of all, that it is seen by the eye of the soul, whose name is Israel. This is difficult to interpret unless one remembers that the name "Israel" is allegorized in several ways for Philo. Here he may be relying on an etymology in which Israel is taken as ʾŠ ŠRWʾH ʾL —"the man who sees God." Therefore Israel is the name which Jacob received only after the theophany at Beth-El, because it is there that Jacob saw God. Yet it is also the name of the angel with whom Jacob fought, since Israel can be a name for the *logos* in Philo. [20] Furthermore what holds for the patriarch can be applied to his namesake, the people Israel, who are descended from him. So Philo can discuss both the people and the divine presence in exile with them, a motif similar to the midrashim associated with this verse in rabbinic writings.

Philo continues, significantly:

> But it is the special mark of those who serve the Existent that theirs are not the tasks of cupbearers or bakers or cooks or any other tasks of the earth ... nor do they mould or fashion material forms like

---

[18] See Fred. L. Horton, Jr., *The Melchizedek Tradition: A Critical Examination of the Sources to the Fifth Century A.D. and in the Epistle to the Hebrews* (Cambridge: 1976). See also Friedländer, *Gnosticismus*, p. 30-33. See also Birger Pearson, "Friedländer Revisited: Alexandrian Judaism and Gnosticism," *Studia Philonica*, 2 (1973) p. 26. Sometimes, Melchizedek is allegorized as the *logos* by Philo. See below, p. 168.

[19] *Conf.* 92, (Loeb, IV, 61), tr. Colson and Whitaker. The continuation of the passage is cited below, p. 168. Also see p. 177 f.

[20] See especially *Conf.* 146. These traditions would seem to parallel those about a divine messenger whose name is Jacob or Israel. See p. 199 f. and J. Smith in *Religions in Antiquity.*

the brickmakers, but in their thoughts ascend to the heavenly height, setting before them Moses, the nature beloved of God, to lead the way. For *then they shall behold the place*, which, in fact, is the *logos, where God stands*, the never changing, never swerving and also what lies under His feet like "the work of a brick of sapphire, like the form of the firmament of the heaven" (Ex. 24 : 10) even the world of our senses, which he indicates in the mystery. [21]

The story serves a further purpose in his argument: to demonstrate that Moses, the true servant of God, can have a mystical vision of God. Philo has used Moses' vision as a paradigm for the mystical vision available to the true believer. According to the LXX translation of **Ex. 24:10 f. Moses** and the elders saw not God, as in Hebrew, but only *"the place where God stands."* LXX has balked at translating a phrase which implies that a man can see God. Instead it substituted the circumlocution "place where God stands." As we have seen, Philo's understanding of the word "place" is *logos*. Therefore, the mystic, here Moses, does not see God himself, but the *logos*, "the place where God stands," who is manifested in the narration at Ex. 24:10 f. as a human figure astride the world. [22]

Philo then takes up the theme of the impossibility of conceiving of God himself. He cautions us not to take the description of the human form literally. "God is not a man" (Nu. 23:19). The form of a man is produced in order to illustrate the concept of *logos*, which otherwise might be unfathomable. But this argument is already familiar from *On Dreams*. The theme of the heavenly figure produced at Ex. 24 here and at *On Dreams* has to do with the "second God." Furthermore, the whole structure of the argument is strikingly parallel in Philonic and rabbinic exegesis. Both traditions posit a contradiction between the vision of God in Ex. 24:10 and other statements about God in scripture. In the rabbinic case, the contradiction is between Ex. 15:3 and Ex. 24:10 f., which is solved by the use of Ex. 20:2. In Philo's case, the contradiction is resolved by use of the *logos* doctrine, followed by the use of contrasting passages Nu. 23:19 and Dt. 8:5 instead of Ex. 15:3. That Philo never used Ex. 15:3 for the same purpose as the rabbis is only an apparent difficulty which can be easily explained by the LXX translation. The LXX toned down the striking anthropo-

---

[21] *Conf.* 95, (Loeb, IV, p. 61, tr. Colson and Whitaker).

[22] This translation is based on the necessary emendation of *delos* to *de logos*, as suggested by Colson (Loeb, IV, 60, n. 2). The simple alteration of the garbled phrase makes clear the identification of *place* and *logos*. Otherwise it comes in too abruptly in section 97.

morphism of the original Hebrew by rendering it "The Lord, bringing wars to nought, the Lord is His name." In the process it made the verse inappropriate for the point that Philo wanted to make, forcing him to rely on other striking statements of God's human form. Philo and the rabbis, then, are relying on the same tradition, but they work with slightly different verses and have different opinions of the helping figure. 23

The *logos* can be present in Philo's exegesis because, both in Gen. 31:13 and in Ex. 24:10 f., the LXX translated the Hebrew with a circumlocution involving the word "place." The usual understanding is that the LXX borrowed language from several biblical citations equating place with the divine. For instance, in Ex. 33:21 God tells Moses to stand in "a place" near Him to see His glory. In Gen. 28:11 Abraham comes to "a place" where he meets an angel. Thus, at the very least, the entire angelic theophany in Exodus (and maybe those in Genesis as well) was seen as a close unit as early as LXX translation in the second century B.C.E.

Philo shared and developed this perspective in striking ways. Philo wants the *logos*, the goal of the mystical vision of God, to serve as a simple explanation for all the angelic and human manifestations of the divine in the Old Testament. 24 Thus Philo hints that, at the burning bush, Moses saw the image of Being, but elsewhere calls it an angel as the scripture requires. 25 Whatever is implied about the status of the tradition at the time of the LXX translation, this angelic manifestation of God is so consistent a character in the biblical drama for Philo that he blithely applies the description of the angel Moses saw to the angel that appeared to Abraham. Again the link is made on the basis of *place*. (Gen. 28:11):

> For as long as he falls short of perfection, he has the Divine Word as his leader, since there is an oracle which says, "Lo I send my messenger before thy face to guard thee in thy way, that he may bring you into the land which I have prepared for thee; give heed

23 See Marmorstein, *Essays in Anthropomorphism*, p. 8 f. The rabbis use Hosea 11:9 against anthropomorphism. There is evidence that the rabbis occasionally associated the word "man" with God, in e.g., Dan. 8:16, Ez. 1:26, Ecc. 2:21. See Gen. R. 27 (T-A, p. 255) Ecc. R. on 2:26, Tanh. Buber i, p. 24. See Marmorstein, *op. cit.*, p. 123 and *ORDOG*, p. 64-65.

24 For the identification of logos and angel, see *Leg. All.* iii 177, *Conf.* 28, *Quis Her.* 205, *Som.* i, 239, *Cher.* 3, 35, *Mut.* 87, *Mig.* 173, *Post.* 91, *Som.* i, 115.

25 *Mos.* i, 66.

to him and hearken to him, disobey him not; for he will by no means
withdraw from you. For My name is in him." (Ex. 23 : 20 f.) [26]

The *logos*, a necessary part of Philo's ontology, is, as "place,"
generally and completely equated with the angel mentioned throughout
Genesis and Exodus. It seems likely that the tradition of a single angelic
messenger can be traced to the LXX itself but it is well developed by
Philo. Furthermore, this angel is a creature who carries "the name of
God", as scripture says (Ex. 23:21). This is the same scripture which
the rabbis found so easily misinterpreted. But not only can Philo refer
to YHWH as the *logos*, he can also interpret other occurrences of
YHWH in scripture to indicate the presence of an angel, not God.
For instance, the Lord (YHWH) standing on top of Jacob's ladder
(Gen. 28:13) is identified as the archangel, the *logos*. [27] Such ideas
are facilitated by (and, in fact, probably mean to explain) a certain
amount of confusion in the biblical narratives as to whether God himself
or an angel appears. [28]

It should be clear by now that the passages which Philo uses to
discuss the *logos* as agent of God are used by the opponents of the
rabbis to discuss God's principal angel. These traditions are similar
to the ones we found later among the merkabah mystics. They discuss
God's angel, Metatron, whose name contains the divine name, YHWH,
(as does Philo's *logos*), and who may have been called Yahoel or
YHWH HQTWN in other traditions.

Now there is a further aspect of Philo's exegesis of Ex. 24:10 f.
and Ex. 23:21 in the LXX that deserves mention. Philo carefully notes
the presence of the word "stands" in the Greek phrase "place where
God stands." The same phrase has been appropriated by the Greek
translator of the LXX at Ex. 24:10 on the basis of its appearance at

---

[26] *Mig.* 174, See also *Som.* i, 115 based on the scriptural citation where Abraham
meets a "place." (Gen. 28:11).

[27] *Mut.* 126, *Mig.* 168, *Som.* i, 57, *Leg. All.* iii, 177, *Mut.* 87, *Quis Her.* 205
and often, in fact, Philo is able to link the two Hebrew words for God, *Elohim* and
YHWH, which he knew by their Greek equivalents *theos* and *kyrios*, with the
Existent One and His *logos* respectively. This is certainly not the only meaning which
he chooses to draw out of the names of God. Other ideas, like linking mercy and
justice with the divine names, which is parallel to rabbinic thought (see p. 38 f.)
will also be relevant to us. But such exegesis is always available to him in analyzing
the Old Testament.

[28] Such confusion is usually explained by modern exegetes as due to differences
between J and E sources of the Bible. Confusion between the angel of YHWH and
God himself can be seen in Gen. 16:7 f., 21:17 f., 22:11, 31:11 f.; Ex. 3:2 f., Ju. 2:1 f.
as well as Ex. 23:21 f. which the rabbis discuss.

Ex. 23:21. Philo takes special notice of it, by stating that "standing" or "establishment" is a particularly important part of the tradition about Moses' theophany. Applied to God, "standing" is an indication of God's immutability. Furthermore, this quality is so superabundantly present in God that Moses was able to share it and become, in a way, divine:

> And Moses too gives his testimony to the unchangeability of the deity when he says: "They saw the place where the God of Israel stood." (Ex. 24 : 10) for by the standing or establishment he indicated His immutability. But indeed so vast in its excess is the stability of the deity that He imparts to chosen natures a share of His steadfastness to be their richest possession. For instance, he says of His convenant filled with His bounties, the highest law and principle, that is, which rules existent things, that this God image shall be firmly planted with just souls on its pedestals. [29]

Nor is the idea of a heavenly journey merely touched on in Philo's thinking. Rather, it forms a major theme of Philo and can be seen in the quotation above from *The Migration of Abraham*. [30] Abraham is allegorized as "he who follows God (173)." Of course, for that journey to God, he has God's principal angel as guide. Elsewhere Abraham is said to have drawn near to God, "the Standing One," by virtue of Gen. 18:22 f.: "He was standing before the Lord and he drew near and said..." Moses, however, is the clearest example of the man worthy of standing with God: "But as for thee, stand thou here by Me." (Dt. 5:31). [31] There can be no doubt that Philo meant to say that rare men of uncommon abilities can share in God's immutability by being summoned into or guided into His presence by means of the *logos*. The *logos*, ambiguously, is also the form of God, which can be seen by the mystic.

Therefore, the phrase "place where God stands" is definitely meant by Philo to imply a divine nature which not only angels and the *logos* but also men of perspicacity can share, if they journey to God with the *logos* as guide. Within Philo's works there is evidence that Abraham, Isaac, Jacob, Israel, and Aaron, Levi and Melchizedek all share some prerogatives of God as exemplars of perfection. [32] Although the doc-

---

[29] *Som.* ii, 222-3. (Loeb V, p. 543, tr. Colson and Whitaker).

[30] See above, p. 170.

[31] *Post.* 28-31. For Moses, as divine mediator, see W. A. Meeks, *The Prophet King*. Moses, is, e.g., said to be the eldest born of the *logos*. *Quest. in Ex.* ii, 44, *Quis her.* 205, cf., *Agr.* 51, *Som.* i, 215.

[32] For a detailed exposition of these "exemplars" see the dissertation of Lala

trine implies immortalization, it is distinctly unlike incarnation in direction. Instead of a god being made flesh, the man is being made divine. However, it is in form not unlike the doctrine of *apotheosis* or *apathanatismos* common to Greek heroes, present in the Greek magical papyri, reported about some of the mystery cults and analogous to Merkabah mysticism.

God's *logos* and the two ways to read scriptures are brought together for Philo at the story of Moses' exaltation in Ex. 24. *Questions and Answers to Exodus* may serve as an example of the intermingling of the motifs in Philo's thought. Philo identifies the angel of Ex. 23:21 with the *logos*, as we have seen before, and says he is sent before the face of man in order to lead him into philosophy, and hence to the presence of God (13). The purpose of the whole theophany is mystical ascent:

> What is the meaning of the words, "They appeared to God in the place and they ate and drank" (Ex. 24 : 11b)? Having attained to the face of the Father, they do not remain in any mortal place at all, for all such (places) are profane and polluted, but they send and make a migration to a holy and divine place which is called by another name, *logos*. Being in this place through the steward they see the master in a lofty and clear manner, envisioning God with the keen-sighted eyes of the mind... (39)

or again:

> Ex. 24 : 12a What is the meaning of the words, "Come up to Me to the mountain and be there? This signifies that a holy soul is divinized by ascending not to the air to the ether or to heaven (which is higher than all) but to a region above the heavens, and beyond the world where there is no place but God. And He determines the stability of the removal by saying "be there (thus demonstrating the placelessness and the unchanging habitation of the divine place ...)

The highest purpose of man is to perceive the face of God or the *logos*. In this way, one sees God in all His power. [33] This is the meaning of the Sinai theophany.

Such relationships suggest a kind of Hellenistic Judaism about which we have little knowledge. Philo attests to a series of traditions involving the divinity of a principal angelic figure who functions as the helper of God. In Philo, these traditions are related to the concept of the

---

K. K. Dey, *The Intermediary World and Patterns of Perfection in Philo and Hebrews*, SBL Dissertation Series 25, p. 65 f.

[33] Notice the ambiguity over whether a man may see God!

logos. But he has also hinted that these doctrines are sometimes held by people who are less wise in philosophy and who actually compromise monotheism, which is precisely the issue in the rabbinic community. Perhaps these more radical traditions were mystical or apocalyptic, for we have seen evidence that they involve a journey to God. Furthermore, this voyage confers a supernatural status upon the voyager on the pattern of the heavenly ascent of Moses described in Ex. 24.

The doctrine of the *logos* is relevant in two further ways to Philo's conception of creation. First, Philo maintains that the *logos* was God's partner in creation. [34] To this effect, he calls the *logos*, "The Beginning," "The Ruler of the Angels," and significantly, "the Name of God." [35] But because the *logos* is an emanation of God, Philo can also talk about him as God's offspring, or the first-born son of God. [36] As such, he is a kind of immortal, heavenly man or the true father of men. [37] For this reason, Philo seems to say in places that God actually put two men into Eden. [38] We remember, of course, that the rabbis opposed ideas that there was more than one Adam, that God had a partner in creation [39] or even that angels helped him. [40] They objected to the idea that there could be more than one Adam, on the grounds that men would begin to boast of their differing lineage, some claiming to have descended from a better man. Of course, most sectarian groups believed themselves better than the common variety of men. But Philo also claims that the virtuous had a better father in that they were descended from the higher Adam. [41] This provides us with a good example of a predecessor to the unstated argument which the tannaim would eventually call heresy, the same argument which was supplied by the amoraim. [42]

Another important aspect of the rabbinic tradition in the Mekhilta which is parallel to Philo has not yet been discussed. That is the doctrine of the mercy and justice of God, based on the interpretation of His divine names. In discussing the early tradition of the Mekhilta, I

---

[34] *Leg. All.* iii, 96; *Cher.* 125, *Mig.* 6, *Spec. Leg.* i, 81.

[35] *Conf.* 146.

[36] *Agr.* 51, *Quis Her., Som.* i, 215, *Conf.* 146.

[37] *Fug.* 72, *Det.* 83, *Quest. in Gen.* i, 4, *Conf.* 41, *Quis Her.* 23-1.

[38] *Leg. All.* i, 31, 53, 55.

[39] See p. 110 f., 117 f.

[40] See p. 137 f.

[41] *Leg. All.* 53. He also uses Cain-Seth typologies to more potent effect in *Post.* 35, 38 f., 42, 43, 45, 78. *Fug.* 64, *Det.* 32, 68, 103.

[42] See p. 110 f.

suggested that this doctrine of God's "two aspects" or "measures" was used by the rabbis to counter a doctrine of "two powers." A doctrine of God's aspects is present in Philo as well, and it is related to the mystical ascent we have noticed in his writings. In exploring Philo's exegesis of the names of God, we will be able to discover more detail about the mystical journey which the true seeker of God must follow.

Philo's alternative method of understanding God's names is also allegorical; they stand for judgment and mercy. For Plato, ideas have a characteristic called power (*dynamis*). Using scripture as a basis, Philo assumes the identification of "power" with "idea" and "form." According to Wolfson, the tradition developed in the following way. [43] In *Ex.* Moses had asked God to let him see His glory (M.T.: KBWD, LXX: *Doxa*). Now, in Ps. 24:9-10, the King of Glory is identified as the Lord of Hosts, which, in turn, was translated by LXX as "Lord of Powers" (*Kyrios tōn dynameōn*). [44] Therefore, Philo can assume that YHWH is equivalent both to the King of Glory and the Lord of Powers. On this basis Philo can understand Moses' request to see God's glory as a request to see His powers or ideas. Of course Philo develops all of his arguments in an exegetical framework, not a systematic one, as Wolfson implies. Alternatively Philo can discuss the *logos* as the sum of the forms, which can be manifested by the visible form of an angel. Philo, therefore, can risk contradiction by assuming that YHWH is Lord of Powers or the *logos*, depending on the needs of his allegory.

When discussing God's powers, Philo maintains they are infinite. But, for convenience, Philo allows them to be categorized into two different kinds. One category is described by the term "goodness" (*agathotēs*) and refers to God's creative power (*dynamis poietikē*) or merciful power (*dynamis eleōs*). [45] But this aspect of God can be identified with the Greek word for God, *theos*, which was the standard LXX translation of *Elohim*. [46] The other power is described by the term "authority" (*exousia*) or "sovereignty" (*archē*). It is often described as the governing or legislative or regal power—in short, those qualities which can be characterized as just. Alternatively, YHWH can

---

[43] Wolfson, *Philo*, I, 219.

[44] Other translations of YHWH ṢBᵓWT in the LXX are *kyrios Sabaoth* and *kyrios pantokrator*.

[45] *Cher.* 9, 27-28, *Fug.* 18, 95, 100, Wolfson, *Philo*, I, 223 f. and n.

[46] Although the formula *kyrios* = YHWH, *theos* = Elohim is standard, there are many places where the LXX translates the tetragrammaton as *theos*. In these places, Philo usually follows the Greek text. This may partially explain the dichotomy between the rabbinic and Philonic traditions.

be allegorized as the just, governing power even though that might contradict the exegesis elsewhere that the tetragrammaton signifies the *logos* or all the powers. [47]

Now, this summary of divine powers sounds suspicuously like the rabbinic doctrine of God's two attributes of mercy and justice, except that Philo's identification of mercy and justice with the names of God is exactly opposite to the standard rabbinic doctrine. YHWH is merciful for the rabbis; *kyrios*, judging for Philo. Conversely, *Elohim* is judging for the rabbis; *theos*, merciful for Philo. However, we have also seen that the Mekhilta passage, which does not actually use the technical terms developed in rabbinic writing, implies a doctrine of mercy and justice identical to the Philonic doctrine and contradictory to the standard rabbinic one. Therefore, the Mekhilta tradition must predate the standardized rabbinic doctrine. The Mekhilta, in reproducing arguments from heretics or in recording a rabbinic doctrine which preceded the official one, has given us an exegesis similar to the Philonic system.

From one point of view, divine powers are abstractions—like the *logos* only convenient ways of discussing vast capabilities of God. However, since their characteristics are fixed, Philo often describes them as living creatures. For instance, the two angels who guard the gates of paradise and the angels who enter Sodom are allegorized as the two powers of God. How these powers relate to the *logos* is ambiguous. Since the *logos* can also signify the sum of all the powers, it logically stands above the two powers in the ascent from concrete to abstract. Yet sometimes Philo uses *kyrios* and *theos* to refer to the two powers of God and other times to refer to the *logos* and the highest God, being-in-itself. Basically he uses whatever exegesis makes most sense in the allegorical context. He may also have received ancient *midrashim*, dictating the use of one tradition rather than another and explaining his similarity with the rabbis.

Not only are such doctrines reminiscent of the rabbinic doctrine, the exegesis of text is parallel. Philo sees Ex. 20:2 as the place where both the creative and ruling powers come together:

> So then He is shown to be the Lord of the foolish in that He holds over them the errors that are proper to a sovereign. Of those who are on the way to betterment he is called in scripture, God, as in the

---

[17] This only points out Philo's exegetical approach. Since his emphasis is exegetical, it seems likely that he is attesting to scriptural traditions which he shares with the rabbis.

present passage. "I am God" or "I am thy God, increase and mul-
tiply." (Gen. 35:11). Of the perfect He is both Lord and God, as
in the Decalogue, "I am the Lord thy God" (Ex. 20 : 2) and elsewhere, "The Lord God of our fathers" (Dt. 4 : 1) for it is His will
that the wicked man should be under His sway as his Lord, and
thus with awe and groaning feel the fear of the Master hanging
over him; that the man of progress should be benefitted by Him as
God. And through the one he remains free from lapses, through
the other he is most surely God's man. [48]

Philo uses Ex. 20:2 for the same reason that the rabbis did—to show
the unification of both God's attributes at the Sinai theophany. [49] This
similarity is especially striking when one notices that otherwise Philo
almost never comments on Ex. 20:2, preferring as a basis for his
exegesis the text of the Ten Commandments which occurs in Deuteronomy.

Several other scriptures seen as dangerous by the rabbis are applied
to the powers by Philo. Gen. 1:26, for instance, is used by Philo to
prove that the creative power is divine:

> Akin to these two is the creative power called God because through
> this the Father, who is its begetter and contriver, made the universe;
> so that "I am thy God" is equivalent to "I am thy maker and arti-
> ficer." And the greatest gift we can have is to have Him for our
> architect, who was also the architect of the whole world, for He did
> not form the soul of the bad, since wickedness is at enmity with Him,
> and in framing the soul which is in the intermediate stage He did not
> serve as the sole agent according to the holiest man, Moses, since
> such a soul would surely admit like wax, the different qualities of
> noble and base. And therefore we read "Let us make man after our
> image" (Gen. 1 : 26), so that according as the wax received the bad
> or the noble impress it should appear to be the handiwork of others
> or of Him who is the framer of the noble and the good alone. [50]

Here Philo flirts with ideas of providence opposed by the tannaim.
Notice too that Philo does not shrink from the idea that God's agents
are called gods themselves, nor from the idea that God had help in
creation—ideas which the rabbis later opposed. Nor is this the only

---

[48] *Mut. 23, 24* (Loeb, V, 155, tr. Colson and Whitaker.)

[49] The point of both questions, regardless of the qualities they identify with
each name of God, is that a mixture of God's qualities (*mixis*), not one quality
alone, was present at the creation or the giving of the law. Henry Fischel has
suggested that this concept parallels conventional Hellenistic philosophy. See Par-
menides (on Empedocles') opposites, Anger (or strife) and love: W. K. C. Guthrie,
A History of Greek Philosophy, II.

[50] *Mut. 29-31*, (V, 159, tr. Colson and Whitaker).

place where Philo uses such arguments. Such interpretations are common. Elsewhere Philo refers to other texts which were seen by the rabbis
to be dangerous because they could imply a plurality of deities: Gen.
11:7 ("Come let us go down to confuse their language"), Gen. 3:22
(Behold Adam has become as one of us"), and Gen. 1:26 are mentioned. [51] Philo maintains that one of God's two powers descends—
in one case, to create man; in another, to punish those building the
tower. He explains that these powers are angels and that their presence
has so impressed some people (even Moses) that they feel no shame
in calling them gods. In other words, Philo depends on his concept of
the powers of justice and mercy to explain scriptural plurals, calling
them both angels and divine. [52]

Therefore in *On the Change of Names*, Philo can offer another
interpretation of what the patriarchs saw when scripture says they saw
God. (6-7). First, he remarks that they saw the same creative power of
God which Moses saw on Sinai for the first time, having already been
privileged to see God's ruling power. We remember that he has
previously said that the elders saw the image of God or the *logos*.
Of course, the two interpretations are not entirely consistent. Yet here,
they are not entirely contradictory, for both the *logos* and the powers
represent summations of all God's emanations. Since Moses has already
known the lesser of God's powers, seeing the higher power as well can
be equivalent to seeing the *logos*, the sum of all the powers. Again we
note the same exegesis as the *Mekhilta* records in rabbinic lore a century
later. This time Philo provides a witness to the doctrine which the
rabbis defend, instead of the one they condemn.

At the beginning of *On the Change of Names*, Philo discusses
seeing God. First, he cautions against understanding "seeing" literally.
"Seeing" means "perceiving," not seeing with the senses. The passage
where Abram was granted a vision of YHWH (Gen. 17:1-5) before
his name was changed to Abraham forms the basis of Philo's discussion,
but he goes far afield in reflecting upon it. At first, Abram only saw
God's sovereign power (15-17). When scripture says that God said
to him "I am thy God" it signified that a vision of the higher, creative

---

[51] *Conf.* 33.

[52] The divine plurals in scriptures are, in fact, consistently understood either as
logos and God or as the two powers of God. See, e.g., Jervell, p. 58 f., Danielou,
p. 135 (for Is. 6) Kretschmar, p. 44. For instance, Gen. 11:5: Conf. 134-149. The
powers are seen to help in creation; *Op.* i, 72-75 (Gen. 1:26); *Fug.* 68, 70 (Dt. 4:7);
Praem. 81-84. For the powers at Sinai, see *QE* 44.

power was given to Abram. Philo again is depending on the distinction between the two names of God. The Existent One may appear in either of two ways to normal men—as Lord YHWH to the bad, when they are punished (hence as the lower-potency), or as "God" to the earnest striver. Only to the perfected can he appear as both "God and Lord" (18-19). Thus he is spoken of as "Lord" to Pharaoh, whom he punished, "God" to Moses (before his ultimate revelation) and "Lord God" to Israel, who in this context is the highest, most perfect believer. Jacob is renamed Israel signifying that he has seen the complete image of God, his *logos*. Only to the higher man, who can understand the allegory, does Got reveal himself as *theos*, the higher power, to whom man must respond with love. To those with lesser powers of intellect, who understand only the literal meaning, God reveals himself as a fearful, punishing deity, *kyrios*. They know no better than to perceive him as a man.

A word remains to be said about the nature of the relationship between Philo and rabbinic writings. The parallel has been clear enough. The question remaining is how the parallel came about. There are many possibilities. First it may be that the two writings are merely coincidentally parallel, that both Philo and the rabbis are interpreting the Bible and have only the text in common. This seems to me to be the least likely possibility because the parallels are exceptionally close; the parallels remain even when the LXX diverges from the MT Bible so the rabbis and Philo do not have a common text. The parallel themes are consistent interests of Philo, not merely the result of fortuitous exegesis. Philo occasionally seems to be aware of a Bible version closer to the Hebrew text than the LXX, implying that he either knew a little Hebrew or some exegetical traditions which were based on a biblical text closer to the Massoretic text than the received LXX. [53] Then too, Philo himself seems to recognize that Palestinian Bible traditions already exist. He uses the term "unwritten law" which may imply a Hebrew meaning of "Oral Law" as well as the Greek meaning. He also says at the beginning of his *Life of Moses* that he is retelling the story as he learned it—both from the sacred books, and from the

---

[53] The Hebrew text cannot often be felt underneath Philo's exegesis, but there are places where he appears to know of translations far closer to the Hebrew than the current LXX. See QG II, 51 on Gen. 8:2-9. Philo's exegesis of Gen. 6:5 in this place depends on the appearance of YHWH alone, but the LXX has *ho theos* and *kyrios ho theos*. In any event, Philo's knowledge of Hebrew is not definitive on the question of whether he knew ancient traditions of exegesis which the rabbis also knew.

elders of the nation, and interweaving the oral teachings with the results of his Bible reading. [54] The parallels between the rabbis and Philo are so complete in the case under consideration as to make it extremely likely that some relationship existed. Furthermore, almost no scholar disputes the conclusion that Philo and the rabbis evince common traditions.

The question of the nature of the influence is much more interesting and difficult. Philo is aware of Jewish "elders," which may be a reference to the technical sense of the word in Palestine. On the other hand, the rabbis never seem to be aware of Philo himself, so any channel of transmission is likely to be indirect. Therefore the various possibilities seem to be: (1) The traditions come from a common source. (2) The traditions have been borrowed from Palestine by Philo or other Alexandrian Jews. (3) Some may have been borrowed by Palestinian Jews from Hellenistic Judaism through various channels of communication. Now these are not mutually exclusive categories, for even the common source implies borrowing in one direction or another. We are not likely to find conclusive evidence for distinguishing between categories with respect to the traditions under consideration. But, since the exegeses under consideration are extremely complex and remarkably parallel, it seems likely that there was a basic tradition common to both Philo and the rabbis which was used in individual ways. This suggests that different issues motivated the exegesis in first century Alexandria and second century Palestine. Philo was interested in showing that the Bible portrayed a God sophisticated enough to make sense in a Greek intellectual climate. Anthropomorphism and God's immutability were his main problems. He needed a way to portray God as immutable yet available to man in the material world so he stressed the traditions of intermediation. The rabbis, on the other hand, were interested in uniting Judaism and preventing extreme applications of the same traditions which had appealed to Philo. There are many explanations for the difference, but it seems to me that it is a mistake to stress differences between Hellenistic and Palestinian Judaism too strongly in this regard. The rabbis were certainly aware of the issue which gripped Hellenistic Jews and showed their sensitivities in most respects. Philo shows sensitivities parallel to the rabbis. There is much more overlap than is usually assumed. Rather, the differences seem

---

[54] See Wolfson, *Philo*, I, 88 f., 190 f., for a more complete discussion of the problem.

to be explainable partially in terms of the epochal events that took place in the Jewish community in the century separating Philo's writings from the first demonstrable rabbinic texts. It is largely to that interval that we must soon turn in an attempt to reconstruct the traditions of God's appearance in the non-rabbinic communities of the first century.

But Philo's arguments will give us a good inkling of the kinds of traditions which must have been current in the Hellenistic Jewish communities of the first century. These traditions set the stage for the rabbinic opposition which we can date with surety only to the early second century but have suspected to have been earlier still. The rabbis too must have known of two different types of traditions about divine providence. In the first, a principal angel was seen as God's primary or sole helper and allowed to share in God's divinity. That a human being, as the hero or exemplar of a particular group, could ascend to become one with this figure—as Enoch, Moses or Elijah had—seems also to have been part of the tradition. In a second tradition, the qualities of divine mercy and justice were hypostasized attributes of the names of God and described the stages on the journey to God. The rabbis opposed the first tradition, with its divine helper and divinization of some earthly heroes. In trying to combat the first they stressed the second set of traditions emphatically. Rather than mention the divine helper at all, they fought against it with the alternative doctrines of God's mercy and justice.

The fact that Philo's doctrine of God's mercy and justice is linked with divine names in just the opposite way to the rabbis is significant. The traditional explanation that Philo did not know Hebrew, and hence confused the midrashic tradition, does injustice to the careful exegesis we know was characteristic of him. Neither is it likely that the rabbis would deliberately change a tradition that had come down to them. Rather, we must remember that the purpose of both traditions was to stress the mixture of justice and mercy in God's governance of the world. Probably the actual identification of divine names was not at first important. It became important within the rabbinic tradition when the rabbis saw that the divine name YHWH was being used to define a second divine creature or angel.

In the second century the sectarians probably continued to use the Philonic identification of divine names with attributes. The rabbis, however, in opposing dualistic views of intermediation, called all such ideas heretical. They wanted to make sure that YHWH, the God of the Jews, was not equated merely with a demiurge. They therefore argued that YHWH should be understood as the merciful aspect of God's providence.

Philo viewed scripture through heavy philosophical lenses. It is difficult from his writings alone to characterize the traditions outside of philosophical discourse and in their developing heretical setting. To describe these traditions adequately we have to survey the inter-testimental and particularly the apocalyptic literature.

CHAPTER TWELVE

JEWISH SECTARIAN TEXTS

A. *Apocalypticism and Mysticism*

Philo understood the descriptions of the "angel of YHWH" in
scripture, together with other passages which the rabbis found dangerous, as references to the *logos* or one of the two principal powers of
God. Based on the Philonic evidence, we should expect traditions
about mediators and principal angels to appear in other writings
contemporary with Philo. The expectation can be confirmed. However,
the variety of conceptions about mediators and principal angels in
intertestamental documents can only be summarized with difficulty,
for the characteristics and names of the mediator differ widely in each
document, suggesting that no single consistent myth underlies the
whole.

In such a dense forest we must rely both on logic and on significant
details gleaned from the rabbinic texts in order to identify those
figures which are likely candidates for the rabbinic charge. Certainly
not all the figures related to the scriptures under consideration can
be automatically included in the heresy. For instance, we have already
seen that many angels and mediators appear in rabbinic literature where
they add color to midrashic stories but where they could not be considered heretical. In order for us to be sure that a mediator was part
of the heresy of "two powers" we would have to find the kind of
scriptural traditions characteristic of the heresy in the rabbinic polemic
and we would have to have both some indication of its independent
existence from God and its divine perquisites.

To start with, these general considerations help us remove some
obvious phenomena from consideration as heresy. *Memra, yekara* and
shekhinah are used in the targumim and midrash in reference to the
dangerous passages to denote the presence of God. But they are never
clearly defined as independent creatures. [1] It rather appears that rabbinic

---

[1] See Moore, *Judaism*, I, 414 f., also "Intermediaries in Jewish Theology" *HTR*,
I, 15 (1922), 41-61 and Strack-Billerbeck, II, (on John 1), 302-333. The opposite
perspective may be found in G. H. Box, "The Idea of Intermediation in Jewish

concepts of *memra, shekhina, yekara* avoid the implications of independent divinity and possibly are meant to combat them. We also know that Philo even saw "the Word" or *logos* as an angel. But there is nothing inherently heretical about such descriptions. It may be anachronistic to apply second century rabbinic categories of heresy to earlier phenomena. The best we can say is that ideas like this might have been seen as heretical in some contexts. More importantly they certainly formed the background out of which heresy arose.

Of course, from the survey of rabbinic documents and Philo, we know that the judgment that a particular conception of mediation violated the canons of monotheism was also partly a matter of individual opinion. Philo could even use the phrase "second God" to describe the *logos* without thinking that he had violated the monotheistic basis of his religion. Because of these perspectival factors, the scriptural passages which we found characteristic of the rabbinic polemic should become especially important in defining the heresy in the apocalyptic communities.

Clearly some of the same issues which Philo discussed were important in first century Palestine as well. Josephus, like Philo, denies that God had any help in creation. [2] After having reviewed the rabbinic traditions we know that God's independence at creation was an issue in the heresy. We can now be sure, from Philo and Josephus, that the issue itself dates back to the first century.

Two further considerations must be addressed. We must, first, discover traditions which deal with the same verses; and, second, we must give attention to the likelihood that heresy was involved. This will be an especially subtle question since even Philo, who was not adverse to the designation "second God" and who describes the *logos* as God's agent manifestation in creation, denies that God had help from assistants in creating.

Let us begin by summarizing the previous findings about scriptural traditions. The dangerous passages include (1) Dan. 7:9 f. and the

---

Theology: A Note on *Memra* and *Shekinah*," *JQR*, 23 (1932-33), 103-119. The history of the argument is summed up by A. M. Goldberg, *Untersuchungen über die Vorstellung von der Schekhinah in der frühen rabbinischen Literatur*, 1-12.

[2] See *Against Apion*, II, 192, where Josephus describes the creation of the natural world. He says: "These God created, not with hands, not with toil, not with assistants (*synergasomenōn*) of whom He had no need." This may profitably be compared with Philo, (*Op.* 72) who uses the same word, *synergasomenos*, as well as the more technical *demiourgos* in excluding unwanted implications from the plural used by God in Gen. 1:26, namely, that God needed any help in creation. The same issue is reflected in rabbinic discussions of ŠWTP. See p. 112, 137, 141.

speculation about the identity of the "son of man," (2) the Ex. 24 theophany, possibly together with other passages in the Bible where God is pictured in the form of a man (3) the related descriptions of the angel of YHWH who carries the divine name [3] (4) scriptural verses which describe God as plural (Gen. 1:26). Of course, the study of these traditions in apocalyptic literature cannot be exhaustive. Hopefully it can be representative of the developments peculiar to apocalyptic.

It is worthwhile to point out that many of these dangerous exegetical traditions may never have been entirely separate at any point in their development. Biblical scholars have recently noticed the relationship between all works describing the divine warrior figure (including both Ex. 15 and Dan. 7) and ancient Near Eastern mythology. [4]

Based on this kind of evidence, it seems likely that the human appearance of the divine mediator was a most important part of the tradition. As Philo has shown us, these ideas can be related to the notion of the image and likeness of God and the problem of anthropomorphism in scripture. The scriptural basis for such discussions in Philo is not only the theophany passages in the Old Testament but also Gen. 1:26 f. which describes the creation of man in the image and likeness of God. The motifs of likeness and image, as well as the identity of the heavenly man, have been studied by several scholars. [5] In the LXX *eikōn* is used for ṢLM (image) and *homoiōsis* is used for DMWT (likeness). The latter, strictly speaking, means "likeness" only in the sense of similarity, not in the sense of an explicit image. However, there are several aspects of its biblical usage which have

---

[3] This might also include the passages in scripture where YHWH and an angel are confused, e.g., Gen. 16:7 f., 21:17 f., 22:11, 31:11 f., Ex. 3:2 f., Ju. 2:1 f., as well as Ex. 23:21 f., though the rabbis themselves do not discuss most of these particular pericopes.

[4] See F. M. Cross, "The Divine Warrior in Israel's Early Cult," in *Biblical Motifs: Origins and Transformations*, ed., Alexander Altman (Cambridge: 1966), pp. 11-30. See also Patrick D. Miller, *The Divine Warrior in Early Israel* (Cambridge: 1973).

[5] See *TDNT*, *eikōn* (Kittel), *homoios* and cognates (Schneider). Also J. Jervell, *Imago Dei* (Göttingen: 1960) and a critique by M. Smith, "On the Shape of God and the Humanity of the Gentiles," *Religion in Antiquity*. R. Mc. L. Wilson, "The Early History of the Exegesis of Gen. 1:26," *Studia Patristica*, 1 (1957), 420-37. F. W. Eltestes, *Eikōn im Neuen Testament* (Berlin: 1958) Harald Hegermann, *Die Vorstellung vom Schöpfungsmittler im hellenistischen Judentum und Urchristentum* (Berlin: 1961); H. M. Schenke, *Der Gott "Mensch" in der Gnosis* (Göttingen: 1962); H. F. Weiss, *Untersuchungen zur Kosmologie des hellenistischen und palästinischen Judentums* (Berlin: 1966). See also Jarl Fossum, dissertation, Utrecht, for a very helpful summary of the Adam traditions.

accounted for a further extension in meaning. For one thing, the Greek word *homoiōsis* appears in other places where heavenly creatures with human characteristics are described. For instance, it appears in Ez. 1:10 with reference to the figure on the heavenly throne who has the likeness of man. It also appears in reference to Dan. 10:16 where it describes the angel Michael who appears like "one who belongs to the sons of men." Thus Gen. 1:26 in Greek can be connected with the throne vision in Ezekiel, "the son of man," and the vision of an angel in Daniel by means of the likeness that Adam (before the fall) and various angelic creatures shared with God. However, one cannot say that these exegetical traditions or the groups which speculated on them were invariably heretical. As in the other cases, we have to look at the context. Some Adam speculation and considerable discussion of Gen. 1:26 and Dan. 7:13 f. occurs in rabbinic writing. As we have seen, [6] the rabbis are willing to posit androgeny of the original Adam and describe the original Adam as having an immense size, which was later reduced on account of his sin. This tradition is probably related to the teaching of several Alexandrian church fathers that *eikōn* is common to all men, but that *homoiōsis* is something for which man was created and after which he should strive. In fact, traditions relating to all the words for "likeness" should be carefully investigated for relationship to sectarian or heretical practices. These would include the terms *homoiōma, paradeigma, typos, rythmos, doxa*, and *morphē* which translate variously ṢLM, DMWT, TBNYT, and KBWD.

We know that the *logos* as well was assumed to be a human figure generally in Hellenistic Judaism. In the *Wisdom of Solomon* 18:15, for instance, the *logos* or Word is a stern warrior who leaps from the throne of God on command. Though the description certainly parallels the description of the human figure who is a "mighty man of war" in Ex. 15, there is no evidence that this is the specific tradition to which the rabbis objected. In this case the scriptural pericope under consideration is the account of the death of the first-born of Egypt in Ex. 12. Occasional clues like this make it probable that traditions of God's primary warrior manifestation are even more widespread than the rabbinic evidence would have us believe.

Another divine creature with human form is Wisdom or Sophia, which is hypostasized as early as Proverbs 8 and 9:1 f. and extensively developed in the apocrypha (Ben Sira 24, W. Sol. 10) and Pseudepi-

---

[6] See p. 114.

grapha (1 Enoch 42). Within the rabbinic community Wisdom is identified with Torah; but wisdom themes sometimes form part of heretical discourse. Sophia is a major figure in gnostic myths, for instance. Obviously then, it is not the tradition itself which defines the heresy but the treatment of the angelic figure or hypostasis as an independent deity. We have no evidence that the early heresy involved a feminine manifestation of God.

We know from the rabbinic texts that some of the beliefs which the rabbis opposed explicitly involved an angel whose function was to guide the believer and who carries, contains, or possesses the divine name (Ex. 23:21 f.). Again, not every belief of this sort will be heretical. But as a preliminary field for inquiry in the intertestamental period, it is reasonable to look among the variety of angelic mediators for some evidence of the kind of beliefs which the rabbis called "two powers" heresy. The idea of a separate hypostasis of the divinity must be functionally equivalent to being an angelic presence. [7]

Because of the complexity of the phenomenon, only the broadest outlines can be suggested. Nor will it always be possible to define a sectarian belief as heresy. Actually, the entire subject of the principal angelic creature demands more systematic investigation than it has hitherto received, and that is a task which cannot be satisfactorily handled within the confines of this work. [8] In the lack of any previously

---

[7] It should be noted that the idea of angel is wider than one might ordinarily think. "Angel" means messenger, therefore prophets (2 Chron. 36:15-16; Is. 44:26; Haggai 1:12-13; cf. Justin Dial 75, including John the Baptist Mt. 11:10; Mk. 1:2; Lk. 7:27) or priests (Malachi 2:7) or kings (2 Sam. 14:17, 20; 19:27; Zech. 12:8) or even the patriarchs (Prayer of Joseph, see below) or Moses as well as the leaders of the people, in their intercessory role, could be referred to as ML³K or *angelos*. We shall see that all of these traditions were used to promote celestial functions for worthies of the past. In the intertestamental age, immortality (or resurrection) could be promised to the righteous in the form of ascent to angelhood. To the righteous is promised: "You shall shine as the lights of heaven... and the portal of heaven shall be opened to you... You shall have great joy as angels of heaven... You shall become companions of the hosts of heaven" (I Enoch 104:2, 4, 6; cf. 39:6-7; Dan. 12:3; Mt. 13:43, 22:30). Therefore, almost any righteous person in the past could be called an angel. Especially righteous men were singled out as paradigms of angelhood. Christianity, as we will see, will appropriate these traditions while denying that the Christ is merely an angel.

[8] See, for instance, the study of W. Lueken, *Michael* (Göttingen: 1898). On the subject of angelologies in general see Kittel, *"angelos"* TDNT; D. S. Russell, *The Method and Message of Jewish Apocalyptic* (Philadelphia: 1964); Moore, *Judaism*, I, 403-413; Michaelis, *Zur Engelschristologie im Urchristentum*; M. Werner, *The Formation of the Christian Dogma* (London: 1957); E. Kaesemann, *Das wandernde Gottesvolk im Hebräerbrief* (Göttingen: 1959); N. Johansson, *Parakletoi* (Lund: 1940); O. Betz, *Der Paraklet* (Leiden: 1963); Joseph Barbel, *Christos Angelos*

completed, disinterested investigation, the discussion here can only be tentative. But it is possible to show that both inside and outside of the rabbinic community, the existence of a principal angelic creature did not seem to be at issue; rather, it was the identity, title and function of the second figure that occupied apocalyptic and mystical Jews' imagination. Among that figure's characteristics we should be especially interested in any that would have impressed the rabbis as compromising monotheism.

A staggering variety of angelic mediators developed during this period. As early as the book of Daniel, angels were identified by name, implying a certain consistency of characterization. Gabriel and Michael, the two named in Daniel (6:21, 8:16, 10:13, 21; 12:1) have the shapes of men and continue to be the most popular of angels, but other angels are also frequent. Of course, Gabriel and Michael are often seen as but two of the several archangels. Yet, whenever a configuration of archangels appears, one or another (often Michael or Gabriel, sometimes Uriel) is designated as the principal angel (often called "Angel of the Presence") or regarded as superior to the others. [9]

A number of common functions of angelic mediators may be summarized from various appearances in literature. Israel's heavenly protagonist and guardian can be spoken of as a principal or archangel. [10] A principal angel often presides over judgment. As an archangel, he may be described as a choirmaster [11] or heavenly scribe [12] or the recorder of the merits of Israel or even the leader of souls (*psychopompos*)

(Bonn: 1941); N. A. Dahl, "Christology Notes," p. 86 f. See especially Gunther, *St. Paul's Opponents*, pp. 172-298; Hengel, *The Son of God*.

[9] Gregory Dix, "The Seven Archangels and the Seven Spirits," *JTS*, 28 (1926), 233-285. In the Old Testament there are ambiguous references to archangels. The Hebrew Bible mentions the prince of the army of YHWH in Jos. 5:14, which the LXX translates as the *archistratēgos dunameōs kuriou*. In Dan. 10:13, 12:1, Michael is one of the *archōns* or the great angels. The first mention of seven special angels is Ez. 9:22 f. See further in Tob. 12:15, Est. 1:8; Gr. En. 20; Tg. J. Gen. 11:7; Rev. 8:2 (cf. also 1:4, 20; 3:1, 4:5, 5:6). Six are mentioned in I En. 20, Tg. Jl Dt. 34:6, and four in I En. 9:1 ff., Sib. 2:215; Pes. R. 46. See Strack-Billerbeck III, 806. The term archangel also occurs in the Prayer of Joseph (Origen, Com. on. *Joh*. II, 25 f.), Gr. En. 20:8, 4 Ezra 4:36 and Philo, who uses it to describe the *logos*, as we have seen (*Conf*. 146, *Quis Her*. 205). See also Iamblichos (*Myst*., 2, 3 p. 70, 10 Parthey) and the Magic Papyri (Preis., *PGM*: IV, 1203; VII, 257; XIII, 744, 929, 973). See Kittel, "*archangelos*," *TDNT*, I, 87. See also H. L. Ginsberg, "Michael and Gabriel," *EJ*.

[10] See Michael in Dan. 10:13, 21; 12:1; Jub. 35:12; I Enoch 20:5; IQ M 17:7 f.

[11] Apoc. Abr. 10, *et passim*.

[12] I En. 89:61 f., 90:14 f.

on visionary ascent, parallel to the ascent at the end of life. [13] Several functions of the angels may be served by men, if they are privileged to assume an exalted, triumphant or immortal form (like Enoch). In apocalyptic writings Enoch, Elijah, and Moses are frequently described as men of God, who are transported to heaven. [14] Enoch traditions were especially elaborate (cf., already Sir. 44:16, 49:14; Wis. 4:10-15; Jub. 4:16-25). In the Enochian cycle Enoch himself is transformed into an angelic being. In III Enoch he is identified with the angel Metatron. But apocalyptic traditions about the translation and enthronement of Levi and Moses also exist, [15] and often involved the principal angel as guide.

It should be noted that the *pneuma* or spirit of the righteous was characteristically thought to take on angelic form upon his death. (See Dan. 12:3; Mt. 13:43; 22:30; I Enoch 104:2, 4, 6 cf. 39:6-7). Therefore principal angels or notables served as role models for the righteous, as well as their guides. In this way, we can speak of an equivalent function for the principal angels and their patriarchal initiates—revealing both wisdom and the mystery of immortality. [16] It is this kind of tradition which best explains the astral journeys reported of the ancient rabbis in the Merkabah texts. It also explains the frequent use of Hebrew angelic names in the magical papyri.

While God is sometimes viewed as using the *yekara*, spirit, word, *memra* or *logos* at creation, early evidence concerning an angel helping God at creation is quite complicated. In late texts, the angelic stature of the agent of God active at creation is not central. We have already noted a number of later Christian traditions in which "the beginning" or "wisdom" helped God in creation. [17] However, there are few clear

---

[13] I En. 71:3; II En. 22; Apoc. Abr. 12 ff.; *Life of Adam* 25:20, 47; Apoc. Mos. 37, Testament Abr. throughout.

[14] See p. 172 f. for Philo. Moses is even called an archangel and eldest *logos*. *Quis Her.* 205; cf., *Agr.* 51; *Som.* i, 215.

[15] For Levi, see *Test. Levi* 2-5, 8. For Moses see Meeks, *The Prophet King*.

[16] See E. R. Goodenough, *Jewish Symbols*, VIII, pp. 121-218 also Ignazio Mancini, *Archaeological Discoveries* relative to the Judaeo-Christians, tr. G. Bushnell (Jerusalem: 1970), Bellarmino Bagatti, *L'Église de la Circoncision*, tr. Storme, (Jerusalem: 1965), p. 113 and compare their archaeological evidence of mystical journey through the cosmic ladder or seven heavens on tomb-stones etc. with the literary evidence in T. Levi 2:2-7, 3 Baruch 2:2, 3:1, 10:1, 11:1-4, Jubilees 32:20-22, T. Isaac (Coptic 67, 70; Arabic 146-47, 148) T. Jacob (Coptic, 83, cf. 82 and Arabic 153), I Enoch 40:2-10, 69 f., T. Abr. 10 f., Apoc. Abr. 12 f. and *Sefer Raziel*, beginning. See Gunther, *St. Paul's Opponents*, pp. 172-298.

[17] See p. 74 f., 83 f., p. 129 f.; See also below, p. 226. See also Gen. R. 1:1.

statements that a principal angel was God's helper in creation. [18] Philo might provide some evidence for identification of the angel with a divine helper in creation because angels can be allegorized as the *logos*. [19]

Adam traditions are especially important in this regard. We have already seen that Philo identifies the heavenly man with the *logos*, which is identified with God's archangel and principal helper in creation. There is an extraordinary amount of Adam speculation in apocalyptic and pseudepigraphical writings, often including descriptions of Adam's heavenly enthronement and glorification. The traditions can be dated to the first century, if an early dating of enthronement of Adam in the Testament of Abraham ch. 11 can be maintained. Adam legends are certainly well ramified later in Jewish, Christian, gnostic, Mandaean and other documents, and even appear at several important junctures in the ascent texts of the magical papyri. [20] As we have already seen, the rabbis themselves record legends about Adam even though they find some of this speculation dangerous, warning specifically against considering Adam God's partner. [21]

Angelic mediation in the giving of the Law is easy to find. It can be seen in Jubilees (Jub. 1:27-3:7) as well as in the New Testament (Gal. 3:19, Acts 7:38, 53, Heb. 2:2). We know that such a doctrine is explicitly criticized by the rabbis, but without special reference to "two powers" heresy.

----

[18] Some relationship between God's principal angel and His agent at creation may be possible in traditions about the angel Adoil in II Enoch 25:1 f.

[19] *Logos* is identified with an angel in *Leg. All*, iii 177; *Conf.* 28; *Quis Her.* 205; *Som.* i, 239; *Cher.* 3, and often but the identification is not stressed when discussing the creation. Rather Philo concentrates on the relationship between the *logos*, the *anthropos* and *hiereus*: *Agr.* 51; *Quis Her.* 119, *Som.* i, 215; *Conf.* 146, see also *Fug.* 72, *Det.* 83, *QG i*, 4, *Conf.* 41, *Quis Her.* 230-31. See also *QG.*, 92, *Conf.* 62, 63 where all the themes converge.

[20] See E. Peterson, "La libération d'Adam de l'*anagke*," *RB*, 1948 and the revised edition, "Die Befreiung Adams aus der *Anagke*," in *Frükirche, Judentums und Gnosis*, (Vienna: 1959). Also, see *PGM*, III, 146 f. where the magician announces that he is Adam, the original father and calls upon the Gods Iaō, Adōnai, Michael, Souriel, Raphael, and Abraxas. In III.211 f. the prayer to Apollo contains similar angelic names while the magician calls Adōnai, "Lord of the world."

[21] For a fuller bibliography and documentary citations see Reitzenstein, *Poimandres* (Leipzig: 1904); W. Bousset, *Hauptprobleme der Gnosis* (reprint Göttingen: 1973); A. Altmann, "The Gnostic Background of the Rabbinic Adam Legends," *JQR*, 1945; G. Quispel, "Der gnostische Anthropos und die jüdische Tradition," *Eranos Jahrbuch*, 22 (1954); for helpful summaries of the primary source material see J. Fossum, dissertation Utrecht and Tardieu, *3 Mythes Gnostiques*, p. 85-139; see above, notes 5 and 8 for further bibliography.

The relationship of the principal angel to the messiah is more problematic. The messiah is essentially an earthly figure. In the Gospel of John, the heavenly *logos* and the earthly messiah are clearly identified for the first time. Furthermore, the earliest correlation of Adam with the messiah may come from Paul, who presented the Christ as the remedy for Adam's fall. [22] This leads one to suspect that Christianity was the first to synthesize the various divine agents at creation by identifying all of them with the Christian messiah. [23]

This summary has necessarily cut across many periods. From it we learned that certain functions of the archangel were common to many groups. To see that the commonality arose by means of exegesis of Old Testament texts, and to judge whether any exegesis could be taken as heretical, the traditions must be investigated in more detail. First we will look at the motifs connecting the manlike angelic figure with the name of God. Then we will look at the "son of man" traditions. Finally, we can look at the Christian movement within this context.

In the Hebrew Bible, both descriptions of the angel of YHWH and of God himself sitting on His throne show up in revelation and ascension texts. Characteristically, the inter-testamental writers interpret any human form in a theophany as the appearance of an angel. For instance, theophanies in Judges, Exodus, and Genesis underlie the description of the angel Raphael's appearance and ascension in Tobit 12. Old Testament texts themselves are not directly quoted but rather assumed as the basis for identifying the angel.

In Tobit 12:14, Raphael reveals his identity as the angel of YHWH who was sent to Abraham to try him.

> And when thou didst not delay to rise up, and leave thy dinner, but didst go and cover the dead, then I was sent unto thee to try thee; and at the same time God did send me also to heal Sarah thy daughter-inlaw. I am Raphael, one of the seven angels, which stand and enter before the glory of the Lord.

Notice the identfication of Raphael with the angel who stands close to the throne and who is able to see the divine form or "glory." The word "glory" is on its way to becoming a technical term for the form of God on the throne as it is in Merkabah mysticism. [24] Furthermore,

---

[22] See Robin Scroggs, *The Last Adam* (Philadelphia: 1966).
[23] See especially below, p. 201 for a discussion of the "son of man" in the Parables of Enoch where the title "messiah" occurs.
[24] See Gruenwald, *Apocalyptic and Merkabah Mysticism*.

in the next chapter, Tobit magnifies God as Father, Lord, and God on account of the angel's appearance. Clearly the anthropomorphisms in the Bible are being reinterpreted in a new context of angelophany.

The entire Enoch cycle, it should be pointed out, is intimately based on theophany passages like Ez. 1 and Dan. 7:13, interpreted as angelophanies. But the books are composite, making it difficult to date some of the traditions to pre-Christian times. This is particularly important with regard to the "Parables of Enoch" which record the most systematic development of the "son of man" outside Christianity, but are not free from the suspicion of being influenced by Christian traditions. The "son of man" traditions will be discussed later. For now it is important to point out that other traditions based on Dan. 7:13 can be found in the pre-Christian parts of Enoch. In I Enoch 14, for instance, Scholem notes an early version of the heavenly journey which later becomes central to Merkabah mysticism. The description of the first palace with its tesselated marble floor gleaming like liquid is the basis for the tradition in b. Hag. 14b where R. Akiba warns his compatriots not to say "water, water" on their heavenly journey, lest they be injured. I Enoch 14 is also replete with imagery taken from the Old Testament theophany scenes. The sight of the palace with its tesselation so frightens Enoch that he falls to the ground and there beholds a vision:

> And I beheld a vision, And lo! there was a second house greater than the former, and the entire portal stood open before me, and it was built of flames of fire. And in every respect it so excelled in splendor and magnificence and extent that I cannot describe to you its splendor and its extent. And its floor was of fire, and above it were lightnings and the path of the stars, and its ceiling was also flaming fire. And I looked and saw therein a lofty throne: its appearance was as crystal, and the wheels thereof as the shining sun, and there was the vision of cherubim. And from underneath the throne came streams of flaming fire so that I could not look thereon. And the Great Glory sat thereon, and His raiment shone more brightly than the sun and was whiter than any snow. None of the angels could enter and could behold His face by reason of the magnificence and glory, and no flesh could behold Him. The Flaming fire was round about Him, and a great fire stood before Him, and none around could draw nigh Him: ten thousand times ten thousand (stood) before Him, yet He needed no counsellor. And the most holy ones who were nigh to Him did not leave by night nor depart from Him. And until then I had been prostrate on my face, trembling: and the Lord called me with His own mouth, and said to me: "Come hither, Enoch, and hear my word." And one of the holy ones came to me and

waked me, and He made me rise up and approach the door: and I bowed my face downwards. 25

The scene is based on Dan. 7:9 together with Exodus 24 and Ez. 1. The figure on the throne is the Ancient of Days, not the "son of man." But there is extreme interest in describing how the divinity can have human shape. The figure is called the "Great Glory," which, as we have already seen, is a technical term for the appearance of God on the throne in Merkabah mysticism and has a similar use in Tobit. This figure is called "Lord" by Enoch as it was by Tobit. The figure is meant to be God manifest since the text states that He needs no counselor. 26 In I Enoch it is Enoch himself who serves as intercessor for the "Watchers." In II Enoch 33:10 f. the angel Michael is mentioned as *archistratēgos* and intercessor for the handwritings of the fathers, Adam, Seth, Enoch, Cainan, etc. Of course, this is another reconstruction of the heavenly judgment scene in Dan. Rather than "the son of man" Enoch himself in I Enoch and Michael in II Enoch are to function as intercessors in front of the throne. As in Philo, men of extraordinary righteousness and purity (e.g., Moses, Melchizedek and Levi) can actually particpate in the divine drama. In the "Parables of Enoch," Enoch is identified as "the son of man." In any event, it is not the angel or mediator figure, but the divine figure on the throne in I Enoch, who has the major role, as does the Lord of the Sheep in I Enoch 90.

There are some cases where angelic mediation can be seen in a growing dualistic context. Usually, the primary figure is seen as the opposition to a demonic figure like Satan, where he pleads the cause of Israel as both heavenly advocate and intercessor. 27

In spite of this early evidence of traditions about a principal angel or manlike figure, there is no way to document a *heresy* involving the divine name as a separate angelic hypostasis in first century dualistic contexts. Some of the least justifiable actions of YHWH

---

25 I Enoch 14:15 f.

26 The Greek text and II Enoch 33:4 are quick to mention that this does not exclude the *logos*, who accomplishes all things for Him, because all things of God are eternal, "not made with hands." It seems clear that the Greek texts have incorporated the same concerns we saw in Philo to explain how God can appear as a man yet be beyond man's ken. The Greek texts remain just as sensitive to the problem of anthropomorphism but can incorporate *logos* conceptions to deal with it, probably arguing, as Philo did, that the *logos* is God himself, not merely a counselor.

27 E.g., Test. Lev.; Test. Dan. 5 f.; I En. 68; 89:76 cf. IQ M. 13:9 f.; Jud. 9; Rev. 12:7. See J. G. Gammie, "Spatial and Ethical Dualism in Jewish Wisdom and Apocalyptic Literature," *JBL*, 93 (1974), 356-385.

in the Bible had been interpreted as being suggested or accomplished by Satan as early as I Chron. 21:1, where Satan proposes the census to David rather than YHWH as in the II Samuel account. In Jubilees 17:16, 48:2 f. and 12 Mastema is reported to have convinced God to initiate the testing of Abraham. These traditions may show that the tetragrammation was already sometimes interpreted in terms of an angel, albeit an evil one.

Further evidence about the archangel Melchizedek at Qumran is exciting but only ambiguously supportive of name of God traditions. At Qumran, the principal angel may be called "The Prince of Light" (1 QS 3:20; CD 5:18), "the Angel of His Truth" (CD 3:24), which is probably the same as "The Spirit of His Truth," and may be identifiable with Melchizedek (11 Q Melch). [28] Melchizedek appears in an incomplete text of Cave XI of Qumran, published by A. S. van der Woude. [29] In this ostensibly first century Hebrew document, Melchizedek appears as an eschatological saviour whose mission is to bring back the exiles at the end of days and to announce the expiation of their sins and liberation. He is identified with Michael who also appears in the scrolls as a celestial being (1QM 17:8). Melchizedek is helped by the celestial armies in his struggle against Belial and the evil angels. It may even be true that an opposing figure, Melkirasha,

---

[28] A word is in order about the general and pervasive importance of angelology at Qumran. The archangels named in the War Scroll are Gabriel, Michael, Sariel and Raphael. No other name is given to the Prince of Lights who aided Moses and Aaron (CD 5:18). The liturgy of the Sabbath from Cave 4 is especially rich in angelic titles and group names, many of which have been derived by detailed exegesis of biblical texts. That the angelic liturgy from Cave 4 pertains to worship within the community in which the angels were actually asked to participate may be deduced from references in other documents: "Praise be to all His holy angels... His holy angels are found in your congregation." (11Q ber. 4-5, 14). Because of this no ritually impure person was allowed in the congregation. See 1 QH 3:20-23, 1QM 12:1-8, 1QH 6:12-13. Also see Ringgren, *The Faith of Qumran*, p. 81 f., John Strugnell, "The Angelic Liturgy at Qumran — 4Q Serek Sirot olat Hassabath," Suppl. to *VT* VII, (Leiden: 1959) 318-345 and L. Schiffmann, "Merkabah Speculation at Qumran: the 4Q Serekh Shirot cOlat ha-Shabbat" Festschrift for A. Altmann, forthcoming.

[29] A. S. van der Woude, "Melchizedek als himmlische Erlösergestalt in den neu-gefundenen eschatologischen Midrashim aus Qumran Hoehle XI," *OTS*, XIV (1965), 354-73. Y. Yadin has made some improvements in the transcription in "A Note on Melchisedek and Qumran," *IEJ*, 15 (1965), 152-54. M. de Jonge and A. S. van der Woude have proposed a new transcription in "11Q Melchizedek and the New Testament," *NTS*, 12 (1966), 301-326. See also J. A. Fitzmyer, "Further light on Melchizedek from Qumran Cave 11," *JBL*, 86 (1967), 25-41 and also M. Delcor, "Melchizedek from Genesis to the Qumran Texts and the Epistle to the Hebrews," *JSJ*, 2 (1971), 115-135.

functioned as Melchizedek's heavenly opponent in place of Satan. [30]
The status of Melchizedek in the heavenly economy is not clear.
His function is based on an exegesis of Is. 61:2 (applied to Jesus
in Luke 4:18) with Ps. 82 and Ps. 7. The Ps. 82 reference is of
particular interest because it contains several words for God. In 11Q
Melch 10a, van der Woude identifies one of the theophoric names with
Melchizedek, translating in this way:

> for that is the time of the acceptable year of Melchizedek ... God's
> holy ones to the reign of judgment, as it is written concerning him
> the hymns of David who says: "The heavenly one (*Elohim*) standeth
> in the congregation of God (*El*); among the heavenly ones (*Elohim*)
> he judges" (Ps. 82 : 1). [31]

This translation applies the divine name "Elohim" to Melchizedek.
However, the translation has been challenged by J. Carmignac. [32]
Carmignac finds no reason to support the suggested identification of
Melchizedek with any celestial being and certainly rejects the identification of Melchizedek with Elohim. While this conclusion seems extreme
in view of Melchizedek's role elsewhere in the apocalypse and his
identification with Michael, Carmignac cogently points out that Ps. 82
may refer to God himself rather than Melchizedek. So we must take
this identification of Melchizedek with Elohim as ambiguous but
certainly not impossible. [33]

---

[30] J. T. Milik, "Milki-sedeq et Milki-rasha dans les anciens écrits Juifs et
Chrétiens," *JJS*, 4 (1972), 95-144 and *RB*, 79 (1972), 77-97.

[31] This is English rendering of van der Woude's transcription taken from
M. Delcor, *op. cit.*, 133.

[32] "Le document de Qumran sur Melchizedek," *RQ*, 27 (1970), 343-378.

[33] The identification of Melchizedek with Elohim would certainly be anomalous,
but it is not totally out of the question, when one looks at the subsequent history of
tradition about this priest-king. In Leg. All, iii, 81 Philo warns against imputing
plurality to God, while discussing Melchizedek. According to Sokolov's Slavonic
manuscript of II Enoch, Melchizedek was conceived and born miraculously (iii,
2,7-21*) and was taken up by Michael to the paradise of Eden for forty days during
the flood (iii, 28-29). There he is called "the great high priest, the Word of God,
and the power to work great and glorious marvels above all that have been"
(iii, 34). The seal of the priesthood on his breast was "glorious in countenance"
(iii, 19). After him another Melchizedek was to arise (iv, 6; iii, 37).

In the modalist controversy within the church, the Asian Theodotus called Melchizedek a great unbegotten power who is mediator and intercessor for angels. (See
Hippolytus *Ref.* 7:36, Epi. *Haer* 55:1, Philaster. *Haer.* 52, Pseudo-Ter. *Adv Omn.* 8).
The teaching that Melchizedek was an angel was also known to Origen and Didymus
according to Jerome, *Epist. ad Evangelium* 73:2 (see Gunther, p. 240). Later still,
a group of Melchizedekian heretics denied "that Melchizedek was a man and not
Christ himself" (Migne, P.G. 65, 112a). They argued the absurdity of the idea that

The Melchizedek documents from Qumran are too fragmentary for definite conclusions, but it does not appear that the scriptural texts central to the Melchizedek traditions are those against which the rabbis explicitly warn. Instead, the Qumranites were primarily concerned with the Jubilee year, and have associated it with the eschaton. In 11 Q Melch., the return and investiture of Melchizedek initiates the judgment of God. Thus Melchizedek is seen as the duly enthroned agent of God who will inaugurate the Jubilee year and the salvation for Zion.

There are other places in the Qumran documents where concepts appear that are otherwise known in later Merkabah speculation. For instance, Is. 6:3 seems to be discussed in 4Q Serek 1. 23. However, in this place KBWD has been substituted for the Biblical KḤ GBWRWTK. This seems to represent an exegesis of the KBWD as the *dynamis* of God, which is well developed in later hekhalot literature. It is important to note that *dynamis* is a standard Greek translation for RŠWT, power. Apparently the Qumranites also believed that a future revelation would be accompanied by MR'WT KBWD ("a vision of the Glory" [34 3,26]), which probably represents another reference to the theophanies of the Old Testament—those of Isaiah, Ezekiel or Moses and the elders having been melded into a single tradition. [34]

There is also other evidence that mystical and apocalyptic traditions of mediation by God's name existed in the first centuries of the common era. It would be appropriate to trace some of that material now, since the surviving fragments are located in Christian, gnostic and

---

Melchizedek was likened (*aphomoiōminos*) to Christ. Instead they asserted that Melchizedek is God by nature (*phusei theos*) (Gunther, p. 241; 1128D; cf. 1136 A, B). Unless he were God, how could he be without father and mother? Melchizedek would no longer be Son but Father. But he is not identical with God, rather he is the divine logos (*theos logos*).

Of course, these traditions ascribing divinity to Melchizedek have not only been affected by Christian thought, they have grown out of it. The *logos* category and the attention to divine perquisites is a result of the modalist and monarchian controversy within the church (see p. 229 f.). But the original angelic category is authentic to the first century and ostensibly free from Christian influence. That Melchizedek was actually called God by anyone in the first century remains a possibility. See the recent book by Fred Horton, Jr. *The Melchizedek Tradition — A Critical Examination of the Sources to the Fifth Century A.D. and in the Epistle to the Hebrews* (Cambridge: 1976). Unfortunately, the book was not available to me until after mine was in press.

[34] See L. Schiffman, "Merkabah Speculation at Qumran: *The 4Q Serekh Shirot Olat Ha-shabat,*" forthcoming Festschrift for A. Altmann. For a discussion of the *dynamis* and GBWRH see Scholem, *Jewish Gnosticism*, 67 f. and Lieberman in Scholem, *Jewish Gnosticism*, 118-126. Scholem suggests that Gen. Apoc. 2:4 MRH RBWT', "great Lord" is also a representation of the GBWRH.

Merkabah literature, which prevents us from dealing with them in a unified fashion elsewhere.

No one can convincingly date the traditions in the Merkabah documents to the first-century rabbinic community. [35] But there is some independent evidence that the ideas in which we are interested were well developed within apocalypticism as early as the first century. This is amply illustrated by the *Apocalypse of Abraham* [36] which is usually dated to the late first century after the destruction of the temple, or early second century. In this work, Yahoel is given a major role. Yahoel himself says in his revelation to Abraham:

> I am called Yahoel by Him who moveth that which existed in me on the seventh expanse upon the firmament, a power in virtue of the ineffable Name that is dwelling in me. [37]

Obviously this, like the YHWH the lesser traditions we have seen, is a reference to the angel of Ex. 23:21. It is evident that the figure is a personification of the name itself. From the text it is quite clear that Yahoel is God's vice-regent, second only to God himself, and is the supreme figure in Jewish angelology. [38]

The *Apocalypse of Abraham* is contemporary or earlier than the first mention of "two powers" heresy in rabbinic literature, but was probably itself not the target, since it is not clearly heretical and the rabbis' earliest reports mention gentiles as the targets. This kind of evidence indicates that the ideas about an angel carrying God's name enjoyed a fairly wide distribution, only some of which was in heretical circles.

In the "Parables of Enoch" there is a long excursus on the value of the hidden, divine name, by which the world was created and which the "son of man" learns. [39]

The work is dated variously to pre-Christian times, to the first,

---

[35] See above, p. 60.

[36] G. H. Box, *Apocalypse of Abraham* (SPCK: 1919).

[37] Apoc. Abr. 10.

[38] See G. H. Box, p. xxv. See also *The Testament of Abraham*, where he is called *archistrategos*, and the *Test. of Job*. In the *Testament of Abraham* ch. 11 Adam is enthroned. See p. 109 f.

[39] I Enoch 69:14 f. R. H. Charles, *The Apocrypha and Pseudepigrapha of the Old Testament in English*, v. 2, pp. 234-235. For more discussion of the passage, see Gilles Quispel, *The Jung Codex and its Significance in Gnostic Studies* (Leiden: 1974), p. 20 f. and also Gershom Scholem, "Die Vorstellung vom Golem," *Eranos Jahrbuch*, 22 (1954), p .246 f.

second and later centuries. What is most important is that there is an explicit reference to the use of God's hidden name as a weapon in an imprecation against demons or fallen angels, as well as in the creation of the world. Because of this name, all aspects of creation do homage to God, yet it becomes the possession of the "son of man." These traditions seem to refer to the tetragrammaton, whose pronunciation was probably already guarded.

Similar traditions based on the tetragrammaton are found in the magical papyri and in esoteric circles in Judaism. Of course, these traditions are datable with any surety only to the third century. In Hekhaloth Rabbati 9, for instance, we can see the same idea of the use of God's name in the creation of heaven and earth: "Great is the Name through which heaven and earth have been created." Similarly, III Enoch is familiar with the same idea:

> He wrote with His finger with a flaming style upon the crown of my head the letters by which were created heaven and earth. 40

> Come and behold the letters by which the heaven and the earth were created. 41

In the *Sefer Yetzira*, written between the third and sixth centuries, the whole creation is described as proceeding from the name of God. In the *Sefer ha-Qoma* 42 the ineffable name is expressly identified with Metatron Yahoel. 43

In III Enoch, Yahoel is also named YHWH the lessor (7, 12:5, 48). YHWH the lessor is also found in the gnostic *Pistis Sophia* (ch. 7). Thus, it seems very likely that, by the beginning of the second century and back into the first century as well, there existed apocalyptic speculations about the name of God as a mediator of creation which probably was very early connected with the idea that this mediation could also be portrayed by a principal angel.

Starting in the second century we see other evidence of speculation about the name of God, used in the gnosticism, described by the church fathers. Irenaeus, for instance, mentions that the Ophites used the Hebrew divine names for the various archons, or angels of the demiurge. 44 This may very well be one kind of belief which the rabbis

---

40 III Enoch 13:1.
41 III Enoch 44:1.
42 *Inyane Merkabah*, Bodl. MS Oppenheimer 467, 61b.
43 Cf., Ödeberg, *III Enoch*, p. 33.
44 Iren. I, 30:5, 11, cf. II, 35:2-3. See Marmorstein, *ZNW*, 25 (1926), 257.

called "many powers in heaven." In one interesting place, the Valentinians mention that Iao has saved himself in Christ: "I redeem my soul from this age, and from all things connected with it in the name of Iao, who redeemed his own soul into redemption in Christ who liveth." [45]

In Origen's *Contra Celsum*, a corrolary report about the Ophites contains the interesting information that, on the mystic journey through the spheres, a prayer is addressed to two different partially contrasting Iao's: "And thou, Archon of the hidden mysteries of Son and Father, who shinest by night, thou Iao, second and first, lord of death." [46]

Simon Magus also is reported to have used some of the same language which is frequent in these reports, calling himself "a power," even identifying himself with a god through use of traditions of "standing" and Ex. 24:10 f. which we noted in Philo. [47]

Samaritans, as well as Christians, may have preserved such ascension traditions. Although the evidence is scanty and speculative, the possible link between "two powers" and Samaritanism in rabbinic literature [48] makes it necessary for us to mention them. The Samaritans, living in the North and rejecting the political control of Judea, did not await the coming of the Davidic Messiah, but the return of Moses or the coming of the "prophet like Moses" described in Dt. 18:15 f. In their glorification of Moses they resembled Philo. [49] In Samaritan scripture a version of this prophecy is even inserted after the Ten Commandments. The fact that the Samaritans are said to deny resurrection does not mean that they necessarily believed the soul to perish after death. Rather they may have believed in angelic or pneumatic bodies which survived to return to heaven. Some New Testament scholars speculate

---

The new material from Nag. Hammadi, especially from tractate 2, is confirming a distinct relationship with Ophism. See below, p. 249.

[45] Iren. I, 21:3. See G. Quispel, "Mandaers en Valentinianen," *Nederlands Theologisch Tijdschrift*, viii: 3 (1954), 144-8.

[46] Orig. *Contra Celsum* 6:31. Chadwick, p. 347. Peterson (*Eis Theos*, p. 307) links the phrase "first and second" with the idea that Iao was identified with light and speculates that the "second" might refer to the light which illuminates Hades at night, as well as the light of the sun during the day (Vergil, *Aen.* VI, 641).

[47] See Acts 8:10; Justin *Apology* I 26, 3; Hippolytus *Refutatio*, VI, 9, 3-18, 7. The authenticity of this tradition is called into question by Roland Bergmeier, "Zur Frühdatierung samaritanischer Theologumena," *JSJ*, V (1974), 121-53, especially 146 f., but the use of the tradition can be demonstrated in heretical Christianity in any event. Its historicity is not the main concern.

[48] See p. 95 f.

[49] See Meeks, *The Prophet King*, pp. 216-257.

that early Christian enthronement traditions came from Samaritan circles. These enthronement traditions could certainly involve Ex. 24 or Dt. 5 as a central ascension text. It would not involve Dan. 7 which was not part of the Samaritan canon. A further link between Samaritanism and the Gospel of John is often theorized. [50] It should also be noted that the New Testament credits the Samaritan, Simon Magus, with a good deal of misinterpretation of Christianity, and later he becomes the first gnostic in the church fathers' account.

A most interesting example of heterodox Judaism has been preserved in the "Prayer of Joseph," which is contained in Origen's commentary on John 2:31. [51] Though only a short fragment of the total work is recorded, almost all of the themes which we have been tracing since Philo are present in it. It is based on the theophany texts of Genesis which deal with Jacob's exploits and possibly is part of the testimony genre of literature which has been preserved in the name of other patriarchs. It is short enough to quote in full.

> If one accepts from the apocrypha presently in use among the Hebrews the one entitled "The Prayer of Joseph," he will derive from it exactly this teaching... (namely) that those who have something distinctive from the beginning when compared to men, being much better than other beings, have descended from the angelic to human nature. Jacob, at any rate, says: "I, Jacob, who am speaking to you, am also Israel, an angel of God and a ruling spirit. Abraham and Isaac were created before any work. But I, Jacob, whom men call Jacob but whose name is Israel, am he who God called Israel, i.e. a man seeing God, because I am the firstborn of every living thing to whom God gives life." And he continues:
>
> "And when I was coming up from Syrian Mesopotamia, Uriel, the angel of God came out and said that I had descended to earth and I had tabernacled among men and that I had been called by the name of Jacob. He envied me and fought with me and wrestled with me saying that his name and the name of Him that is before every angel was to be above mine. I told him his name and what rank he held among the sons of God: 'Are you not Uriel, the eighth after me and I, Israel, the archangel of the power of the Lord and the

---

[50] Charles Scobie, "The Origins and Development of Samaritan Christianity," p. 309 f. for survey of works. Also Bowman, "Early Samaritan Eschatology," *JJS*, (1955), 63-72. G. W. Buchanan, "The Samaritan Origin of the Gospel of John," *Religions in Antiquity*, (E. R. Goodenough Festschrift), 149-175. James D. Purvis, "The Fourth Gospel and the Samaritans," *SBL* section on John, Annual Meeting, Washington, D.C., October, 1974 and response by Wayne Meeks. Ödeberg speculated that the whole fourth Chapter of John was intended primarily for Samaritan circles, *Fourth Gospel*, p. 185 f.

[51] Jonathan Z. Smith, "The Prayer of Joseph," in *Religions in Antiquity*.

chief captain among the sons of God? Am I not Israel, the first minister before the face of God?' And I called upon my God by the inextinguishable name ... But we have made a lengthy digression in considering the matter of Jacob and using as evidence a writing not lightly to be despised to render more credible the belief concerning John the Baptist which maintains that he ... being an angel, took a body in order to bear witness to the light. [52]

Here it is an archangel of the power of the people of God who is called Israel and is also identified with the patriarch Jacob. He was created before all the works of creation and claims ascendancy over Uriel on the basis of his victory in personal combat by which he ostensibly possesses the divine name. To sum up the issues, as reported by J. Z. Smith, the fragment is dominated by three themes: (1) the lofty role of Israel (called Jacob, an angel of God, a ruling spirit, a man who sees God, the first-born of all life, the archangel of the power of the Lord, the heavenly chief captain, the high-priest before the face of God); (2) the conflict between Jacob and Uriel, each claiming ascendancy over each other; and (3) the myth relating to the descent of the angel to a flesh-like existence. Although this material is contained in a Christian source, no doubt its origin was Jewish sectarianism. Nor is it the only evidence that traditions about angelic keepers of the name were common in Jewish-Christianity. Cardinal Danielou cites considerable evidence that traditions associating Michael and Gabriel with the name of God were recorded in Christian writings, often with the titles transferred to Christ. [53]

In this quick tour of apocalyptic and mystical literature we have established certain things. First, it seems obvious that traditions similar to the ones which the rabbis dismissed as "two powers" heresy in the second century can be seen in sectarian literature of the first century. However, just when and where the traditions become heretical is a vexing question. It is certainly true that many of the traditions about the angel of YHWH would not have been taken as heretical by the rabbis. For instance, there is no convincing evidence that Merkabah mystics were ever called heretical, although the rabbis warned against exegesis of Ezekiel as early as the compilation of the Mishnah. While the evidence abounds for the existence of dangerous scriptural tradi-

---

[52] J. Z. Smith, "The Prayer of Joseph," *ibid.*, p. 256 f. See also Martin Hengel, *The Son of God*, p. 48.

[53] Danièlou, *The Theology of Jewish Christianity*, pp. 119-131. See also E. R. Goodenough, "The Pseudo-Justinian *Oratio ad Graecos*," *HTR*, 18 (1925), 185-200.

tions there is not much evidence that angelic or hypostatic creatures were considered independent enough to provide definite targets for the "two powers" polemic. Of course, our knowledge of first century Judaism is quite limited. In the extreme gnostic systems, where the power with the Hebrew name opposed a higher power, the heresy is clear. But we have no solid evidence that such systems existed in apocalyptic literature before the early second century. Then too, to a certain extent the application of the term "heresy" is anachronistic because the earliest witness to the rabbinic charge is the second century, and we cannot be sure that the rabbis were firmly in control of Judaism until the second century. So we cannot be sure that any of the systems would have been called heresy in the first century or even if there was a central power interested to define it. But we cannot altogether dismiss the possibility that some apocalyptic groups posited an independent power as early as the first century or that other groups, among them the predecessors of the rabbis, would have called them heretics.

Once this general structure of traditions is clear we can hesitantly approach the thorny problem of the "son of man." We must certainly deal with the "son of man" traditions while we are discussing human manifestations in heaven in "apocalyptic Judaism." While most scholars agree that the "son of man" is not yet a specific title in Dan., there is little agreement about the character of the figure. Recently J. J. Collins has suggested anew that the "son of man" in Dan. means only a "manlike figure" who appears in the vision and is logically to be identified with Gabriel, the "manlike" angel (8:15; 9:21) or even Michael, the angel like God but with a human form, who appears in the next vision. [54] This would be in keeping with the archangels' role in the Enoch-Metatron literature. So it is growing more plausible that a whole constellation of traditions existed which speculated about the identity and character of the heavenly human figure. In its original mythological context before it appeared in Daniel it may have been a reflection of another Near Eastern god, as the holy war and divine warrior traditions have shown, [55] but this figure not a consistent personage in Jewish tradition.

Evidence for heterodox speculation about Daniel 7:9 f. in Jewish

---

[54] See Fossum, p. 92, J. J. Collins, "The Son of Man and the Saints of the Most High in the Book of Daniel," *JBL*, 93 (1974), 50-66 and H. L. Ginsberg, "Michael and Gabriel," *EJ*. Fossum argues persuasively for Gabriel because in 10:13 the angel speaks about Michael.

[55] See Altman, Cross and Miller, as cited on p. 184, n. 4.

thought may be recorded in some of the versions of the LXX. The original LXX translation of Daniel was very free and should appropriately be considered a commentary rather than a translation of Daniel. Because of this, it was eventually replaced in the Greek Bible by Theodotion's more literal translation. The LXX apparently translated "the son of man" vision in such a way as to make one suspicious that very early "two powers" traditions were being challenged. One version says that the "son of man" approached *as* the Ancient of Days, instead of *until* the Ancient of Days, coalescing the two divine figures by changing *heos* to *hos*. [56] Such a change can be explained as a scribal error, but since the text is well-attested, it may also have been a purposeful change to defend against heretics.

In the Parables of Enoch, which may bear Christian influence, the emphasis turned to the manlike figure, or the "son of man." Most of the portrayals of judgment in the Parables of Enoch (I Enoch 37-71)— as in all the Enoch literature—involve a detailed exegesis of the Daniel 7:13 passage. However the "son of man" in the Parables is a salvific figure of some prominence, having many divine perquisites. But whether "son of man" is actually the title of this savior or merely a semitic idiom describing "a manlike figure" has remained a scholarly puzzle. [57] Adapted from the Daniel pericope, the story of the "son of man" seems to involve the following scenario: (1) the wicked oppress the righteous (which is given as the reason for punishment); (2) the "son of man" enters God's throneroom and is enthroned (alternatively he is already enthroned before the scene opens); (3) whereupon the "son of man" passes judgment on God's behalf; (4) the wicked are justly punished by one of the two figures, usually the "son of man," and (5) scenes of triumph follow. [58] Of course, this is only the general scenario; the events are not always narrated in that order, nor are all the parts always expressed. [59] Whereas in other apocalyptic judgment scenes outside of the Parables, God is perfectly capable of

---

[56] See Montgomery, *Daniel*, ICC, p. 316. Recent publications appearing after this manuscript was in press, suggest that Enoch speculation may be quite old, older than Daniel, and form the basis of the Daniel speculation. See below, n. 65 for the evidence.

[57] Carsten Colpe, *"huios tou anthropou,"* TDNT.

[58] This is adopted from the scheme of Lars Hartman, *Prophecy Interpreted: The Formation of Some Jewish Apocalyptic Texts and of the Eschatological Discourse in Mark 13* (Uppsala: 1966).

[59] See e.g., outside of the Parables in I Enoch 47:1-48 where parts of the pattern have been shuffled and some are missing.

carrying out the whole plan himself, [60] in the Parables the "son of man" is usually the instrument of God's justice. This fact only points out the importance of the character of the "son of man" in the Parables. But nowhere is it certain that the "son of man" is a title. We may only have a series of traditions concerning Dan. 7:13.

In I En. 48:2 f. there is further description of this divine figure. He is casually named messiah and he (or only his name and office) are described as premundane, having been foreordained before the Lord of Spirits created the stars. Never before in this material has the figure been identified as the messiah, which leads many scholars to assume Christian influence (whether friendly or polemical), or authorship. In I En. 70 and 71 Enoch and his name are elevated to become the "son of man." He tours heaven, which contains the new paradise (I En. 70:4) (the *pardes*?) and is guided before the throne of the Ancient of Days by Michael; whereupon Enoch himself is proclaimed the "son of man." [61] At the last judgment the "son of man" will be brought before God and His name before the Ancient of Days. Because of this parallelism between the name and function of the figure of the "son of man," we are probably warranted in saying that from one perspective the "son of man" is a pre-existent being—but not in every respect, because the point of the story is to tell the mystical events by which Enoch learns of his future role. It seems clear that the figure has been human and becomes both divine and messianic, although his heavenly enthronement aspects are far better described than his earthly tasks. There is no evidence that a separate human messiah is to bring national redemption while this cosmic figure will bring cosmic justice.

The roots of the images in these verses should not concern us. Whether they are closest to ancient Canaanite, Babylonian, or Persian mythology is not specifically relevant. [62] Since the Prophets and the book of Daniel, the traditions were squarely within Israelite thought and underwent transformations peculiar to Israelite culture. I Enoch

---

[60] E.g., 1 Enoch 25:3-6, 100:1-9.

[61] That the figures became one is as sure as it has been troublesome. R. H. Charles assumed that a copyist had erred in transcribing the pronouns, hence he changed the pronouns to make the conversation appear to be taking place between the "son of man" and God. Mowinckel has also denied any identification of the two figures. Note his description of the scene in *He That Cometh* (New York: n.d.) p. 383 f. and especially 442 f.

[62] See Montgomery, *Daniel: A Critical and Exegetical Commentary on the Book of Daniel* (Edinburgh, 1927), p. 317-322. Also Borsch, *The Son of Man in Myth and History* (London: 1970); Carson Colpe, *"uios tou anthropou,"* in *TDNT*.

would be the next chronological occurrence of the tradition of the "son of man" after Daniel, exclusive of the gospels, if the early dating could be maintained. Yet the date of the Parables of Enoch, in which these traditions occur, is a great scholarly *desideratum*. It would be convenient to be able to assume that the book was pre-Christian, as many scholars have maintained. [63] But the evidence is hardly conclusive and the suspicious absence of "son of man" traditions at Qumran argues rather for a post-Christian date. [64] Until some definite evidence confirms a pre-Christian date, we must be satisfied with a post-Christian theory of origin. Even the scholarly consensus that the Parables are non-Christian has been seriously questioned. J. T. Milik has suggested that the parables are a Christian invention, designed to substitute for the "Book of Giants" attested at Qumran. [65]

Though we learn much about the Daniel traditions from this writing, more prudent dating of the Parables requires us to take the New Testament as the earliest document which understands that the "son of man" as a title (though possibly not consistently), in turn identified with Christ. Of course, Philo does describe the heavenly Adam in terms which are elsewhere used of the "son of man." He also evidences similar ideas about the heavenly *logos*. So we must allow that some sort of "son of man" traditions preceded the gospels. It would not be surprising to find that the pre-Christian traditions were a variety of conflicting exegeses of Dan. 7:13, all describing an unnamed figure, possibly God's human hypostasis or a principal angel who carries the name of God. There is no clear evidence that the figure was proclaimed "son of man" as a title or that his coming was predicted before the eschaton. Instead there is some evidence that special people might be translated to heaven to appear before the throne, whereupon they are

---

[63] The pre-Christian son of man is integral part of the Bultmann thesis that the son of man is a representative of pre-Christian, gnostic-salvation myth.

[64] Ragnar Leivestad, "Exit the Apocalyptic Son of Man," *NTS*, 18 (1972), 243. J. C. Hindley, "Towards a Date for the Similitudes of Enoch: An Historical Approach," *NTS*, 14, 551-65.

[65] See Milik, "Problèmes de la littérature hénochique à la lumière des fragments araméens de Qumran," *HTR*, 64 (1971), 333-78; "Turfan et Qumran: Livre des Géants juif et manichéen," *Tradition und Glaube: Das frühe Christentum in seiner Umwelt: Festgabe für K. G. Kuhn* (Göttingen: 1971), pp. 117-27. His new edition of *The Book of Enoch: Aramaic Fragments of Qumran Cave 4* (with the collaboration of Matthew Black) (Oxford: 1976) suggests that Enoch is older than Daniel and forms the basis of the Daniel speculation. The dating of the Son of Man title, however, remains unaffected. See Matthew Black, "The Parables, of Enoch (1 En. 37-71) and the 'Son of Man.'" *Expository Times*, 78 (1976), 5-8.

identified with the manlike figure or are granted immortality and use the name of God to gain vindication for themselves and their followers.

B. *New Testament Christianity*

Of all the forms of religion in Palestine in the first century, New Testament Christianity is the best documented, most controversial, and most often studied. Even so, there is little that can be said in certainty about the roots of Christian doctrines. This lack of sure knowledge will be especially frustrating in studying "two powers" tradition, as we shall see, because many traditions found heretical by the rabbis in the second century were intimately connected to the apostolic understanding of Jesus. Yet, it is a mistake to assume that Christianity was a unified social movement which contained a consistent, theological perspective, even in its earliest stages. [66] The most we can say is that some kinds of Christianity found "two powers" traditions favorable to their perspective. The relationships between these traditions of angelic mediation and Christianity are significant enough to call for a more complete study of the problem as background for Christology than has yet been attempted.

It is fair to begin with the observation that Jesus is never called merely an angel in the New Testament. Nor is there any clarity about the first titles applied to Jesus. In spite of these disclaimers, Christianity is the most extensive developer of the "son of man" traditions. As opposed to the Enoch traditions, the gospels certainly understand Jesus as "the son of man." It would not be exaggerating to say that one purpose of the gospel is to identify Jesus as the "son of man." However, the identification is neither clear nor consistent. The term does not always appear to be a title, nor is it proclaimed of Jesus since it only occurs in his own speeches. Yet, when the total picture is taken into account, the identification of Jesus with the "son of man" is so characteristic of the gospels that many scholars take the occasional *logion* of Jesus in which he does not equate himself with the "son of man" (or does so in some ambiguous way) to be undoubtedly authentic. Since a distinction between Jesus and the "son of man" could not reflect the bias of the early church, according to this perspective, it may reflect the authentic words of Jesus, because there would have

---

[66] J. M. Robinson and Helmut Koester, *Trajectories Through Early Christianity* (Philadelphia: 1971).

been no reason to preserve the statements, were they not from Jesus. Furthermore, the title itself quickly went to disuse, superceded by more understandable titles like "Son of God" and "Messiah" (*Christos*). Yet, whether or not Jesus meant anything apocalyptic in calling himself "son of man" has not been settled. A non-apocalyptic possibility for the meaning of Jesus' "son of man" sayings must be mentioned. It is possible that he used the phrase in a self-referential way only because it was a possible, self-referential Aramaic idiom, having no direct relationship to the manlike figure of Daniel. [67] In short, even accepting the argument which makes "son of man" an authentic self-designation of Jesus does not clarify what Jesus might have meant by it. One school of critics accepts the eschatological statements as primary; another accepts the self-referential ones as primary. All agree that neither the self-referential nor the eschatological statements can be clearly distinguished from the perspective of the church. Therefore some of the statements may have been attributed to Jesus by Christians who had already accepted the titles and found it impossible to imagine that Jesus may have thought of himself in other ways.

There is probably no possible historical solution to the question of Jesus' self-consciousness. There is a greater chance of discovering how various christologies developed.

It is clear that the "son of man" traditions refer back to *Dan.* 7:13, which is a text important for "two powers" investigation. So we should mention the uses of Dan. 7:9 f. in the New Testament. Certainly the most interesting use of Dan. 7:13 in the gospels for our purposes is its combination with Ps. 110. [68] Ps. 110, the most quoted Old Testament scripture in the New Testament, has recently been studied

---

[67] Geza Vermes, "Appendix E: The Use of Bar Nasha/BarNash in Jewish Aramaic," in Matthew Black, *An Aramaic Approach to the Gospels and Acts* (Oxford: 1967), pp. 310-330. However, criticism of this theory is persuasive, see J. Jeremias, *New Testament Theology* (New York: 1971), p. 261, n. 1. J. A. Fitzmyer has reported that BRNŠ꜐ is evidenced at Qumran as a designation for the collectivity "mankind" or the individual belonging to a collectivity (i.e., II Qtg Job 26:3). But there is no evidence of its being used (a) as a surrogate for "I," (b) as a form of address, or (c) as an eschatological title. The full evidence is forthcoming in "Methodology in the Study of the Aramaic Substratum of Jesus' Sayings in the New Testament," *Jésus aux origines de la Christologie*, Bibliotheca ephemeridum theologicarum lovaniensum, (Gembloux: Ducalot, 1975).

[68] See Mk. 2:32 f., 8:56 f., 13:26, 14:62. Norman Perrin, *A Modern Pilgrimage in New Testament Christology* (Philadelphia: 1974), has been very helpful in this section.

by David Hay. [69] Many N.T. uses stress Jesus' exaltation after death, represented as a vindication by God. Other uses of the psalm stress Christ's enthronement as the basis for ecclesiology or for a priestly christology. But when used in connection with Dan. 7:13, the first clause of psalm 110 was certainly a support for the christological interpretation of the "son of man." No less, it served as testimony to the supreme dignity of the one whom the Christians called "My Lord" and promised vindication for the believers. The question is how such a concept developed. It may be that messianic interpretations already lay behind these scriptures when the Christians adopted them. But we do not have any firm evidence for that. Rather all that is necessary to be presupposed in the tradition is that Jesus be identified with the second "lord" in Ps. 110:1. This identification would be based on the Hebrew text, where both ᵓDWNY, (my lord) and tetragrammaton, YHWH, appears. Bousset had assumed that the use of the euphemism, "Lord," for the tetragrammaton was not known in Palestine in the first century. However, this theory has been challenged. [70] It is at least possible that believers said "lord" twice in quoting Ps. 110:1 in Hebrew in the first century. It is certainly true that anyone speaking Greek or Aramaic would have used two "Lords" in the psalm. This much seems sensible. But it is fascinating to speculate further. We know that the ascension and heavenly enthronement of Jesus was assumed on the basis of Ps. 110, which had the function of an eschatological promise for the believer and a vindication which countered Jesus' crucifixion. Might it be that the connection between the earthly Jesus and the son of man was made because Jesus was believed to have ascended to the throne in heaven—thus identifying him with the manlike figure (BRNŠᵓ "son of man") who fought against the unjust, and who was seated on His divine throne? Immortality or resurrection were often stressed in reports of martyrdom, [71]

---

[69] David M. Hay, *Glory at the Right Hand: Ps. 110 in Early Christianity*, SBL monograph 18 (New York: 1973).

[70] J. A. Fitzmyer, "Qumran Aramaic and the New Testament," *NTS*, 20 (1974), 390. See now, Martin Hengel, *The Son of God*, p. 77-83.

[71] See G. W. E. Nickelsburg, Jr. *Resurrection, Immortality, and Eternal Life in Intertestamental Judaism* (Cambridge: 1972). For the significant relationship between martyrdom, resurrection and the story of the sacrifice of Isaac in Jewish tradition, see Shalom Spiegel, *The Last Trial: On the Legends and Lore of the Command to Abraham to Offer Isaac as a Sacrifice: The Akedah.* tr. J. Goldin (New York: 1967). Geza Vermes, *Scripture and Tradition in Judaism.* (Leiden: 1961) and N. A. Dahl, "The Atonement—An Adequate Reward for the Akeda?" in *Neotestamenta et Semitica* (festschrift M. Black) ed. Ellis and Wilcox (Edinburgh: 1969).

while Philo wrote that men of special ability could mystically ascend to participate in divine immutability. The novelty of some Christian understandings would then have been to stress the divine title given to Jesus on the basis of Ps. 110, and thereby to associate the martyred messiah with the divine warrior who carried the name of God. While only a hypothesis, it has two advantages over the gnostic savior hypothesis. It does not need to predicate a well-defined but unevidenced myth into which Jesus was fit. Rather it assumes that many different traditions about mediators, human figures in heaven and angelic mediators were eventually identified with Jesus, after he was believed to have survived death and ascended to heaven. These traditions may or may not have been associated with the messiah before Jesus. But certainly Jesus' life provided one definite link with messianic expectations since he was crucified as "King of the Jews"—that is, as a messianic pretender, even if he had no messianic consciousness. [72]

While the scriptural traditions with which Jesus was associated were not "gnostic," the motif can certainly be said to be mythical in the current, anthropological use of that term. Before Christianity there is evidence of many different exegetical traditions but no central, single redemption myth. It looks as if the unity was reached by applying all the traditions to Jesus.

As central and ancient as were these beliefs, they were by no means the whole story. It is not my purpose to elaborate a theory of the evolution of christological titles. But it should be pointed out that the christological titles (and even Son of God) can be partially understood as a combination of traditions of exegesis about various angelic figures with messianic prophecies. [73] All of these titles can be explained

---

[72] See the title essay in N. A. Dahl's recently translated *The Crucified Messiah and other Essays* (Minneapolis: 1974).

[73] Martin Hengel, *The Son of God*, argues that Son of God was not a purely Hellenistic title. It would appear that in the Old Testament "My son" was a title of the king while "son of God" originally denoted other gods, which became subservient as angels under the pressure of biblical monotheism (see Föhrer, *TDNT*, "huios," 347 f.). The singular form occurs only late for Old Testament references, in Dan. 3:25. In the New Testament there are a few, uncertain traces of similar terminology. Rev. 2:18 introduces Christ as "the son of God" with features similar to Dan. 10:5 f. In Hebr. 7:3, Melkizedek is described as resembling the son of God. However, much more often the christological title "son of God" is linked up with messianic prophecies of the Old Testament—like Ps. 2:7 f. and 2 Sam. 7:14 f.—where God calls the Davidic king, "my son." It seems likely that "sonship" developed both to discuss Jesus' messianic mission and to define his relationship to the father. For instance, in Paul, Hebrews and Johannine writings, the term 'son of God' includes the idea of pre-existence. It is used in connection with terms like *"logos"* and "image

without any necessary messianic or salvational self-proclamation by Jesus during his life. They all may be seen as part of the church's conviction that Jesus' death was vindicated by his ascension which, in turn, was the sign of the future vindication of all believers.

After this identification, the church could easily present the authority of Jesus in his ministry to stem from his identification with the "son of man." In Mark 2:10 and 2:28 the authority of Jesus, as "son of man," extends even to abrogating the law and forgiving sins. The latter claim is especially significant in view of R. Idi's argument with the heretics.

Besides the themes of vindication and authority apparent in the "son of man" sayings of Jesus, another exegesis of the book of Daniel figures prominently in the synoptic apocalypse, edited by the church during the time of the destruction of the Second Temple (ca. 70 C.E.). By now, Jesus, as Son of Man, was considered to have passed judgment on Jerusalem (Mk. 13:26 with Mk. 14:62). Nor could the destruction of Jerusalem fail to have been taken as a sign by the Christian community that the Jews were punished for opposing the Church and its message, a doctrine which was maintained even after the prophesied apocalyptic end failed to materialize.

Still other uses of "two powers" traditions may be found in the synoptic gospels. For instance, the Sinai theophany, together with Dan. 7:9 f. has often been suggested as the background for the synoptic account of the transfiguration, especially prominent in the Lukan version. [74] Of course these exegeses were not invented by Christianity. The early Christians referred to several other intertestamental texts which picture the appearance of angels and describe their functions on earth. We have seen that the appearance of angels in Jud. 6

---

of God" (Hebr. 1, Rom. 8:29, Col. 1:13-18, John 1:1-3, cf., John 1:1-18). Obviously, many associations have become part of this title but it cannot be said to have originated to express the pre-existence of Jesus. Like *Kyrios* and unlike *Christos*, the term "Son of God" would have remained meaningful to people who were not aware of its Jewish background. It should be noted that the divine connotation of "Son of God" is one way of explaining the charge of blasphemy at the trial. See D. Catchpole, *The Trial of Jesus: a Study in the Gospels and Jewish Historiography from 1770 to the Present Day* (Leiden: 1971), pp. 72-148. "Son of God" has been reported as a human title for the Messiah at Qumran by Milik, though the text has not yet been published. See Fitzmyer, "Qumran Aramaic and the New Testament," *NTS*, 20 (1974), 382-407.

[74] The strongest proponent of this idea is Davies, *He Ascended into Heaven: A Study in the History of Doctrine* (1958), pp. 25, 185. See also Gerhardt Lohfink, *Die Himmelfahrt Jesu: Untersuchungen zu den Himmelfahrts und Erhöhungstexten bei Lukas* (München: 1971), pp. 64, 191. Also Borsch, p. 383.

and 13 as well as the theophanies (understood as angelophanies) in the pentateuch underlie the description of the angel Raphael's appearance and ascension in Tobit 12. These, in turn, are likely to have formed the basis for Markan transfiguration. Interesting too is the recent suggestion by Anitra Kolenkow that these traditions may also underlie and give form to some of the healing and feeding stories in Mark as well as the post-resurrection epiphany stories in later gospels. [75]

The identification of Jesus with the "son of man" was not the end of the matter. Rather it was the beginning of a long discussion of the status of Jesus in the heavenly economy. Jesus is not called an angel in the New Testament because he was not believed to be *merely* an angel. So it is not surprising to see the figure of Jesus begin to take over divine titles in the Pauline and Johannine corpora.

> Therefore God has highly exalted him and bestowed upon him the name which is above every name, that at the name of Jesus every knee should bow in heaven and on earth and under the earth, and that every tongue confess that Jesus Christ is Lord to the glory of God the father. [76]

On the basis of his ascension and translation Jesus has been raised higher even than the angels. The divine names and titles used by II Isaiah have been transferred to Jesus. Furthermore, though this occurs in the writings of Paul, which are certainly early (middle first century) and earlier than much of the gospel material, there is no reason to believe that Paul was the first to think of Jesus in this manner. This section in Paul's writing bears all the characteristics of a separate liturgical fragment which Paul inserted into his argument because it was relevant to his discussion of patience and humility. Note too that, true to this theme, the beginning of the psalm seems to deny Jesus' equality with God: "Christ Jesus, who, though he was in the form of God, did not count equality with God a thing to be grasped." [77] This represents a fairly early stage in the development of christology, similar in many respects to Philo, because though traditions about the name of God were applied to Jesus, Jewish sensibilities about the preservation of monotheism remained strong. In fact, Paul himself seems to use a polemic against some kinds of first century

---

[75] Anitra Kolenkow, "The Coming and Ascent of a Heavenly Healer—Tobit and Mark," a paper delivered to the SBL Gospel of John seminar, October, 1974.

[76] Phil. 2:9-11.

[77] Phil. 2:6.

Jews which we also find characteristic of the rabbinic "two powers" discussion in the second century.

> Why then the law? It was added because of transgressions, till the offspring should come to whom the promise had been made; and it was ordained by angels through an intermediary. Now an intermediary implies more than one, but God is one. [78]

Paul's total argument in this passage is ambiguous and baffling. He seems to be relying on Jewish argument in a peculiar way. He accepts the idea that the Law was given by angels, a position which is explicitly denied by the rabbis for reasons that are already apparent. Though Paul's point is opposite to theirs, his argument is rather similar to the rabbis. Both agree that some ideas of mediation dilute strict monotheism but argue toward different remedies: Paul claims that the Law is inferior. The rabbis will claim that the Law is given directly by God. Whatever else it proves, this seems to show that a polemic against angelology already existed in Jewish circles in the first century and could be applied in various, different ways, depending on the perspective of the exegete.

The pattern is characteristic of most Pauline letters as well as those of the Pauline School. We need not go into Paul's angelology in detail. [79] Generally speaking, it is fair to say that for Paul and his school Christ had brought the reign of both the Law and the angels to its close, since Christ had broken the power of sin and overthrown the cosmic spirits. It is interesting to note the common words that Paul uses to describe the various kinds of angelic creature. These are *archē, exousia,* and *dynamis* (see e.g., I Cor. 15:24-26, and freq.) as well as *thronos* (Col. 1:16) and *kosmokrator* (Eph. 6:12). These are identical with the words for angels in apocalyptic literature. [80] They are also the common Greek equivalents of the Hebrew term

---

[78] Gal. 3:19-20. See N. A. Dahl, "Widersprüche in der Bibel, ein altes hermeneutisches Problem," *Studia Theologica,* 25 (1971), 1-19.

[79] For more detail on Paul's concept of angels see W. D. Davies, "A Note on Josephus, *Antiquities* 15:136," *HTR,* 47 (1954); Bo Reicke, "The Law and the World according to Paul," *JBL,* 70 (1951), 261-63; Fred Francis, "Visionary Discipline and Scriptural Tradition at Colossae," *Lexington Theological Quarterly* 2 (1967); F. Francis and W. Meeks, *The Colossian Controversy* (SBL: 1974); G. MacGregor, "Principalities and Powers: The Cosmic Background of Paul's Thought," *NTS,* 1 (1954), 22; Andrew John Bandstra, *The Law and the Elements of the World* (1964), pp. 158-68; Edward Langton, *The Angel Teaching of the New Testament* (London: n.d.); H. Berkhof, *Christ and the Powers* (Scottdale, Pa.: 1962); M. Jones, "St. Paul and the Angels," *Expositor,* vii-15 (1918), 415.

[80] See T. of Solomon 20:12-15, cf. I Enoch 61:10.

RŠWT. Paul uses such terms to stress the inferior status of the celestial beings. It seemed reasonable to assume that the rabbis used these terms, rather than the infrequent "two gods," for the same reason. However, we shall also find language similar to "two gods" in the New Testament. [81] In Ephesians, Christ's victory over the angelic powers is stressed. And in 1:21 it appears as if the Pauline author describes Christ with the ineffable name of God:

> They are measured by his strength and the might which he exerted in Christ when he raised him from the dead, when he enthroned him at his right hand in the heavenly realms, far above all government and authority, all power and dominion, and any title of sovereignty that can be named, not only in this age, but in the age to come. [82]

Many "two powers" themes have come together. Jesus is raised from the dead and enthroned as Christ far above the status of any man or angel. He is sovereign in this age and the age to come, a claim explicitly reserved for God according to rabbinic tradition. Furthermore, Christ has been exalted beyond any title that can be named, implying that he has been awarded the secret name of God.

The process of transferring divine names and titles to Jesus is especially characteristic of the Revelation of John where the identification of the Christ with the tetragrammaton is even more obvious. For instance, Rev. 22:12-13:

> Behold I am coming soon bringing my recompense to repay every one for what he has done. I am the alpha and the omega, the first and the last, the beginning and the end. [83]

We have seen that such titles from Isaiah and Deuteronomy are particularly important in the rabbinic polemic. [84] These traditions present some plausible targets for the rabbis' attack. The same can be said of the Christ's victorious coming in Rev. 19.

> Then I saw heaven opened, and behold, a white horse! He who sat upon it is called Faithful and True, and in righteousness he judges and makes war. His eyes are like a flame of fire and on his head are many diadems; and he has a name inscribed which no one knows but himself. He is clad in a robe dipped in blood, and the name by which he is called is the Word of God. And the armies of heaven

---

81 See p. 216 f.
82 Eph. 1:20 f. according to NEB.
83 Rev. 22:12-13.
84 See p. 60 f., 84 f.

arrayed in fine linen white and pure, followed him on white horses. From his mouth issues a sharp sword with which to smite the nations and he will rule them with a rod of iron; he will tred the wine press of the fury of the wrath of God the almighty. On his robe and on his thigh he has a name inscribed, King of Kings and Lord of Lords. [85]

Many different images are jumbled together in this description. Divine warrior imagery is prominent but the divine warrior has been identified with the messiah (Ps. 2) and Jesus, based on the "son of man" tradition in Daniel. Furthermore, many divine titles are applied to the figure: "true and faithful," "King of Kings," "Lord of Lords" are all divine attributions in Judaism. Lastly and more importantly, he has appropriated the ineffable name, which is identical with "Word of God" (v. 13). On this basis, it seems safe to consider that many Christians identified the Christ with God's principal angel, who carried the divine name, because of his resurrection.

It is in this context that we should see the arguments in the Epistle to the Hebrews that Jesus is more sublime a mediator than the angels or Moses. In Hebrews there is no complete polemic against angel worship. Rather Christ, as "Son" (1:4-2:10), is reputed to be better. Significantly the Son is reputed to be the "Elohim" enthroned in Ps. 45:7 (Heb. 1:8). The notion that the Lord will rule the world to come is transferred to Christ (2:5). [86] The book is probably directed against some Christians who did not see Jesus' role as unique, rather as merely one more example of a special intercessor who had been taken into the presence of God.

These ascension and theophany themes, placed in a polemical setting, show up in the Gospel of John. In John 6:46 the gospel states: "No one has ever seen God, except His son," which amounts to a new interpretation of Ex. 33:20 in the Sinai theophany. We saw that the solution to the contradiction between God's appearance to the elders at Sinai (Ex. 24:10 f.) and the statement that "no one can see Him and live" (Ex. 33:20) was the purpose of the rabbinic and Philonic exegesis of the passage. In Philo's case, reconciling the contradiction necessitated positing a second divine figure. In the rabbinic case, it occasioned a polemic against a second figure. [87] In the Johannine

---

[85] Rev. 19:11-16.

[86] This seems related to the rabbinic insistence that the God of Israel will rule in the age to come as well. See p. 60 f.

[87] Peder Borgen, *Bread from Heaven* (Leiden: 1965), p. 415. Also see Ödeberg, *The Fourth Gospel* and John 3:3-13. One should note the similarity to Abahu's com-

version a new argument is discovered in that theophany story. Since
Moses was not allowed to see the face of God (for no mortal can see
God and live), John proclaims that only a specific heavenly figure
can have had a full vision of God—he who was from God, Jesus.
Probably John was speaking against opposing ascension views. The
statement that "No one has gone to heaven except he who is descended
from heaven" is probably designed to disallow any ascension traditions
excepting the Christian one.

Neither are controversies like the one in John 12:37 f. innocent
of "two powers" ramifications:

> In spite of many signs which Jesus had performed in their presence
> they would not believe in him, for the prophet Isaiah's utterance had
> to be fulfilled: "Lord, who has believed what we reported, and to
> whom has the Lord's arm been revealed?" So it was that they could
> not believe, for there is another saying of Isaiah's: "He has blinded
> their eyes and dulled their minds, lest they should see with their
> eyes, and perceive with their minds, and turn to me to heal them."
> Isaiah said this because he saw His glory and spoke about Him.
> ... So Jesus cried aloud: "When a man believes in me, he believes
> in Him who sent me. I have come into the world as Light..." [88]

The purpose of this passage is to identify Jesus as both messiah
and as the "glory of God." It does so by identifying the Christ as the
glory of God which Isaiah saw in Is. 6. [89] Isaiah's prophecies of woe
on Israel can then be transferred by the gospel writer to the Jews who
did not perceive Jesus as God's glory. To make the matter clear Jesus
even cries aloud that in viewing him, men also view the Father. The
rabbis had partially insisted on the use of "glory" as a metonymy
for God in order to remove any heretical implications from the Sinai
theophany. They expressly forbad the interpretation of the theophany
as an angelophany. The New Testament adopts the targumic language
but not the entire rabbinic sensibility.

In a sense, it is no surprise to see so many of the themes of the

---

ment against the person who attempts to go to heaven or who calls himself the
son of man:

> R. Abahu said: If a man say to you "I am God," he is a liar; if (he says,
> "I am) the son of man," in the end people will laugh at him; if (he says)
> "I will go up to heaven, he says so, but shall not perform it." (j Taan. 65b).

In Abahu's time, Christianity of the gnostic or even Johannine type, is the most
likely referent for the heresy.

[88] John 12:37 f according to the NEB.

[89] See McNamara, *Targum and Testament*, p. 98 f. and p. 50 above. Also Is. 12:42
for a discussion of the targumic background for these traditions.

the phrase "son of God" means more than this basic designation and that the Old Testament reference had found fulfillment in Jesus. [93] What is important for our purposes is to see that by the time of the Gospel of John, the Jewish community is already described as opposing Christianity on the issue of the divinity of Jesus. It was the divinity of Jesus, rather than the messianic claim (though both were issues), that is portrayed as separating the two communities. The Jews criticize the Christians of "ditheism," rather than "two powers" which also foreshadows a christological problem in later Christianity.

Some of the social bases of the opposition between Jew and Christian can also be seen. The Johannine gospel reflects a time when the cleavage between Jews and Christians had become irremediable. This must refer to the end of the first century, although John explicitly says that the hostility started during the time of Jesus (see, e.g., 12:42). The gospel reports that Jews were already applying ostracism to the Christian community. If anyone should confess Jesus as messiah, according to Jn. 9:22, he was excluded from the synagogue. [94] We already have good evidence about the doctrinal and exegetical issues that separated Jew from Christian. Now some of the social consequences can be seen. Lou Martyn has made the very cogent suggestion that the Johannine texts refer to the imposition of the *Birkat ha-minim*, the curse against sectarians which was expanded in this period to include the *minim*. [95]

But the Christian community is also very bothered by the Jewish reaction, for the gospel contains an anti-Jewish polemic of extreme ferocity, culminating in the charge that the Jews are offspring of the devil, while Jesus and his followers are from God. (8:42 f.) This extreme, opposing dualism in the fourth gospel seems parallel to the highly irritated social situation and suggests that such dualism may sometimes arise out of situations of severe social conflict. More can be said about the correlation between polemic and dualism when discussing the extreme gnostics of succeeding cenutries. [96]

What is most important is that the New Testament attests to traditions which, by the methodological assumptions necessary in

[94] See N. A. Dahl, "The Johannine Church and History," in W. Klassen and G. F. Snyder, eds., *Current Issues in New Testament Interpretation* (Nashville: 1962), p. 125 f.

[95] See J. Louis Martyn, *History and Theology in the Fourth Gospel* (New York: 1968).

[96] See below, p. 244 and my article "'Lord of the World' — Angel or Devil?" forthcoming.

studying midrash, could only be dated to the second century actually date to the first century, both in the Greek-speaking philosophical-Hellenistic environment which Philo represented, and the Aramaic and Greek speaking environment described by the gospels. Apparently the categories which the rabbis used to describe heretics in the second century are somewhat serviceable even to more objective historiography of the first century. But since there is no uniquely anti-Christian theme in the rabbinic attack, we cannot conclude that Christians were the only offending group.

One may disagree as to whether or when these groups began to compromise monotheism, which was the force of the rabbinic criticism, since many different positions in Judaism defended themselves with "two powers" arguments. But the terminology itself is apt, because it tells us the categories in which the development of Christianity was seen. It tells us that Christianity was probably one of a number of similar sects. It may have been unique in that it identified a messianic candidate with the manlike figure in heaven who was going to judge the world. But the theme itself was apocalyptic (and possibly mystical) in nature. It may also have been unique to identify a contemporary rather than a hero of the past with an angelic being. [97] But the theme was not, insofar as anyone can prove, the Christian application of a redeemer myth of a single, gnostic pre-existent, divine savior who was going to descend to earth, save those who received him, and reascend to heaven. Rather Christianity was one among a plethora of different sects with similar scriptural traditions. The single gnostic pattern, if there is one, seems to be a rather sophisticated re-understanding of the Christian model.

To summarize, the one sectarian movement in Judaism about which we have considerable evidence is Christianity. There is warrant to believe that "two powers" heresy was manifested in some kinds of Christianity in the first century. The evidence seems to show that Johannine Christianity, at least, was condemned by Jews as "ditheism" and would have considered itself to be "binitarian." There is some evidence that the Greek vocabulary for "two powers" would have been understandable to Paul. He did not use the actual term against his opponents but argued against their concepts of the angelic powers on the basis of God's unity. It is beginning to look like it was Christianity, in its zeal

---

[97] It does not seem likely to me that this was a great innovation. Personages of the recent past, far past, antedeluvian heroes and even angels, were all equally part of the thought-world of first century Judaism.

to apply all Hebrew designations of divinity to Christ, which first put together the complete myth of the redeemed redeemer who descended to earth to save his followers.

The New Testament never overtly identifies Jesus with an angel. On the other hand, the church fathers identify Jesus as an angel quite frequently. Whatever one may say about the variety of Christianity manifested in the New Testament, it seems quite certain, as we shall see, that the Christianity of Justin Martyr and other church fathers would have been condemned by the rabbis as "two powers" speculation.

CHAPTER THIRTEEN

THE CHURCH FATHERS

We have seen that the rabbinic classification of heretics describes sectarian life sensibly, albeit from the rabbinic perspective, from the time of Philo and before through the apocalyptic and gnostic periods. Of course, Christianity was the most important heresy, not only because it was the most successful of the sects, but because it defined the divinity and personality of the "second power" in the clearest and most emphatic way. Since the Christian tradition is manifold and complex, [1] we cannot expect that the concept of an angelic mediator influenced every aspect of it. However, it seems possible, in light of the rabbinic description of Christianity, that such influence is greater than is usually assumed.

Luckily, much of the history of angelic christologies has already been chronicled in the process of tracing the origin of ancient Arianism. [2] In the next few sections on the church fathers, then, I can afford to be even more schematic and selective than previously. I must be content only to mention the angel in the Shepherd of Hermas, which should be seen as intimately related to the principal angel traditions in apocalyptic literature. Hermas talks in many places of a highest angel worthy of reverence, whom most commentators have identified as the Son of God. [3] The angel is given the name Michael, [4] yet the conclusion that he is equivalent to the Son of God or the Christ, is difficult to escape. [5] Both are invested with supreme power over the people of God; both pronounce judgment on the faithful; both hand sinners over to the angel of repentance to record them. [6]

---

[1] See, e.g., J. Robinson & H. Koester, *Trajectories through Early Christianity* (Philadelphia: 1971).

[2] W. Michaelis, *Zur Engelschristologie in Urchristentum*; Werner, *The Formation of the Christian Dogma* (London: 1957), cf., Barbel, *Christos Angelos* (Bonn: 1941), see p. 186 n. 8.

[3] See Barbel, p. 47, n. 4.

[4] Sim. 8, 3, 3.

[5] See Sim. 8, 3, 3 and 5, 6, 4.

[6] Sim. 5, 2-7; 9, 6, 3-6; 9, 10, 4; 8, 2, 5; 8, 4, 3; 9, 7, 1. For a more detailed exposition of the relationship between the angel in Hermas and the angel of YHWH see H. Moxnes, "God and His Angel in the Shepherd of Hermas," *Studia Theologica*,

Justin, the gentile Christian, is the one church father whose relationship to the "two powers controversy" has been noted previously by several scholars. [7] Justin Martyr was born at the beginning of the second century in Shechem, then called Flavia Neapolis, in Samaria. He called himself a Samaritan, which meant only that he was descended from people living in that part of the country and not part of that religious sect, [8] because he stated that he was uncircumcized. [9] The details of Justin's life add evidence for the relationship we have already suspected between Samaritans and early gentile Christianity. Justin's *Dialogue with Trypho* also evinces real polemical use of almost all the scriptural exegesis which the rabbis thought dangerous.

The setting for the *Dialogue* was Ephesus whence Justin had migrated in his Christian mission. The date for the *Dialogue* must have corresponded closely with the Bar Kokhba Revolt, for Justin mentions it often [10] and Trypho is described as a Jewish fugitive who escaped from the turmoil.

Justin's use of midrashic traditions has sometimes been taken as evidence that the *Dialogue* is fictional, serving as a purely literary framework for presenting Justin's views. [11] Yet it certainly reflects one side of the debate between Judaism and Christianity in the early second century, whether the immediate incident be wholly fact, embellished incident, or pure fiction.

The clearest parallel between Justin and the enemies of the rabbis has been mentioned before. [12] By means of Gen. 19:24 Justin procedes to show that a second divine figure, Christ, is responsible for carrying out divine commands on earth:

> "The previously quoted Scriptural passages will make this evident to you," I replied. "Here are the words: 'The sun was risen upon the earth, and Lot entered into Segor. And the Lord rained upon

---

28 (1974), 49-56. He shows that language normally used of God, e.g., as the sender of angels, has been transferred to the principal angel.

[7] **Several scholars** have pointed out Justin's relationship to the aggada. See A. H. Goldfahn, *Justinus Martyr und die Agada*, (Breslau: n.d.). Friedländer, "Patristische und talmudische Studien." Büchler has further emphasized the relevance of Justin for the two powers controversy around Sepphoris & Tiberius, see *Minim*. Also Ginzberg, *Die Aggada bei den Kirchenvätern*.

[8] *Dial.* 120.

[9] *Dial.* 29.

[10] *Dial.* 108; *Apol.* I, 31, for example.

[11] E.g., Weissäcker, *Jahrbuch für Theol.*, 13 (1867), p. 63.

[12] See p. 13 f. and p. 118.

Sodom brimstone and fire from the Lord out of Heaven. And He destroyed these cities and all the country round about.' "

Then the fourth of the companions who remained with Trypho spoke up: "It must therefore be admitted that one of the two angels who went down to Sodom, and whom Moses in the Scriptures calls Lord, is different from Him who is also God, and appeared to Abraham."

"Not only because of that quotation," I said, "must we certainly admit that, besides the creator of the universe, another was called Lord by the Holy Spirit. For this was attested to not only by Moses, but also by David, when he said: 'The Lord said to my Lord: Sit Thou at My right hand, until I make Thy enemies Thy footstool,' and in other words: 'Thy throne, O God is forever and ever; the sceptre of Thy kingdom is a sceptre of uprightness. Thou hast loved justice, and hated iniquity; therefore God, Thy God hath annointed Thee with the oil of gladness above Thy fellows." (Ps. 45:7-8). [13]

It is a Jew, not Justin, who admits that another divine being, "The Lord," was present at the destruction of Sodom and Gomorah, and that this divine being was different from God. From our previous discussion, there is no reason to doubt that such heterodox Jews existed as early as Philo. Justin only endeavored to prove that this second divinity is the Christ. It is significant that the angelic figure is accepted by the Jew—only his messianic status is questioned. This is another piece of evidence that Christianity was the first to connect the messiah and the principal angel. In this place he relies primarily on the various descriptions of vindication and enthronement found in the Psalm texts. Subsequently in the *Dialogue*, he relies on the various theophany texts where a man-like figure appears to the Israelites and their prophets: Gen. 31:10-14 (ch. 58); Gen. 32:22-31 (ch. 58); Gen. 35:6-10 (ch. 58); Ex. 2:23; Ex. 3:16, 3:2-4 and Gen. 35:7 (ch. 60). His conclusion is:

> When the Scripture here states that an angel of the Lord appeared to Moses, and then announced that He is Lord and God, it refers to the same person who is identified in many of our earlier quotations as the minister to God who is above the world and above whom there is no God. [14]

Since Justin understands the appearance of God in Jacob's dreams, wrestlings and even at the burning bush as a single consistent figure, he is able to promote both the independent personality of the being

---

[13] *Dial*. 56.
[14] *Dial*. 60 end and 61.

manifested and his divine nature. [15] Like Philo Justin calls the *logos*
another God (*heteros theos*), distinct in number, if not in essence.
(ch. 56). The sharply drawn personality of this manifestation (together
with the doctrine of the incarnation) is the element which most
distinguishes Justin's concept of *logos* from Philo's. But, as Goodenough has persuasively argued, both Justin and Philo should be seen
as evidencing examples of the same Hellenistic Jewish traditions. [16]
Like Philo, Justin believes that the *logos* is an angel in that it is a
power (*dynamis*) radiating from God. Like the angels it has freedom
of choice, but unlike the angels, Justin's *logos* has self-direction.
(ch. 88). Therefore, although Justin implies that the *logos* is the
same as an angel, he prefers to emphasize its distinctiveness in ways
that never occurred to Philo.

As further evidence that these traditions had a background in
Hellenistic Judaism before they were put to Christian use, Goodenough
shows that most of the titles applied to the *logos* by Justin are the same
as those used by Philo and other Hellenistic Jewish writers: *theos,
kyrios, angelos, dynamis, anatolē, litha, petra, archē, hemera (phos),
sophia, anēr, anthrōpos*, Israel, Jacob etc.: [17]

As Justin says:

> "So my friends," I said, "I shall show from Scripture that the God
> has begotten of Himself a certain rational power as a beginning be-
> fore all other creatures. The Holy Spirit indicates this power by
> various titles, sometimes the Glory of the Lord, at other times, Son
> or Wisdom or Angel or God or Lord or Word. He even called him-
> self commander-in-chief when he appeared in human guise to Josue,
> the son of Nun." [18]

To substantiate the claim of the *logos*'s primacy in the divine economy, Justin points to the grammatical plural referring to God in
Gen. 1:26 and Gen. 3:22. [19] After this he adduces passages to support
the incarnation from the virgin birth to the ascension. [20] Of course,
the argument is not well received by his Jewish opponents, even those
who admitted the existence of the second power, and Justin is required

---

[15] E. R. Goodenough, *The Theology of Justin Martyr: An Investigation into the
Conceptions of the Earliest Christian Literature and its Hellenistic and Judaistic
Influences* (Jena: 1923), p. 143 f.

[16] E. R. Goodenough, *The Theology of Justin Martyr*, p. 147 f.

[17] E. R. Goodenough, *The Theology of Justin Martyr*, p. 168-172.

[18] *Dial.* 61, p. 244.

[19] *Dial.* 62.

[20] *Dial.* 63-65.

to emphasize his argument by coming at essentially the same scripture from a variety of different perspectives. At one point he goes into a rather fanciful exegesis to show that the name of God, which the angel in Ex. 23:21 carried, is: "Jesus:"

> Now from the book of Exodus we know that Moses cryptically indicated that the name of God himself (which He says was not revealed to Abraham or to Jacob) was also Jesus. For it is written: "And the Lord said to Moses, say to this people: Behold, I send my angel before thy face, to keep thee in thy journey, and bring thee into the place that I have prepared for thee. Take notice of him, and obey his voice; do not disobey him, for he will not pardon thee, because My name is in him." Consider well who it was that led your fathers into the promised land, namely he who was at first named Auses (Osee), but later renamed Jesus (Josue). If you keep this in mind, you will also realize that the name of him who said to Moses, "My name is in him," was Jesus. Indeed he was also called Israel, and he similarly bestowed this name upon Jacob. [21]

While it is clear that Justin is using "two powers" traditions to discuss Jesus, the traditions could have hardly originated with the identification of Jesus as the angel in Exodus. The attempt to see Jesus as the angel's name is secondary. Rather, Justin is taking over a previous exegetical, possibly mystical tradition, applying the name of his particular savior, and defending his belief against the other candidates for the office of angelic mediator. The tradition itself, without the Christian coloring, can be seen as early as Philo.

Nor did Justin neglect the Dan. 7:9 passage. [22] He returned to that theme again and again, leaving no doubt it forms one central point of his faith. Since these are the very passages against which the rabbis warned, we should conclude that the rabbinic polemics against "two powers in heaven," by the middle of the tannaitic period, were directed against gentile Christians like Justin. Chronologically, it would correspond with the first written level of tradition in rabbinic writing and may be preserved at the core of the Mekhilta traditions where the opponents are actually called gentiles. Although Justin was Christian and could even call himself a Samaritan, he and people like him could easily have been seen as gentiles by the rabbis. This demonstrates that the reports of "two powers" do not merely put scripture in the mouths of the gentile opponents; they report actual scriptural debates.

---

[21] *Dial.* 75. Probably, another form of the traditions evinced in the **Prayer of Jacob** lies behind this argument. See p. 199 f.

[22] E.g., *Dial.* 76.

It is likely that the first fixed copy of the rabbinic traditions in the Mekhilta (which seems to come from exactly this time, as indicated by internal evidence, [23]) was a response to people like Justin who were promulgating their doctrine of the Christian savior.

As was just concluded, Justin did not invent the arguments he used, nor was he the first to use them. The rabbinic texts, however, begin to appear at the time in which Justin was alive and reflect enemies of Judaism like Justin who were contemporary with the Bar Kochba revolt. [24]

Several traditions corresponding to the rabbinic ones are found in another second century church father, Theophilus of Antioch. [25] His relationship with midrashic traditions has been noticed before, but no conclusions have previously been drawn about his relationship to the "two powers" controversy. He too uses Christ as equivalent to *logos*, on the basis on John 1, but he uses several interesting scriptural quotations to prove his point. [26] He witnesses to the traditions we saw in Philo in which the *logos* is described as God's "place:"

> Since the *logos* is God and derived his nature from God, whenever the Father of the Universe wills to do so, He sends him into some place where he is present and is heard and seen. [27]

Further, after claiming that another title for the *logos* is "light," Theophilus could posit the idea that the *logos* helped God in the process of creation:

> The unique spirit occupied the place of light and was situated between the water and the heaven so that, so to speak, the darkness might not communicate with the heaven which was nearer to God, before God said: "Let there be light." [28]

---

23 See p. 47 f.

24 We know, of course that Christian gentiles were not the only gentiles to listen to the words of Jewish scriptures. Many people came to hear the scriptures read in synagogues. Judaism of that day had attracted many interested observers, even though it had not undertaken as zealous a proselytizing program as had Christianity. There is considerable evidence that Christian success in part depended on the attraction of that faith to gentiles already conversant with Judaism but unable to become completely Jewish either because they feared circumcision or because some Jews put other constraints and restrictions upon them. So we must not rule out the God-fearers or *sebomenoi* as the gentiles in these texts, even though we have no independent texts from them. See Paul Donahue, dissertation, Yale 1974.

25 Barbel, *Christos Angelos* (Bonn: 1941), p. 61 f.

26 See Theophilus *Ad Autolycum* I, 3; II 22; also Gen. 1:26 is used in II, 18.

27 *Ad Autolycum* 2:22.

28 *Ad Autolycum* 2:13.

For him, "In the beginning," the first words of Genesis, has the meaning of "by means of the beginning," [29] which is yet another name for the *logos* and characterizes it as Lord and agent of God in the creation. Traditions like this which have Philonic antecedents may well be the kind of doctrine opposed by use of the tradition about Ishmael and Akiba.

However, he is much opposed to those who can derive *a multiplicity* of gods in creation:

> And Moses, who lived many years before Solomon, or rather the Logos of God speaking him as an instrument, says: "In the beginning God made heaven and earth." (Gen. 1 : 1) First he mentioned beginning and creation and only then did he introduce God, for it is not right to mention God idly and in vain (id. Ex. 20 : 3). For the divine Sophia knew in advance that some persons were going to speak nonsense and make mention of a multiplicity of non-existent gods. Therefore, in order for the real God to be known through his work and to show that by his *logos* God made heaven and earth and what is in them, he said: "In the beginning God made heaven and earth." Then after mentioning this creation, he gives an explanation: "And the earth was invisible and formless and darkness was above the abyss and spirit of God was borne above the water" (Gen. 1 : 2). [30]

Theophilus does not identify his opponents. But he talks about them as if they, to use the rabbinic term, believe in "many powers in heaven." His use of Gen. 1:1 sounds like the debate between Ishmael and Akiba, or at least, the ways in which Ishmael and Akiba's exegesis was understood by later rabbis. [31] This points out that someone whom the rabbis would have called a believer in "two powers" and who believed in a divine partner in creation nevertheless opposed other traditions about the creation which he described as "many powers." It would not be too rash to attempt to identify the "many powers" groups with the varieties of gnosticism and Jewish Christians that elaborated grand schemes of the cosmic spheres, inhabited by myriads of angels.

Theophilus also opposes the idea that two different gods were involved in creation—one creating man, therefore masculine in nature; the other creating woman, therefore feminine in nature:

> You shall be like Gods—so that no one would suppose that one god made man and another made woman, He made the two together. Moreover, He formed only man from the earth so that thus the

29 *Ibid.*
30 *Ad Autolycum* II, 10.

expected. However, in a sudden turn, Hippolytus also accuses Callistus of the same crime, even though the latter was presumably aware of the dangers of patripassionism. Most interesting of all, Hippolytus records one of the charges made against him by Callistus as ditheism, (*ditheous*). [49] Now, it is difficult to show the exact nature of the relationship of this polemic to the rabbinic one. But the great similarity in terms and scriptures may point to influence. It seems likely that the church continued to use the stronger term "two gods" because of the polemical context. This would suggest that the synagogue must have ceased to be actively involved in polemic when it prudently changed to the designation "two powers" at the end of the tannaitic and beginning of the amoraic period.

A philosophical context for the argument, corresponding to the exegetical context, is to be noticed in the writing of Origen (ca. 185-250). As an Alexandrian, he was heir to the Philonic tradition and is clearly also in the tradition of middle Platonism represented by Albinus. He felt that the Son of God, as *logos*, could be called a *deuteros theos*. [50] In his *Dialogue with Heraclides*, the issue between the two men is centered on the Eucharist. Apparently, they both agreed that Christianity could be said to believe in "two Gods," although only in a special way: "We are not afraid to speak, in one sense of two Gods, in another sense of one God." [51]

His reservations against describing Christianity as believing in "two Gods" are understandable. Jews, Christian modalists and even pagans could accuse him of violating monotheism. In fact, he is forced to defend himself from such a charge levelled by Celsus, who says that Christians believe that two lords rule the world. [52] By now, many different groups of people were using the same arguments in a variety of contrasting ways. Of course, wherever the charge of "two gods" was brought, the familiar scriptural passages from Dt. and Is. as well as "I and my father are one" from the New Testament were the corrective. Origen can bring them in to defend the monotheism of Christianity, even while maintaining "two Gods" elsewhere. [53]

---

[49] *Ref.* IX, 11, 12.

[50] *Contra Celsum* V, 39; VI, 61; VII, 57; *De Oratione* XV, 1; *Com. ev. Joh.* II, 2; X, 37 (21).

[51] *Dial Heracl.* 2, 3 Oulton, ed., Library of Christian Classics, v. 2 *Alexandrian Christianity*, p. 438, 1. 124-125.

[52] *Contra Celsum*, VIII, 12 .

[53] Comp. *Contra Celsum* II, 24 where he shows that the same god both smites and heals, based on Dt., with the places in which he maintains "two gods."

Aphrahat also reviewed the scriptural exegesis against Christians which he has heard from the Jews. He said the Jews use Ex. 34 and Dt. 32:39 to show that God has no son, [54] as indeed the rabbis do in Sifre and Mekhilta. [55] At a fairly late period of time, the argument against God having a son continued in use against Christians.

Equally interesting is the polemic against Christians developed by Julian in the pagan revival. The surviving fragments of Julian's writing against Christians show that he criticized Christians for having given up the belief in God's unity when they adopted the doctrine of the trinity, while the Jews continued to preach the original idea. [56] Against Christians who protested that they did not worship more than one God, Julian quoted the New Testament: "And the Word was with God and was God" (John 1:18). [57] Obviously Julian had learned Christian scripture. Nor did his training stop with the New Testament; he knew the Old Testament and evidently was even familiar with rabbinic writings. There is a definite relationship between the arguments of Julian and the Jewish opponents of Justin in the *Dialogue with Trypho* although modalism may have provided the channel of transmission. Julian's observation that Gen. 49:10 could not be said about Jesus is the same as the comment of the Jewish sage to Justin. So Dt. 18:18 and Nu. 24:17, other of Julian's proof-texts against christology, may also have been in use in Jewish, anti-Christian polemic. [58] Even more to the point is Julian's use of rabbinic or modalist polemic when he charged the Christians with worshipping, "a second god." Julian showed that Moses repeatedly forbad such worship by citing Dt. 4:35-39, Dt. 6:4 and Dt. 32:39——the very passages which are developed for use against "two powers" in rabbinic literature. By the time of Julian therefore, the "two powers" argument was quite normally used both by and against Christians. This points to the existence of firm literary traditions but we know from the apocalyptic and Philonic evidence that the history of such traditions extended back as early as the first

---

R. Kimelman, dissertation in progress at Yale University, has pointed out that Origen and R. Yohanan interpret the Song of Songs in such corresponding ways that it is likely that they actually heard of each other's arguments in third century Caesaria.

[54] Aphrahat I, 785.

[55] See also Git. 57b; b. Pes. 68a; b. San. 91b. Neusner, *Aphrahat*, 159. See p. 11 f., p. 139 f. where we inferred that Christianity was the target, though it was not mentioned by name.

[56] Julian *c. Christ.* (p. 2133, Lehrman) and Lactantius IV, 29, 1.

[57] *c. Christ.* 55; 120.

[58] J. Gager, *Moses in Greco-Roman Paganism* (Nashville: 1972) p. 109.

century, even when we can only date the earliest rabbinic recension of these arguments to the second century. In comparing the use of the terms of the polemic in rabbinic and Christian settings, it has seemed logical to assume that "two gods" is a better term for battling with heretics, while "two powers" is better for instructing the faithful. If so the change from "two gods" to "two powers" in rabbinic writings would signal a change in the function of the tradition. It would have been done by rabbis more interested in warning their constituents than actually in battling the heretics.

CHAPTER FOURTEEN

MARCION

Only when the scope of the "two powers" controversy has been outlined within both the Christian and Jewish communities, can one hope to approach the figure of Marcion. Certainly he is a key figure in the debate concerning dualism. The complexities that attend serious study of Marcion might justify a whole book on this aspect of his thought. Again we are in the position of having to deal with issues very selectively, primarily in order to date the rabbinic evidence, in the hope that some of the issues ignored or only touched upon now can be investigated more fully at a later date.

Marcion has been seen as a prime candidate for the rabbinic polemic against two powers. [1] However, we have already seen evidence that the controversy has roots that go back considerably earlier than he. It is growing clear that the rabbinic texts present us with a palimpsest of different traditions. Yet the Marcionite polemic has certain characteristics which will affect our identification of the targets of the rabbinic polemic. We shall see that, although he and his followers were participants in polemics, Marcion's method makes it unlikely that he himself could have been the original target of the rabbinic charges. In studying Marcion, then, we shall uncover merely one more layer of the development of the polemic, not the origin of the issue.

In his *Letter to the Phillipians* (7:1) Polycarp of Smyrna warned that he who denied that there can be either judgment or resurrection should be considered "the first-born of Satan." We realize that such issues were characteristic of both rabbinic and early Christian communities. By the time of Irenaeus, a legend had developed that Marcion had asked Polycarp for recognition as bishop only to be rebuffed by the words "I recognize you—as the first-born of Satan!" [2]

The term "first-born of Satan" has a Hebrew equivalent (BKWR STN) which seems to have had a similar and contemporary use within Jewish exegesis—as a term of reproach for someone who did not

---

[1] See Marmorstein, *Background*, pp. 141-204.
[2] *Adv. Haer.*, III 3, 4.

follow the accepted tradition of scriptural interpretation. [3] (In the rabbinic occurrence, the offender had followed Shammaite *halakha*.) Since the first-born of Satan is Cain, as we discovered previously, [4] the term probably alluded to the tradition we noted as early as Philo that the human race was descended from two different genealogies—the good from Seth and the bad from Cain. [5] It seems likely that the term was developed in Jewish sectarian life and was later applied to Marcion. If we believe Harnack, [6] there was good reason for this term of derision to have been applied to Marcion. What made Marcion extreme in his belief according to Harnack, and what would make him a good target for the term "first-born of Satan," was the idea that only those who had been rejected by the creator (e.g., Cain and his descendents) could be led out from the lower world by Christ, while Abraham and those justified by the creator must remain unredeemed. [7]

Apparently Marcion accepted the traditions that those who did not follow the "orthodox exegesis" were descended from Cain, but he transvalued that tradition so that Cain became the ancestor of those elected of Christ, in turn, the messenger of a good, saving God yet unknown and unprophesied in the Old Testament. [8]

Such common terminology between Jewish and Christian communities is important to us because it points to a relationship between them. We already have good evidence that such relationships existed, based on corresponding terminology and exegesis in the rabbis and church fathers. Although the church's use of language parallel to rabbinic practice in calling Marcion names appears now to tell us nothing specific about the "two powers" controversy, the reversal theme will provide a

---

[3] b. Yeb. 16a, j. Yeb. 3a.

[4] See N. A. Dahl, "Der Erstgeborene Satans und Der Vater des Teufels (Polyk 7:1 and John 8:44)," in *Apophoreta* (Berlin: 1964), pp. 70-84. See p. 81 f., p. 255.

[5] See p. 173 f. Philo in *Post.* 35, 38 f., 42, 43, 45; *Det.* 32, 68, 78, 103; *Fug.* I 64. See also Armenian Adam 63. 64.

[6] See Harnack, *Marcion: Das Evangelium vom fremden Gott: Eine Monographie zur Geschichte der Grundlegung der katholischen Kirche* (Leipzig: 2nd ed., 1924). In Harnack's opinion, based on the reports of Irenaeus, Marcion believed that Christ's function was to be judge at the end of the world, redeeming the good men from among the living and from the grave. If so, this would have been an idea he held in common with orthodox Christianity.

[7] Cf., see Iren., *Haer.*, I, XXV, 1; Origen, *Contr. Cels.*, IV, 10 and E. C. Blackman, *Marcion and his Influence* (London: 1948), p. 102.

[8] Marcion was not alone in this; the Cainite gnostics also had such a belief, as noted previously, p. 82 f.

model for a hypothesis about mutual dependence later on. [9] Previously in this discussion, it has always seemed more plausible to reconstruct the transmission of a tradition from an original context in Judaism into Christianity. From Marcion onwards, the case is no longer clear. Since Marcion is primarily a Christian heretic, and since he represented fully as much a danger to the Christian community as to the Jewish one, the original source of the defense against him should remain open. If the rabbis were concerned with Marcionite theology they might have been dependent on the church fathers for their defense against him. It is also possible that each community developed its defense against Marcion independently.

We know about Marcion's doctrines from various polemics against him within the church fathers. Justin probably wrote the earliest treatise devoted solely to discrediting Marcion. Although scholars have detected parts of it in Irenaeus' discussion of Marcion, Justin's work has not survived intact. Irenaeus, in turn, wrote little as compared to the systematic work by Tertullian afterwards. Therefore, most of the evidence about Marcion is not contemporary with him and may testify not to Marcion's own doctrine but to what Marcion's later adherents believed as well as the extent to which the church fathers were willing to villify their opponents. Justin Martyr is the first to mention him, saying:

> One Marcion, a man of Pontus, who is even now alive, teaching those who believe in him to pay honor to a different god, greater than the creator; and this man has by the assistance of demons caused many of every nation to utter blasphemies denying the God who made this universe and professing that another, a greater than He, has done greater things. [10]

Irenaeus said that Marcion was a follower of Cerdo and that both taught that the god discussed in Torah is just or righteous (*dikaios*) but that he is not the father of Jesus, who was descended from an unknown and wholly good (*agathos*) god. [11] The Old Testament god is "just" or "righteous" in the sense of being the administrator of justice—simply paying men what they deserve for their actions. Besides this retributive aspect he is also the creator of the world. On the other hand, the New Testament god is good in the sense of being

---

[9] See below, p. 245 f.

[10] Apology, 1:26.

[11] Iren., *Haer.*, I, XXV, 1. Since Marcion is a true dualist, I have chosen not to capitalize his references to biblical divinity.

noble or generous or kind. Corresponding to the Old Testament god's role at creation, the New Testament god is the author of salvation. Then Irenaeus tells us that Marcion believed Jesus to have been an emissary of the good god, appearing suddenly in human shape at the start of his mission. Marcion only accepted those parts of Christian writings which substantiated his point. He accepted Luke alone of the gospels but abridged it to avoid any annunciation or birth narratives. Likewise, he edited the letters of Paul in such a way as to eliminate any inference that an Old Testament prophecy was fulfilled by Jesus or that the Christ aided in the work of creation. Lastly, Irenaeus tells us that Marcion made all the villains of the Old Testament into heroes.

Tertullian begins his treatise by saying that Marcion, like other heretics of Tertullian's day, [12] was perplexed by the problem of evil, especially as it was expressed in the book of Isaiah: "It is I who create evil things" (Is. 45:7). This testimony about the value of Isaiah 45 to heretics parallels the rabbis sensitivity to a similar passages in liturgy. But it does not make Marcion the first target of the heretical charges. It only makes clear that there were a variety of heretical notions which the rabbis wished to avoid and that Marcion promulgated one of them. It also clarifies rabbinic interest in arguments about God's justice and mercy.

Though he was strictly dualistic, many of Marcion's disciples followed more moderate routes. For instance, Apelles reduced the dualism of Marcion to a single god with one power (*dynamis*) who yet created a principal angel, called variously a second principle or second god, (*deuteros theos*). [13] Whereas the followers of Marcion would seem uncontestably to have used some of the dangerous ideas and scriptures characteristic of the "two powers" controversy, the same cannot necessarily be said of Marcion himself.

Pure Marcionite dualism then was a special, unique and shortlived development in the history of dualism and should involve identifiably different uses of scripture. Because his superior god is a stranger whose existence was previously unknown and unexpected, Marcion had to reject the Old Testament as irrelevant to the process of salvation, yet not as historically inaccurate. There could be no prophecies of the advent of the true Christ in the Old Testament, since the Christ was

---

[12] "Quod et nunc multi et maxime haeretici," *Adv. Marc.* 1:2.

[13] See Harnack, *Marcion*, pp. 188-92. Apelles' god has a single power as described in Epiph., *Haer.*, 44, 1. His principal angel, like the *logos* of Philo, is called *deuteros theos* in Hipp.. *Ref.*, X, 20.

absolutely unknown until he appeared. [14] In fact, Marcion felt that the Jewish messiah, as a representative of the just god, was prophesied and would appear as a kind of anti-Christ. Furthermore, Marcion disallowed the kind of allegorical interpretation which was so popular in Philo and the church fathers. [15] Therefore all Old Testament prophecies were either fulfilled in their time or refer to the Jewish messiah who was to be a national (albeit also a supernatural) deliverer. Thus, one can immediately observe that Marcion's understanding of Dan. 7:9 f. and the theophany passages in Gen. Ex. or Ez. would not have anything to do with the god of salvation. He might even have agreed with the messianic interpretation of Dan. 7 given by Akiba, but he certainly would not have used the passage to discuss anything beyond the national deliverance of Israel. These aspects of Marcion's thought help us understand the ferocity of the church fathers' opposition to him. They did not mind his deprecation of the Israel of the flesh. Rather his canon of New Testament writings was dangerous and the church required the Old Testament authority in order to foretell the coming of the Christian messiah.

Because Marcion's writings have not come down to us directly, it is difficult to draw firm conclusions about the scriptural passages which were most important to him. However, from the reports about the *Antitheses* which Harnack collected, some of Marcion's techniques of exegesis and certain of his favorite scriptures can be inferred. According to the church fathers he found those scriptures important which speak of the Old Testament god as the author of evil. This would include Isaiah 45:7 (which Tertullian placed at the center of his thought), but also Jeremiah 18:11 and the several other passages which discuss the power of God to do evil. [16] Still, Marcion does not want to describe the Old Testament god as purely evil. Rather, he wants to show that his justice is inferior to the goodness of the New Testament god. Therefore, he emphasizes those aspects of Old Testament narrative which imply divine ignorance or inferiority. The god of the Old Testament has to ask Adam where he is. He has to ask Adam and Eve what they have done (Gen. 3:9). He has to ask Cain where his

---

[14] Harnack, *Marcion*, pp. 188-92. In his strict adherence to the principle that the Old Testament prophecies refer to events congruent with their context, Marcion had a rather modern perspective on the Old Testament.

[15] Ter. *Adv. Marc.*, V, 18; see Harnack, *Marcion*, p. 260*.

[16] Harnack, p. 260. Ter. *Adv. Marc.*, II, 13 f., 24 and frequently.

brother Abel is (Gen. 4:9). [17] He must descend in order to see what the outcry of Sodom and Gomorrah signifies (Gen. 18:21). [18] Marcion further points out that the Old Testament god does and says many contradictory things, showing that he is inconstant. For instance, he repents. [19] Now these passages turn out to be generally similar to the scriptural passages used by the critics of the Torah against whom both the rabbis and Philo polemicized. But they are not used by Marcion to develop "two powers" arguments.

In fact, Marcion seems to agree with the rabbis that one god speaks through the whole of the Jewish canon. The rabbis would say that God is both merciful or just. Marcion would say that he is by nature just but this would include being cruel on occasion. [20] However much the rabbis disagreed with his opinion of the Old Testament and the character of the divinity described therein, they would not have used "two powers" arguments to defeat him. Marcion himself, in the context of his own thought, finds principal support from the sayings of Jesus in Lk 16:13, (Mt. 6:24) and Lk 6:43 (Mt. 7:18) which warn against serving two masters or against a divided household. [21]

Accordingly, rabbinic and Marcionite beliefs appear similar enough to Tertullian that he sometimes groups them both together:

> It is now possible for the heretic to learn, and the Jew as well, what he ought to know already, the reason for the Jew's errors: . . . [22]

Also:

> Let the heretic now give up borrowing poison from the Jew—the asp as they say, from the viper: let him from now on belch forth the slime of his own particular devices, as he maintains that Christ was a phantasm: except that this opinion too will have had other inventors, those so-to-speak premature and abortive Marcionites whom the apostle John pronounced antichrists, who denied that Christ was come in the flesh but not with the intention of setting up the law of a second god [alterius deus]—else for this too they would have been censured (by the apostle)—but because they had assumed it incredible that God (should take to him human) flesh. [23]

---

[17] Harnack, p. 269*. This resembles the gnostic arguments reported by Irenaeus. See p. 227 f. It is opposed by the rabbis, see p. 57.

[18] See Harnack, p. 269*. This may explain some of the language of the Targumim, p. 84 f., p. 373 f.

[19] Harnack, p. 268 f. See, e.g., Gen. 6:6.

[20] Harnack, p. 271*.

[21] Harnack, p. 260*.

[22] *Adv. Marc.*, III, 7, Evans, I, 187.

[23] Ter., *Adv. Marc.*, III, 8; (Evans, I, p. 191).

This section of Tertullian's work is known to have circulated independently under the title of *adversus Iudaeos*! [24] Evidently the Tertullian's interpretation of the Old Testament prophecies in a Christian sense attempts to be no less valid against Jews, who deny the incarnation and the truth of the New Testament, than against Marcionites who deny the Christian value of the Old Testament by asserting that there are two gods. The syntax is quite ambiguous, but Tertullian here seems to me ironically not to understand "a second God" as a term of derision against Marcionites. However, Tertullian asserts as counter-arguments to Marcion (and Jews) the very Old Testament passages which the rabbis found dangerous as grounds for "two powers" interpretations. It is clear, then, that the accusation has became conventional, having different meanings in different contexts.

Tertullian compares the Old Testament references to the "son of man" with the New Testament "son of man" sayings of Jesus to show that the Old Testament did, indeed, foretell the coming of Christ. [25] In one place he uses Ps. 110:1 to proclaim the "son of man" as identical with Jesus who has been raised in power to be seated next to God. [26] Furthermore, to prove that Christ is present in the Old Testament he has to retreat from the antinomianism of some of his predecessors. [27] He maintains that the good God was present at the giving of the Ten Commandments, by asserting that the Christ, even there, was God's intermediary. As proof of this, he quotes Ex. 23:20, one of the passages which gave the rabbis such trouble: "I send my angel before thy face, to guard thee in the way and to bring thee into the land which I have prepared for thee: give heed to him and hear him, disobey him not." [28]

---

[24] The wording of Tertullian's work so closely parallels the anonymous *adversus Iudaeos* that it is possible to correct the defective reading of either one from the other. Several theories have been propounced about the relationship between them. Professor Gilles Quispel, *De bronnen van Tertullianus' adversus Marcionem* (1943) suggests that the author of the *adversus Iudaeos* is the Christian apostate whom Tertullian condemns for having pirated his work in *Adv. Marc.* I, 1. H. Traenkle, in his edition of *adversus Iudaeus* (1964), says that it is Tertullian's own work, but is earlier than *Adv. Marc.* See Evans, I, p. xix.

[25] *Adv. Marc.*, IV, 10, 9; (Evans, II, p. 301 f.) and IV, 39, 11; (Evans, II, p. 489).

[26] Ter., *Adv. Marc.*, IV, 41, 4 f.; (Evans, II, p. 497).

[27] On this problem of the abrogation of the law and the church fathers' retreat from the doctrine, see G. M. Werner, *The Formation of the Christian Dogma*, pp. 71-94.

[28] Ter. *Adv. Marc.*, III, 16, Evans, I, p. 219. Note dependence on Justin who used a similar argument against the Jews. See p. 224.

Similarly, Tertullian uses Ps. 22:2 to show that Jesus communicated with his Father in heaven while on the cross.

Not only is Marcion's exegesis of scripture similar to the rabbinic exegesis in some respects, but also Tertullian, as an opponent of Marcion, exhibits many of the characteristics of "two powers" heresy which offended the rabbis. Of course, this is to be expected, in part, since Tertullian is usually seen to have developed his defense against Marcion out of writings which came down to him from Justin, Irenaeus, and Theophilus, all of whom have assumed candidacy for the charge of "two powers" heresy. [29] It also implies that some modalists may have accused Christian orthodoxy of believing in a second God in order to group it together with Marcionism. The exegeses typical of this heresy in Judaism thus came to be completely revalued in Christianity.

As his use of "alterius deus" seems to imply, Tertullian can also use anti-dualism arguments against Marcionism which are familiar to us from rabbinic writings themselves:

> To such a degree is this justice, even plentitude of divinity itself . . . God Father and Lord, Father in clemency, Lord in discipline ... Thou shall love God and Thou shall fear Him . . . The same God who smites also heals: He kills and also makes alive, He brings down, He rises up: He creates evil, but also makes peace. So that on this suggestion too I have to answer the heretics. "See," they say, "He himself claims to be the creator of evil things when He says: 'It is I who create evil' . . . " [30]

It is surprising to see Tertullian marshall what look like Philonic or rabbinic arguments against "two powers" to defeat Marcion. The backbone of the passage is Dt. 32:39 which was central to the rabbinic exegesis against "two powers." Nor is it the only time that Tertullian relies on this passage:

> Why need you explain a difference of facts as an opposition of *authorities*? Why need you distort against the Creator those antitheses in the evidences, which you can recognize also in His own thoughts and affection? *I will smite*, He says, and *I will heal. I will slay*, He says and also *I will make alive* by establishing evil things and making peace. [31]

In this case Tertullian might be relying on a rabbinic tradition directly or indirectly through other church fathers, who had used it in

---

[29] See, e.g., Evans, I, p. xx.
[30] Tert. *Adv. Marc.*, II, 14; (Evans, I, p. 125). Note the similarity to the Philonic exegesis of the names of God.
[31] Tert., *Adv. Marc.*, IV, 1; (Evans, II, p. 261).

their battles with heretics. It seems most likely, however, that Tertullian is trying to reinterpret Deut. 32:39 because it is a scriptural passage Marcion himself used. [32] In Marcion's system, the statement of Dt. 32:39 can only be said by the inferior god of the Old Testament. Tertullian is trying to prove that the Old Testament God is good as well as just. Notice that in doing so he promulgates a distinction between YHWH and God, denying only the opposition between the powers. Marcion used Dt. 32:39 to show the ignorance and inferiority of the god of the Jews. Tertullian wishes to disprove dualism but does not necessarily object to a binitarian interpretation. When viewed together with the christological conflicts outlined in the last chapter we see the subtlety of the argument in a Christian context.

This is a special example of the inter-relationship between Christian and Jewish communities because Dt. 32 is especially important to the rabbinic polemic against "two powers." It is evidenced often in tannaitic writings as proof against binitarianism entirely. It seems obvious that the rabbis could not have brought up this passage originally to defeat Marcion, because Marcion would have been able to agree to all the rabbinic arguments against the doctrine of "two powers" within the Old Testament. If the rabbinic use is in any way related to the Christian and Marcionite use, it would have had to evolve earlier than Marcion. Marcion himself need never have heard the rabbinic use of Dt. 32 at all because he could have heard it from a source within the church. It may even be that the church's usage contributed to the evolution of standard terminology within Judaism. The exegetical issue dates from the first century but the terminology was standardized in this context. The most important point is to note that Marcion's statement of the ignorance of the Old Testament god becomes a typical refutation of the rabbinic understanding of Dt. 32, both for Marcion's followers and for other groups of his day. The rabbis stress God's unity by means of Dt. 32. Some gnostics will attribute these passages to the demiurge who promulgated his uniqueness only because he is ignorant.

We are left with the conclusion that the rabbinic polemic against "two powers" may oppose Tertullian's theology but could not have arisen to combat Marcion. In many respects Marcion's exegesis resembles some of the critics of the Torah in Philo's time. No doubt philosophical discussions about the nature of evil influenced him significantly. Many rabbinic traditions about justice and mercy may have had Marcion in

---

[32] See Harnack, p. 264* who relies on Origen for this conclusion.

mind. But the debate over "two powers" must be earlier than Marcion since Marcion's use of scripture, when relevant at all, presumes that the debate has already reached a certain stage. Since Marcion himself lived in the first half of the second century, we have more evidence that the debate antedates the earliest references in rabbinic literature and seems appropriate to the first century. Some of Marcion's followers, like Apelles, certainly become relevant to the polemic when they give up the radical dualism of Marcion and turn the inferior god into a helping angel or *deus secundus*. In this respect they are no different from a host of gnostic sects proliferating during this period. It is to gnosticism that we must now turn our attention.

CHAPTER FIFTEEN

GNOSTICISM

By the end of the second century, at least two different kinds of heretics were opposed in rabbinic polemic. The earliest polemic was designed to counter apocalyptic, mystical or Christian identifications of a manlike figure enthroned as judge next to God, as described in various epiphany texts. The second to emerge involved the claim that the creator was ignorant of a higher god and that there was a complete separation of divine mercy from divine justice, even to the extent of making them properties of two different gods. The first tradition could be seen as early as Philo in Hellenistic Judaism and was continuously employed by mystics, apocalyptists and Christians. It was opposed by the rabbis in traditions which antedate the first midrashic recensions of the post-Bar Kochba times. The second theme (divine mercy and justice) was present in Philo and the rabbis but it developed as a separate polemic only after "two powers" traditions had already started—in fact, as the rabbinic corrective to "two powers" heresy. It may have been asserted by the rabbis strenuously in opposition to Marcion. Based on the synoptic apocalypse, early Christianity may well have felt that the function of the second figure was to judge the world, not be merciful to it as in Marcion's system. So Marcion's doctrine represents a clear break from Christian conceptions as well as from the exegetical traditions in Judaism.

Is there any historical relationship between binitarian "two powers" heretics and dualistic "two powers" heretics? Were they historically related or merely classified together by the rabbis? It may be that Christians and gnostics (who are reportedly the best examples of binitarian and dualistic "two powers" heretics) are entirely different movements which were put together by the rabbis because of certain gross similarities. Yet, complete separation of the two communities should not be seen as probable because, in characterizing gnostics as Christian heretics, even the church fathers admitted an intimate relationship between the two.

If it is true that only the second angelic figure in heaven has a continuous history in heterodox exegesis and that the argument about mercy and justice was used extensively first by the rabbis against

Christians, gnostics and Marcion, then we are faced with the difficulty of explaining how some "two powers in heaven" heretics changed the early concept of co-operating deities into the two antagonistic deities characteristic of later gnosticism.

Is there anything in the rabbinic evidence which helps us understand the relationships between gnosticism and Christianity? The answer, I feel, is "Yes." There are some clues about the relationship between them in the scriptures they use. Gnosticism is an extremely widespread phenomenon in the late Hellenism occurring in many different communities—Jewish, Christian and pagan—so no history of traditions in any one community can account for the whole development definitively. Nor can any single argument be viewed as absolute in such a complex situation. Nevertheless, one significant aspect of the development of gnosticism in the Jewish and Christian communities is highlighted by the scriptural traditions which we have been tracing, when seen together with the gnostic texts found in the church fathers and those from Nag Hammadi. The change from binitarian to dualistic and gnostic systems seems more closely related to polemical exaggerations between groups than to the earlier sectarian dualisms (like Qumran, for example). Several intermediate systems will have to be mentioned before the reason for the change from binitarianism to dualism in sectarian literature will become clear.

The *Poimandres* is one of the earliest examples of these traditions. C. H. Dodd dates it just prior to the time of Valentinus (130-140 C.E.) but remarks that its exact date cannot yet be fixed. [1] As Dodd shows, the work is an amalgam of the creation story based on the Bible and various conceptions current in stoic and Platonic thought. At the base of the cosmos there is only a primal God, *Nous* or Mind, who is manifested to the seer as the figure Poimandres. Creation is carried out by the primary manifestation of the highest being, the *logos* or Word. This *logos* is personified as the Son of God in ways similar to those we have seen in Philo and the Wisdom of Solomon (18:15-16). [2] It is clear that, whatever else may be of interest in the document, it would be considered "two powers in heaven" by the rabbis. We can see that those powers are complementary.

Among the Greek philosophers, just as among the theosophists who produced the hermetic literature, the concept of "second god"

---

[1] *The Bible and the Greeks*, p. 209.
[2] C. H. Dodd, *The Bible and the Greeks*, pp. 117-119.

appears to have achieved some limited use, partially based on Plato's idea of the demiurge in the Timaeus and partially based on the application of the idea to the *logos* by Philo. Numenius of Apamaea, for instance, though he survives only in fragments, is known to have been influenced by Jewish scriptures. [3] Origen, in the *Contra Celsum*, remarks that Numenius was familiar with the scriptures of the Hebrews, which he endeavored to synthesize with Greek philosophy by means of allegory. [4] Numenius calls the first divinity "The Good" or "Reason or Thought, [5] even "the Standing God." [6] But because Numenius also distinguishes radically between God and matter, he finds it necessary to assume a "second god" who mediates the chasm while participating both in divinity and matter. With this cosmology, Numenius has appeared to many scholars as a gnostic. [7] However, he can hardly be a radical gnostic, for the soul, while divine in origin, is distributed in sentient beings through the rational agency of the second god. [8] Thus, Numenius' second god is hardly the evil demiurge of the radical gnostics. However, when seen together with the *Hermetic Literature* and possibly even the *Chaldaean Oracles*, Numenius' writing suggests that there was a healthy interest in Jewish thought among the pagan mystics and incipient neo-Platonists of the second century. [9] Perhaps some philosophers like Numenius, as successors to Philo, together with gentile Christians were included among the "nations of the world" identified by the rabbis as believing in "two powers in heaven." This philosophical usage of the term "second god" in the successors of Philo may be the basis of the use of the term in rabbinic literature and the christological controversies of the second and third centuries.

Some of the documents called gnostic in the writings of the church

---

[3] For the history of scholarship on Numenius, see the new edition of the *Fragments*, edited by Édouard des Places (Paris: 1973). The numbering of the fragments will be according to des Places' system, not according to the numbering of Leemans.

[4] Origen, *Contra Celsum*, IV, 52.

[5] Fr. 16-17.

[6] Fr. 15. Notice the affinities with Philo's discussion of God, based on the LXX phrase, "place where God stands." In fact, since the study of K. S. Guthrie, *Numenius of Apamea: The Father of Neo-Platonism* some relationship between Philo and Numenius has been generally assumed.

[7] See, for example, the study of Beutler in Pauly-Wissowa, Supplement 7 (1950).

[8] Fr. 13. In this fragment Numenius uses the metaphor of a plantor of a vinyard for God, as is common in Philo and Jewish tradition in general.

[9] For a more detailed study of this question see Le R. P. Festugière, *La révélation d'Hermès Trismégiste*, 4 Vols., (Paris: 1950-53), especially Vol. III and IV.

in the apocalyptic literature of the first century, in some of the gnostic and much of the Christian literature—the independence of the second power is a moot question. It is often possible that the later traditions in heretical literature are survivals of heterodox but not necessarily heretical exegesis, brought into a new context.

In the untitled document from Codex II, often called the *Origin of the World*, and in *The Hypostasis of The Archons* there are long descriptions of the heavenly throne which depend to a great degree on the traditions we have been discussing from Ex. and from the begining of Ezekiel. In both documents, as in those described by the church fathers, proto-Merkabah traditions abound. We see that the chariot is used as a throne surrounded by a glorious palace inhabited by a plethora of angels. The major cherubim have four faces—that of a lion, a bull, an eagle, and a man, as adduced from Ezekiel 1, the most important Merkabah text. Similar chariots are also employed by the seventy-two gods who give man the seventy-two languages of the world.

Sabaoth, in *The Untitled Work*, has many of the characteristics of the second figure in heaven. His name is evidently derived from the Hebrew YHWH ṢBᵒWT, Lord of Hosts or Powers. In UW 152:10 he is said to be "over all the forces (*dynameis*) of Chaos." He also shares some of the characteristics given to Jesus in various traditions. Like Christ in the *Sophia Jesu Christi*, he is said to have created the angels. [19] Yet the parallel between the documents is not complete, since Jesus is himself one of the created angels, seated at the right of Sabaoth in the *Untitled Work* (UW 153:25-29), whereas in the *Hypostasis of the Archons*, it is Zoē who sits on the right of Sabaoth. Apparently, only the figure of the primary angel is consistent in the documents, not his name or identity.

In *UW*, Sabaoth is the son of Yaldabaoth, the demiurge. As in Valentinian thought, Sabaoth is to function as a savior. He has learned that what his father told him—namely, that his father is lord of all—is untrue. Upon realizing this, he is taken to the seventh heaven and enthroned. Some of the "two powers" traditions have been applied to the gnostic savior and the reason is clear. Sabaoth functions as the role model for the ideal believer, who is to move beyond Judaism (and Christianity) to true gnostic belief.

Other parts of these esoteric Jewish traditions have been applied to the demiurge. This development points out a transformation charact-

---

[19] See H. A. Bullard, p. 110; (also SJC 99:18-100:3). Also now a new edition by Bentley Leyton, "The Hypostasis of the Archons," *HTR*, 67 (1974) p. 351 f.

eristic of gnostic interpretation of these traditions. Throughout the document we are informed that Yaldabaoth, the demiurge, had exclaimed at his creation: "There is no other god but me"—paraphrasing the same verses in Ex., Dt. and Is., which the rabbis had used to defend their God. In the gnostic text, the claim of the demiurge is patently false, because he is ignorant of the higher, good deity above him.

The pattern is far from unique. It occurs many times in the Nag Hammadi corpus. In every case, the ignorant demiurge (often Yaldabaoth) boasts that he is the only god, quoting or paraphrasing Dt. 32:29, Is. 44:6, or 46:4. In every case the boast is ironic because the reader knows that there is a god higher than he. [20] Therefore, gnostic interpretation also took over the claims of uniqueness of Israel's God, but applied them to a demiurge. Apparently gnostic exegesis split the tradition we find opposed by the rabbis into two parts. The traditions about a second figure were transmuted into the gnostic savior, while the scripture characteristic of the rabbinic polemic against "two powers" was associated with the evil demiurge who is still the god of Israel, but not the high god.

It is conceivable that "negative value" Judaism developed independently, and not in response to orthodox disapproval. Deuteronomy and Isaiah had been available for many centuries. But several consideration make it more probable that the specifically gnostic arguments date from a period considerably later, when the rabbinic polemic against "two powers" had already been developed. First of all, even a quick reading of gnostic texts reveals that the scriptural focus of the gnostic mind was on the first few chapters of Genesis rather than on Deuteronomy, Exodus or II Isaiah. The rabbis were the first sure witnesses to the use

---

[20] See H. Jonas, *History of Religion*, p. 267 who locates the following texts: #27 (p. 149), #39 (134:27-135:4; 143; 407), #4 (UW: 148:27-33; 151- 3-28 155: 17-37), #2 (Sacred book of the Invisible Great Spirit or Gospel of the Egyptians), p. 178; #4 (Sophia of Jesus, SJC in BG 125:10-126:5); #1, 6, 36 in Apoc. of John. (BG 44:8-16 cf., 45:11f, 45:20-46:9). According to the more recent numbering of the Nag Hammadi corpus the vain claim of the demiurge can be found in clear form also in "The Hypostasis of the Archons," (II, 1) 86:28-87:3; 94:20-28; 94:34-95:7 in "The Origin of the World" (II, 2) 103:6-20; "The Apocryphon of John" (II, 3) 11:18-21; 13:5-13 (with parallels to BG 44:9-17); "The Gospel of the Egyptians" (II, 4) 58:23-59:4 and often elsewhere. My thanks to Anne Maguire and N. A. Dahl for providing further references for the Nag Hammadi section of the 1976 SBL meeting. See also H. M. Schenke, *Der Gott "Mensch" in der Gnosis*, p. 87f. Also see Gilles Quispel, "The Origins of the Gnostic Demiurge" *Kyriakon: Festschrift for Johannes Quasten*, I (Leiden: 1970) 271-276, and H. A. Wolfson "The Pre-existent Angel of the Magharians and Al-Nahawandi," *JQR*, XI (1960), for exceedingly cogent discussions of gnostic roots in Jewish sectarianism.

of Deuteronomy passages together with the principal angel passages. Since they brought them in for polemical purposes, there is little possibility that gnostics could have brought in the same traditions for any purposes other than polemical ones. It makes good sense to see these distorted claims about the ignorance of Israel's God as a polemical answer to the rabbinic polemic against "two powers" which relied heavily on Dt. 32 and on Is. 44-47.

Final conclusions will have to await the publication of the remainder of the Nag Hammadi library. But some striking ramifications of the evidence in the library already seem to be clear. The Jewish sectarian milieu for gnostic origins, postulated by Quispel, Wolfson and others seems confirmed. [21] For instance, two documents from the library, which give primary importance to Shem or Seth as revealers, clarify an essentially Jewish sectarian setting for many of the gnostic documents by showing Christian influence to be secondary. In the *Apocalypse of Adam*, [22] Seth functions as the prophet to whom *gnosis* is given after creation, paralleled by Shem after the flood. Adam is quite important in this treatise. He helps in creation and is higher in rank than the god who created him and Eve. The demiurge attempts to stamp out *gnosis* by causing a deep sleep of forgetfulness to come over Adam but *gnosis* later triumphs. Adam is emphasized throughout the text, but he is not the redeemer, only an angelic carrier of the *gnosis*. Several other figures, including an "illuminator," function as redeemer. Persian themes are present in the birth of the illuminator, like Mithras, from a rock. Yet there is no single myth of a redeemed redeemer or *anthropos*, because Adam and the redeemer remain separate figures. If any Christian material relating the redeemer to Adam is present at all, it is well disguised. We are therefore justified in describing this document as a non-Christian, heterodox, Jewish-gnostic document, though there is no reason to assume it is pre-Christian in origin.

The same evidence seems to be emerging in reports about *The Paraphrase of Shem*. [23] In this case as well, we have evidence for a primarily Jewish sectarian document in the Nag Hammadi library. Almost no Christian influence can be seen. On the other hand, the dependence on the Hebrew Bible is obvious. Not only are Sodom and the Sodomites mentioned in a favorable sense, but the flood, and the tower of Babel

---

[21] See above p. 252 n. 20 and p. 19.

[22] See Foerster, *Gnosis*, II, p. 13-23.

[23] See Frederik Wisse, "The Redeemer Figure in the Paraphase of Shem," *NT*, 12 (1970), 130-140.

also play a role. All of these contain primary places where the doctrine of "two powers" could be derived. In this case, the major character is called Derdekeas and functions primarily as a redeemer. He is also supposed to be the creator of heaven and earth, rather like Poimandres, except that the atmosphere is now anti-Jewish. [24]

Instead of evidence of de-Christianization, we have some evidence that the tractate was Christianized. Hippolytus seems to use a form of the *Paraphrase of Shem* as his main source for the doctrine of the Sethians. [25] He calls it *the Paraphrase of Seth*, but the document is essentially the same. In Hippolytus' version, however, several Christological interpretations have been added. [26] Epiphanius knew of an early gnostic sect, the Archontici (many powers?) who, like the believers of this document, considered water anathema in baptism. [27] A preliminary study seems to be showing that this document is an example of non-Christian, Jewish sectarian gnostic work which was later Christianized. Like the *Poimandres* it makes use of material from the Hebrew Bible but in this case it is radically transformed into a "negative value" Judaism for polemical purposes.

It is now possible to speak of the later history of the polemic. Just as the rabbis were passionately trying to preserve their faith, so too some "two powers" sectarians were passionately trying to preserve theirs. They refuted the forceful rabbinic charge against dualism, based on Dt. 32, by revaluing the biblical creation to make their god or hero come out on top. We have already seen examples of this creative exegesis. Cainite and Marcionite circles accepted the appro-

---

[24] Fred Wisse seems to find that the notion of a pre-Christian savior myth is confirmed in this material, even though the document is not pre-Christian. It seems to me more warranted to say that many of the aspects of what is called "the gnostic salvation myth" are present, but the late date makes it impossible to decide when or how all the themes—helper in creation, Adam, angelic mediation and redemption—came together.

[25] Hippol. *Philosophoumena*, V, 19-22.

[26] See V, 19, 20. Since Sethians identified Seth with Christ, this identification of Shem with Christ indicates a peculiar relationship of Shem and Seth. We must also remember that Shem and Melchizedek are firmly connected with Samaritanism by Pseudo-Eupolemos. Shem and Melchizedek are also equated by the rabbis. In the Sethian documents of the Nag Hammadi corpus, the vain claim of the demiurge appears often. In *The Second Logos of the Great Seth* (VII, 2), for instance, the Cosmocrator says to the angels "I am God" but was scorned. The savior in this case has the Hebrew theophoric name "Adonaios" and gnostics ridicule orthodox christians for believing in "two lords, even a multitude."

[27] These Archontici lived in Palestine and were closely related to the Sethians. For further reports about this sect in the church fathers, see Wisse, p. 139.

bation "first born of Satan." In doing so, they revalued the dishonorable epithet into a positive term. Similarly, gnostic distortion of the original "two powers" tradition—the bifurcation of the second figure into a gnostic savior and evil demiurge—can be seen as a response to the aggravated atmosphere created by rabbinic polemic on the one side and incipient orthodox Christian polemic on the other. [28] The heretics must have reasoned that Israel's God and Christian orthodoxy's God who claimed to be unique as recorded in monotheistic statements of Exodus, Deuteronomy and Isaiah, was only an ignorant god. He did not know about the gnostic god, who was going to save only those who recognized him—that is, only the "two powers" heretics who were "gnostics." The church offered a possible haven from the battle because some varieties of Christianity maintained christologies which were very close to the gnostic idea of the redeemer, and Christianity shared the experience of expulsion from the synagogue for violating the doctrine of monotheism. But both church and synagogue reacted antagonistically to the gnostics. Thus we actually have a three-cornered battle. Extreme anti-Jewish gnosticism can be seen to arise in circumstances where groups holding "two powers" traditions run headlong into the polemics against "two powers" and "many powers" which developed in the rabbinic academies, but which were used by church fathers as well. In a real sense then, both orthodoxy and heresy were trying to manipulate scripture in order to demonstrate the veracity of their own beliefs and the authority of their own clergy. The rabbis attempted to use highly rationalized methods of exegesis to show that the stories of the heretics were completely faulty. Their method, midrash, was derived from the discussions of the academies and the sermons of the synagogues. The extreme gnostics countered by developing a massively polemical mythology. [29] The church fathers used both methods against both sides.

---

[28] This idea is an extension of the kind of development of traditions portrayed by N. A. Dahl, *Erstgeborene Satans*, see p. 137 f. and p. 234 f. We have jointly developed these themes further, together with a response from Birger Pearson in a forthcoming volume of proceedings from the SBL seminar on Nag Hammadi studies.

[29] The whole issue of polemical mythology deserves more serious study, both phenomenologically within history of religions circles and exegetically among scholars of this particular period. In this case, for instance, Dt. 32:39 occurs as the boast of the demiurge in such a variety of gnostic systems that one cannot escape the conclusion that the claim itself antedates any mythological setting. Probably many artificial myths were created in order to explain how the claim of the demiurge (that he was the only God) was to be treated. For an analogy see A. Kragerud, *Die Hymnen der Pistis*

The transformation of values seen in Nag Hammadi is not limited to the third century, when gnosticism was already full grown. The story of the arrogance of the demiurge was known to the early church fathers. It is reported in Irenaeus, [30] Hippolytus, [31] and Epiphanius [32] —indicating that the process of transvaluing Judaism to create an evil demiurge in contrast to the saving grace of the gnostic redeemer was already underway by the middle of the second century. Such arguments, in turn, might call forth the kind of defense seen in the latest level of rabbinic polemic. For instance in passage 2, R. Nathan's argument, may be understood to oppose the idea that the god who created the world claimed his uniqueness in secret. [33]

Furthermore, not all groups wanted to use the solution of the radical gnostics. Many (probably those who continued to attract Jews) remained in an intermediate position where the text of the Old Testament was not so thoroughly revalued. We can see more evidence for them in the latest body of writing significant to the "two powers" controversy, the Pseudo-Clementine literature. Though the literature comes from the fourth century in its present form, earlier traditions have been recognized in it. The literature tries to defeat gnostic arguments; nevertheless, it contains many traditions common to Jewish esoteric teachings and various non-orthodox Christian communities. For instance, its division of the cosmos into masculine and feminine syzygies could easily have been the doctrine opposed by Theophilus [34] In form, it is a collection of narratives and homilies attributed to the apostle Peter and transcribed by Clement, all polemicizing against the gnostic Simon. Yet the Christianity offered as a corrective to gnosticism is not equivalent to what has

---

Sophia (Oslo: 1967) especially 159-220. In that case, the myths about Sophia were created to provide a setting for the Psalms and Odes of Solomon texts which the sect wanted to clarify and interpret. Elaine Pagels reports in "The Demiurge and his Archons—Gnostic Views on the Bishop and Presbyters?" *HTR*, (1976), p. 1, that a similar battle can be seen between Christian and gnostic bishops. She suggests that the real issue was over the authority and polity of the bishops, but was translated into a mythological battle over whose god was higher! This is a very persuasive argument about the social context of gnostic polemics. We should not assume that the battles were merely exegetical. For instance, the social dimension of Johannine dualism may be discoverable in the polemic against their Jewish neighbors, who oppose their faith and have excluded them from the synagogue. See my article on the "Lord of the World-Angel or Devil?: Towards a Sociology of Gnosticism," and also p. 189 n. 20.

[30] Iren. *Adv. Haer*. I, 5, 2-4 and I, 30, 1-6.
[31] Hippol. *Refut*. vi, 33 and vii 25:3.
[32] Epiphan. Pan. 26:2.
[33] See p. 57 f.
[34] See p. 225 f.

become orthodoxy. Rather it has many "Jewish-Christian" character-istics. For instance, the statements of Christ's divinity in the New Testament are reinterpreted to mean that all men's souls are divine. After death they will all shine as stars in heaven. According to Peter, neither is Jesus himself a god. Instead he has been adopted as "the Son of God," and is called Adam, an angelic prince or a variety of other terms. Such doctrines, as well as Christian orthodoxy, may have been countered by rabbinic statements that God has no son, but they probably would not be considered "two powers" heresy by the rabbis.

Many other issues which we have been tracing were also discussed in this literature. Simon argues, for instance, that the plural used in Gen. 1:26 indicates that there were many creators, or at any rate, more than one. [35] Peter replies that the verse refers not to another creator but to God's *Wisdom*, who was present with God at the creation. Peter typically defends his monotheistic Christianity against the charges of his enemies by relying on many of the scriptures used by the rabbis against "two powers" and also some used by the church fathers against gnostics. [36]

The heretical side of the dialogue is represented by Simon Magus. His doctrine also attests to the idea of *place* as another name for the *logos* or principal divine manifestation on earth. Simon allowed that two different areas have been separated in the cosmos; the second area, (*deutera chora*), being a second place, is also a second being. [37] In this system there are also two rulers (*hegemones*) who govern the two areas, [38] who are in turn related in time to this world and the next. The prince of this world is evil, while the prince of the world to come will be good. [39] So the high god, having delimited two areas or dominions, has also ordained two cosmic periods. [40] The total number of gods is then three. It is as if the Simon of this document has split the second god of Marcion into a creator and a legislator in a manner reminiscent of Philo. Therefore, the higher god has sent two gods, one of whom created the world, the other of whom gave the Law. [41]

---

[35] 16:11 also 38 for a similar use of Gen. 18:21 conflated with Gen. 11:7.

[36] 16:6 contains the following passages. Gen. 3:1-22, Ex. 22:28, Dt. 4:34. Jer. 10:10, Dt. 13:6, Josh. 23:7 (LXX) 24:7 (MT) Dt. 10:17, Ps. 86:8 (LXX 85) Ps. 50:1. Notice the presence of Jer. 10:10 which, in another way, was as important to R. Isaac's exegesis against the heretics. See p. 135 f.

[37] H 17:8 Souiville, p. 323.

[38] 20:3.

[39] On the Prince of the World, see p. 51, 67, 189, 214, 256.

[40] H 20:2, see also 15:6, 7.

[41] H 3:2.

Here is an occurrence of the two exegetical traditions—the second figure and the mercy and justice traditions—coming together in heresy, rather than in anti-heretical polemic. Apparently in the position attributed to Simon, traditions about the justice and mercy of God are combined with the notion of the high god and his helper. He is operating with the same issues which surround the rabbinic defense of "two powers" speculation. Unlike Marcion, Simon uses Old Testament references to prove his case. Therefore heretics like the Simon of this document may certainly among those that the rabbis condemned.

But they are also distressing to Peter! He attempts to counter them with the same scriptural passages which the rabbis would have used. One of his comments about Simon is a quite important:

> Whilst I betake myself to the heathen who say there are many gods, to preach and proclaim the one and only God who made heaven and earth and all that is therein, that they may love and be saved, wickedness has anticipated me according to the laws of the syzygies and has sent Simon ahead in order that those men who, rejecting the gods assumed to exist on the earth, speak no more of their great numbers, may believe that there are *many gods in heaven*. Thus, would men be brought to dishonor the monarchy of God and to meet severe punishment and eternal perdition. [42]

The writer of this document may have been familiar with the term "many powers in heaven." He used rabbinic defenses against "two powers" arguments and the designation "many powers" so the "many powers" must certainly be seen as a species of "two powers" and not a wholly different heresy. He compared "many powers in heaven" with "many powers on earth," synonymous with paganism. The rabbis never use the term to contrast with paganism, and instead contrast "no power in heaven" with "two powers in heaven" and "many powers in heaven." Nevertheless the terms may not be unrelated. Though the method of definition differs, the basic identification by both Jews and Jewish Christians of sectarian groups (rather than gentile nonbelievers) is good evidence that both the rabbis and the Jewish Christians are dealing with similar opponents and the same traditions. In a work that relies so heavily both on rabbinic and Christian traditions, the ironic complaint of Peter cannot be purely coincidental. It seems as if "many powers in heaven" is meant to refer to the Simonian gnosticism with its complex system of archons and creators.

---

[42] H. 3 (59:2) Hennecke-Schneemelcher, p. 552.

These traditions are fully in agreement with the traditions about "many powers in heaven" which we found in the rabbinic legends. They probably dated from the same time and confirm our suspicions that the basic category of heresy involved "two powers" ideas expanded by an elaborate angelic cosmology.

CHAPTER SIXTEEN

CONCLUSIONS

Having surveyed several varieties of extra-rabbinic literature in the Hellenistic period to find texts relevant to the "two powers" controversy, it is now time to return to the original questions of the inquiry: Which extra-rabbinic groups are most likely to have been the targets of the rabbinic polemic? How early is the "two powers" controversy? The extra-rabbinic evidence has provided much information helpful for answering both of these questions. All the data and many of the conclusions have already been mentioned. But the various findings of the study need to be summarized so that avenues for future research can be defined.

In the rabbinic evidence, dating was an especially difficult problem, because the traditions crystallized over a long period of time, forming texts with complicated lattices and strata. Even when we could date a document with relative certainty, we could not be sure that the earliest form of that tradition was present in it. In such cases previous scholars have felt relatively free to assume a long and sometimes fanciful pre-history. With more careful attention to the text we were forced to conclude that the rabbinic polemic against "two powers," like most rabbinic traditions, can not be dated earlier than the time of Ishmael and Akiba. While even such an early dating has problems in rabbinic texts, there were many hints of greater antiquity.

In the rabbinic evidence, we discovered that the earliest issue concerned the identity and status of a human figure in heaven. The issue might have originally been the anthropomorphic language used of God or the meaning of the two Hebrew words for deity, YHWH and Elohim. It was difficult to tell which problem was the most basic, since both were based on the same exegetical context and were discussed together. In the late tannaitic period, but not before, we found a certain amount of evidence for an opposing, configuration of deities in the heretical theology. (R. Nathan).

Once the extra-rabbinic evidence was consulted it became obvious that the rabbis' second century opponents had first century forebears. In apocalyptic literature as well as in the Philonic corpus it was often difficult to say whether the borderline between sectarian strife and heresy was actually crossed. No doubt the line was drawn subjectively, depending on the perspective of the observer.

It is now possible to construct a coherent, synchronized history of the tradition. The early biblical theophanies which picture God as a man or confuse YHWH with an angel are the basis of the tradition. The book of Daniel, usually dated to Maccabean times, is the earliest witness in the Bible to the existence of apocalyptic traditions of a heavenly figure, though it is possible that some Enoch traditions are older. Yet neither Daniel nor the early Enoch material give the figure a title. Most attributes of the "son of man" or "manlike" figure are undefined. Instead the tradition grew through differing exegeses of a variety of theophany texts. The events narrated in Dan. 7:9 f. may be part of the Israelite Holy War and Divine Warrior traditions—mythological motifs which Israel shared with its neighbors. If so, Israelite culture, as is normal in cases of cultural contact, not only shared the ideas, but transformed them to fit its own scheme of things. The mythology recorded in early Daniel and Enoch traditions was monotheistic and was fitted through exegesis to the events of Maccabean times, stimulating the development of an eschatology suited to Maccabean partisans. The speculation continued among a number of groups and was later canonized by the rabbinic community. In no way can every occurrence be considered heretical.

Some traditions which became part of the "two powers" controversy were known by Philo, who used the term "second god" (*deuteros theos*) to describe the *logos*. The Hebrew equivalent "two gods" or "second god" was used infrequently by the rabbis as a term of reproach. It did not become the preferred title for heresy within the rabbinic movement, possibly because of the risk of blasphemy merely in saying it. The usual rabbinic terminology "two powers in heaven" was standardized at the end of the tannaitic period, although alternatives continued to enjoy a certain currency in the amoraic period, apparently in polemical settings. "Two powers," on the other hand, was better suited for informing the community of the dangers of heresy without revealing too much of the content. It is impossible to speculate on how the Pharisees would have reacted to Philo's system.

Within the Palestinian community, with its many sects, polemics for monotheism were used in a variety of ways. Paul seems to use anti-"two powers" polemic against Jews whom he charged with venerating angels while he himself could have been charged with the identical crime by rabbinic Jews.

One heretical candidate was sure. The christological statements in Johannine literature are clearly heretical because the fourth gospel represents the Jews as opposing Jesus when he equates himself with God. Johannine Christians, if not Jesus himself, were charged with the crime. "Two powers" seems to be one of the basic issues over which Judaism and Christianity separated.

Therefore the evidence is that opposition to Christian exegesis preceded opposition to extreme gnostic exegesis. In this case, the key factor in separating radical gnosticism from earlier exegesis is the negative portrayal of the demiurge. Whenever the second figure in heaven is seen as negative, we are dealing with a radically gnostic system. Not until then can we say definitively that a gnostic heresy is present. In all the earliest traditions, the second figure is always seen as a complementary figure, suggesting that the notion of a divine helper who carried God's name is the basic concept which developed into heresy, not a redeemed redeemer.

Marcion's system is not a likely candidate for the original target of the rabbinic attack against "two powers," for the rabbinic attack was exegetical at base, while Marcion does not allow any Old Testament references to the savior God. Although the best candidates for the heresy, both on internal and external evidence, are Christians there is no distinctively anti-Christian polemic at first. Therefore we should continue to assume that the Christians were but one of a number of apocalyptic or mystical groups who posited a primary angelic helper for God. The rabbinic attack against these groups had two thrusts. It damned the sectarian groups for having violated Jewish monotheism, using Dt. 32 and Is. 44-47, and Ex. 20 while suggesting that the dangerous scripture used by the sectarians really concerned God's aspects of justice and mercy or His *shekhina*.

The rabbis did not invent the exegesis that God's Hebrew names stood for mercy and justice. They used ancient traditions of God's mercy and justice to defeat the heresy. These traditions were also attested by Philo, who understood the names of God as symbols for His attributes. No doubt Philo was relying on more ancient traditions as well. We have no conclusive evidence about the form these traditions took within the Palestinian, semitic-language-speaking community. The early Palestinian scholars may have followed the Philonic identification of the names of God or they may have followed the opposite identification, the normative tradition in rabbinic literature. Probably they just emphasized that the mixture, both mercy and justice, was present at the creation and at Sinai. Such arguments became even stronger during the gnostic controversy. The received rabbinic identification of justice and mercy with Elohim and YHWH respectively is attested by the second century. It was a convenient weapon against Christianity, gnosticism and Marcionism because it emphasized that YHWH was a merciful God, making mercy the aspect of God which was most often manifested to Israel. While the argument made sense against Christianity, it was a very powerful argument against gnosticism, which maintained that Israel's god was ignorant and arbitrary.

During the later stage of the heresy, which is better evidenced in the rabbinic texts, almost any doctrine incompatible with monotheism was understood by the rabbis as "two powers" speculation. Such may already have been the case during the second century (Passage 1) but it certainly is true in the Mishnah (Passage 7, Chapter 7). It also seems clear that several church fathers evinced "two powers" heresy in the second century. Justin especially, but also Theophilus, maintained doctrines of the *logos* and Christ supported by scriptural traditions which the rabbis opposed. The "two powers" polemic was related to christological controversies between many of the early fathers as well.

By the end of the second century, arguments like R. Nathan's (Passage 2) were probably being used against dualists and gnostics, though it is unclear whether R. Nathan himself had gnostics in mind. He may have only been defending Torah against its critics. "Many powers in heaven" was also singled out for censure. Groups espousing this belief must have included any sectarians who provided an intricate mythological context for their angelology by using the first chapters in Genesis. Many second century gnostics and most third century gnostics were prominent members of this heresy. By the end of the second century complementary and antagonistic dualists were both evidencing "two powers" traditions, but before that time there was no evidence for any opposing configuration of deities either among the heretics or among the rabbinic traditions.

The rabbinic texts, which recorded only the rabbinic side of the argument, ordered and related the traditions thematically or by scriptural reference. This unintentionally obfuscated the historical progression of the debate. When both sides of the tradition have been presented and compared according to their use of scripture, the original order of the debate can be reconstructed.

Once the debate is reconstructed, we are able to understand some of the historical issues affecting the exegesis. By the time of the consolidation of rabbinic authority at Yavneh and the attempt at a new Jewish orthodoxy, mediation traditions were seen as a clear and present danger within rabbinic Judaism. No doubt the rabbis' concern was linked to the political events which immediately preceded. The war had stimulated a terrible crisis of faith. Furthermore Christians and others had taken the fall of Jerusalem as proof of the end of the Jewish dispensation. Such ideas were heinous to the majority of the Jewish community. A new set of standards was necessary to insure survival. In asserting further control over the synagogue, the rabbis excluded any sectarian who compromised monotheism from participating in the service. This meant that Christians, among others, were excluded from Jewish life. The growing emphasis on strict monotheism characterizes the rabbinic movement and sets it off from the other sects of its time.

The earliest reports about "two powers" in the rabbinic texts were associated with gentiles. This may further indicate that proto-gnostic interpretations of angelic mediation originated in a thoroughly Hellenized kind of Judaism or among gentiles attracted to synagogue services. But "two powers" heresy has a clear Jewish sectarian setting as well. Apparently, along with the Jewish sectarians, gentiles who had been drawn to the synagogue to hear the Bible proclaimed were attracted to biblical monotheism in a form that distinguished between the supreme God and a divine agent, possibly in a more extreme form than the system that Philo had described. All such doctrines, whether in apocalypticism, Christianity or philosophical speculations, were probably condemned by the rabbis as early as the end of the first century and the beginning of the second. But the gentiles continued to hear the Christian message.

The response of the excluded groups varied. Orthodox Christianity claimed both that the legal aspects of the Torah were void and that the Jews stubbornly refused to hear the message of the fulfillment of their own scriptures. A few Christians even relied on the teachings of men like Marcion and Cerdo, who argued that the god of salvation was unknown to the Jews. But that was atypical. Others claimed that the god of the official synagogue, in whose name they had been excluded from worship, was not the high god. By his own intransigence he proved he was an ignorant and vain god. For these gnostics, a higher god was envisioned, one who was the author of salvation. These arguments might be phenomenologically similar to Marcion's, but they differed in their use of Jewish scripture. Unlike Marcion, gnostics used familiar Old Testament verses to help prove their contention of the arrogance of the creator. Condemned by the standards of strict monotheism, some of these "gnostics" transformed the distinction between the transcendent God and His agent manifestation on earth into a contrast between the high god and the vain demiurge god of the Jews.

The gnostics drew mainly upon the early chapters of Genesis to prove their point. They inherited many ancient traditions congenial to their perspective. But they also created new interpretations: They elaborated cosmogonic myths in order to provide a setting for their claim that Israel's god is ignorant. They also found ways to turn the insults hurled at them into compliments. However, their knowledge and use of other parts of scripture was more limited. The gnostic use of Isaiah and Deuteronomy passages seems to have arisen as a defense against the previous Jewish and Christian use of those scriptures against them.

There is further evidence that some who cherished moderate "two powers" traditions did not adopt anti-Jewish arguments. Jews who had a closer connection to the legal traditions of the community and were not part of the fierce polemic were able to give the traditions a limited form of acceptability in Merkabah mysticism.

Most others, having been linked together with the Christians by the rabbis, found refuge in the church and incorporated Christian elements into their systems. However, Christianity immediately found itself faced with the same problem that the rabbis were facing. Using the same traditions, Christians began to define orthodoxy and heresy along much more complicated lines. Tertullian claimed that Marcionites, who postulated a second god, were anti-christs like Jews. Monarchians and modalists claimed that "orthodoxy," like the gnostics and Marcionites, had compromised Christianity's monotheistic center. Therefore they used "two gods" as a term of approbation against "orthodox" Christianity, just as the rabbis did.

Obviously this is not meant to be *the* authoritative reconstruction of events. But it seems to be a credible account of the complete evidence. Besides a general chronological scheme, a new hypothesis is assumed— namely, *that the radicalization of gnosticism was a product of the battle between the rabbis, the Christians and various other "two powers" sectarians who inhabited the outskirts of Judaism.* The battle was recorded as a debate over the meaning of several scriptural passages, among which were all the angelic or theophany texts of the Old Testament, followed closely by the plurals used by or about God in scripture.

Of course, it took many sides to make this argument. The rabbis' polemical statements were justified from their perspective by sectarian readiness to dilute strict monotheism in order to support traditions which applied to their ancestors, heroes and saviors. From the other perspectives, the attempt to establish a "normative" Judaism was seen as exclusivist and caused the radicalization of the sectarian community. Therefore, it is possible to say that gnosticism arose in Judaism out of the polarization of the Jewish community over the issue of the status of God's primary angel.

One advantage of this new hypothesis for describing the gnostic debate is that it not only accounts for the large quantity of Jewish material in gnosticism and the phenomenological similarity between various proto-gnostic groups but it also accounts for the anti-Jewish bias of extreme gnosticism. Phenomenologically and historically the gnostic demiurge is the second deity of the earlier "two powers" theology. Usually he has appropriated half of the traditions about the second power, yielding the honorable traditions to the gnostic savior. The agent manifestation of God was therefore identified with the limited god of the Jews while the high god, unknown to Jews or Christians, was reserved only for the gnostics.

This theory, of course, does not address the history of gnostic and anti-gnostic speculation within pagan philosophy. Many of the concepts employed by the heretics were also developed in neo-Platonism, for example. But the theory does give a good account of the history of the phenomenon as it existed within its Jewish context. One ramification of this hypothesis lies in the area of New Testament scholarship. This history of traditions seems to show that radical gnosticism superceded rather than preceded Christianity as a target for the rabbinic debate.

Continued study is needed in almost every area to decide whether the hypothesis deserves further scholarly support. Of particular interest is the relationship of the angelic figure to early christology. Perhaps angelic christologies will turn out to be more important to the thought of the first century than the New Testament leads us to believe. Then too, the use of Enoch and Daniel traditions needs to be traced in detail in sectarian and proto-gnostic thought. Furthermore philosophical issues connecting divine anthropomorphism with the term "second god" need to be studied more closely. Hellenistic concepts of divine justice and mercy need to be explored in greater detail. It has often seemed plausible that a Hellenistic Judaism, like Philo's but less sophisticated, was the background for Justin's and Theophilus' writing.

Throughout this work, the central thread uniting all the early traditions has been God's theophany at the Sea, Sinai, in the Temple, in the Song of Songs, Daniel, Psalms and the prophets. It is quite evident that these traditions, contributing to what will be known as Merkabah mysticism in Judaism, have been a major factor in the development of the Jewish-Christian-gnostic polemic. Much more work is needed to uncover the fascinating subject of early Jewish mystical traditions.

The use of the term "second god" in Christian and pagan Platonism should also be investigated further. Perhaps philosophers like Numenius, who had some contact with Hebrew thought, will become an important link in understanding the relationship between the church fathers and the rabbis. It may turn out that the issues with which the rabbis were concerned were of general interest to all educated men at that time, while the exegetical issues were formulated by those intellectuals interested in combining Greek and Hebrew thought.

Further research is certainly necessary to uncover the social dynamics of this hostility. The exegetical nature of our texts should not preclude such inquiry. In the early post-war confusion, many groups were doubtlessly making claims for the authority to speak for the entire Jewish community. The conflict, as we have it recorded in "religious texts," was expressed in theological rather than political or social terms. No doubt, some social and political forces were being expressed in the religious controversies. For instance, strict dualism seems to appear where the most ferocious social antagonisms are expressed and seems to function as an explanation of opposition

This study began by admitting that the reports about "two powers in heaven" were obscure. It is not likely that the preceding description and analysis has altered anyone's opinion about their obscurity. However, it does not necessarily follow that the reports are unimportant. Not until the reports were collected, collated, arranged and dated could the full significance of the "two powers" controversy become evident. It seems to have been one of the primary rabbinic categories for describing heresy. Furthermore, hidden within the reports is the Jewish witness to the rise of Christianity, even though the texts date from centuries later. They certainly give us a good idea of the issues over which Christianity and Judaism separated. Continued close study of rabbinic evidence may reveal more of this epoch-making period of history for all the religious traditions of the West.

BIBLIOGRAPHY

PRIMARY SOURCES

Altjüdisches Schrifttum ausserhalb der Bibel. Ed. and Tr. Paul Riessler. Heidelberg: F. H. Kerle Verlag, 1966.

Die Apokalypse Abrahams und das Testament der vierzig Maertyrer. Ed. and Tr. Gottlieb Nathanael Bonwetsch. Aalen: 1972, Neudruck der Ausgabe Leipzig: 1897.

Aboth de R. Nathan. Ed. S. Schechter. New York: Feldheim, 1945.

The Apocalypse of Abraham: from the Roumanian text. Ed. M. Gaster. *Transactions of the Society of Biblical Archaeology,* IX: 1887.

Apocalypse of Adam. Ed. George MacRae. SBL: 1972.

The Apocrypha and Pseudepigrapha of the Old Testament in English with Introductions and Critical and Explanatory Notes to the Several Books. Ed. R. H. Charles, *et al.* Two Volumes. Oxford: Oxford University Press, 1968.

Apostolic Fathers. Ed. and Tr. Lightfoot. (Completed by J. R. Haimer.) Grand Rapids: 1956.

The Babylonian Talmud. Ed. Rabbi Dr. I. Epstein. London: Soncino Press, 1961.

Biblia Hebraica. Ed. Rud. Kittel, et al. Stuttgart: Württembergische Bibelanstalt, 1962.

The Bible in Aramaic. Ed. A. Sperber. Volume I: *The Pentateuch according to Targum Onkelos.* Leiden. Brill, 1959.

The Bible in Aramaic. Ed. A. Sperber. Volume III: *The Latter Prophets according to Targum Jonathan.* Leiden: Brill, 1962.

The Book of Tobit: An English Translation with Introduction and Commentary. Ed. Frank Zimmerman. New York: Harper & Row, 1958.

Clemens Romanus. *First and Second Clement.* Ed. R. M. Grant and H. H. Graham. New York: 1965.

Clemens Romanus. [Spurious and Doubtful Works] *Die syrischen Clementine mit griechischem parallel Text; eine Vorarbeit zu dem literargeschichtlichen Problem der Sammlung von Wilhelm Frankenburg.* 1937.

Clemens Romanus. [Spurious and Doubtful Works]. *Clementina.* Ed. Paul de Lagarde. Osnabruck: 1966.

Clemens Romanus. [Spurious and Doubtful Works]. *Die Pseudoklementinen.* Ed. Bernhard Rehm. Berlin: 1953-65.

Clemens, Romanus. [Spurious and Doubtful Works]. *Les Homélies Clementines: Première traduction française avec une introduction et des notes par A. Siouville.* Paris: 1933.

Daily Prayer Book (Ha-Siddur Ha-Shalem). Ed. Philip Birnbaum. New York: 1949.

The Dead Sea Scrolls in English. Ed. Geza Vermes. Harmondsworth: Penguin Books, 1968.

The Dead Sea Scriptures in English Translation. Ed. and Tr. T. H. Gaster. Anchor Doubleday: 1964.

The Dead Sea Scrolls College Text and Study Guide. Ed. M. Mansoor. Leiden: Brill, 1966.

Eusebii Pamphili. *Evangelicae Praeparationis.* Ed. Gifford. Oxford: 1903.

L'Évangile de Verité. Ed. J. Ménard. Leiden: Brill, 1972.

Evangelien aus dem Nilssand. Ed. W. C. van Unnik. Frankfurt-am-Main: 1960.

The Fathers According to Rabbi Nathan. Tr. Judah Goldin. New Haven: Yale University Press, 1955.

Fontes Historiae Religionis Persicae. Ed. C. Clemen. Bonn: 1920.

Studies and Texts in Folklore, Magic, Medieval Romance, Hebrew Apocrypha and Samaritan Archaeology. Ed. Moses Gaster. 3 Volumes, n.d.

Gnosticism: A Source Book of Heretical Writings from the Early Christian Period. Ed. Robert M. Grant. New York: Harper & Row Brothers, 1961.

Hermes Trismégiste. *Corpus Hermeticum.* Texte par A. D. Nock, Traduit par A.-J. Festugière. Volumes One, Two, Three, Four. Paris: Société d'Édition "Les Belles-Lettres," 1960.

Hermetica. The Ancient Writings Which Contain Religious or Philosophic Teachings Ascribed to Hermes. Ed. W. Scott. Oxford: 1926.

Hippolytus. *The Ante-Nicene Fathers: Translation of the Writings of the Fathers down to A.D. 325.* Ed. A. Roberts and J. Donaldson. New York: Scribners', 1899.

The Hymns of Zarathustra: Being a Translation of the Gathas together with Introduction and Commentary. Ed. and Tr. J. Duchesne-Guillemins. Trans. from the French by Mrs. M. Henning. Boston: Beacon Press, 1963.

Hypostasis of the Archons: The Coptic Text with Translation and Commentary by Roger Aubrey Bullard. Berlin: De Gruyter, 1970.

Iamblichus on the Mysteries of the Egyptians, Chaldeans, and Assyrians. Ed. Thomas Taylor. London: Dobell, Reeves and Turner, 1895.

Irenaeus. *The Writings of Irenaeus.* Ed. and Tr. Alexander Roberts and W. H. Rambaut. Edinburgh: T. & T. Clark, 1869.

Isbell, Charles. *Corpus of the Aramaic Incantation Bowls.* Missoula, SBL Press, 1975.

Jamblique: Les mystères d'Égypte. Ed. and Tr. E. des Places. Paris: Société d'Édition "Les Belles-Lettres," 1966.

Josephus with an English Translation. Ed. and Tr. H. St. J. Thackeray. Cambridge: 1961.

Justin Martyr. *The First Apology, the Second Apology, Dialogue with Trypho, Exhortation to the Greeks, Discourse to the Greeks, the Monarch, or the Rule of God.* Ed. Thomas Falls. New York: Christian Heritage, 1948.

Justin Martyr. *Justin: Dialogue avec Tryphon. Texte grec, Traduction française, introduction, notes et index par Georges Archambault.* Tomes I, II. Paris: Librairie Alphonse Picard et Fils, 1909.

Koptisch-gnostische Schriften. Erster Band. Die Pistis Sophia, die beiden Bücher des Jeu, unbekanntes altgnostisches Werk. Ed. C. Schmidt. Berlin: Akademie Verlag, 1959.

Koptisch-gnostische Schriften aus den Papyrus-Codices von Nag Hammadi. Ed. Johannes Leipoldt and Hans Martin Schenke. Hamburg: 1960.

Die koptisch-gnostische Schrift ohne Titel aus Codex II von Nag Hammadi im koptischen Museum zu-altkairo. Ed. and Tr. A. Böhlig and P. Labib. Berlin: Akademie Verlag, 1962.

The Letter of Aristeas, translated: with an Appendix of Ancient Evidence on the Origin of the Septuagint. Ed. H. St. J. Thackeray. SPCK: MacMillan, 1918.

Mechilta d'Rabbi Sim'on b. Jochai. Ed. J. N. Epstein and E. Z. Melamed. Fragmenta in Geniza Cairensi reperta digessit. Jerusalem: American Academy for Jewish Research, 1955.

Mekilta de-Rabbi Ishmael. A Critical Edition on the basis of manuscripts and early editions with an English translation introduction and notes. Ed. J. Z. Lauterbach. Philadelphia: JPS, 1949.

Mechilta d'Rabbi Ishmael. Ed. J. H. Weiss. Vienna: 1865.

Mechilta d' Rabbi Ismael. Ed. M. Friedmann. Vienna: 1870.

Bet ha-Midrasch. Sammlung kleiner Midraschim und vermischter Abhandlungen aus der ältern jüdischen Literatur . . . nach Handschriften und Druckwerken gesammelt und nebst Einleitungen herausgegeben. Dritte Auflage. Ed. A. Jellinek. Jerusalem: Wahrmann, 1967. First pub. in Leipzig (1853-77).

Mechilta d' Rabbi Ismael. Ed. H. S. Horowitz and A. Rabin. Jerusalem: Bamberger & Wahrmann, 1960.

Midrash Bereshit Rabba. Critical edition with notes and commentary (in Hebrew). Ed. J. Theodor and C. Albeck. 2nd printing, corrected. Jerusalem: Wahrmann, 1965.

Midrash Debarim Rabba. Edited for the first time from the Oxford Ms. No. 147 with an introduction and notes. 2nd edition with additions and corrections. Ed. S. Lieberman. Jerusalem: Wahrmann, 1964/65.

The Midrash on Psalms. Tr. William G. Braude. Two volumes. New Haven: Yale University Press, 1960.

Midrash Rabbah. Ed. and Tr. under the direction of H. Freedman and M. Simon. Ten volumes. London: Soncino Press, 1961.

Midrasch Tanchuma; Ein agadischer Commentar zum Pentateuch von Rabbi Tanchuma ben Rabbi Abba. Zum ersten male nach Handschriften aus den Bibliotheken zu Oxford, Rom, Parma und München herausgegeben. Kritisch bearbeitet, commentirt und mit einer ausführlichen Einleitung (auf Hebräische) versehen. Ed. S. Buber. Wilna: Romm, 1885. Reprinted in Wilna, 1913, and in Jerusalem, 1963/64. The edition is based on Oxford Opp. 20 (= Neubauer Cat. 154).

Midrash Tanchuma: Ein Agadischer Commentar zum Pentateuch von Rabbi Tanchuma ben Rabbi Abba. Ed. S. Buber. Vilna, Jerusalem, 1963/64. From Vilna: Romm, 1885.

Midrasch Tannaim zum Deuteronomium. Ed. D. Hoffmann. Berlin: M. Poppelaver, 1908-09.

Midrash Tehillim (called Sohar Tob). Ed. Solomon Buber. Vilna: 5651.

Midrash Tehillim. Ed. Mahari Cohen. Jerusalem: 5728.

Midrash Wayyikra Rabba. A Critical Edition Based on Mss. and Geniza Fragments with Variants and Notes. Ed. M. Margulies. Jerusalem: Ministry of Education and Culture, 1953-60.

Miqraot Gedolot [Rabbinic Bible]. Jerusalem: Schocken, 1958-59.

The Six orders of the Mishnah [in Hebr.] Ed. E. Albeck and H. Yalon. 6 volumes. Jerusalem: Bialik Institute and Tel Aviv: Dvir, 1952-56.

The Mishnah. Tr. Herbert Danby. London: Oxford University Press, 1964.

New Testament Apocrypha. Ed. E. Hennecke and W. Schneemelcher. Tr. R. McL. Wilson. Philadelphia: Westminster Press, 1963-64.

Oracles Chaldaiques avec un choix de commentaires anciens. Ed. and Tr. E. des Places. Paris: Société d'Édition "Les Belles-Lettres," 1971.

Origenes. *Contra Celsum.* Tr. Henry Chadwick. Cambridge: 1965.

Origenes. *Dialogue of Origen with Heracleides* in *Alexandrian Christianity.* Ed. H. Chadwick and J. L. Oulton. Philadelphia: The Westminster Press, 1954.

Papyri Graecae Magicae. Ed. K. Preisendanz *et al.* 1928-31.

Patrologiae Cursus Completus Series Graeca. Ed. Jacques Paul Migne. Paris: 1928-36.

The Writings of St. Paul. Ed. W. A. Meeks. New York: 1972.

Pesikta Rabbati: Midrash für den Fest-Cyclus und die ausgezeichneten Sabbathe. Ed. M. Friedmann. Tel Aviv: 1962/63. Reprint of Vienna, 1880 edition.

Pesikta Rabbati: Discourses for Feasts, Fasts, and Special Sabbaths. Tr. William G. Braude. Two volumes. New Haven: Yale University Press, 1968.

Philo in Ten Volumes and Two Supplementary Volumes. Tr. F. H. Colson and G. H. Whitaker and R. Marcus. Cambridge: Harvard University Press, 1971.

Philonis Alexandrini. *Opera Quae Supersunt.* Ed. Leopoldus Cohn. Berolini: 1896.

Pirke de Rabbi Eliezer. [The Chapters of Rabbi Eliezer the Great] According to the text of the manuscript belonging to Abraham Epstein of Vienna. Tr. Gerald Friedländer. New York: Hermon Press, 1970.

Siphre d'Be Rab. Fasciculus primus: Siphre ad Numeros adjecto Siphre zutta. Ed. H. S. Horovitz. Schriften herausgegeben von der Gesellschaft zur Forderung der Wissenschaft des Judentums: (Corpus Tannaiticum, 3:3) Jerusalem: Wahrmann, 1966. Reprint of Leipzig: G. Fock, 1917 edition.

Sifre debe Rab: Der älteste halachische und hagadische Midrasch zu Numeri und Deuteronomium. Ed. M. Friedmann. Vienna: 1864. Reprinted in New York, 1947.

Sifre on Deuteronomy. (Corpus Tannaiticum, 3:3: Siphre d'be Rab, Fasciculus alter) Ed. L. Finkelstein (using notes of H. S. Horovitz). New York: JTSA, 1969. Reprint of Berlin: Gesellschaft zur Forderung der Wissenschaft des Judentums, 1939.

Sources of Sectarian History in the Second Commonwealth. [in Hebr.] Ed. R. Rokeah. Jerusalem: Reproduction Association Hebrew University, n.d.

The Rule of Qumran and Its Meaning. Tr. A. R. C. Leaney. London: SCM Press, 1966.

Die samaritanische Liturgie (Auswahl der wichtigsten Texte). Ed. and Tr. H. Heidenheim. Leipzig: Schulze, 1885.

The Stoic and Epicurean Philosophers. The Complete Extant Writings of Epicurius, Epictetes, Lucretius, Marcus Aurelius. Ed. W. J. Oates. New York: Random, 1940.

Talmud Bavli. Vilna: Romm, 1886.

Talmud Bavli. Tractate *Sanhedrin* with Rashi, Tosafot, etc. according to the Venice Text. Jerusalem, n.d.

Talmud Bavli. Tractate *Hagigah* with Rashi, Tosafot, etc. according to the Venice Text. Jerusalem: 5730.

Talmud Yerushalmi. (In Hebr.) Wilna: Romm, 1922.

Le Talmud de Jerusalem. Traduit pour la première fois en français par Moise Schwab. Paris: Maisonneuve, 1960.

The Talmud of Jerusalem. Volume One *Berakhoth.* Tr. Moses Schwab. New York: Hermon Press, 1969.

The Targums of Onkelos and Jonathan ben Ussiel on the Pentateuch with Fragments of the Jerusalem Targum. Tr. J. W. Etheridge. New York: Ktav, 1968.

The Targum to the Five Megilloth. Ed. Bernard Grossfeld. New York: Hermon Press, 1973.

Tertullianus. *Adversus Marcionem.* Ed. and Tr. Ernest Evans. Oxford: Clarendon Press, 1972.

The Ante-Nicene Fathers: Translations of the Writings of the Fathers down to A.D. 325. Ed. Alexander Roberts and James Donaldson. New York: Scribner's, 1899.

The Testament of Abraham. Tr. G. H. Box. London: 1927.

Die Texte aus Qumran: Hebräisch und Deutsch. Ed. and Tr. E. Lohse. München: 1971.

The Thanksgiving Scroll: A Scroll from the Wilderness of Judaea. Text, Introduction, Commentary and Glossary. Ed. J. Licht. Jerusalem: Bialik Institute, 1957.

Théophile D'Antioche: Trois livres à Autolycus. Ed. G. Bardy. Tr. J. Sender. Paris: 1948.

Theophilus of Antioch Ad Autolycum. Text and Tr. R. M. Grant. Oxford: 1970.

Third Enoch or the Hebrew Book of Enoch. Ed. H. Ödeberg. Cambridge: 1928.

Tosefta. Based on the Erfurt and codices with parallels and variants. Ed. M. S. Zuckermandel. 2nd Edition with supplement to the Tosefta by Saul Lieberman. Jerusalem: Bamberger & Wahrmann, 1937.

"The Visions of Ezekiel." *Temirin: Texts and Studies in Kabbalah and Hasidism.* Ed. I. Gruenwald and I. Weinstein. 1972.

SECONDARY SOURCES

Aalen, S., *Die Begriffe 'Licht' und 'Finsternis' im AT, im Spätjudentum und im Rabbanismus.* Oslo: 1951.

Abrahams, Israel, *Studies in Pharisaism and the Gospels.* New York: Ktav, 1967.

Alon, Gedaliah, *Studies in Jewish History in the time of the 2nd Temple, the Mishnah and the Talmud.* [in Hebr.] Jerusalem: 1967.

Altmann, A., "The Gnostic Background of the Rabbinic Adam Legends." *JQR*, NS 35 (1944-45), 371-391.

Altmann, A., "Gnostic Themes in Rabbinic Cosmology." *Essays Presented to J. H. Hertz*. Ed. J. Epstein, E. Levine, and C. Roth. London: 1942, 19-32.

Angus, B., *The Mystic Religions and Christianity: A Study in the Religious Background of Early Christianity*. New York: Charles Scribner's Sons, 1925.

Anz, Wilhelm, *Zur Frage nach dem Ursprung des Gnosticismus*. Ein religionsgeschichtlicher Versuch. Leipzig: 1897.

Apocalypticism. Ed., R. Frank. *Journal for Theology and the Church*. Number 6, New York: Herder and Herder, 1969.

Aptowitzer, V., "Christliche Talmudforschung." *MGWJ*, 57 (1913), 10-23.

Aptowitzer, V., "Geschichte einer liturgischen Formel." *MGWJ*, 73 (1929), 93-118.

Aptowitzer, V., "The Heavenly Temple according to the Aggadah." [in Hebr.]. *Tarbiz*, 2 (1930-31), 137-276.

Aptowitzer, V., *Kain und Abel in der Agada: den Apocryphen, der hellenistischen, christlichen und muhammedanischen Literatur*. Vienna and Leipzig: R. Lowit, 1922.

Aptowitzer, V., "Die rabbinischen Berichte über die Entstehung der Septuaginta." *Ha-Kedem*, 2 (St. Petersburg: 1908), 11-27, 102-122.

Aptowitzer, V., "Die rabbinischen Berichte über die Entstehung der Septuaginta." *Ha-Kedem*, 3 (St. Petersburg: 1909), 4-17.

The Cambridge History of Later Greek and Early Medieval Philosophy. Ed. A. H. Armstrong. Cambridge: 1967.

Bacher, W., *Die Agada der Palästinischen Amoräer*. Strassburg: 1892.

Bacher, W., *The Legends of the Tannaim*. [Hebr. tr. of *die Agada der Tannäiten*] Tel Aviv: 5682.

Bacher, W., *Die exegetische Terminologie der jüdischen Traditionsliteratur*. Zwei Teile. Darmstadt: Wissenschaftliche Buchgesellschaft, 1965. [Reprint of Leipzig 1899 & 1905].

Bacher, W., "Die Gelehrten von Caesarea." *MGWJ*, 45 (1901), 298-311.

Bamberger, Bernard J., *Fallen Angels*. Philadelphia: Jewish Publication Society of America, 1952.

Bandstra, A. J., *The Law and the Elements of the World*. n.p.: 1964.

Baneth, Eduard, *Ursprung der Sadokäer und Boethosäer*. Frankfort: Kauffman, 1882.

Barbel, J., *Christos Angelos: Die Anschauung von Christus als Bote und Engel in der gelehrten und volkstümlichen Literatur der christlichen Altertums*. Bonn: Hanstein, 1941. [Reprint, 1964].

Baron, S. W., *A Social and Religious History of the Jews*. New York: 1958.

Barrett, C. Kingsley, "Stephen and the Son of Man," *Apophoreta: Festschrift—Ernst Haenchen*. Berlin: 1964, 32-38.

Baumgarten, J. M., "Form Criticism and the Oral Law." *JSJ*, v (1974), 34-41.

Bauer, Walter, *Orthodoxy and Heresy in Earliest Christianity*, appendices by Georg Strecker, ed., Robert Kraft and Gerhard Krodel [Trans. by a team from the Philadelphia Seminar on Christian Origins]. Philadelphia: Fortress Press, 1971.

Bergmeier, R., "Zur Frühdatierung samaritanischer Theologoumena." *JSJ*, v (1974), 121-153.

Bergmann, J., *Jüdische Apologetik im neutestamentlichen Zeitalter*. Berlin: Georg Reimer, 1908.

Berkhof, H., *Christ and the Powers*. Tr. John Howard Yoder. Scottsdale, Pa.: 1962.

Betz, Otto, *Der Paraklet: Fürsprecher im häretischen Spätjudentum, im Johannes-evangelium und neu gefundenen gnostischen Schriften*. Leiden: Brill, 1963.

Beutler, Rudolf, "Numenios" in *Supplements to Pauly-Wissowa Realencyclopedie der classischen Wissenschaft*. Stuttgart: 1894.

Bianchi, U., Ed. *Le Origini delle Gnosticismo*. Leiden: Brill, 1967.

Biblical Motifs: Origins and Transformations. Ed. A. Altmann. Cambridge: Harvard University Press, 1966.

Bickerman, Elias, *From Ezra to the Last of the Maccabees: Foundations of Post-Biblical Judaism*. New York: Schocken Books, 1968.

Bietenbard, H., *Die himmlische Welt*. Tübingen: 1951.

Bigg, Charles, *The Christian Platonists of Alexandria*. Oxford: 1913, 1968.

Black, Matthew, *An Aramaic Approach to Gospel and Acts*. Oxford: 1967 (c. 1946).

Black, Matthew, "The Son of Man Problem in Recent Research and Debate." *Bulletin of John Rylands Library*, XIV (1962-63), 305-318.

Blackman, E. C., *Marcion and His Influence*. London: SPCK, 1948.

Blau, Ludwig, *Das altjüdische Zauberwesen*. Strassbourg: Trubner, 1898.

Blau, Ludwig, "Gnosticism," *JE*.

Blau, Ludwig, "La récitation du Schema et de la Haftara." *REJ*, 55 (1908), 209-220.

Blumenkranz, Bernhard, *Die Judenpredigt Augustins: ein Beitrag zur Geschichte der jüdisch-christlichen Beziehungen in der ersten Jahrhunderten*. Basel: 1946.

Böhlig, Alexander, *Mysterion und Wahrheit: gesammelte Beiträge zur spätantiken Religionsgeschichte*. Leiden: Brill, 1968.

Boers, H. W., "Apocalyptic Eschatology in I Corinthians 15: An Essay in Contemporary Interpretation." *Interpretation*, 21 (1967), 50-65.

Bonsirven, Joseph, S. J., *Palestinian Judaism in the time of Jesus Christ*. New York: Holt, Reinhart and Winston, n.d.

Borgen, Peder, *Bread from Heaven*. Leiden: Brill, 1965.

Borsch, F. H., *The Christian and Gnostic Son of Man*. London: SCM Press, 1970.

Borsch, F. H., *The Son of Man in Myth and History*. Philadelphia: Westminister Press, 1967.

Bousset, W., "Die Himmelsreise der Seele." *Archiv für Religionswissenschaft*, 4 (1901), 136-273.

Bousset, W., *Die Religion des Judentums im späthellenistischen Zeitalter*. Tübingen: Mohr (Siebeck), 1926.

Bousset, W., *Kyrios Christos: A History of the Belief in Christ from the Beginnings of Christianity to Irenaeus*. Tr. John E. Steely. Nashville: Abingdon Press, 1970.

Bowker, John, *Jesus and the Pharisees*. Cambridge: Cambridge University Press, 1973.

Bowker, J. W., " 'Merkabah' Visions and the Visions of Paul." *JJS*, 16 (1971), 157-173.

Bowker, J., *The Targums and Rabbinic Literature: an Introduction to Jewish Interpretations of Scripture*. Cambridge, UK: Cambridge University Press, 1969.

Bowman, J., "Early Samaritan Eschatology." *JJS*, (1955), 63-72.

Box, G. H., "The Idea of Intermediation in Jewish Theology: A Note on Memra and Shekinah." *JQR*, 23 (1932-33), 103-119.

Brandon, S. G. F., *The Fall of Jerusalem and the Christian Church: A Study of the Effects of the Jewish Overthrow of A.D. 70 on Christianity*. London: SPCK, 1957.

Brann, G., "Erklärung zu einer Mischna im Traktat Megilla." *MGWJ*, 18 (1869), 313-315.

Braun, H., *Spätjüdisch-häretischer und frühchristlicher Radikalismus: Jesus von Nazareth und die essenische Qumransekte*. 2 vol. Tübingen: Mohr (Siebeck), 1957.

Braver, A. J., "The Debate between a Sadducee and Pharisee in the Mouths of Cain and Abel." *Beth Mikra*, 44 (1971), 583-85 (Hebr.)

Bréhier, E., *The Hellenistic and Roman Age*. Tr. Wade Baskin. Chicago: The University of Chicago Press, 1965.

Brock, S. P., "Early Syrian Ascetics." *Numen*, 20 (1973), 1-19.

Brown, R. E., *The Gospel According to John*. Garden City: 1966.

Buchanan, George W., "The Samaritan Origin of the Gospel of John." *Religions in Antiquity* (Festschrift for E. R. Goodenough), 149-175.

Büchler, A., "La Kedouscha du Yoçer chez les Geonim." *REJ,* 53 (1907), 220-230.

Büchler, A., "The Minim of Sepphoris and Tiberias in the Second and Third Centuries." From the Adolf Büchler memorial volume, *Studies in Jewish History.* Oxford: Oxford University Press, 1956, 245-274.

Büchler, A., *Studies in Sin and Atonement in the Rabbinic Literature of the First Century.* New York: Ktav, 1967.

Büchler, A., *Types of Jewish-Palestinian Piety: from 70 B.C.E. to 70 C.E. The Ancient Pious Men.* Oxford: Jews College Publication #8, n.d.

Bultmann, R., *Primitive Christianity in its Contemporary Settings.* Tr. R. H. Fuller. Cleveland: World, 1969.

Catchpole, D., *The Trial of Jesus: A Study in the Gospels and Jewish Historiography from 1770 to the Present Day.* Leiden: Brill, 1971.

Charles, R. H., *Eschatology: The Doctrine of a Future Life in Israel, Judaism, and Christianity.* New York: Schocken Books, 1963.

Clemen, C., *Die griechischen und lateinischen Nachrichten über die persische Religion.* Giessen: 1920.

Collins, J. J., "Apocalyptic Eschatology as the Transcendence of Death." *CBQ,* 36 (1974), 21-43.

Collins, J. J., "The Son of Man and the Saints of the Most high in the Book of Daniel." *JBL,* 93 (1974), 50-66.

Colpe, Carsten, *Die Religionsgeschichtliche Schule.* Göttingen: Vandenhoeck & Ruprecht, 1961.

Colpe, Carsten, "New Testament and Gnostic Christology." *Religions in Antiquity,* 227-243.

Cooke, G., "The Sons of the God(s)." *ZAW,* 76 (1964), 22-47.

Cross, F. M., *The Ancient Library of Qumran and Modern Biblical Studies.* Garden City: Anchor Books, 1961.

Cross, F. M., "Yahweh and the God of the Patriarchs." *HTR,* 55 (1962), 225-259.

Cullman, O., *Le problème littéraire et historique du roman Pseudo-Clémentin: Étude sur le rapport êntre le gnosticisme et la Judéo-Chrétiennisme.* Paris: Felix Alcan, 1930.

Cumont, F., *After Life in Roman Paganism.* New York: Dover, 1959.

Cumont, F., *Astrology and Religion Among the Greeks and Romans.* New York: Dover, 1960.

Cumont, F., "Le mysticisme astrale dans l'antiquité." *Bulletins de la classe des lettres et des sciences morales et politiques et de la classe des beaux arts de Académie Royale de Belgique,* 58 (1909), 256-286.

Cumont, F., "La Théologie solaire du paganisme romaine". *Mémoires présentés par divers savants à l'Academie Des Inscriptions et Belles-Lettres de l'Institut de France.* Tome XII, Deuxième partie: Paris, 1913, 448-481.

Dahl, N. A., *The Crucified Messiah and other essays.* Minneapolis: Augsburg Publishing House, 1974.

Dahl, N. A., "Der Erstgeborene Satans und der Vater des Teufels (Polyk. 7:1 und Joh. 8:44), *Apophoreta: Festschrift—Ernst Haenchen.* Berlin: 1964.

Dahl, N. A., "Eschatology and History in the Light of the Dead Sea Scrolls," *The Future of our Religious Past.* Festschrift for Bultmann, ed. J. M. Robinson, 3-18.

Dahl, N. A., "Form-Critical Observations on the Early Preaching to the Church." unpublished paper.

Dahl, N. A., "The Fragment 2 Corinthians 6:14-7:1 and its Context." unpublished paper.

Dahl, N. A., "The Johannine Church and History." Ed. Klassen & Snyder. *Current Issues in New Testament Interpretation.* New York: 1962.

Dahl, N. A., *Das Volk Gottes: Eine Untersuchung zum Kirchenbewusstsein des Urchristentums.* Darmstadt: Wissenschaftliche Buchgesellschaft, 1963.

Dahl, N. A., "Widersprüche in der Bibel, ein altes hermeneutisches Problem." *Studia Theologica,* 25 (1971), 1-19.

Dahl, N. A. and A. Segal, "Philo and the Rabbis and the Names of God," seminar paper *SBL* convention, Washington, October, 1974.

Danielou, J., *The Theology of Jewish Christianity.* (vol. I of the *Development of Christian Doctrine before the Council of Nicaea)* Tr. and Ed. by J. A. Baker. London: Darton, Longman and Todd, 1964. Chicago: Henry Regnery, 1964.

Danielou, J., "Les traditions secrètes des apôtres." *Eranos Jahrbuch,* 31 (1962), 199-215.

Davies, J. G., *He Ascended into Heaven: A Study in The History of Doctrine.* New York: Association Press, 1958.

Davies, W. D., "A Note on Josephus' *Antiquities* 15:136." *HTR,* 47 (1954), 135.

Davies, W. D., *Torah in the Messianic Age and/or the Age to Come.* Philadelphia: Society of Biblical Literature, 1952.

DeJonge, M., "The Use of the Word 'Anointed' in the Time of Jesus," *NT,* 8 (1966), 132-148.

DeJonge, M. et A. S. van der Woude, "11 Q Melch. and the New Testament." *NTS,* 12 (1956), 301-326.

Delcor, M., "Melchizedek from Genesis to the Qumran texts and the Epistle to the Hebrews." *JSJ,* 2 (1971), 115-135.

Dey, Lala K. K., The Intermediary World and Patterns of Perfection in Philo and the Hebrews. Missoula: SBL dissertation series, 1975.

Dieterich, A., *Abraxas: Studien zur Religionsgeschichte des späteren Altertums.* Leipzig: Teubner, 1891.

Dieterich, A., *Eine Mithrasliturgie.* Leipzig: Teubner, 1923.

Dix, Gregory, "The Seven Archangels and the Seven Spirits." *JTS,* 28 (1926), 233-285.

Dodds, C. H., *The Bible and the Greeks.* London: Hodder & Stoughton, 1935 (3rd printing, 1964).

Dodds, E. R., *Theurgy, JRS,* 37 (1948).

Dodds, E. R., *The Greeks and the Irrational.* Berkeley. University of California Press, 1968.

Dodds, E. R., "New Light on the Chaldaean Oracles." *HTR,* 54 (1961), 272 f.

Dodds, E. R., *Pagan and Christian in an Age of Anxiety: Some Aspects of Religious Experience from Marcus Aurelius to Constantine.* New York: W. W. Norton, 1965.

Doresse, J., *The Secret Book of the Egyptian Gnostics.* New York: 1960.

Drijvers, H. J. W., "The Origins of Gnosticism." *Nederlands Theologisch Tijdschrift,* 22 (1967/68), 321-51.

Duchesne-Guillemin, J., *Symbols and Values in Zoroastrianism: Their Survival and Renewal.* New York: Harper & Row, 1970.

Duncan, G., *The Epistle of Paul to the Galatians.* New York: 1934.

Dupont-Sommer, A., "The Essenes in Ancient Literature." *The Essene Writings from Qumran.* Tr. G. Vermes. Oxford: Blackwell, 1961.

Edsman, Carl-Martin, *Le baptême de feu.* Leipzig: Lorentz, Uppsala: Lundequistska, 1940.

Eissfeldt, O., *The Old Testament: An Introduction.* Tr. Peter R. Ackroyd. New York: Harper and Row, 1965.

Elbogen, I., *Der jüdische Gottesdienst in seiner geschichtlichen Entwicklung.* Hildesheim: Georg Olms, 1962.

Eltester, F. W., *Eikōn im Neuen Testament*. Berlin: A Topelmann, 1958.

Emerton, J. A., "The Origin of the Son of Man Imagery." *JTS*, 9 (1958), 225-242.

Fascher, E., *Prophētēs: Eine sprach- und religionsgeschichtliche Untersuchung*. Giessen: Topelmann, 1927.

Festugière, André-Jean, R. P., *Personal Religion Among the Greeks*. Berkeley: University of California Press, 1960.

Festugière, R. P., *La révélation d'Hermes Trismégiste I*: L'Astrologie et les sciences occultes. Paris: Libraire Lecoffre, 1950.

Festugière, R. P., *La révélation d'Hermes Trismégiste II*: Le dieu cosmique. Paris: Libraire Lecoffre, 1949.

Festugière, R. P., *La révélation d'Hermes Trismégiste III*: Les doctrines de l'âme. Paris: 1953.

Festugière, R. P., *La révélation d'Hermes Trismégiste IV*. Paris: J. Gabalda, 1954.

Fiedler, M. J., *Dikaiosunē im der diaspora-jüdische und intertestamentarischen Literatur*. *JSJ*, 1, 120-143.

Finkelstein, L., "The Development of the Amidah." *JQR*, *NS* 16 (1925-26), 1-43, 127-170.

Finkelstein, L. (Ed.), *The Jews*. Three volumes. New York: Schocken Books: 1972.

Finkelstein, L., *Introduction to the treatises Abot and Abot of Rabbi Nathan*. New York: 1950.

Finkelstein, L., "La Kedouscha et les bénédictions du Schema," *REJ*, 93 (1932), 1-26.

Finkelstein, L., "*Miscellen*." *JQR*, 10 (1929-30), 362f.

Finkelstein, L., *The Pharisees: The Sociological Background of their Faith*. Two volumes. Philadelphia: The Jewish Publication Society of America, 1962.

Fischel, Henry, *Rabbinic Literature and Greco-Roman Philosophy: A Study of Epicurea and Rhetorica in Early Midrashic Writings*. Leiden: Brill, 1973.

Fitzmyer, J. A., "The Contribution of Qumran Aramaic to the Study of the New Testament." *NTS*, 20 (1974), 382-407.

Fitzmyer, J. A., *Essays on the Semitic Background of the New Testament*. London: Geoffrey Chapman, 1971.

Fitzmyer, J. A., "Further Light on Melchizedek from Qumran Cave 11." *JBL*, 86 (1967), 25-41.

Fitzmyer, J. A., *The Genesis Apocryphon of Qumran Cave I: A Commentary*. Rome: Biblical Institute Press, 1971.

Fitzmyer, J. A., "Methodology in the Study of the Aramaic Substratum of Jesus' Sayings in the New Testament." *Jesus aux origines de la christologie* (Biblioteca ephemeridum theologicarum lovaniensium: Gemloux, Duculot), 1975.

Fitzmyer, J. A., "Qumran and the Interpolated Paragraph in 2 Cor. 6:14-7:1." *CBQ.*, 23 (n.d.), 271-280.

Flusser, David G., "The Social Message From Qumran." *Cahiers de l'histoire mondiale*, XI n. 1-2 (1968), 107-115.

Ford, J. M., "He That Cometh and the Divine Name: Apocalypse 1:4, 4:8." *JSJ*, 1 (1970), 144-47.

Forkman, Goeran, *The Limits of Religious Community*. Lund: CWK Gleerup, 1972.

Francis, F., "Visionary Discipline and Scriptural Tradition at Colossae." *Lexington Theological Quarterly*, 2 (1967).

Freimann, M., "Die Wortführer des Judentums in den ältesten Kontroversen zwischen Juden und Christen." *MGWJ*, 55 (1911), 555-585.

Frickel, J., "Eine neue Deutung von Gen. 1, 26 in der Gnosis," in *Ex Orbe Religionum: Studia Geo Widengren Oblata I*. Ed. Bleeker, C. J. Brandon, S. G. F. and M. Simon. Leiden: Brill, 1972, 413-423.

Friedländer, M., *Geschichte der jüdischen Apologetik als Vorgeschichte des Christentums*. Amsterdam: 1903.

Friedländer, M., "La propagande religieuse des Juifs grecs." *REJ*, 30 (1895), 161-181.

Friedländer, M., "Der Minaismus," *Die religiosen Bewegungen innerhalb des Judentums im Zeitalter Jesu.* Berlin: 1905.
Friedländer, M., *Vorchristliche jüdische Gnosticismus.* Göttingen: Vandenhoeck & Ruprecht, 1898.
Frye, R., "Reitzenstein and Qumran Revisited by an Iranian." *HTR,* 55 (1962), 266.
Gager, J., "The Dialogue of Paganism with Judaism: Bar Cochba to Julian." *HUCA,* 44 (1973), 89-118.
Gager, J., "The Gospels and Jesus: Some Doubts about Method." *JR,* 54 (1974), 244-272.
Gager, J., "Marcion and Philosophy." *Vigilae Christianae,* 26 (1972), 53-59.
Gager, J., *Moses in Graeco-Roman Paganism.* Nashville: Abingdon Press, 1972.
Galavaris, G., *Bread and the Liturgy: The Symbolism of Early Christian and Byzantine Bread Stamps.* Madison: University of Wisconsin Press, 1970.
Gammie, J., "Spatial and Ethical Dualism in Jewish Wisdom and Apocalyptic Literature." *JBL,* 93 (1974), 356-385.
Geiger, A., *Nachgelassene Schriften:* Herausgegeben von Ludwig Geiger. IV Band. Berlin: 1876.
Gerhardsson, B., *Memory and Manuscript: Oral Tradition and Written Transmission in Rabbinic Judaism and Early Christianity.* Lund: 1961.
Gershevitch, I., "Zoroaster's Own Contribution to Zoroastrianism." *JNES,* 23 (1964), 12-31.
Ginzburg, "Merkabah" *JE,* 5 (138-139).
Ginzburg, L., *The Legends of the Jews.* Tr. Henrietta Szold. Philadelphia: The Jewish Publication Society of America, 1968.
Ginzberg, L., *Die Haggada bei den Kirchenvätern.* Erster Theil. Die Haggada in den pseudohieronymianischen "Quaestiones". Amsterdam: 1899.
Gnilka, J., "2 Cor 6:14-7:1 in the Light of the Qumran Texts and the Testaments of the Twelve Patriarchs." *Neutestamentliche Aufsätze* (Festschrift J. Schmid) E. J. Blinzer et al., Regensburg: 1963, 86-99.
Goldberg, A. M., *Untersuchungen über die Vorstellung von der Schekhinah in der frühen rabbinischen Literatur: Talmud und Midrash.* Berlin: Walter De Gruyter, 1969.
Goldfahn, A. H., *Justinus Martyr und die Agada.* Breslau: Glutsch, n.d.
Goldin, J., "Not By Means of an Angel and Not By Means of a Messenger". *Religions in Antiquity.* Ed. J. Neusner. Leiden: 1968.
Goldin, J., *The Song at the Sea: Being a Commentary on a Commentary in Two Parts.* New Haven: Yale University Press, 1971.
Goodenough, E. R., *By Light, Light: The Mystic Gospel of Hellenistic Judaism.* New Haven: Yale University Press, 1935.
Goodenough, E. R., *An Introduction to Philo Judaeus.* Oxford: Basil Blackwell, 1962.
Goodenough, E. R., "Literal Mystery in Hellenistic Judaism," *Quantalacumque: Studies Presented to Kirsopp Lake.* London: 1937, 227-241.
Goodenough, E. R., "The Pseudo-Justinian 'Oratio Ad Graecos.' " *Harvard Theological Review,* 18 (1925), 187-200.
Goodenough, E. R., "Psychopomps" Ch. 11 of *Jewish Symbols in the Greco-Roman Period.* Princeton: 1958.
Goodenough, E. R., *The Theology of Justin Martyr.* Jena: 1922.
Goodspeed, E. J., *Index Apologeticus to Justin.* Chicago: 1912.
Graetz, H., *Gnosticismus und Judenthum.* Krotoschin: Monasd und Gohn, 1846.
Graetz, H., *History of the Jews.* Philadelphia: 1893.
Grant, F. C., *Ancient Judaism and the New Testament.* New York: Macmillan, 1959.
Grant, R. M., *Gnosticism and Early Christianity.* Revised edition. New York: Harper & Row, 1966.

Green, A., "The Children in Egypt and the Theophany at the Sea: Interpretation of an Aggadic Motif." unpublished paper.

Gruenwald, I., *Apocalyptic and Merkabah Mysticism: A Study of the Jewish Esoteric Literature in the Time of the Mishnah and Talmud.* Jerusalem: Unpublished dissertation of the Hebrew University, 1968-69.

Gunther, J. J., *St. Paul's Opponents and Their Background: A Study of Apocalyptic and Jewish Sectarian Teachings.* Leiden: Brill, 1973.

Guthrie, W. K. L., *A History of Greek Philosophy.* Cambridge: Cambridge University Press, 1962.

Haardt, R., Ed. *Gnosis: Characters and Testimony.* Tr. J. F. Hendry. Leiden: Brill, 1971.

Hadas, Moses & M. Smith, *Heroes and Gods: Spiritual Biographies in Antiquity.* New York: Harper & Row, 1965.

von Harnack, Adolf, *Die Altercatio Simonis Judaei et Theophili Irani, nebst Untersuchungen über die anti-jüdische Polemik in der alten Kirche.* Berlin: 1883.

von Harnack, Adolf, *Marcion: Das Evangelium vom fremden Gott. Eine Monographie zur Geschichte der Grundlegung der katholischen Kirche. Neue Studien zu Marcion.* Darmstadt: Wissenschaftliche Buchgesellschaft, 1960.

von Harnack, Adolf, und Schmidt, Carl, *Texte und Untersuchungen zur Geschichte der altchristlichen Literatur.* Leipzig: Hinrich'ssche Buchhandlung, 1913.

Hartman, Lars, *Prophecy Interpreted: The Formation of Some Jewish Apocalyptic Texts and the Eschatological Discourse, Mark 13.* Lund: Gleerup, 1966.

Hay, David M., *Glory at the Right Hand: Psalm 110 in Early Christianity.* Nashville: Abingdon Press, 1973.

Hegerman, Harald, *Die Vorstellung vom Schöpfungsmittler im hellenistischen Jüdentum und Urchristentum.* Berlin: Akademie, 1961.

Heinemann, J., *Prayer in the Period of the Tannaim and Amoraim* (in Hebr.) Jerusalem: 1966.

Heintzel, E., *Hermogenes: Der Hauptvertreter des philosophischen Dualismus in der alten Kirche: Ein Beitrag zur Geschichte der patristischen Philosophie.* Berlin: 1902.

Hengel, Martin, *Judentum und Hellenismus: Studien zu ihrer Begegnung unter besonderer Berüchsichtigung Palästinas bis zur Mitte des 2 Jh. s. v. Chr.* Tübingen: Mohr (Siebeck), 1973.

Hengel, Martin, *Der Sohn Gottes: Die Entstehung der Christologie und die jüdisch-hellenistische Religionsgeschichte.* Tübingen; Mohr, 1925—[tr. by John Bowden Philadelphia: Fortress, 1976].

Hengel, Martin, *Victory over Violence: Jesus and the Revolutionists.* Tr. David E. Green. Introduction by Robin Scroggs. Philadelphia: Fortress, 1973.

Herford, R. Travers, *Christianity in Talmud and Midrash.* London: Williams and Norgate, 1903.

Hilgenfeld, A., *Judentum und Juden-Christentum: Eine Nachlese zur der Ketzergeschichte des Urchristentum.* Hildesheim 1966. (Reprint of 1886 edition.)

Hilgenfeld, A., *Die Ketzengeschichte des Urchristenthums.* Leipzig: 1884.

Hindley, J. C., "Towards a Date for the Similitudes of Enoch: An Historical Approach." *NTS,* 14 (1967-68).

Herschberg, Harris, "Allusions to the Apostle Paul in the Talmud." *JBL,* 62 (1943), 73-87.

Herschberg, Harris, "Once Again The Minim." *JBL,* 67 (1948), 305-318.

Holscher, Uvo, *Anfängliches Fragen: Studien zur frühen griechischen Philosophie.* Göttingen: 1968.

Hulen, Amos, B., "The 'Dialogues with the Jews' as Sources for the Early Jewish Argument Against Christianity." *JBL,* 51 (1932), 58-71.

Inge, W. R., *The Philosophy of Plotinus.* London: 1923.

The Interpreter's Dictionary of the Bible: An Illustrated Encyclopedia in Four Volumes. Ed. George Arthur Buttrick, et al. New York: Abingdon Press, 1962.

Jastrow, Marcus, *A Dictionary of the Targumim, the Talmud Babli and Yerushalmi and the Midrashic Literature.* Two volumes. New York: Pardes Publishing House, 1950.

Jeremias, *The Eucharistic Words of Jesus.* New York: Scribners, 1966.

Jeremias, J., *New Testament Theology.* New York, 1976.

Jervell, J., *Imago Dei: Gen. 1,26 f im Spätjudentum, in der Gnosis und in den paulinischen Briefen.* Göttingen: Vandenhoeck & Ruprecht, 1960.

Jervell, J., *Luke and the People of God: A New Look at Luke-Acts.* Minneapolis: Augsburg Publishing House, 1972.

The Jewish Encyclopedia: The History, Religion, Literature, and Customs of the Jewish People from the Earliest Times to the Present Day. Isidore Singer, Projector and Managing Editor. New York: Funk and Wagnalls, 1912.

Joël, M., *Blicke in die Religionsgeschichte zu Anfang des zweiten christlichen Jahrhunderts.* Breslau: Schottlaender, 1880.

Johansson, N., *Parakletoi: Vorstellungen von Fürsprechern für die Menschen vor Gott in der alttestamentlichen Religion, im Spätjudentum und Urchristentum.* Lund: Ohlssons, 1940.

Johnson, N. B., *Prayer in the Apocrypha and Pseudepigrapha: A Study in the Jewish Concept of God.* Philadelphia: Society of Biblical Literature, 1948.

Jonas, H., *Gnosis und spätantiker Geist.* Göttingen: 2te durchgesehene Auflage, 1954.

Jonas, H., *The Gnostic Religion: The Message of the Alien God and the Beginnings of Christianity.* Boston: Beacon Press, 1963.

Jonas, H., "Myth and Mysticism: A Study of Objectification and Interiorization in Religious Thought." *JR,* 49 (1969), 315-29.

Jonas, H., "The Secret Books of the Egyptian Gnostics." *JR,* 42 (1962), 262-73.

Jones, M., "St. Paul and the Angels." *Expositor,* viii-15 (1918), 415.

Jongeling, B., *A Classified Bibliography of the Finds in the Desert of Judah 1958-1969.* Leiden: Brill, 1971.

Juel, Donald, *The Messiah and the Temple.* Missoula, Montana: Scholars Press, 1977.

Jung Codex: A Newly Recovered Gnostic Papyrus, 3 Studies by H.-ch. Puech, G. Quispel, and W. C. Van Unnik. Tr. by F. L. Cross. London: 1955.

Jungmann, J. A., *The Early Liturgy.* Tr. by F. A. Brunner. South Bend: Notre Dame, 1959.

Kaesemann, E., *Das wandernde Gottesvolk im Hebräerbrief.* Göttingen: 1959.

Kaplan, M., "Philo and the Midrash." *JQR,* 23 (1933), 285-291.

Kelly, J. N. D., *Early Christian Doctrines.* New York: Harper & Row, 1958.

Kimelman, R., "Some Rabbinic Responses to Gnosticism." Paper.

Kimelman, R., "R. Yohanan and Origen on Canticles." Paper.

Klausner, J., *Jesus of Nazareth: His Life, Times, and Teaching.* Tr. from Hebrew by H. Danby. New York: Macmillan, 1929.

Klijn, A. F. J. and G. J. Reinach, *Patristic Evidence for Jewish-Christian Sects.* Leiden: Brill, 1973.

Kolenkow, A., "The Angelology of the Testament of Abraham." Philadelphia: *IOSCS Pseudepigrapha Proceedings,* 1972.

Kolenkow, A., "The Coming and Ascent of a Heavenly Healer—Tobit and Mark." Unpublished paper for *Gospel of John* Seminar, SBL Meeting, October, 1974.

Kasouwski, H. J., *Concordance to the Targum Onkelos.* 5 vols. in 2. Jerusalem: Rab Cook Foundation, 1939/40.

Kossowsky, B. (Ed.), *Concordance to the Tosefta.* Jerusalem: 1966.

Kossowsky, B. (Ed.), *Concordantiae Verborum Quae in Mechilta d'Rabbi Ismael.* Jerusalem: JTS, 1966.

Kraeling, C. H., *Anthropos and Son of Man.* New York: Columbia University Press, 1927.

Kragerud, A., *Die Hymnen der Pistis Sophia.* Oslo: 1967.

Krause, M. (Ed.), *Essays on the Nag Hammadi Texts in Honor of Alexander Böhlig.* Leiden: Brill, 1972.

Krauss, S., Un fragment polémique de la geniza." *REJ*, LXIII, 63-74.

Krauss, S., *Griechische und lateinische Lehnwörter in Talmud, Midrash und Targum.* Berlin: Calvary, 1898-99.

Kretschmar, Georg, *Studien zur frühchristlichen Trinitätstheologie.* Tübingen: Mohr, 1956.

Kretschmar, G., "Zur religionsgeschichtlichen Einordnung der Gnosis." *Evangelische Theologie,* 13 (1953), 354-61.

Krochmal, N., *More Nevukhe ha-Zeman.* Lemberg: 1851.

Kuhn, K. G., *Konkordanz zu den Qumrantexten.* Göttingen: Vandenhoeck & Ruprecht, 1960.

Kummel, W. G. (Ed.), *Introduction to the New Testament.* Tr. A. J. Mattill, Jr. Nashville: Abingdon Press, 1965.

Kropp, A. M., *Der Lobpreis des Erzengels Michael.* Bruxelles: 1966.

Kuntz, J. K., *The Self-Revelation of God.* Philadelphia: Westminster Press, 1967.

Laubscher, F. du T., "God's Angel of Truth and Melchizedek, A Note on 11Q Melch 13b." *JSJ*, 3 (1972), 46-51.

Langdon, E., *The Angel Teaching of the New Testament.* London: n.d.

Lauterbach, J., *Rabbinical Essays.* New York: Ktav, 1973, c 1951.

Lauterbach, J., "Some Clarifications on the Mekhilta." (Heb.) *Sefer Klausner: A Collection of Science and Belles-Lettres gathered for Professor Yoseph Klausner on his Sixtieth Jubilee.* Ed. N. H. Torchyner, A. Tcherikover, A. A. Kubed, B. Shortman. Tel Aviv: 1940.

Lauterbach, J., "Zur Erforschung des Jelamdenu-Problems." *MGWJ*, 74 (1930), 266-284.

Leany, A. R. C., *The Rule of Qumran and its Meaning.* London: 1966.

Le Déaut, R., "Aspects de l'intercession dans le Judaisme ancien." *JSJ*, 1 (1970), 35-57.

Lehmann, J., "Les sectes Juives mentionnées dans la Mischna de Berakhot et de Meguilla." *REJ*, 30 (1895), 182-203.

Leivestad, R., "Exit the Apocalyptic Son of Man." *NTS*, 18 (1972), 243-267.

Levine, L., *A History of Caesarea under Roman Rule.* New York: Unpublished dissertation, Columbia University, 1970.

Levey, S., "The Best Kept Secret of the Rabbinic Tradition." *Judaism,* 21 (1972), 454-69.

Levy, J., *Chaldäisches Wörterbuch über die Targumim und einen grossen Theil des rabbinischen Schriftthums.* Cologne: J. Melzer, 1859.

Levy, J. (Ed.), *Neuhebräisches und chaldäisches Wörterbuch über die Talmudim und Midrashim.* Leipzig: 1876-9.

Lewy, H., *Chaldean Oracles and Theurgy: Mysticism, Magic and Platonism in the Later Roman Empire.* Cairo: Imprimerie de l'institut français de l'archéologie orientale, 1956.

Lewy, H., *Sobria Ebrietas, Untersuchungen zur Geschichte der antiken Mystik.* Giessen: Topelmann, 1929.

Liber, M., "La récitation du Schema et les Bénédictions." *REJ*, 54 (1909).

Lieberman, S., *Greek in Jewish Palestine: Studies in the Life and Manners of Jewish Palestine in the II-IV Centuries C.E.* New York: Philipp Feldheim, 1965.

Lieberman, S., *Hellenism in Jewish Palestine: Studies in the Literary Transmission Beliefs and Manners of Palestine in the I Century B.C.E.-IV Century C.E.* New York: Jewish Theological Seminary of America, 1962.

Lieberman, S., "How Much Greek in Jewish Palestine?" *Biblical And Other Studies.* Ed. A. Altmann. Cambridge: 1963, 123-141.

Lieberman, S., "The Martyrs of Caesarea." *JQR,* 36 (1946), 239-253.

Lieberman, S., "Palestine in the Third And Fourth Centuries." *JQR,* 36 (1945-46), 329-370; cont. in *JQR,* 37 (1946-47), 31-55.

Lietzmann, H., *Der Menschensohn: Ein Beitrag zur neutestamentlichen Theologie.* Leipzig: Freiburg i. B., 1896.

Lindars, Barnabas, *New Testament Apologetic: The Doctrinal Significance of the Old Testament Quotations.* Philadelphia: Westminster, 1961.

Ljungman, H., *Guds Barmhärtighet och Dom: Fariseernas Lära om de två mätten.* Lund: 1950. (With an English summary).

Lohfink, G., *Die Himmelfahrt Jesu: Untersuchungen zu den himmelfahrts- und Erhöhungstexten bei Lukas.* München: Kosel, 1971.

Loewy, M., *La Gnose dans le Talmud.* Budapest: 1885.

McEleney, N. J., "Orthodoxy in Judaism of the First Christian Century." *JSJ,* IV (1973), 19-42.

Macgregor, G., "Principalities and Powers: the Cosmic Background of Paul's thought." *NTS,* 1 (1954).

McKnight, Edgar V., *What is Form Criticism?* Philadelphia: Fortress Press, 1971.

MacMullen, R., *Enemies of the Roman Order: Treason, Unrest and Alienation in the Empire.* Cambridge: Harvard University Press, 1966.

McNamara, Martin, *Targum and Testament: Aramaic Paraphrases of the Hebrew Bible: A Light on the New Testament.* Grand Rapids: William B. Eerdmans, 1972.

Macrae, G. W., "Jewish Background of the Gnostic Sophia Myth." *NT,* 12 (1970), 86-101.

Macrae, G. W., "A Nag Hammadi Tractate on the Soul." *Ex Orbe Religionum Studia Geo Widengren Oblata* I. Leiden: Brill, 1972, 471-479.

Mack Burton L., *Logos und Sophia: Untersuchungen zur Weisheitstheologie im hellenistischen Judentum.* Göttingen: Vandenhoeck & Ruprecht, 1973.

Mann, J., *The Bible as Read and Preached in the Old Synagogue.* V. 1, New York: Ktav, 1971.

Maier, J. "Das Gefährdungsmotiv bei der Himmelreise in den jüdischen Apocalyptus und 'gnosis.' " *Kairos,* 5 (1963), 18-40.

Mancini, I., *Archaeological Discoveries Relative to the Judaeo-Christians.* Tr. G. Bushell. Jerusalem: 1970.

Mantel, H., *Studies in the History of the Sanhedrin.* Cambridge: Harvard University Press, 1965.

Marcus, R., "Judaism and Gnosticism." *Judaism,* 4 (1955), 360-64.

Margalioth, M., *Encyclopedia of the Sages of the Talmud and the Geonim.* (In Hebr.) Tel Aviv: 1970.

Marmorstein, A., "The Background of the Haggadah." *HUCA,* 6 (1929), 141-204.

Marmorstein, A., "Deux renseignements d'Origine concernant les Juifs." *REJ,* LXX (1920), 190-99.

Marmorstein, A., *The Doctrine of Merits in Old Rabbinic Literature and the Old Rabbinic Doctrine of God.* New York: Ktav, 1920 (copyright, with new material, 1968).

Marmorstein, A., "The Emperor Julianus in the Aggada of R. Aha." *Melilah: A Volume of Studies.* Ed. Edward Robertson and Meir Wallenstein, 1 (1944), 93-120.

Marmorstein, A., "Les Épicuriens dans la littérature talmudique." *REJ,* LIV (1907), 181-193.

Marmorstein, A., *Essays in Anthropomorphism: Vol. 2 of The Old Rabbinic Doctrine of God.* New York: 1937.

Marmorstein, A., "Jews and Judaism in the Earliest Christian Apologies." *Expositor*, VIII, 17 (1919), 100-116.

Marmorstein, A., "Judaism and Christianity in the Middle of the Third Century." *HUCA*, 10 (1935), 223-363.

Marmorstein, A., "Miscillen." *ZNW*, 25 (1925), 249-58.

Marmorstein, A., *The Old Rabbinic Doctrine of God.* London: Oxford University Press, 1937.

Marmorstein, A., "Philo and the Names of God." *JQR*, 22 (1931-32), 295-306.

Marmorstein, A., "Les rabbins et les Évangiles." *REJ*, XCII (1931), 31-54.

Marmorstein, A., *Religionsgeschichtliche Studien: Die Bezeichnungen für Christen und Gnostischen im Talmud und Midras.* Schotschau (Ost Schlesien): Sebst Verlag des Verfasser, 1910.

Marmorstein, A., *Studies in Jewish Theology.* Ed. J. Rabbinowitz and M. S. Lew. Oxford: Oxford University Press, 1950.

Marmorstein, A., "Zur Erforschung des Jelamdenu Problems." *MGWJ*, 74 (1930), 266-284.

Marmorstein, A., "The Unity of God in Rabbinic Literature." *HUCA*, I, 467-499.

Marks, Luther H. Jr., "The Anti-Philosophical Polemic and Gnostic Soteriology in the Treatise on the Resurrection (CG I, 3)." *Numen*, 20 (1973), 20-37.

Martyn, J. Louis, *History and Theology in the Fourth Gospel.* New York: Harper Row, 1968.

Martyn, J. L., "Source Criticism and Religionsgeschichte in the Fourth Gospel" in *Jesus and Man's Hope.* Pittsburgh Festival on the Gospels, 1970. Pittsburgh: Pittsburgh Theological Seminary, 1970.

Marxsen, W., *Mark the Evangelist: Studies on the Redaction History of the Gospel.* Tr. James Boyce, et al. Nashville: Abingdon Press, 1969.

Meeks, Wayne, " 'Am I a Jew?' Johannine Christianity and Judaism," *Christianity, Judaism and other Greco-Roman Cults.* Studies for Morton Smith at Sixty, ed. J. Neusner. I, 168-186.

Meeks, Wayne, "Moses as God and King." *Religions in Antiquity: Festschrift for E. R. Goodenough,* Ed. J. Neusner. Leiden: Brill, 1968.

Meeks, Wayne, *The Prophet King: Moses Traditions and the Johannine Christology.* Leiden: Brill, 1967.

Meeks, Wayne, "Samaritans, Magicians, and the Fourth Gospel." (Response to J. Purvis, "The Fourth Gospel and the Samaritans." 10/26/74.) paper SBL meeting, October, 1974.

Michaelis, W., *Zur Engelschristologie im Urchristentum.*

Michl, J., *"Engel" Reallexicon für antike und Christentum.* Ed. T. Klauser. Stuttgart: 1962, 66-67.

Mielziner, M., *Introduction to the Talmud with a new Bibliography 1925-1967.* Ed. Alexander Guttman. New York: Bloch, 1968.

Milik, J. T., "4Q Visions de 'Amran et une citation d'Origène." *RB*, LXXIX (1972), 77-97.

Milik, J. T., "Milki-şedeq et Milki-reša dans les ancient écrits juifs et chrétiens." *JJS*, 3 (1972), 95-144.

Milik, J. T., "Problèmes de la littérature hénochique à la lumière des fragments araméens de Qumran." *HTR*, 64 (1971), 333-78.

Milik, J. T., "Turfan et Qumran: Livre des Géants Juifs et Manichéen." *Tradition und Glaube: Das frühe Christentum in seiner Umwelt: Festgabe für K. G. Kuhn.* Göttingen: 1971, 117-27.

Miner, D. F., "A Suggested Reading for 11Q Melch." *JSJ*, 2 (1971), 144-148.

Moore, G. F., "Christian Writers on Judaism." *HTR*, 14 (1921), 197-254.

Moore, G. F., *Judaism in the First Centuries of the Christian Era: The Age of the Tannaim.* Cambridge: Harvard University Press, 1954.

Moxnes, H., "God and his Angel in the Shepherd of Hermas." *Studia Theologica*, 28 (1974), 49-56.

Neher, A., "Le voyage mystique de quatre." *Révue de l'histoire des religions*, CXL (1951), 59-82.

Neusner, Jacob, *Aphrahat and Judaism. The Christian-Jewish Argument in the Fourth Century Iran*. Leiden: Brill, 1971.

Neusner, Jacob, "Babylonian Jewry and Shapur II's Persecution of Christianity from 339 to 379 A.D." *HUCA*, XLIII (1972), 77-102.

Neusner, J., "The Development of the Merkabah Tradition." *JSJ*, 2 (1971), 149-160.

Neusner, J., *Eliezer b. Hyrcanus: The Tradition and the Man*. Leiden, Brill, 1974-5.

Neusner, J., *First Century Judaism in Crisis: Yohanan ben Zakkai and the Renaissance of Torah*. Nashville: Abingdon, 1975.

Neusner, J., *The Formation of the Babylonian Talmud*. Leiden: Brill, 1971.

Neusner, J., *A History of the Jews in Babylonia*. 5 Volumes. Leiden: Brill, 1965-1970.

Neusner, J., "The Idea of Purity in Ancient Judaism." *JAAR*, 43 (March, 1975), 15-27.

Neusner, J., "Judaism in a Time of Crisis; Four Responses to the Destruction of the Second Temple." *Judaism*, 21 (1972), 313-27.

Neusner, J., "Pharisaic Law in N.T. Times." *USQR*, 26 (1971), 331-40.

Neusner, J., *From Politics to Piety: The Emergence of Pharisaic Judaism*. Englewood Cliffs: Prentice-Hall, 1973.

Neusner, J., *A Life of Rabban Yohanan ben Zakkai Ca 1-80 C.E.* Leiden: Brill, 1962.

Neusner, J., "Pre-70 C.E. Pharisaism: The Record of the Rabbis." *CCARJ*, 19 (1972), 53-70.

Neusner, J., "Rabbinic Judaism in Early Sasanian Babylonia." *A History of the Jews in Babylonia*. Leiden: Brill, 1966, 147-51.

Neusner, J., "The Rabbinic Tradition about the Pharisees before 70 A.D.: The Problem of Oral Transmission." *JJS*, 22 (1971), 1-18.

Neusner, J., "Rabbis and Community in Third Century Babylonia." *Religions in Antiquity*. Ed. J. Neusner. (Festschrift for E. R. Goodenough). Leiden: Brill. 1968.

Neusner, J., "The Traditions Concerning Johanan ben Zakkai: Reconsiderations." *JJS*, 24 (1973), 65-73.

Neusner, J., "Types and Forms in Ancient Jewish Literature: Some Comparisons. *HR*, 11 (1972), 354-90.

Nickelsburg, G. W. E. Jr., *Resurrection, Immortality and Eternal Life in Intertestamental Judaism*. Cambridge: Harvard U. Press, 1972.

Newman, L. I., *Jewish Influence on Christian Reform Movements*. New York: Columbia University Press, 1925.

Nock, A. D., *Conversion: The Old and the New in Religion from Alexander the Great to Augustine of Hippo*. Oxford: Oxford University Press, 1969.

Nock, A. D., *Early Gentile Christianity and its Hellenistic Background*. New York: Harper & Row, 1964.

Nock, A. D., "Review of *By Light, Light: The Mystic Gospel of Hellenistic Judaism*." *Gnomon*, 1937, 156-65.

Nock, A. D., "Paul and the Magus." *The Beginnings of Christianity*. Ed. F. J. Foakes Jackson and K. Lake. Grand Rapids: Baker, V, 164-189.

L'Orange, H. P., *Art Forms and Civic Life in the Late Roman Empire*. Tr. Dr. and Mrs. Knut Berg. Princeton: Princeton University Press, 1972.

L'Orange, H. P., *Studies on the Iconography of Cosmic Kingship in the Ancient World*. Oslo: H. Aschehough & Co. (W. Nygaard), 1953.

Ödeberg, H., *The Aramaic Portions of Bereshit Rabba with Grammar of Galilean Aramaic I*. Lund: Gleerup, 1939.

Ödeberg, H., *The Fourth Gospel: Interpreted in its Relation to Contemporaneous Religious Currents in Palestine and the Hellenistic-Oriental World*. Amsterdam: B. R. Gruner, 1968.

Ödeberg, H., "Fragen von Metatron, Schekina und Memra." K. Human. Vetenskaps-samfundet i Lund Årsberättelse: 1941-42, 31-46.

Ödeberg, H., *Pharasaism and Christianity*. Tr. J. M. Moe. Saint Louis: Concordia Publishing House, 1964.

Oesterley, W. O. E., *The Jewish Background of the Christian Liturgy*. Oxford: Clarendon Press, 1925.

Pagels, Elaine H., *The Johannine Gospel in Gnostic Exegesis: Heracleon's Commentary on John*. Nashville: Abingdon Press, 1973.

Pagels, Elaine H., "The Demiurge and His Archons," *HTR*, 69 (1976).

Parkes, James, *The Conflict of the Church and the Synagogue*. New York: 1934.

Pearson, B. A., "Friedländer Revisited: Alexandrian Judaism and Gnostic Origins: *Studia Philonica*, 2 (1973), 23-29.

Pearson, B. A., "Jewish Haggadic Traditions in 'The Testimony of Truth' from Nag Hammadi (CG IX, 3)." from *Ex Orbe Religionum: Studia Geo Widengren Oblata*. Ed. C. J. Bleeker, S. G. F. Brandon, and M. Simon. Leiden: Brill, 1972, 457-70.

Pepin, *Mythe et allégorie*. Paris: 1958.

Perrin, N., *What is Redaction Criticism?* Philadelphia: Fortress Press, 1969.

Perrin, N., *A Modern Pilgrimage in New Testament Christology*. Philadelphia: Fortress Press, 1974.

Peterson, E., *Heis Theos: Epigraphische, formgeschichtliche und religionsgeschichtliche Untersuchungen*. Göttingen: Vandenhoeck & Ruprecht, 1926.

Peterson, E., "La libération d'Adam de l'*ananke*." *RB*, LV (1948), 199 f.

Peterson, E., *Der Monotheismus als politisches Problem: Ein Beitrag zur Geschichte der politischen Theologie im Imperium Romanum*. Leipzig: Hegner, 1935.

Plöger, O., *Theocracy and Eschatology*. Tr. S. Rudman. Richmond: John Knox Press, 1968.

Pokorny, P., "Der Ursprung der Gnosis." *Kairos*, 9 (1967), 94-105.

Porton, Gary G., "The Artificial Dispute Ishmael and ᶜAqiba" *Christianity, Judaism and other Greco-Roman Cults*. Leiden: Brill, 1975, 18-29.

Purvis, J. D., "The Fourth Gospel and the Samaritans." *SBL* seminar on John, Annual Meeting, Washington, D.C. October, 1974.

Quispel, Gilles, "The Birth of the Child: Some Gnostic and Jewish Aspects." *Eranos Jahrbuch*, 40 (1971).

Quispel, Gilles, "The Doctrine of Basilides" from *The Mystic Vision: Papers from the Eranos Yearbooks*. Princeton: Princeton University Press, 1968, 210-246.

Quispel, Gilles, "Das ewige Ebenbild der Menschen: Zur Begegnung mit dem Selbst in der Gnosis." *Eranos Jahrbuch*, 36 (1967), 9-30.

Quispel, Gilles, "Der gnostische Anthropos und die jüdische Tradition." *Eranos Jahrbuch* v. 22, *Mensch und Erde*. Princeton: Princeton University Press, 1953, 195-234.

Quispel, Gilles, "Gnosticism and the New Testament." From *The Bible in Modern Scholarship*. Ed. J. Philip Hyatt. Nashville: 1965, 252-271.

Quispel, Gilles, *Gnosis als Weltreligion*. Zurich: Origo Verlag, 1951.

Quispel, Gilles, *Gnostic Studies* I. Istanbul: 1974.

Quispel, Gilles, "The Jung Codex and its Significance." from *The Jung Codex: A Newly recovered Gnostic Papyrus: 3 Studies by H.-ch. Puech, G. Quispel and W. C. van Unnik*. London: 1955, 35-78.

Quispel, Gilles, "The Original Doctrine of Valentinus." *Vigiliae Christianae*, 1 (1947), 43-73.

Quispel, Gilles, "The Origins of the Gnostic Demiurge." *Kyriakon*: Festschrift Johannes Quasten, I. Leiden: Brill, 1970, 271-276.

Recheis, P. A., *Engel, Tod und Seelenreise das Wirken der Geister beim Heimgang des Menschen in der Lehre der alexandrinischen und kappadokisch Väter.* Roma: 1958.

Reitzenstein, Richard, *Die hellenistischen Mysterienreligionen: nach ihren Grundgedanken und Wirkungen.* Stuttgart: Teubner, 1956.

Reitzenstein, R., *Das iranische Erlösungsmysterium: religionsgeschichtliche Untersuchungen.* Bonn: A. Marcus & E. Weber, 1921.

Reitzenstein, R., *Poimandres: Studien zur griechisch-agyptischen und frühchristlichen Literatur.* Leipzig: B. G. Teubner, 1904.

Reicke, B., "The Law and the World according to Paul." *JBL*, 70 (1951), 261-63.

Ringgren, H., *The Faith of Qumran: Theology of the Dead Sea Scrolls.* Tr. Emilie T. Sander. Philadelphia: Fortress Press, 1963.

Rinkin, E., "Defining the Pharisees: The Tannaitic Sources." *HUCA*, 40 (1970), 205-250.

Robinson, J. A. T., "The Earliest Christology of All." *Twelve New Testament Studies.* Philadelphia: SCM Press, 1962.

Robinson, J. and H. Koester, *Trajectories through Early Christianity.* Philadelphia: Fortress Press, 1971.

Rubin, S., "The Belief in Two Powers." (in Hebr.) Krakow: 1908.

Rudolph, K., "Randerscheinungen des Judentums und das Problem der Entstehung des Gnosticismus." *Kairos*, 9 (1967), 105-22.

Russell, D. S., *The Method and Message of Jewish Apocalyptic 200 B.C.-A.D. 100.* Philadelphia: Westminster Press, 1964.

Schachter, J., *Otsar ha-Talmud.* Tel Aviv: Dvir, 1963.

Scheffczyk, L., *Der Mensch als bild Gottes.* Darmstadt: Wissenschaftliche Buchgesellschaft, 1969.

Schiffmann, L., "Merkabah Speculation at Qumran. The 4Q Sereq Shiroth ᶜOlat Ha-shabat," Festschrift for Alexander Altmann, forthcoming.

Schenke, Hans-Martin, *Der Gott "Mensch" in der Gnosis: Ein religionsgeschichtlicher Beitrag zur Diskussion über die paulinische Anschauung von der Kirche als Lieb Christi.* Göttingen: 1962.

Schoedel, W. R., " 'Topological' Theology and Some Monistic Tendencies in Gnosticism." *Essays on Nag Hammadi Texts in Honor of Alexander Böhlig.* Leiden: Brill, 1972, 88-108.

Schoeps, Hans Joachim, *Jewish Christianity: Factional Disputes in the Early Church.* Tr. Douglas R. A. Hare. Philadelphia: Fortress Press, 1969.

Scholem, G., *Bibliographica Kabbalistica: die Jüdische Mystik (Gnosis, Kabbala, Sabbatianismus, Frankismus, Chassidismus) Behandelnde Bücher und Aufsätze von Reuchlin bis zum Gegenwart.* Berlin: Schocken, 1933.

Scholem, Gershom, *Jewish Gnosticism, Merkabah Mysticism and Talmudic Tradition.* New York: The Jewish Theological Seminary of America, 1965.

Scholem, G., "Ein Fragment zur Physiognomik und Chiromantik aus der Tradition der spätantiken jüdischen Esoterik." *Liber Amicorum*: Studies in honour of Professor Dr. C. J. Bleeker. Leiden: Brill, 1969.

Scholem, G., *Major Trends in Jewish Mysticism.* New York: Schocken Books, 1961.

Scholem, G., "Merkabah Mysticism or Ma'aseh Merkavah." *Encyclopedia Judaica*, Vol. 11, 1386-1390.

Scholem, G., *The Messianic Idea in Judaism and Other Essays on Jewish Spirituality.* New York: Schocken Books, 1972.

Scholem, G., *On the Kabbalah and Its Symbolism.* New York: Schocken Books, 1970.

Scholem, G., Ursprung und Anfänge der Kabbala." *Studia Judaica*, II, Berlin: 1962.

Scholem, G., "Die Vorstellung vom Golem." *Eranos Jahrbuch*, 22 (1954).

Scholer, D. M., *Nag Hammadi Bibliography* 1948-1969. Leiden: Brill, 1971.

Scroggs, R., "The Earliest Hellenistic Christianity." *Religions in Antiquity* (Festschrift for E. R. Goodenough). Ed. J. Neusner. Leiden: Brill, 1968, 176-208.

Scroggs, R., *The Last Adam: A Study in Pauline Anthropology.* Philadelphia: Fortress Press, 1966.

Sèd, N., "Les traditions secrètes et les disciples de Rabban Yohanan b. Zakkai." *Révue de l'histoire des religions,* 184 (1973), 49-66.

Shaked, S., "Qumran and Iran: Further Considerations." *Israel Oriental Studies,* 2 (1972), 433-446.

Shotwell, W. A., *The Biblical Exegesis of Justin Martyr.* London: SPCK, 1965.

Simon, M., "Essenes, Gnostics and Jewish Christians." *Jewish Review,* 2 (1944).

Simon, M., *Verus Israel: Étude sur les relations entre Chrétiens et Juifs dans l'empire romain.* Paris: Éditions É. de Boccard, 1964.

Simonsen, D., "Tobit-Aphorismen." *Gedenkbuch zur Erinnerung an David Kaufmann.* Herausgegeben Dr. M. Brann and Dr. F. Rosenthal. Breslau: 1900, 106-116.

Sjöberg, E., *Der Menschensohn im Äthiopischen Henochbuch.* Lund: Gleerup, 1946.

Smith, J. Z., "Birth Upside-down or Right-side Up?" *HR,* 9 (1969-70), 281-303.

Smith, J. Z., "Book Review: Native Cults in the Hellenistic Period." *HR,* 10 (1971), 236-249.

Smith, J. Z., "The Garments of Shame." *HR,* 5 (1966), 217-238.

Smith, J. Z., "The Prayer of Joseph." *Religions in Antiquity: Festschrift for E. R. Goodenough.* Ed. J. Neusner. Leiden: Brill, 1968, 253-293.

Smith, M., *Clement of Alexandria and A Secret Gospel of Mark.* Cambridge: Harvard University Press, 1973.

Smith, M., "II Isaiah and the Persians." *JAOS,* 83 (1963), 415-421.

Smith, M., "Image of God." *Bulletin of J. Rylands Library,* 40 (1958), 473-512.

Smith, M., "Observations on Hekhalot Rabbati." in *Biblical and Other Studies.* Ed. Alexander Altmann, Cambridge: 1963, 142-160.

Smith, M., "On the Shape of God and the Humanity of Gentiles." *Religions in Antiquity* (Festschrift for E. R. Goodenough). Ed. J. Neusner. Leiden: Brill, 1968, 315-326.

Smith, M., *Palestinian Parties and Politics that Shaped the Old Testament.* New York: Columbia University Press, 1971.

Smith, M., *Tannaitic Parallels to the Gospels.* Philadelphia: Society of Biblical Literature, 1951.

Smith, M., "What is Implied by the Variety of Messianic Figures." *JBL,* 78 (1959), 66-72.

Smith, M., "Zealots and Sicarii." *HTR,* 64 (1971).

Sonne, I., "Use of Rabbinic Literature as Historical Sources." *JQR,* 36 (1924), 163 f. and *JQR,* 37 (1925), 318 f.

Sowers, S. G., "The Hermeneutics of Philo and Hebrews; A Comparison of the Interpretation of the Old Testament in Philo Judaeus and the Epistle to the Hebrews." Zurich: NLUJ, 1965.

Stone, M., "Paradise in 4 Ezra 4, 8; 7, 36; 8, 52." *JJS,* 17 (1968), 85-88.

Stone, M., "The Concept of the Messiah in IV Ezra." *Religions in Antiquity.* Ed. J. Neusner. Leiden: Brill, 1968, 295-312.

Strack, H., *Introduction to the Talmud and Midrash.* New York: Atheneum, 1969.

Strack, H. L., *Introduction to the Talmud and Midrash.* Translated from the 5th German edition and revised on the basis of the revisions in the author's copy. Philadelphia: JPSA, 1945.

Strack, H. L. und Billerbeck, Paul, *Das Evangelium nach Matthäus erläutert aus Talmud und Midrash.* Vols. I, II, III, IV, IV 2, V, VI. München: Beck'sche, 1922.

Strecher, G., *Das Juden-Christentum in den Pseudoklementinen.* Berlin: Akademie-Verlag, 1958.

Strugnell, J., "The Angelic Liturgy at Qumran-4Q Serek Šîrôt ᶜOlat Haššabbāt."
    Supplement to *VT* VII. Leiden: Brill, 1960, 318-345.
Studies on the Testament of Moses: Seminar Papers. Ed. G. W. E. Nickelsburg. Sep-
    tuagint and Cognate Studies, Number Four. Cambridge: Society of Biblical
    Literature, 1973.
Teeple, H. M., *The Mosaic Eschatological Prophet.* Philadelphia: Society of Biblical
    Literature, 1957.
Testa, P. E., *Il Simbolismo dei Giudeo-christiani.* Jerusalem: Studium Biblicum
    Franciscanum 14, 1962.
Thompson, L., "Cult and Eschatology in the Revelation of John." *JR*, 49 (1969),
    334-342.
Tiede, D. L., *The Charismatic Figure as Miracle Worker.* Missoula: Society of Biblical
    Literature, 1972.
Towner, W. S., "Form-Criticism of Rabbinic Literature." Unpublished paper.
Towner, W. S., *Rabbinic Enumeration of Scriptural Examples.* Leiden: Brill, 1973.
Turdeanu, E., "L'apocalypse d'Abraham en slave." *JSJ*, 3 (1972), 153-180.
Townsend, J. T., *Bibliographia Rabbinica in The Study of Judaism: Bibliographical
    Essays.* New York: B'nai Brith Anti-defamation League, Ktav, 1972.
van Unnik, W. C., "Die jüdische Componente in der Gnosis." *Vigiliae Christianae*,
    15 (1961), 65-82.
van Unnik, W. C., *Newly Discovered Gnostic Writings: A Preliminary Survey of
    the Nag-Hammadi Find.* London: SCM Press, 1960.
Urbach, E., "Jesus." *Encyclopedia Hebraica*, 10-18.
Urbach, E., "The Sages' Teaching about the Gentile Prophets and about the Balaam
    Prophecies." (in Hebr.) *Tarbiz*, 24 (5715), 286-287.
Urbach, E., *The Sages, Their Concepts and Beliefs.* (in Hebr.) Jerusalem: 1969.
Urbach, E., "The Tradition of Secret Torah during the Tannaitic **Period**." *Studies in
    Mysticism and Religion presented to Gershom G. Scholem on his 70th Birthday
    by Pupils, Colleagues and Friends.* Jerusalem: 1967.
Vansina, J., *Oral Tradition: A Study in Historical Methodology.* Tr. H. M. Wright.
    Chicago: Aldine, 1965, c 1961.
Vermes, G., "The Use of Barnasha/Barnash in Jewish Aramaic." Appendix E in M.
    Black. *An Aramaic Approach to the Gospels and Acts.* Oxford: 1967.
Völker, W., *Quellen zur Geschichte der christlichen Gnosis.* Tübingen: Mohr, 1932.
Wagner, S. M., *Religious Non-Conformity in Ancient Jewish Life.* Unpublished
    dissertation (Yeshiva University, 1964).
Weiss, H. K., *Untersuchungen zur Kosmologie des hellenistischen und palästinischen
    Judentums.* Berlin: 1966.
Weiss, I. H., *Dor Dor we Dorshaw.* 5 Volumes. Wilno: Zawadski, 1911.
Werblowski, R. J. Z., "Philo and the Zohar: A Note on the Methods of the *Scienza
    Nuova* in Jewish Studies." *JJS*, 10 (1959), 25-135.
Werner, E., *The Sacred Bridge: Liturgical Parallels in Synagogue and Early Church.*
    New York: Schocken Books, 1970.
Werner, M., *The Formation of Christian Dogma: An Historical Study of its Problem.*
    London: Adam & Charles Black, 1957.
Westermann, C., *Isaiah 40-66.* Philadelphia: 1969.
Widengren, G., "Heavenly Enthronement and Baptism: Studies in Mandaean Baptism."
    Religions in Antiquity. Ed. J. Neusner. Leiden: Brill, 1968, 551-581.
Wilde, R., *The Treatment of the Jews in the Greek Christian Writers of the First
    Three Centuries.* Washington: 1949.
Wilder, A., "Social Factors in Early Christian Eschatology." *Early Christian Origins.*
    Ed. Wikgren. Chicago: Quadrangle, 1961, 67-76.
Wilken, R. L., *Judaism and the Early Christian Mind: A Study of Cyril of Alexandria's
    Exegesis and Theology.* New Haven: Yale University Press, 1971.

Williamson, R., *Philo and the Epistle of the Hebrews*. Leiden: Brill, 1970.

Wilson, R. McL., "The Early History of the Exegesis of Gen. 1.26." *Studia Patristica*, I:1 (1957), 420-437.

Wilson, R. McL., *Gnosis and the New Testament*. Philadelphia: Fortress Press, 1968.

Wilson, R. McL., *The Gnostic Problem: A Study of the Relations between Hellenistic Judaism and the Gnostic Heresy*. London: Mowbray & Co., 1958.

Winston, D., "The Iranian Component in the Bible, Apocrypha, and Qumran: A Review of the Evidence." *HR*, 5 (1966), 183-216.

Wisse, F., "The Epistle of Jude in the History of Heresiology." *Essays on the Nag Hammadi texts in Honor of Alexander Böhlig*. Ed. M. Krause. Leiden: Brill, 1972, 133-143.

Wisse, F., "The Nag Hammadi Library and the Heresiologists." *Vigiliae Christianae*, 25 (1971), 205-223.

Wisse, F., "The Redeemer Figure in the Paraphrase of Shem." *NT*, 12 (1970), Leiden: Brill, 130-140.

Wolfson, H. A., *Philo: Foundations of Religious Philosophy in Judaism, Christianity, and Islam*. 2 Volumes. Cambridge: Harvard University Press, 1947.

Wolfson, H. A., "The Pre-existent Angel of the Magharians and Al-nahawandi." *JQR*, 51 (1960), 89-106.

van der Woude, A. S., "Melchizedek als himmlische Erlösergestalte in den neugefundenen eschatologischen Midrashim aus Qumran Höhle XI." *OTS*, 14 (1965).

van der Woude, A. S., *Die messianischen Vorstellungen der Gemeinde von Qumran*. Assen: Van Gorcum & Co., 1957.

Yadin, Y., "A Note on Melchizedek and Qumran." *IEJ*, 15 (1965), 152-154.

Yamauchi, E. M., *Pre-Christian Gnosticism: A Survey of the Proposed Evidence*. Grand Rapids: 1973.

York, A. D., "The Dating of Targumic Literature." *JSJ*, 5 (1974), 49-62.

Zaehner, R. C., *The Dawn and Twilight of Zoroastrianism*. London: Weidenfeld and Nicolson, 1961.

Zeitlin, Solomon, "Les principes des controverses halachiques entre les écoles de Schammai et de Hillel: Étude sur la jurisprudence tannaitique." *REJ*, 93 (1932), 73-84.

Zeller, E., *Geschichte der deutschen Philosophie seit Leibniz*. München: 1873. 2nd Edition, 1875.

Zeller, E., *The Stoics, Epicureans, and Sceptics*. Tr. O. J. Reichil. New York: Russell & Russell, Inc., 1962.

INDICES

I. RABBINIC WRITINGS

II. EXTRA-RABBINIC WRITINGS

III. SCRIPTURAL REFERENCES

OLD TESTAMENT

NEW TESTAMENT

IV. SUBJECTS

OLYMPIC**STEEL**

1. Covenant Christian school Application Tuition Assistance

2. Lean Six Sigma Certification

3. House hunting

4. ~~Loan~~ application {HELOC}

5. House sale

6. Kaizen Biz

7. Resume update

8. Career highlights + achievements writeup

9. Apply for margin @ sureprosperity

10. Plan for Kachinywe's land.

11. Indiana College Choice 529 Accounts for Zamilamane, Flehaombe Adja & Eliezer.

12. General plan for family.

1251 North Clark Road, Gary, Indiana 46406 • 219.359.3900 • www.olysteel.com